OTHER A TO Z GUIDES FROM
THE SCARECROW PRESS, INC.

The A to Z of United States Intelligence

Michael A. Turner

The A to Z Guide Series, No. 79

The Scarecrow Press, Inc.
Lanham • Toronto • Plymouth, UK
2009

Published by Scarecrow Press, Inc.
A wholly owned subsidiary of
The Rowman & Littlefield Publishing Group, Inc.
4501 Forbes Boulevard, Suite 200, Lanham, Maryland 20706
http://www.scarecrowpress.com

Estover Road, Plymouth PL6 7PY, United Kingdom

British Library Cataloguing in Publication Information Available

Library of Congress Cataloging-in-Publication Data

The hardback version of this book was cataloged by the Library of Congress as
follows:

Turner, Michael A., 1947–
 Historical dictionary of United States intelligence / Michael A. Turner.
   p. cm.—(Historical dictionaries of intelligence and counterintelligence ;
   no. 2)
 Includes bibliographical references.
  1. Intelligence service—United States—History—Dictionaries. 2. Military
intelligence—United States—History—Dictionaries. I. Title. II. Series.
 JK468.I6T863 2006
 327.1273'03—dc22   2005016699

ISBN 978-0-8108-6866-3 (pbk. : alk. paper)
ISBN 978-0-8108-7029-1 (ebook)

$\otimes$™ The paper used in this publication meets the minimum requirements of
American National Standard for Information Sciences—Permanence of Paper
for Printed Library Materials, ANSI/NISO Z39.48-1992.

Printed in the United States of America

Contents

Editor's Foreword

The A to Z of United States Intelligence follows the one on British intelligence, perhaps rightly so since the Americans actually got started while throwing off the British yoke during the Revolution and later cooperated very closely with the British. While the Americans could certainly learn a trick or two about espionage during the early period, it quickly became apparent that no one could outperform them in most areas and especially not for technical collection of intelligence. And there is no question that intelligence was decisive in defeating the Axis during World War II and the Soviet Union and communism during the Cold War. Alas, since 11 September 2001 and the war on terrorism, the United States is pitted against an enemy in which old-fashioned human intelligence is far more important than any fancy gadgetry, and it will have to revamp its intelligence organizations and train more agents to face a tenacious and bitter foe. Thus, once again, the United States intelligence community is undergoing realignment and tighter oversight, in the midst of a crisis that has certainly shaken the faith in its ability to do the job.

The chronology follows the twists and turns of over two centuries of history. The introduction explains just what intelligence is and does and shows how U.S. intelligence operations have evolved over those centuries. The dictionary then looks at essential aspects more closely, including the various organizations, the persons who created and managed them, who worked for or defied them, and the many reforms and laws adopted to improve their operations or bring them under government control. This section includes entries on the successes, and also on the failures, as well as the present challenges, which are very different and particularly difficult to cope with. The bibliography is helpful for those who want to learn more. Meanwhile, the list of acronyms is there for anyone who needs to figure out which letters represent which organizations or functions.

This book was written by Michael A. Turner, who has learned about U.S. intelligence from within and without. After a brief stint as professor, he joined the Central Intelligence Agency and spent nearly 15 years in various positions, including analysis, congressional liaison, and public affairs. He has spent the past decade in academia as Cannon Professor of International Relations and Peace Studies at Alliant International University. So he is well placed to know about the trade and also to explain it to others, which he has been doing in lectures to his students, and books and articles in learned journals. While not revealing any secrets, he has performed the precious task of making sense of a very complicated and increasingly vital activity.

Jon Woronoff
Series Editor

Preface

Preparing a historical dictionary on U.S. intelligence is a formidable task, for two reasons. First, the subject matter is not what it seems: while the United States has had some kind of intelligence capability throughout its history, its intelligence apparatus is young, dating only to the period immediately after World War II. Yet, in that short a time, it has undergone enormous changes—from the labor-intensive espionage and covert action establishment of the 1950s to an enterprise that today relies heavily on technologically advanced information pathways and seriously expensive gadgets like satellites, airborne collection platforms, and unmanned aerial vehicles.

Second, writing about intelligence matters invariably is fraught with difficulties, not the least of which is the secrecy surrounding intelligence activities. Secrecy is a bulwark of any intelligence service, and this is no different for U.S. intelligence. Therefore, some of what could be known about U.S. intelligence and its activities simply is shrouded in the mists of classification schemes and is unavailable to the public. However, the United States is one of the few countries on the globe that allows discussion and debate, albeit sometimes grudgingly, about its intelligence agencies and their activities. As a result, a surprisingly large number of authors, both from inside and outside the U.S. intelligence community, have written about U.S. intelligence in all its guises. This burgeoning literature makes virtually all facets of the American intelligence enterprise readily available to the public. The richness of this literature is evident in the fact that, even though the author is a former intelligence officer, everything in this dictionary came from publicly available materials.

There is a third complication in writing historically about intelligence—that of coming to terms with the myriad conceptions of intelligence. Appreciating the history of U.S. intelligence requires an understanding of intelligence as an essential governmental activity. The public understandably focuses on its most alluring aspects, gleaned often from fictional works that provide grist for the entertainment industry. This is the world of fantasy, far removed from the real world of secret intelligence, although it has had an enormous impact on public perceptions of American intelligence. Those among the public who are suspicious of government in all its forms see intelligence as a source of evil, a dark world of secrecy and deception that overthrows legitimate governments, assassinates political leaders, and tramples the civil liberties of Americans. When these two images are combined, they produce a view of intelligence that is simultaneously titillating and exciting, and nefarious, uncontrolled, and uncontrollable.

Occasionally, discussions on intelligence are mired in additional conceptual difficulties, owing to the fact that intelligence, as a governmental activity, exists to illuminate and support the foreign policy objectives of whichever administration is in office, and so, logically, comes to be identified with that administration's foreign policy. Critics of administration policy then quickly focus on the role intelligence plays in that process and typically associate intelligence with sinister activities that illegally further a dubious foreign policy.

However, intelligence has little to do with implementing policy. There is a part of secret intelligence, covert action, that is designed to execute specific aspects of American foreign policy, but it is only a small — although, unfortunately, the most infamous — part of intelligence.

Acknowledgments

Writing a dictionary almost certainly is a team effort, and *Historical Dictionary of United States Intelligence* is no exception. I would not have been able to complete the project in an expeditious manner if it were not for the meticulous and determined efforts of my two research assistants, Sara Grace Petite and Samer Elchahabi. My friend Dr. William Perry, of Western Carolina University, edited the manuscript and made invaluable contributions to its content and style. Margaret Billy's comments and editorial suggestions certainly strengthened the manuscript. Last but not least Jon Woronoff, of Scarecrow Press, the editor of this series, went out of his way to ensure the integrity of the book and to hasten its publication at this critical time when intelligence is such an important political issue. I am grateful to all of them for their help. Thank you all.

Acronyms and Abbreviations

ABM	antiballistic missile
ACDA	Arms Control and Disarmament Agency
ACIS	Arms Control Intelligence Staff
AEC	Atomic Energy Commission
AFIO	Association of Former Intelligence Officers
AFIWC	Air Force Information Warfare Center
AIC	American Intelligence Command
AINTA	Army Intelligence Agency
APNSA	assistant to the president for national security affairs
ARPA	Advanced Research Projects Agency
ASA	Army Security Agency
ASAS	All Source Analysis System
AVG	American Volunteer Group
BOE	Board of Estimates
BND	Bundesnachrichttendienst
BNDD	Bureau of Narcotics and Dangerous Drugs
BNL	Banca Nazionale del Lavorno
CAPG	Covert Action Planning Group
CARG	Covert Action Review Group
CAT	Civil Air Transport
CCB	Community Counterterrorism Board
CCP	Consolidated Cryptologic Program
CFE	Conventional Armed Forces in Europe
Cheka	All Russian Extraordinary Commission for Combating Counterrevolution and Sabotage
CI	counterintelligence
CIA	Central Intelligence Agency
CIC	Counterintelligence Center
CIC	Counter Intelligence Corps

CIG	Central Intelligence Group
CIO	Central Imagery Office
CIPA	Classified Information Procedures Act
CMA	Current Management Account
CMS	Community Management Staff
CNC	DCI Crime and Narcotics Center
COI	coordinator of information
COMINT	communications intelligence
COMIREX	Committee on Imagery Requirements and Exploitation
COMOR	Committee on Overhead Reconnaissance
COMSEC	communications security
COS	chief of station
CSA	Confederate States of America
CSI	Center for the Study of Intelligence
CTBT	Comprehensive Test Ban Treaty
CTC	Counterterrorism Center
DARO	Defense Airborne Reconnaissance Office
DARPA	Defense Advanced Research Projects Agency
DCI	director of central intelligence
DCID	director of central intelligence directive
DCP	Defense Cryptologic Program
DDCI	deputy director of central intelligence
DDO	deputy director of operations
DDP	deputy director for plans
DDPO	Defense Dissemination Program Office
DEA	Drug Enforcement Administration
DEC	DCI Environmental Center
DGIAP	Defense General Intelligence and Program
DH	Defense HUMINT Service
DHS	Department of Homeland Security
DI	Directorate of Intelligence
DIA	Defense Intelligence Agency
DIC	Defense Intelligence College
DIAMP	Defense Imagery and Mapping Program
DIO	defense intelligence officer
DIRINT	director of intelligence (Marine Corps)
DIS	Defense Investigative Service

DMA	Defense Mapping Agency
DNI	director of national intelligence
DO	Directorate of Operations
DOD	Department of Defense
DOE	Department of Energy
DP	Directorate of Plans
DS	Bureau of Diplomatic Security
DSS	Defense Security Service
DSS	Diplomatic Security Service
DS&T	Directorate of Science and Technology
ELINT	electronic intelligence
EO	executive order
EPIC	El Paso Intelligence Center
ERTS	Earth Resources Technology Satellite
EXDIR/ICA	executive director for intelligence community affairs
EXCOM	executive committee
FAA	Federal Aviation Administration
FARA	Foreign Agents Registration Act
FBI	Federal Bureau of Investigation
FBIS	Foreign Broadcast Information Service
FCO	Foreign and Commonwealth Office
FinCEN	Financial Crimes Enforcement Network
FISA	Foreign Intelligence Surveillance Act
FOIA	Freedom of Information Act
FSB	Federal Security Service (Russian Federation)
FSLN	Frente Sandinista de Liberacion Nacional
GAO	Government Accounting Office
GCHQ	Government Communications Headquarters
GDIP	General Defense Intelligence Program
GEOINT	geospatial intelligence
GRU	Glavnoe Razvedyvatel'noe Upravlenie (Chief Intelligence Directorate)
HPSCI	House Permanent Select Committee on Intelligence
HSPD	homeland security presidential directive
HUAC	House Un-American Activities Committee
HUMINT	human intelligence
IAEA	International Atomic Energy Agency
IC	intelligence community

ICBM	intercontinental ballistic missile
ICJ	International Court of Justice
ICS	Intelligence Community Staff
IIC	Interdepartemental Intelligence Committee
IICT	Interagency Intelligence Committee on Terrorism
IMINT	imagery intelligence
INF	intermediate nuclear force
INR	Bureau of Intelligence and Research
INS	Immigration and Naturalization Service
INSCOM	Army Intelligence and Security Command
IOB	Intelligence Oversight Board
IRA	intelligence-related activities
IRS	Internal Revenue Service
ISR	Intelligence, Surveillance, and Reconnaissance (Air Force)
IWG	interagency working groups
JCS	Joint Chiefs of Staff
JIC	Joint Intelligence Committee
JMIC	Joint Military Intelligence College
JMIP	Joint Military Intelligence Program
KGB	Committee on State Security
KH	Keyhole
LNTBT	Limited Nuclear Test Ban Treaty
MASINT	Measurement and Signature Intelligence
MCIA	Marine Corps Intelligence Activity
MIB	Military Intelligence Branch
MID	Military Intelligence Division
MIS	Military Intelligence Service
MSSI	Master of Science in Strategic Intelligence
NAIC	National Air Intelligence Center
NASA	National Aeronautics and Space Administration
NATO	North Atlantic Treaty Organization
NCC	National Counterterrorism Center
NCIX	National Counterintelligence Executive
NDIC	National Drug Intelligence Center
NFAC	National Foreign Assessment Center
NFIB	National Foreign Intelligence Board
NFIP	National Foreign Intelligence Program

NFOSG	Naval Field Operations Support Group
NGA	National Geospatial-Intelligence Agency
NIA	National Intelligence Authority
NIC	National Intelligence Council
NICB	National Intelligence Collection Board
NID	national intelligence daily
NIE	national intelligence estimate
NIMA	National Imagery and Mapping Agency
NIO	national intelligence officer
NIPB	National Intelligence Production Board
NIPC	National Infrastructure Protection Center
NKVD	People's Commissariat of Internal Affairs
NMIC	Navy's National Maritime Intelligence Center
NPC	DCI Nonproliferation Center
NPIC	National Photographic Interpretation Center
NPT	Nonproliferation Treaty
NRO	National Reconnaissance Office
NROC	National Resettlement Operations Center
NSA	National Security Agency
NSAM	national security action memorandum
NSC	National Security Council
NSCD	National Security Council directive
NSC/DC	National Security Council's Deputies Committee
NSD	national security directive
NSDD	national security decision directive
NSDM	national security decision memorandum
NSEP	National Security Education Program
NSPD	national security presidential directive
NSRs	national security reviews
NST	Nuclear and Space Arms Talks
NSTL	National Security Threat List
NTIS	National Technical Information Service
OMB	Office of Management and Budget
ONE	Office of National Estimates
ONI	Office of Naval Intelligence
OPR	Office of Political Research
OPC	Office of Policy Coordination
OPEC	Organization of Petroleum Exporting States

ORA	Office of Research and Analysis
ORE	Office of Reports and Estimates
OSINT	open-source intelligence
OSO	Office of Special Operations
OSS	Office of Strategic Services
PD	presidential directive
PDB	president's daily brief
PDD	presidential decision directive
PFIAB	President's Foreign Intelligence Advisory Board
PHOTINT	photographic intelligence
PHSAC	President's Homeland Security Advisory Council
PICL	president's intelligence check list
PRC	People's Republic of China
PRD	presidential review directive
PRM	presidential review memoranda
PSYWAR	psychological warfare
RFE	Radio Free Europe
RL	Radio Liberty
SALT	Strategic Arms Limitation Talks
SAR	synthetic aperture radar
SASC	Senate Armed Services Committee
SAT	Southern Air Transport
SCAP	Supreme Commander of the Allied Powers
SCIF	Special Compartmented Intelligence Facility
SDI	Strategic Defense Initiative
SDIO	Strategic Defense Initiative Office
SEIB	senior executive intelligence brief
SFRC	Senate Foreign Relations Committee
SIG	Senior Interdepartmental Group
SIGINT	signals intelligence
SIS	Special Intelligence Service
SLBM	submarine-launched ballistic missile
SNIE	special national intelligence estimate
SOE	Special Operations Executive
SSCI	Senate Select Committee on Intelligence
START	Strategic Arms Reduction Treaty
SVRR	Sluzhba Vneshney Rasvedki Rossii (Russia's foreign intelligence service)

TELINT	telemetry intelligence
TIARA	tactical intelligence and related activities
TSA	Transportation Security Administration
TTAC	Technology Transfer Assessment Center
TTIC	Terrorism Threat Integration Center
UAV	unmanned aerial vehicle
UN	United Nations
USAINTA	U.S. Army Intelligence Agency
USAINTC	U.S. Army Intelligence Command
USAISA	U.S. Army Intelligence Support Activity
USASE	U.S. Army Security Agency
USGS	United States Geological Survey
USIA	United States Information Agency
USIB	United States Intelligence Board
USICA	United States International Communications Agency
USIS	United States Information Service
USSOCOM	U.S. Special Operations Command
USSR	Union of Soviet Socialist Republics
VOA	Voice of America
WMD	weapons of mass destruction

Chronology

1765   Sons of Liberty, the first American dissident group, established.

1772   Beginning of organized resistance by the Patriots, in the form of Committees of Correspondence, against the British.

1775   **29 November:** Continental Congress establishes Committee of Secret Correspondence, headed by Benjamin Franklin, to gather secret intelligence.

1776   **April:** Committee of Secret Correspondence sends first American agent abroad to secure weapons. **4 July:** Declaration of Independence. **12–22 September:** Nathan Hale's disastrous espionage mission behind British lines in New York City. **27 November:** Continental Congress appropriates first intelligence funds.

1777   George Washington organizes first intelligence service by initiating contacts with Committees of Security in each state.

1778   George Washington organizes the "Culper Spy Ring" and other spy networks.

1780   **September:** Benedict Arnold defects to the British.

1783   **3 September:** Treaty of Paris ends the Revolutionary War with Britain.

1790   **1 July:** Congress establishes Contingent Fund to pay for American agents abroad.

1798   Congress passes Alien and Sedition Acts.

1804   **May:** The Lewis and Clark "Corps of Discovery" expedition begins. Lewis and Clark carry secret orders to make accurate maps of the West. Attempt to overthrow the ruler of Tripoli in order to end the taking of American hostages; effort fails and affair ends in 1805 in a negotiated settlement.

1811 Congress passes secret resolution authorizing President James Madison to temporarily occupy Spanish Florida. Florida becomes American in 1813.

1812 The War of 1812 with Britain; ends in 1814.

1815 U.S. Navy takes action against Barbary Coast pirates; navy sinks Algerian warship, kills Algerian admiral, and puts an end Barbary Coast terrorism.

1822 House of Representatives makes Committee on Foreign Affairs a standing committee.

1845 President James Polk authorizes covert operation to induce California to declare independence from Mexico.

1848 **22 February:** Treaty of Guadalupe-Hidalgo cedes a large chunk of Mexico to the United States.

1861 The Civil War begins; ends in 1865. First use of balloons for reconnaissance; intercepts of telegraph messages; visual flag signals; ciphers to protect communications; and deception and disinformation campaigns. U.S. government establishes National Detective Bureau to engage in counterespionage; evolves into the Secret Service.

1862 Confederacy establishes Signal and Secret Service Bureau.

1863 Army establishes Bureau of Military Information.

1865 **5 July:** The federal government establishes the Secret Service.

1882 **23 March:** U.S. Navy establishes Office of Intelligence, soon after renamed Office of Naval Intelligence (ONI).

1885 **October:** War Department establishes Military Information Division.

1889 First military attaches sent abroad.

1898 **25 January:** American battleship Maine arrives in Havana, Cuba. **15 February:** The sinking of USS *Maine* in Havana Harbor. **19 April:** Congressional resolution authorizing President William McKinley to use military force against Spain in Cuba. **24 April:** Military Intelligence Section agents sent to Cuba to assist Cuban insurgents against the Spanish. **25 April:** United States declares war on Spain over Cuba. **1 May:** Destruction of Spanish fleet in Manila Harbor. **22–24 July:** U.S. Army lands in Cuba. **10 December:** Treaty of Paris ends Spanish-American War.

1905   Russo-Japanese War; Japanese victory.

1906   Japanese war scare in U.S. prompts intelligence gathering against Japan; ends in 1907.

1908   Military Intelligence Section files transferred to Army War College, ending War Department intelligence activities. Department of Justice establishes Bureau of Investigation.

1911   **February:** German deception operation to provoke war between U.S. and Mexico by claiming alliance between Mexico and Japan.

1912   Contingency Plans developed; Green Plan for intervening in revolutionary Mexico; Orange Plan for war with Japan.

1914   **July:** Austro-Hungarian Empire and Germany declare war against Serbia, Britain, and France. U.S. taken completely by surprise.

1915   Plan of San Diego, an aborted German plan to foment an uprising by Mexican Americans, Native Americans, and African Americans in the American Southwest.

1916   U.S. Army incursions into Mexico to catch Pancho Villa; U.S. intelligence based only on interrogations of refugees. **1 July:** Congress authorizes Bureau of Investigation to engage in counterespionage on behalf of the Department of State.

1917   The Industrial Workers of the World (IWW) Labor Federation foments strikes and labor unrest to prevent U.S. entry into World War II. IWW used by German intelligence for sabotage in U.S. **February:** British turn Zimmerman telegram over to President Woodrow Wilson; German scheme to seek an alliance with Mexico in a war with U.S. **March:** American Protective League begins to act as auxiliary to the Bureau of Investigation. **4 April:** U.S. entry into World War I. **April:** War Department establishes Military Intelligence Section as well as the

Cipher Bureau, first American agency to collect communications intelligence (COMINT). **April–May:** President Wilson invokes federal laws restricting the movements of enemy aliens in the U.S. Bureau of Investigation is beefed up. U.S. Army establishes G-2 appellation for intelligence within military units; G-2 establishes liaison with foreign counterparts. **15 June:** President Wilson signs the Espionage Act into law. **5 September:** IWW offices raided by Bureau of Investigation agents and American Protective League auxiliaries. **September:** President Wilson takes steps to establish "the Inquiry." **October:** Trading-with-the-Enemy Act passed; allows federal government to open and censor mail, the print press, and other communications. **12 October:** President Wilson establishes National Censorship Board to implement Trading-with-the-Enemy Act. **7 November:** The Bolshevik Revolution in Russia. **November:** Military Intelligence Section begins to incorporate American Protective League auxiliaries into its ranks.

1918 February: Military Intelligence Section establishes unit to study enemy propaganda and engage in counterpropaganda. **April:** President Wilson endorses a strengthened Espionage Act, making spying for a foreign nation and speaking out against the U.S. and the war federal offenses. **3 August:** American military landings in Murmansk and Archangel, Russia, to engage the Red Army. **26 August:** Military Intelligence Section taken out of the Army War College, renamed Military Intelligence Division, and reestablished as independent unit under General Staff. **September:** Military Intelligence Division establishes unit to screen travelers to and from the U.S. **October:** Congress passes the Immigration Act, allowing the government to deport aliens advocating the violent overthrow of the U.S. government. **11 November:** World War I ends; Armistice Day. **December:** "Inquiry" becomes the Division of Political and Territorial Intelligence of the American Peace Commission.

1919 Agreement worked out between Military Intelligence Division (MID) and the State Department to keep code-breaking operations (Cipher Bureau) within MID. Cipher Bureau moves to New York City under cover name Code Compilation Company; begins collecting telegram traffic from cable companies. **February:** Peace Commission establishes the Division of Current and Diplomatic Correspondence, which sends agents abroad to collect current intelligence. State Department creates "U-1" to carry out intelligence coordination and liaison. **June:** Attorney general creates Radical Division, soon renamed General Intelligence Division, within Bureau of Investigation to compile intelligence on anarchists; headed by J. Edgar Hoover.

1919–1922 Anticommunist raids by General Intelligence Division.

1920s Office of Naval Intelligence steps up efforts to collect intelligence against Japan and updates War Plan Orange.

1921 November: Naval Disarmament Conference in Washington, D.C.; Cipher Bureau reads Japanese negotiators' diplomatic traffic.

1922 November: MID prohibited from collecting domestic intelligence.

1924 General Intelligence Division disbanded. **January:** Office of Naval Intelligence (ONI) begins intercepting Japanese communications; unaware of activities of Cipher Bureau. **10 May:** J. Edgar Hoover named director of Bureau of Investigation and is restricted to investigating violations of federal law.

1927 Congress passes tough law prohibiting unauthorized interception or disclosure of the contents of electrical and electronic communications. State Department's "U-1" abolished and responsibilities allocated to geographic divisions.

1929 The army's Signal Intelligence Service established to break foreign codes. **March:** Secretary of State Henry L. Stimpson orders Cipher Bureau closed.

1930s State Department maintains the only domestic counterintelligence operation in the U.S. government.

1931 Herbert Yardley, former director of Cipher Bureau, publishes book disclosing U.S. ability to read Japanese diplomatic traffic.

1933 President Franklin D. Roosevelt establishes diplomatic ties with Union of Soviet Socialist Republics. Adolf Hitler becomes chancellor of Germany.

1934 Japan denounces 1922 Naval Treaty.

1937 Japan begins occupation of China.

1938 Army chief of staff secretly authorizes the Signal Intelligence Service to intercept radio communications and provide crypto-analytic services.

1938 British prime minister Neville Chamberlain announces Munich Agreement with Adolf Hitler, ceding Czechoslovakia.

1939 Japanese government switches to "Purple" code machine. **June:** President Franklin D. Roosevelt issues secret directive, placing all espionage, counterespionage, and sabotage matters under jurisdictions of the Federal Bureau of Investigation (FBI), Military Intelligence Division (MID), and Office of Naval Intelligence (ONI); also establishes Interdepartmental Intelligence Committee (IIC) to coordinate these activities. **June:** President Roosevelt gives the FBI authority to carry out counterintelligence and security operations against Axis agents in Latin America. **29 August:** Nazi-Soviet Nonaggression Pact signed; ONI and MID begin daily intelligence briefings of the president. **1 September:** Nazi Germany attacks Poland; World War II begins.

1940 Japan joins the Axis. President Roosevelt sends William J. Donovan to Britain to assess its ability to withstand Germany. **April:** Prime Minister Winston Churchill sends William Stephenson to establish liaison and urge U.S. to counter Axis sabotage and subversion in U.S. **24 June:** President Franklin D. Roosevelt orders the establishment of the Special Intelligence Service within the Federal Bureau of Investigation to engage in espionage in Latin America. **August:** Signals Intelligence Service breaks Japan's "Purple" code; intercepted messages given code name MAGIC. **December:** William Donovan, accompanied by William Stephenson, visits Mediterranean and Balkans.

1941 President Roosevelt establishes informal intelligence network operated out of the White House. U.S. government freezes Japanese assets in the U.S. **February:** The British reveal to U.S. that they had broken the German "Enigma" code; decryptions code-named ULTRA. **March:** Donovan proposes an intelligence agency to analyze intentions of enemies; opposed by ONI, MID, and FBI. **11 June:** President Roosevelt appoints Donovan as coordinator of information (COI) to collect and analyze national security information. **22 June:** Germany attacks the Soviet Union. **7 December:** Japanese attack on Pearl Harbor; the U.S. enters World War II.

1942 U.S. establishes Foreign Broadcast Information Service (FBIS) to collect radio broadcasts and press information. **1 January:** President Roosevelt forms "grand alliance" against Axis powers through the "Declaration of the United Nations" to fight collectively. **11 February:** Joint Chiefs of Staff (JCS) establishes the Joint Intelligence Committee (JIC). **9 March:** Military Intelligence Service (MIS) established as the operating arm of the Military Intelligence Division. **April:** President Roosevelt signs order to intern Japanese Americans. **13 June:** President Roosevelt abolishes the coordinator of information position and establishes the Office of Strategic Services (OSS).

1943 Britain's Special Operations Executive (SOE) and OSS launch Jedburgh teams behind enemy lines in Europe. **27 January:** OSS Detachment 101 launches mission against the Japanese in Burma.

1944 **6 June:** Allied landings in Normandy, France after OSS deception operation to convince the Germans that landing would take place in Calais. **Early November:** President Roosevelt asks William Donovan to prepare a plan for a permanent postwar intelligence agency. **18 November:** Donovan sends President Roosevelt a secret memo calling for a permanent intelligence organization much like the OSS, with no law enforcement powers at home.

1945 **9 February:** American press discloses Donovan's plan, effectively killing the proposal. **February:** Project VENONA initiated. **April:** President Roosevelt dies. **May:** Germany surrenders unconditionally. **6 August:** First atomic bomb dropped on Hiroshima, Japan. **9 August:** Second atomic bomb dropped on Nagasaki, Japan. **15 August:** Japan surrenders. **1 October:** President Harry Truman abolishes the OSS.

1946 **22 January:** President Truman establishes the National Intelligence Authority (NIA) and within it the Central Intelligence Group (CIG), headed by Director of Central Intelligence (DCI) Sydney W. Souers. **March:** Army, navy, and air force intelligence directed to join CIG in producing assessment of Soviet military capabilities. House of Representatives establishes the House Armed Services Committee. The Senate establishes the Senate Armed Services Committee (SASC). **June:** Lt. General Hoyt S. Vandenberg succeeds Souers as DCI. **23 July:** First national intelligence estimate on Soviet strategic posture produced by CIG. **July:** Director of Central Intelligence Hoyt Vandenberg establishes the Office of

Special Operations (OSO) to conduct espionage and the Office of Reports and Estimates (ORE) to engage in analysis, both within the CIG.

1947   February: President Truman proposes National Security Act. **12 March:** President Truman enunciates "Truman Doctrine." **19 April:** Military Intelligence Service absorbs Military Intelligence Division. **26 July:** Congress passes National Security Act. **August:** Rear Admiral Roscoe H. Hillenkoetter becomes DCI. **18 September:** Central Intelligence Agency (CIA) established. **December:** National Security Council (NSC) issues National Security Council Directive (NSCD) 4-A, giving the CIA authority to engage in covert actions.

1948   CIA propaganda campaign in Italy to keep the communists from gaining power. **May:** George F. Kennan proposes independent Office of Policy Coordination (OPC) to carry out covert operations; established by National Security Council Directive 10/2 and headed by Frank Wisner. **18 June:** National Security Council (NSC) issues NSCD 10/2 authorizing the creation of the Office of Policy Coordination. **1 September:** OPC established to conduct covert operations.

1948–1949   Berlin Crisis; Berlin Airlift.

1949   Communist takeover in China. **4 April:** North Atlantic Treaty Organization (NATO) is established.

1950   Radio Free Europe (RFE) goes on the air. DCI Smith establishes Office of National Estimates (ONE); takes over the Office of Policy Coordination. **February:** Wisconsin senator Joseph McCarthy assumes chairmanship of the House Un-American Activities Committee. **April:** National Security Council issues NSC 68, setting forth American principles for confronting the Soviet Union in the Cold War. **June 27:** Korean War breaks out; surprises the CIA. **19 October:** The People's Republic of China (PRC) enters the Korean War.

1952   OPC officially incorporated into the CIA. CIA's Office of Policy Coordination combines with CIA's Office of Special Operations to form the Directorate of Plans (DP). **November:** Congress establishes the National Security Agency (NSA).

1953   CIA establishes Photographic Intelligence Division. U.S. government sets up United States Information Agency (USIA). **April:** Operation

MKULTRA initiated. **27 July:** Korean truce takes effect. **16 August:** CIA overthrows Iranian prime minister Mohammad Mossadegh.

1954 Soviet NKVD renamed KGB. Geneva Accords on Vietnam. **2 June:** CIA overthrows Guatemalan president Jacobo Arbenz. **24 November:** President Dwight D. Eisenhower approves the building of the U-2 spy plane. **2 December:** Senate censures Wisconsin senator Joseph McCarthy.

1955 Milstar military communications satellites launched. **1 May:** Warsaw Pact is established.

1955–1956 Berlin Tunnel Operation.

1956 President Dwight D. Eisenhower establishes President's Board of Consultants on Foreign Intelligence Activities. U-2 flights begin. **February:** Premier Khrushchev's secret speech to the Twentieth Congress of the Communist Party. **June:** CIA acquires Premier Nikita S. Khrushchev's secret speech and makes it public. **4 July:** U-2 spy plane makes its first flight. **26 July:** Egyptian president Gamel Abdul Nasser nationalizes the Suez Canal, sparking a crisis. **August:** CIA begins development of SR-71 supersonic spy plane to replace the U-2. **October:** Revolt in Hungary against Soviet forces. **29 October:** Israeli forces attack Egypt. **31 October:** A combined Franco-British military force attacks Egypt. **15 November:** United Nations Emergency Force arrives in Egypt, thereby defusing Suez Crisis.

1957 **27 June:** Ploughshares Program approved. **4 October:** Soviet Union launches Sputnik, first man-made satellite in earth orbit.

1958 CIA's National Photographic Interpretation Center (NPIC) established; incorporates Photographic Intelligence Division. CIA-backed attempt to overthrow President Sukarno of Indonesia. Joint Intelligence Committee disbanded. Soviet Union launches the Sputnik satellite.

1959 **January:** Fidel Castro comes to power in Cuba. **29 May:** Congress passes the National Security Act of 1959.

1960 CIA authorized to assassinate Patrice Lumumba of the Congo; operation aborted. Air force establishes Office of Missile and Satellite Systems. **March:** President Eisenhower approves covert operation to infiltrate guerrillas into Cuba. Viet Minh guerrillas begin full-scale revolt in Vietnam. **Spring:** Castro signs trade agreement with USSR. **1 May:** Soviet Union downs a U-2 plane flown by Francis Gary Powers. **July:** First CIA plan to assassinate Fidel Castro; plan called off. **10 August:** First successful launch of CORONA spy satellite. **25 August:** Central Intelligence Agency and the air force agree to establish the National Reconnaissance Office (NRO).

1961 CIA and air force agreement to establish the NRO comes into effect. The Soviet Union erects a wall in Berlin separating its sector from that of the Western powers. National Security Council creates the National Photographic Interpretation Center (NPIC) from CIA's Photographic Interpretation Center to serve national customers. Secretary of Defense Robert McNamara establishes the Defense Intelligence Agency (DIA). **May:** CIA supplies weapons to Dominican dissidents, who assassinate Rafael Trujillo. **17 April:** Bay of Pigs invasion of Cuba. **June:** President John F. Kennedy meets with Soviet premier Khrushchev in Vienna. **30 November:** President Kennedy authorizes "Operation Mongoose," covert operation to remove Castro.

1962 Defense Intelligence School established. **10 February:** Soviet spy Rudolph Abel (William Fischer) is exchanged for U-2 pilot Francis Gary Powers. **April:** SR-71 spy plane makes its first flight. **14 October:** CIA discovers Soviet medium-range missiles in Cuba. **27 October:** President Kennedy goes on nationwide television to announce "quarantine" of Cuba; the height of Cuban Missile Crisis. **29 October:** The Soviet Union backs down and agrees to remove its missiles from Cuba. **October:** President Kennedy terminates Operation Mongoose. **22 November:** President Kennedy assassinated in Dallas, Texas.

1963 **10 October:** Limited Nuclear Test Ban Treaty (LNTBT) takes effect.

1963–1966 "Confrontation," undeclared war between Britain, Malaysia, and Indonesia; Indonesia attempts to break up Malaysian Federation through guerrilla insurgency; Britain beats attempt back through successful counterinsurgency techniques.

1964 **7 August:** Congress adopts Gulf of Tonkin Resolution.

1965 President Johnson orders American troops into Dominican Republic.

1966 **June:** Richard Helms becomes DCI.

1967   *Ramparts* reveals CIA funding of National Student Association. **8 June:** USS *Liberty* attacked by Israeli gunboats.

1968   **January:** The Tet Offensive in Vietnam. **23 January:** North Korea seizes the USS *Pueblo*. **Summer:** Soviet invasion of Czechoslovakia. **23 December:** North Korea releases crew of USS *Pueblo*.

1970   **5 March:** Nonproliferation Treaty enters into force. **4 September:** Salvador Allende Gossens popularly elected president of Chile. **15 September:** President Richard M. Nixon orders the CIA to prevent Salvador Allende's election in Chile. **22 October:** General Rene Schneider of Chile assassinated. **November:** National Security Council issues National Security Directive (NSD) Memorandum 93, authorizing the destabilization of the government of Chilean president Allende.

1972   CORONA satellite system terminated. **February:** President Nixon visits the People's Republic of China. **17 June:** Break-in at the Democratic National Committee offices in the Watergate building in Washington, D.C. **23 July:** LANDSAT Satellite launched. **December:** DCI Helms fired by President Nixon for saying no to assisting in the Watergate break-in.

1973   **February–June:** James Schlesinger serves as DCI. **8 August:** President Nixon resigns presidency. **September:** DCI William Colby disbands Office of National Estimates and establishes the National Intelligence Council (NIC). **11 September:** General Augusto Pinochet mounts a coup in Chile against Salvador Allende.

1974   Hughes-Ryan Amendment, banning CIA assassinations and requiring findings. **12 August:** *Glomar Explorer* retrieves parts of sunken Soviet submarine in Pacific.

1975   Senate creates Select Committee on Intelligence; House creates its own panel to investigate CIA abuses. Iranian Shah reaches understanding with Iraq's Saddam Hussein against the Kurds. CIA Station Chief in Athens, Richard Welch, murdered by terrorists. **4 January:** President Gerald R. Ford establishes the Rockefeller Commission to investigate activities of the Central Intelligence Agency. **February:** Senate establishes the Select Committee on Intelligence to Investigate Allegations of Illegal or Improper Activities of Federal Intelligence Agencies (later the Church Committee). **30 April:** North Vietnamese forces overrun Saigon, effectively bringing the Vietnam War to an end.

12 May: Cambodian Khmer Rouge gunboats seize American merchant ship USS *Mayaguez* and imprison its crew. **15 May:** U.S. marines free the *Mayaguez*. **6 June:** Rockefeller Commission issues its report.

1976 Intelligence Oversight Board (IOB) established to oversee legality and propriety of U.S. intelligence operations. DCI George H. W. Bush authorizes the development of space-based imaging satellite systems codenamed INDIGO, later renamed LACROSSE. **18 February:** President Ford issues Executive Order (EO) 11905, reorganizing the U.S. intelligence community, enhancing the position of the director of central intelligence, and establishing the Operations Advisory Group to review and approve covert actions. **19 May:** Senate establishes Senate Select Committee on Intelligence (SSCI). **June:** Team A–Team B exercise authorized.

1977 **14 July:** House of Representatives establishes the House Permanent Select Committee on Intelligence (HPSCI). **October:** "Halloween Massacre" at CIA; DCI Stansfield Turner fires over 800 operations officers.

1978 **10 June:** U.S. government launches CHALET (later VORTEX) signals intelligence satellite.

1979 DCI Stansfield Turner establishes National Intelligence Production Board. **16 January:** The Shah of Iran leaves the country. **1 February:** Ayatollah Khomeini returns to Iran. **17 July:** Nicaraguan Sandinistas oust strongman Fulgencio Batista. **4 November:** Iranian militants seize and occupy American Embassy in Tehran. **December:** Soviet Union invades Afghanistan.

1980 CIA ordered to make covert assistance available to Afghan resistance. Intelligence Oversight Act passed.

1981 Soviet intelligence goes on alert fearing surprise U.S. nuclear attack. Defense Intelligence School receives congressional charter and becomes the Defense Intelligence College (DIC). **23 September:** Radio Marti established to beam news reports to Cuba. **20 October:** President Ronald Reagan issues Executive Order 12331 reestablishing the President's Foreign Intelligence Advisory Board (PFIAB). **4 December:** President Reagan issues Executive Orders 12333 and 12334.

1982 **January:** INDIGO radar imaging satellite tested.

1983   Truck bombing in Beirut kills 241 U.S. Marines. U.S Embassy in Beirut bombed by Islamic extremists. **23 March:** President Reagan announces the Strategic Defense Initiative (SDI). **1 September:** Soviet fighter jets shoot down Korean civilian airliner KAL 007.

1984   **4 January:** National Security Council issues National Security Council Directive 17, approving CIA assistance to the Contra rebels in Nicaragua. **March:** CIA officer William Buckley taken hostage by terrorists in Lebanon; is subsequently murdered. **November:** Iran sounds out U.S. through intermediaries about possibility of ransoming hostages in Lebanon in exchange for weapons. U.S. government covertly ships weapons to Iran in exchange for hostages held in Lebanon.

1985   **July:** Iran secretly makes known to U.S. that it would exert its influence on extremists in Lebanon to release hostages in exchange for arms. **August–September:** First shipment of weapons to Iran by Israel; one hostage released. **December:** President Reagan calls off arms sales to Iran.

1986   Congress enacts the Goldwater-Nichols Department of Defense Reorganization Act. **17 January:** President Reagan signs "finding" ordering resumption of arms sales to Iran from U.S. stocks. **2 November:** Lebanese newspaper in Beirut reveals the arms-for-hostages deal. **1 December:** President Reagan authorizes the Tower Commission to investigate the Iran-Contra Affairs.

1988   **18 March:** Indictment of Iran-Contra personalities.

1990   **August:** Iraq invades Kuwait.

1991   Soviet Union dissolves. **January:** The Persian Gulf War. Federal Bureau of Investigation establishes the National Security Threat List (NSTL). **8 March:** Second version of LACROSSE radar imaging satellite launched. **May:** President George H. W. Bush signs "finding" for covert operations in Iraq to overthrow Saddam Hussein. (Clinton administration initially discontinues program but then reactivates it in face of congressional pressure.) **1 July:** Warsaw Pact disbanded.

1992   Intelligence Community Staff (ICS) becomes the Community Management Staff (CMS).

1993   Defense Intelligence College renamed Joint Military Intelligence College (JMIC). American peacekeepers killed in Somalia. President's

Foreign Intelligence Advisory Board absorbs the Intelligence Oversight Board. President Bush establishes the National Drug Intelligence Center (NDIC) within the Department of Justice. **3 February:** Senate votes to confirm James Woolsey as DCI.

1995 Department of Defense (DOD) establishes a new budget category, the Joint Military Intelligence Program (JMIP). **17 April:** President William J. Clinton signs Executive Order 12958 overhauling government secrecy rules. **12 June:** DCI establishes National Intelligence Collection Board (NICB).

1996 1 October: Congress establishes the National Imagery and Mapping Agency (NIMA). **19 December:** KH 11, first U.S. digital satellite, deployed.

1997 19 May: President Clinton names George J. Tenet DCI. **Fall:** Third version of LACROSSE radar imaging satellite launched.

1998 DCI Tenet reveals U.S. intelligence budget. **11 May:** India tests nuclear weapons.

1999 DCI Tenet reverses himself and reclassifies U.S. intelligence budget. **February:** CIA establishes In-Q-Tel. **1 October:** Clinton administration abolishes United States Information Agency.

2001 1 April: U.S. Navy spy plane collides with Chinese fighter and makes emergency landing on Chinese soil. **May:** National Counterintelligence Executive (NCIX) comes into being to protect from foreign industrial espionage. **6 June:** DCI Tenet mission to the Middle East. **11 September:** Terrorist attacks on World Trade Center towers in New York City and the Pentagon in Washington, D.C. **8 October:** Governor Tom Ridge is sworn in as director of Office of Homeland Security. **25 October:** Congress enacts the USA PATRIOT Act.

2002 4 February: Predator reconnaissance drone attacks convoy of terrorists in Afghanistan. **14 February:** Leaders of congressional intelligence committees announce joint inquiry into the terrorist attacks of 11 September 2001. **19 March:** President George W. Bush establishes President's Homeland Security Advisory Council (PHSAC). **23 March:** Arabic-language Radio Sawa authorized. **14 June:** House-Senate panel opens inquiry into 9/11 intelligence failure. **3 November:** CIA Predator drone kills al Qaeda operatives in Yemen. **19 November:** U.S. Senate passes Homeland Security Bill, establishing the Department of Homeland Security (DHS). **16 December:** James S. Gilmore III, chair of the Federal Terrorism Commission, issues report.

2003 **March:** President Bush launches military operations against Iraq to oust Saddam Hussein. **24 November:** The National Geospatial-Intelligence Agency (NGA) replaces the National Imagery and Mapping Agency. **28 November:** Radio Free Europe and Radio Liberty (RL) closed down.

2004 **22 July:** 9/11 Commission releases its report, criticizing the performance of U.S. intelligence. **27 August:** President Bush establishes the National Counterterrorism Center (NCC). **December:** Congress passes the Intelligence Reform and Terrorism Prevention Act, which reorganizes U.S. intelligence by creating the position of the director of national intelligence (DNI) and allowing for the establishment of interagency centers.

2005 **17 February:** President Bush appoints John D. Negroponte as the first DNI. **1 March:** Presidential commission issues report finding the intelligence community to have been "dead wrong" in its assessment of Iraq's weapons of mass destruction capabilities. **18 April:** President Bush issues Executive Order (EO) 13376, replacing the DCI with the DNI on the President's Foreign Intelligence Advisory Board (PFIAB).

Introduction

The public perceives intelligence to be all action, with freewheeling agents either doing dastardly deeds or saving the world. This is a limited view of intelligence, in which the media feeds the public only depictions of covert actions that have gone wrong or of fictional characters stealing secrets, thwarting terrorists, nabbing the bad guys, and producing general mayhem—all, of course, for the common good. The media promotes this erroneous view in order to publicize its television programs or to boost newspaper and magazine readership. Intelligence professionals probably secretly wish that at least some of this were true. However, they also know that what the media puts out for public consumption is for fun and generally a misrepresentation of the world of intelligence.

Some intelligence supports covert actions—the notorious part of intelligence—but the bulk of intelligence activities have more to do with collecting, processing, analyzing, and disseminating intelligence information to decision makers. Indeed, intelligence agencies provide specific services and products to political leaders—consumers—who use intelligence information to make national security and foreign policy decisions. More specifically, intelligence is policy-relevant information, collected through open and clandestine means and subjected to analysis, for the purposes of educating, enlightening, or helping American decision makers in formulating and implementing U.S. national security and foreign policy. This, at least, is the theory behind intelligence, and there is a good deal of truth to it.

THE MISSION

According to the definition, the mission of intelligence is to gather "raw" information based on "requirements" identified by political leaders, analyze that information to make it relevant and actionable, and disseminate "finished" intelligence information in usable form to policymakers. This suggests several functional aspects of intelligence.

First, intelligence seeks to identify threats, gather information about the plans and capabilities of adversaries, and assess their intentions toward the United States. In so doing, intelligence fulfills the role of a safety valve, providing information to decision makers that would reduce their informational gaps and levels of uncertainty. Second, intelligence is employed to protect secrets by identifying those who want to uncover them, steal them, or put them in jeopardy. This counterintelligence function has both defensive and offensive components to it, involving everything from physical and personnel security to counterespionage against foreign agents or Americans working for foreign governments against the United States. Third, some American intelligence activities involve implementing elements of the president's foreign policy. Covert action—special activities, from a legal standpoint— employs intelligence resources to influence events and behaviors abroad for legitimate national security reasons in ways that mask the involvement of the United States government.

THE INTELLIGENCE CYCLE

The principal tasks of intelligence, however, are the gathering, processing, and analysis of intelligence information and the production of intelligence materials that meet policymaker needs. This suggests an intelligence process comprised of several steps, normally referred to as the "intelligence cycle": a cycle of identifying needs; collecting information based on those needs; subjecting the information to analysis; producing finished intelligence based on such analysis; and disseminating the analysis to political leaders, who may then identify additional needs that start the cycle all over again.

The first stage—setting the requirements and priorities and providing direction—is the point where decision makers express their "needs" and relay the "tasking" to the intelligence agencies. This presumes that decision makers know what it is they need and can communicate their requirements effectively, both of which are faulty assumptions. Intelligence professionals frequently find themselves in the position of having to identify gaps in intelligence for political leaders and relate that information to decision makers, a very sensitive issue given that intelligence officers work for politicians and are reluctant, like their bosses, to admit a lack of knowledge.

Indeed, the awkward relationship between policymakers and intelligence officials raises questions about politicization of intelligence. Intelligence professionals in the United States like to portray themselves as objective arbiters of information and as disinterested participants in the policy process. Yet, organizational arrangements, even informal ones like the policy-intelligence relationship, surely exert pressure on intelligence analysts to toe the political line in ways that may jeopardize their policy neutrality.

Collecting and processing intelligence information—the second step in the cycle—is no easy task. Collecting intelligence is subject to several intangible factors, such as whether the information exists in identifiable form in the first place and whether it can be accessed in a reasonably cost-effective way. Gathering intelligence spans a variety of collection disciplines—such as signals intelligence (SIGINT), imagery intelligence (IMINT), and human intelligence—and is subject to institutional and budgetary considerations. Acquisition of intelligence is also highly sensitive to political and technological constraints. Even if the information is collected, it may not be the right information and therefore may not directly address the issues formulated in the requirements process. Technological and human constraints may even thwart the gathering of information on a particular issue altogether. Worse still, there may be policy questions, which have no answers. Former director of central intelligence (DCI) Robert M. Gates once claimed that there are secrets and there are mysteries; secrets can be acquired by using intelligence methods, but mysteries simply defy collection, analysis, and explanation.

The third stage of the cycle—analysis—is the point at which the gathered and processed information goes through rigorous evaluation and analysis. Without analysis, raw intelligence stands on its own, outside its context, and with little relevance. Information that has not been analyzed may also be misinterpreted and misused. Some policymakers prefer to do their own analysis. Undoubtedly, policymakers possess substantial analytic capabilities, but there is a critical difference—policymakers perform analysis within the context of their political world and their policy preferences, which may skew and bias their evaluations. Intelligence analysts are better placed objectively to evaluate raw intelligence. Analysts themselves often are subject to political pressures—after all, the intelligence analyst operates in a political world—but good analysts are able to extricate themselves sufficiently from policy concerns and conduct their analyses in a politically neutral environment.

Intelligence analysis leads to the next step in the intelligence cycle—production—where intelligence information finds its way into "finished" intelligence products. Because policymakers have their own preferences about how they absorb information, intelligence analysts study the consumption patterns of their consumers as well as the intelligence questions they pose. Intelligence analysts also have the obligation to ensure that their intelligence products—whether in manuscript form, oral briefings, or video teleconferencing—are engaging enough to draw the attention of policymakers. Above all, intelligence products must be timely, accurate, and relevant. Policymakers may otherwise not understand or deliberately ignore intelligence information, or even turn to other sources of information, all of which defeat the purposes of intelligence.

Factors such as cost, time, and the availability of information certainly affect whether intelligence serves the policy consumer well. Finished intelligence is relayed to the consumer on a "need to know" basis—that is, it is disseminated, the last stage in the cycle—to answer the policymakers' questions as completely and accurately as possible in a timely manner. While finished intelligence usually seeks to be thorough, it may only answer questions partially or not at all. It may also raise new questions. The theory of the intelligence cycle suggests that these new questions then serve as new requirements, along with new foreign policy crises, national security threats, and other policy concerns.

HISTORY

The United States government has had to deal with and address these issues in varying degrees throughout its history. In fact, the United States government engaged in intelligence activities from the inception of the republic, but the quality of the capability has varied over time, largely owing to the fact that Americans generally have been suspicious of such European balance of power tactics as espionage. For much of the history of the United States, Americans rejected anything associated with nefarious European politics, and intelligence suffered as a result.

The historical antipathy to intelligence is now part of the political culture and still affects the American psyche. The history of U.S. intelligence can be broken down into three historical periods. The first period spans the nascent years just before the onset of the Revolutionary War in 1776 until the end of the Civil War in 1865 and can best be described as one during which intelligence remained largely in the background, providing services to individual decision makers—particularly to military commanders or specific presidents—who wanted to avail themselves of its services but rejected the notion of having a formal and centralized intelligence establishment. The second period, from 1865 until the end of World War II in 1945, was one of transition, in which the United States, an emerging power in world politics, made piecemeal and largely unsuccessful attempts to establish an ongoing and permanent intelligence capability. The third period, spanning the years 1945 until the present, is the one in which the United States developed a permanent, professional, and civilian intelligence apparatus that took into account American unease with intelligence while bowing to the realities of the modern world, such as the Cold War and the more complicated global environment that followed it.

Nascent Period, 1776–1865

Intelligence—both the capability and the services it provides—is a tool available to presidents for use in conducting foreign policy. Precedents for presidential use of intelligence were set early in the history of the United States, beginning with the Sons of Liberty organizations that were created in 1775 to bring patriots together in common cause and to gather information against the British foe. These organizations later were transformed into the Committees of Correspondence, which acted as the first American intelligence agencies. The Continental Congress incorporated the Committees of Correspondence into its legislative structure and then evolved them into the House Committee on Foreign Affairs, which until World War II was the principal congressional committee responsible for overseeing American foreign relations.

During the Revolutionary War, General George Washington ran his own spy group—the Culper Ring—and successfully laid down principles governing intelligence secrecy and the provision of secret funding of intelligence. By the time Washington became president, the young United States already had a hero in the person of Nathan Hale, whose statue, with the inscription "I only regret that I have but one life to lose for my country," now stands in front of the Central Intelligence Agency (CIA) headquarters in McLean, Virginia. Benjamin Franklin also ran his own spies in London, where he was an emissary, and made arms deals with the French. He also engaged in double-agent operations, which were common in the late 1700s, inaugurating the field of counterintelligence that would not be fully incorporated into U.S. intelligence until two hundred years later.

George Washington's successors also undertook ad hoc intelligence operations, mostly to accommodate the young country's expansionist aims, or what later became known as "manifest destiny." For example, President Thomas Jefferson commissioned the Lewis and Clark expedition in 1803 to scout out the American Northwest and bring back detailed information and maps about the lay of the land and the people living on it. In 1811, President James Madison approved a covert operation to steal Florida from the Spanish and sent an agent to negotiate with the Spaniards to bring Florida into the United States peacefully. Instead, the agent, against orders, fomented rebellion by the English-speaking inhabitants, prompting President Madison to disavow the agent and his operation. The debacle caused a rift with Spain, but the United States acquired Florida in 1819.

This kind of ad hoc and unformulated intelligence effort remained the norm until after the Civil War. Taking advantage of discontent among Mexican citizens, for example, American military commanders during the Mexican-American War (1845–1848) were able to form temporary intelligence units to serve their military needs. The Mexican Spy Company was one of the more successful.

The Civil War accelerated intelligence activities on both sides to some degree, principally because of the impact of new technologies. The railroad made long-distance travel economical and easy. The observation balloon and the telegraph created opportunities for intelligence collection. That both sides had a common language and culture helped make espionage a prominent feature of the strategic landscape. Yet, most intelligence operations were the personal efforts of various military commanders, even though both sides tried to establish formal intelligence capabilities, with little success. The South's Confederate Secret Service and Allan Pinkerton's efforts on behalf of the Union are examples of this.

As the side rebelling against an established government, the Confederates undertook more intelligence operations than the Union, engaging in such covert actions as shipping arms and supplies to sympathizers, guerrilla warfare, and sabotage. For example, Confederate president Jefferson Davis created an intelligence operation that involved the opening of a land route between Maryland and Virginia for the covert movement of people and money to finance the South's war effort. In addition, according to one account, the assassination of President Abraham Lincoln was a Confederate covert operation, intended to kidnap Lincoln and hold him hostage.

Transitional Period, 1865–1945

The Civil War was a watershed for U.S. intelligence, for it exposed the risks of haphazard intelligence operations. The beginning of the modern American intelligence structure can be traced to the period immediately after the Civil War. Technological developments were the main impetus for the growth of America's nascent intelligence apparatus, incorporating such techniques as collecting aerial intelligence by means of surveillance balloons and other types of craft. Moreover, innovations in the communications industry, such as the development of the telegraph, sparked interest in encryption and decoding capabilities. The navy established a permanent intelligence unit—the Office of Naval Intelligence (ONI)—in 1882, and the army's intelligence unit—the Military Intelligence Division (MID)—came into being in 1885.

During the World War I, U.S. intelligence efforts were limited to supporting the new American foreign policy doctrine of "open diplomacy," reflecting the openness that permeated the thinking of U.S. policymakers at the time. To promote this new way of doing things, the State Department assumed the responsibility of coordinating all intelligence information, an effort that lasted until 1927. Even though there is general agreement that intelligence barely made an impression on policy leaders, many precedents were set in these early years, including civilian control of intelligence.

In the interwar years between 1918 and 1941, code making and code breaking became important enterprises, involving the State Department, the army, and the navy, all of which concentrated on breaking the codes of foreign governments in order to read their secret correspondence and to make their own more secure. The State Department established the "Black Chamber" in New York City for such a purpose, and this operation managed to decode or decipher more than 45,000 telegrams from 19 countries over a period of 12 years. Secretary of State Henry Stimpson was informed of the operation in 1929, upon which he ordered the closure of the Black Chamber, claiming that gentlemen do not read each other's mail. This assertion has become part of American intelligence folklore, and intelligence officials today often allude to Stimpson's claim as an illustration of the politicians' naiveté and folly. After Stimpson closed the Black Chamber, its director, Herbert O. Yardley, wrote a book revealing the secrets of American code-breaking operations, prompting the Japanese—who were deemed the main threat to the United States—to change their codes.

The army and the navy surreptitiously continued interception programs despite the closing of the State Department's cryptologic program, and they successfully broke the Japanese codes once again. The U.S. government gave the acronym MAGIC to the intercepted Japanese material. In 1941, MAGIC provided information that a Japanese attack was imminent, but did not say where or when. The ensuing Japanese surprise attack on Pearl Harbor and the failure of U.S. intelligence to detect it ahead of time shocked the American people and provided the impetus for the establishment of a centrally organized civilian intelligence organization after the war.

However, before the Japanese attack, the British had persuaded President Franklin D. Roosevelt to establish the Office of the Coordinator of Information (COI), which was to carry out "when requested by the President, such supplementary activities as may facilitate the securing of information important for national security not now available to the Government." The president appointed William Donovan to be COI, whose mandate was to gather intelligence information, but Donovan considered analytical work only a "cover" for secret operations. In early 1942, soon after America's entrance into the war, President Roosevelt established the Office of Strategic Services (OSS) and designated Donovan to head it. Donovan employed the OSS principally for operations like infiltrations and sabotage, although he also commissioned some notable analytic efforts that were later published and made available to the public.

Period of Professionalization, 1945–Present

At the end of the war, President Harry S. Truman and his advisors followed American tradition and demobilized the armed forces, including the OSS. Even with the emergence of the USSR as a serious threat and the rapidly changing strategic situation, the Truman administration was slow to recognize the need for the United States to have an intelligence capability. As a stopgap measure, and bowing to the realities of the emerging Cold War, Congress in January 1946 established the National Intelligence Authority (NIA) and the Central Intelligence Group (CIG) to coordinate intelligence, primarily among the feuding military services and the Federal Bureau of Investigation (FBI), while the civilians debated the merits of establishing a permanent professional civilian intelligence organization.

A good deal of public and policy opposition to a central civilian organization focused on possible threats to civil liberties and constitutional government. Even President Truman wanted to be certain "that no single unit or agency of the Federal Government would have so much power that we would find ourselves, perhaps inadvertently, slipping in the direction of a police state." The military also opposed the creation of a central intelligence organization for bureaucratic reasons, fearing some loss of turf, access, authority, and money if strategic military intelligence were to be taken away by a new intelligence-gathering agency. The FBI was opposed, too, because it did not want to lose the foreign intelligence and espionage capabilities in Latin America that it had acquired in the 1930s.

Yet, Congress enacted the National Security Act in August of 1947, setting up the National Security Council (NSC), a coordinating and policy-planning body consisting of the president, vice president, and the secretaries of defense and state. It also established the Central Intelligence Agency (CIA) to coordinate intelligence analysis so that never again would the government suffer from too many intelligence agencies working at cross-purposes. The act specified the CIA as an independent agency reporting to the president through the NSC to coordinate intelligence activities, provide intelligence analysis to political leaders, and engage in special activities that the National Security Council may direct. The director of central intelligence (DCI), whose position was created in 1946 to coordinate intelligence information, was designated under the act the advisor to the president on intelligence matters. The act also gave the DCI command of the CIA. The CIA's limited mandate—the act denied the CIA any police, subpoena, law-enforcement powers, or internal security functions—spoke to the concerns of those who feared for American liberties.

The National Security Act of 1947 also created the National Military Authority and the Office of the Secretary of Defense, with little authority over the autonomous military services. A 1949 amendment to the law established the Department of Defense (DOD) and incorporated the services within it. The Joint Chiefs of Staff (JCS) was also created out of the loose arrangements that existed during World War II and before. The act did not abolish the intelligence units of the army, the Military Intelligence Division (MID), or the navy, the Office of Naval Intelligence (ONI), or other departmental intelligence services. Instead, the act stipulated each would continue to perform its own more specialized intelligence functions.

The Central Intelligence Agency became the spearhead for intelligence operations during the Cold War. However, given the bureaucratic tensions over the creation of the CIA, it surprised no one that the CIA quickly became enmeshed in bureaucratic fights to expand its authorities into areas not mentioned in the National Security Act and into covert operations designed to thwart Soviet designs in the European theater. As a matter of fact, the late 1940s and the entire decade of the 1950s were later to be known as the CIA's Golden Age, when the agency engaged in a series of successful covert operations that built its reputation as the "quiet option" available to American presidents for wielding power. For example, the CIA's operations secured Italy away from the communists in 1948; overthrew Prime Minister Mohammad Mossadegh in Iran in 1953 (Operation Ajax); and ousted the elected government of Alfonso Arbenz in Guatemala in 1954 (Operation Success). U.S. intelligence also managed to get hold of Soviet premier Nikita Khrushchev's secret 1956 speech to the Communist Party Congress, denouncing Stalin's abuses. In addition, the CIA forecast the launching of the Soviet Sputnik in 1957. However, the CIA failed in many respects to anticipate key developments during this time. For example, it failed to forecast the North Korean invasion of South Korea in 1950; the People's Republic of China's (PRC's) entry into the Korean War; the defeat of the French in Vietnam; the British-French-Israeli invasion of Egypt that led to the Suez Crisis in 1956; and the Soviet invasion of Hungary in 1956.

Technological innovations in the post–World War II environment prompted new intelligence advances. The National Security Agency (NSA) was established in 1952 to consolidate cryptology (or interception of communications), code making and code breaking (on which cryptology depends), and communications security (COMSEC). Combining all these activities in a single agency meant that the other intelligence agencies would have to depend on the NSA for their needs in these areas. Thus, the NSA became a service agency for the entire U.S. government, in and out of the intelligence community, providing services in encryption, communications interception, and secure communications. The NSA continues to function in this capacity today.

The launching of the Sputnik satellite in 1957 inaugurated the space age and gave U.S. intelligence the incentive to delve into new technological areas. The Sputnik energized U.S. intelligence in the area of aerial and space reconnaissance, especially the satellite program that was already in the works within the Advanced Research Projects Agency (ARPA) of the Department of Defense. Meanwhile, the CIA had contracted and built the U-2 aircraft in the mid-1950s. The CIA had also begun to develop the CORONA satellite project that would in the 1960s return photographic images in film canisters. The CIA soon established the National Photographic Interpretation Center (NPIC) to analyze the information gleaned from these new technologies.

The urgency of attaining an operational satellite program increased with the downing of Francis Gary Powers and his U-2 aircraft over the Soviet Union in 1960. In that year, the air force established the Office of Missile and Satellite Systems to direct, supervise, and control satellite development for the military. To facilitate this development, the CIA and the air force signed an agreement in 1961 to establish the National Reconnaissance Office (NRO) to oversee and fund research and development for reconnaissance aircraft and their sensors, procure space systems and their associated ground stations, determine launch vehicle requirements, operate spacecraft after they attained orbit, and disseminate the data collected. Because of satellites, overhead reconnaissance rapidly became the principal source of American intelligence. The NRO remained an official state secret until 1994, when the Department of Defense and the CIA acknowledged its existence but refused to declassify anything else about the organization.

A joint study group in 1958 recommended the consolidation of military intelligence agencies within the Office of the Secretary of Defense. However, President John F. Kennedy's secretary of defense, Robert McNamara, decided to allow the services to retain tactical intelligence and transfer strategic military intelligence to the Defense Intelligence Agency (DIA), which was established in 1961 as the intelligence arm of the Joint Chiefs of Staff.

The energetic use of new collection technologies enabled U.S. intelligence agencies to score some impressive successes during the 1960s. For example, U.S. intelligence did forecast the Sino-Soviet split in 1962, the development of the Chinese atomic bomb in 1964, the deployment of new Soviet strategic weapons, the Arab-Israeli War in 1967, and the Soviet antiballistic missile (ABM) system in 1968. However, there is also an equally impressive list of intelligence failures during the 1960s. The Bay of Pigs invasion of Cuba in 1961, intended to oust Fidel Castro from power, turned into a disaster. In quick succession thereafter, U.S. intelligence failed to forecast developments in Vietnam, although intelligence officials were split on various issues, with the CIA assessing the war as unwinnable and the military holding on to the view that sufficient force could conclude the war. American intelligence also failed to foresee the toughness of the Vietnamese guerrillas—the Viet Cong—and the Tet Offensive of 1968, which is generally considered the watershed event that turned the American public against the U.S. political leadership and the conduct of the Vietnam War. U.S. intelligence failed in 1968 to forecast the Soviet invasion of Czechoslovakia.

The decade of the 1970s ushered in an era that weakened U.S. intelligence. Soon after the decade began, American intelligence was mired in defending itself against a public outcry about its illegal activities. Revelations came in quick succession—assassination attempts against Castro, an assassination program in Vietnam (the Phoenix Program), spying on antiwar activists in the United States (COINTELPRO), dirty tricks against civil-rights leaders and liberal politicians, and the overthrow of democratically elected governments. The public as well as political leaders demanded curbs on U.S. intelligence, which were quickly set in place.

In 1974, the Hughes-Ryan Amendment, an amendment to the Intelligence Authorization Act, prohibited the Central Intelligence Agency from engaging in assassinations and initiated the "finding" process. Executive orders during the Gerald R. Ford and Jimmy Carter administrations put additional restrictions on intelligence operations. The U.S. Congress also began a series of hearings in the late 1970s on U.S. intelligence activities, which culminated in the establishment of formal congressional oversight. The Senate Select Committee on Intelligence (SSCI) was established in 1977, and the House Permanent Select Committee on Intelligence (HPSCI) was established in 1978. Both committees considered and rejected the notion of an intelligence charter for the CIA, but Congress passed the Intelligence Oversight Act of 1980, which put in place, for the first time, a process for the approval of covert action by the U.S. Congress.

Despite preoccupation with survival, intelligence agencies forecast the India-Pakistan War of 1971; the Turkish invasion of Cyprus in 1974; and the Chinese invasion of Vietnam in 1978. However, they failed to foresee the Arab-Israeli war in 1973; the Soviet invasion of Afghanistan in 1979; and the fall of the Iranian shah in 1979.

In 1981, President Ronald Reagan issued Executive Order 12333, which still is the legal instrument governing U.S. intelligence activities. President Reagan's order described the agencies of the U.S. intelligence community and their activities, set in place oversight mechanisms in both the executive and legislative branches, and extended the prohibition of assassination to the rest of the U.S. government.

Stringent congressional and executive branch oversight did not inhibit U.S. intelligence from becoming embroiled in the Contra War in Nicaragua and the Iran-Contra Affair in the mid-1980s. These developments gave further credence to those who believed that U.S. intelligence could not refrain from illegal activities despite statutory safeguards.

U.S. intelligence agencies were in no position in the late 1980s to accurately forecast the breakup of the USSR and the fall of communism. On the one hand, there is substantial evidence that agencies like the DIA and CIA did produce finished intelligence that marked the slow but steady deterioration of the Soviet system. On the other hand, the media has long claimed that U.S. intelligence agencies failed to call the Soviet breakup. Preoccupation with Soviet developments probably accounted for the failure of the U.S. intelligence community to anticipate Iraq's invasion of Kuwait in 1990.

The end of the Cold War in the early 1990s brought a call to downsize the national security apparatus in the U.S. government, including the intelligence agencies. Anticipating the "peace dividend," each of the agencies began programs of reducing staff and activities, such that by the mid-1990s staffing numbers were at levels not seen since the early 1970s. At the same time, a process of "openness" ushered in a period of public debate and discussion about intelligence and its role in the American society.

Rapid technological advancements, especially in information technologies, also contributed to organizational innovations in the 1990s. Yet, the American intelligence establishment did not forecast the intertribal conflict in Somalia that led to the killing of American peacekeepers in 1993, and it performed poorly in Bosnia and Kosovo. It even missed the Indian nuclear tests in 1998. Because of widespread perceptions of a steady deterioration of U.S. intelligence capabilities, the administration of President William J. Clinton reversed itself and began making substantial investments in intelligence capabilities. By the end of the 1990s, U.S. intelligence was making a comeback from the sloth into which it had sunk in the early parts of the decade. The 11 September 2001 terrorist attacks propelled U.S. intelligence into the forefront of the national fight against terrorists and thrust the U.S. intelligence community into the center of American national security policy.

Despite its prominence in the national security front, U.S. intelligence came under intense scrutiny for its failure to anticipate the 9/11 terrorist attacks. First, a congressional joint intelligence inquiry in 2002 found America's intelligence agencies to have performed poorly in collecting and analyzing terrorism information and criticized the loose management of the intelligence community. The independent national commission investigating the terrorist attacks, established in 2003, came to similar conclusions, focusing on the lack of centralized direction and control as the key ingredient in making for the 9/11 intelligence failure. Subsequently, Congress passed the Intelligence Reform and Terrorism Prevention Act of 2004, which established the position of the director of national intelligence (DNI) and provided for various fusion centers as palliatives for the historic drawbacks of the American intelligence community.

ORGANIZATION, MANAGEMENT, AND CONTROL

The Intelligence Reform and Terrorism Prevention Act now endows the DNI with the authority to control and direct the U.S. intelligence community, including most of its money and personnel. The director of central intelligence (DCI), who was the titular head of the intelligence community (IC) for 58 years, stays on as the head of the CIA, which is part of an intelligence community of 15 departments, bureaus, and agencies. The IC today, as in the past, is an informal confederation—more a cartel, really—of autonomous agencies with a structure intended to divide authority among them. Indeed, the organization of American intelligence reflects the dominant political culture—that it is desirable to "divide and rule" an establishment that potentially could affect freedoms and civil liberties. The IC today comprises 15 separate entities:

- Defense Intelligence Agency (DIA)
- National Security Agency (NSA)
- Intelligence units of the army, navy, air force, and marines
- National Geospatial-Intelligence Agency (NGA)
- National Reconnaissance Office (NRO)
- Department of Homeland Security (DHS) and, separately, the Coast Guard, part of the Department of Homeland Security
- Counterintelligence unit of the Federal Bureau of Investigation (FBI)
- Intelligence division of the Department of the Treasury
- Intelligence division of the Department of Energy (DOE)
- Bureau of Intelligence and Research (INR) in the Department of State
- Central Intelligence Agency (CIA)

These agencies are organizationally scattered throughout the executive branch, further fragmenting the community. In addition, their disparate and specialized missions, structures, and institutional affiliations guarantee that they all compete against each other to secure benefits for themselves. For example, the DIA; NSA; army, navy, air force, and marine intelligence; NGA; and NRO all fall under the Department of Defense (DOD) and therefore reflect the missions and priorities of the military establishment. The other intelligence units—with the exception of the CIA—either are or belong to a cabinet-level policy department in the executive branch and so reflect the bureaucratic imperatives of their cabinet secretaries. The CIA, on the other hand, is an independent U.S. government agency, much like the Federal Reserve Bank, the Interstate Commerce Commission, and hundreds of others, now reporting to the president through the DNI and the NSC. Each IC agency contributes to the broader intelligence mission in discrete and specialized ways, while simultaneously participating in the larger effort of providing policy leaders with the comprehensive and collective judgment of the intelligence community—neither an easy nor an inexpensive task.

Between 1946 and 2004, the DCIs performed three functions. First, the DCI was authorized to put together, submit, and control the National Foreign Intelligence Program (NFIP) budget (one of three intelligence budgets, the other two controlled by the secretary of defense), which is the intelligence community budget, integrating intelligence requirements that policymakers feel are necessary during any given budgetary cycle. Second, the DCI managed the country's counterintelligence programs, a responsibility shared by some IC agencies. Third, the DCI as IC chief was responsible for protecting sources and methods. Most of what is secret about the intelligence process is the way it is done—the sources from which information is obtained and the methods used to obtain it. This secrecy is mainly for the protection of these sources and methods; otherwise, U.S. intelligence would be unable to gather and analyze the information necessary to understanding adversaries and issues relevant to U.S. security. "Protecting sources and methods" forms the basis for all classification and compartmentation schemes in the government, an area over which the DCI retains complete control.

These three responsibilities—submitting a community budget, conducting counterintelligence, and protecting sources and methods—were the only ones the DCI exercised in his statutory role as head of the intelligence community. Even in this capacity, however, the DCI was more a coordinator, only able to exercise soft power techniques like persuasion and influence. To overcome this deficiency, the typical DCI needed to bring to his office attributes that enabled him better to manage the community—a personal relationship and access to the president, the skills of an excellent negotiator, and the patience of a mediator. Some DCIs were very successful in doing this, but most lacked these qualities and therefore were less successful in their community responsibilities.

Because the heads of IC agencies—except the CIA—reported directly to their policy principals, the DCI's relative position in the White House pecking order also came into play in the bureaucratic politics of the intelligence community. This was especially so regarding the Pentagon's intelligence units, over which the secretary of defense loomed—and still looms—large. From time to time, a particular secretary of defense would give lip service to allowing the DCI greater authority over the defense-related intelligence organizations, but no defense secretary ever relinquished any significant amount of power to the DCI. It took an act of Congress and substantial compromise finally to get the Department of Defense to relinquish some authority and moneys to the new DNI in 2004.

The DNI's ability now to manage the IC in an effective way depends largely on the president's backing. This is so because the 2004 act provides for a substantially weaker DNI than that sought by the 9/11 Commission report. Consequently, while the act endows the DNI ostensibly with substantial power, the wielding of that power depends on presidential endorsement. Short of that, the DNI is a mere coordinator, reminiscent of the role the DCIs played for 58 years as titular heads of the IC.

The DNI's authorities are now limited. Under the law, the DNI has a say in hiring the heads of the intelligence agencies but has no authority to fire them. The DNI can move money from one agency to another to meet needs, but always within strict limits. Under the law, the DNI has only limited authority to reprogram funds and transfer personnel from the Defense Department, while the department still keeps control over its massive intelligence agencies as well as 30 percent of intelligence moneys. The DNI, under the law, is supposed to develop and determine all agency budgets, but he is only empowered to monitor the implementation and execution of intelligence spending. Moreover, while the legislation puts the new national intelligence chief in the position of commanding the attention of agency heads, weakened authorities do not assure greater intelligence coherence and effectiveness. Indeed, given the weakness of law, the new position constitutes an additional bureaucratic layer, further separating the titular head of U.S. intelligence from collectors and analysts who reside within the agencies.

Given the fluidity of the international order and the response of the American government to it, it is almost certain that American intelligence will continue to evolve in unpredictable ways in the near future.

Some of the changes that U.S. intelligence will experience are already in the offing, what with the establishment of the position of a new national intelligence director and consolidation of the country's counterterrorism institutions. Undoubtedly, American intelligence 20 years from now will look considerably different from the way it does now, for new challenges will compel it to reinvent itself to meet them. However, the history of American intelligence as illustrated in its people, institutions, and actions shows that its fundamental principles at least are immutable and an essential part of the American democratic enterprise.

The Dictionary

– A –

ABEL, RUDOLPH (1903–1971). Rudolph Abel was a Soviet illegal agent who organized spy networks and acquired atomic secrets in the United States from 1946 until 1957. Born as William Fischer to radical parents, Abel began working for Soviet security in 1927 and served primarily as a radio operator in Norway and Britain in the 1930s. During **World War II**, Fischer lived in Moscow with his friend, the real Rudolph Abel, also a Soviet agent who died in 1955. On 12 October 1946, the Soviet **GRU** sent Fischer to the United States, under the code name ARACH, to reorganize the system of illegals, set up communications with Moscow, and create sabotage networks.

In 1948–1949, Fischer approached several American nuclear scientists, such as Theodore Alvin Hall, for atomic secrets. During the **Korean War**, Fischer also served as a possible saboteur, calling all Soviet explosive experts in Latin America to the United States for possible action. However, his primary mission continued to be the acquisition of information on American nuclear weapons. One of Fischer's subordinates in the United States finally betrayed him to the **Federal Bureau of Investigation** (FBI), and the FBI arrested Fischer on 21 July 1957. Fischer spent five years in prison and was exchanged on 10 February 1962 for **Francis Gary Powers**, the pilot of the **U-2** spy plane that was shot down over the **USSR** on 1 May 1960.

ACCOUNTABILITY REVIEW BOARD. Unit within the **Central Intelligence Agency** (CIA), composed of selected senior managers, that reviews the agency's activities and performance, assigns blame for misdeeds and failures, and recommends disciplinary actions and corrective measures. The board works closely with the CIA's independent inspector general, who is nominated by the president and confirmed by the Senate.

AFGHANISTAN. *See* MUJAHIDEEN, AFGHAN.

AIR AMERICA. A front company, formally known as a **proprietary**, of the **Central Intelligence Agency** (CIA), Air America was established in the early 1950s essentially to support American military operations in **Vietnam**, Laos, and Thailand. It hauled refugees, ammunition, and troops through Laos; inserted and extracted reconnaissance teams; worked with Thai police to stem communist guerrilla infiltrations; and carried refugees and CIA agents between Hanoi and Saigon from 1954 until the end of the war. An Air America helicopter was the last to leave Saigon, now Ho Chi Minh City, with a load of passengers before the city fell to Viet Cong guerrillas and North Vietnamese troops in 1975.

AIR FORCE INTELLIGENCE, SURVEILLANCE, AND RE-CONNAISSANCE (ISR). A formal member of the **intelligence community** (IC), Air Force ISR specialists are embedded in each air force component, preparing for and conducting operations that range from disaster and humanitarian relief, peacekeeping, counterterrorism, and counternarcotics, to full-scale conflict. The air force acquired its own intelligence capability soon after the **National Security Act of 1947** established the air force as an independent service within America's military structure.

Air Force ISR is the latest iteration in the evolution of air force intelligence. It now has the responsibility to provide accurate, timely intelligence on air and space forces for U.S., allied, and coalition forces at all echelons and levels of command. It does so by employing analytic tools and dissemination systems to tailor intelligence information for all levels of the air force, including theater commanders.

ISR contains several subordinate elements, the most important of which is the National Air Intelligence Center (NAIC), which exploits and analyzes adversary air, space, and long-range ballistic missile systems using all-source information. Another major subordinate unit is the Air Force Information Warfare Center (AFIWC), which works on the development of information warfare concepts, tools, and a wide array of support services. In addition, Air Force ISR contributes to national intelligence capabilities by operating a worldwide array of ground-based, airborne, shipborne and space-based high-technology sensors.

AJAX (OPERATION). A **covert action** by the **Central Intelligence Agency** (CIA) in 1953 to overthrow the government of Prime Minister Mohammad Mossadegh in **Iran**. Both the American and British governments were angered by Mossadegh's nationalization of the Anglo-Iranian Oil Corporation in 1952. In addition, the Iranian Communist Party was gaining influence, and President **Dwight D. Eisenhower** feared that the Iranian political climate, if left unchecked, would enable the **Union of Soviet Socialist Republics** (USSR) to have a stronghold on Iranian oil. A CIA operative, Kermit Roosevelt (grandson of President Theodore Roosevelt) headed a joint U.S.-British operation that incited a revolt against Mossadegh, overthrowing him and restoring Shah Reza Pahlavi to power. This action, though lauded as a successful covert operation at the time, engendered resentment of the United States and the United Kingdom among Iranians and sparked an insurgent religious movement that eventually ousted the shah in 1979 and led to the Iranian hostage crisis, during which Iranian students held 54 American officials hostage for 444 days. The hostages were released on 20 January 1981.

ALIAS. A fictitious name employed by an officer of the **Central Intelligence Agency** (CIA) to mask his identity when conducting operations. A CIA officer may use many aliases during an operation. *See also* PSEUDONYM.

ALIEN REGISTRATION ACT. *See* McCARTHY ERA.

ALL AMERICAN SYSTEM. The All American system was an innovative agent extraction procedure employed by the British toward the end of **World War II**. The procedure involved the use of a modified version of a mail pickup system used by All American Aviation before America's entry into the war. The mail package to be picked up was secured to a transfer line, strung between two wheel poles, set 54 feet apart. The aircraft designated to do the pickup approached the ground in a gentle glide of 90 miles per hour, while a mechanic in the airplane let out a 50-foot steel cable, with a four-finger grapple at the end. As the aircraft pulled up, the grapple engaged the transfer line, and the mechanic winched the mail package into the airplane.

The British revised the All American system in September 1943 to retrieve human beings behind enemy lines. The modified grapple yanked the transfer line off the ground, and the agent soared off behind the airplane. While the British used the system to retrieve agents, United States forces occasionally used the method to retrieve objects, such as downed gliders. During the **Korean War**, the **Central Intelligence Agency** (CIA) used the system to retrieve agents as part of **Operation Tropic**. It modified and adapted the system even further toward the end of the 1950s, employing it as part of the **Skyhook system** and **Operation Coldfeet**.

ALLENDE, SALVADOR (1908–1973). President of **Chile** from 1970 until 1973, when a coup fomented by Chilean military officers, who were backed by the **Central Intelligence Agency** (CIA), ousted him from office. Prior to his presidency, Allende served as minister in a previous government and was for a time chairman of the Chilean Senate. He ran for president of Chile three times and succeeded in 1970 as leader of the Unidad Popular coalition party.

The U.S. government, along with American commercial interests in Chile, had long opposed left-leaning politicians and supported the Chilean Right, especially the Christian Democrats. Declassified documents show that beginning in 1963 the CIA spent $2.6 million on propping up the Christian Democratic presidential aspirant, Eduardo Frei. Allende was a thorn in the sides of both the Christian Democrats and the CIA, especially because Allende, a physician by profession, was an ardent Marxist and an outspoken critic of the capitalist system. Even before his election, Allende had declared his intention for far-reaching socialist reforms but was vague about how exactly he planned to implement them.

President **Richard M. Nixon** made his displeasure with Allende's prospective election known very early in his administration and instructed the CIA to engage in **covert actions** to prevent Allende's election. Consequently, the CIA spent an additional $3 million on propaganda activities to turn Chilean voters away from Allende. When that failed, the Nixon White House authorized the CIA to oust Allende from office. General **Augusto Pinochet** overthrew the Allende government in a CIA-engineered military coup on 11 September 1973, and Allende committed suicide soon thereafter. *See also* COVERT ACTION; FUBELT (OPERATION); KISSINGER, HENRY A.; NATIONAL SECURITY DECISION MEMORANDUM 93.

ALL SOURCE ANALYSIS SYSTEM (ASAS). ASAS is a computerized battlefield intelligence collection system developed by the Jet Propulsion Laboratory (JPL) of Pasadena, California, and operated by **Army Intelligence and Security Command** (INSCOM). The system receives intelligence information by radio or from battlefield sensors, analyzes it, and provides real-time results to tactical commanders. The army first used the system in the 1991 Persian Gulf War by employing more than a dozen workstations in the battlefield. *See also* TACTICAL INTELLIGENCE.

AL QAI'DA. Also commonly referred to as al Qaeda, it is an umbrella organization of worldwide terrorist groups that espouse *jihad* (or holy war) against the West, or what Islamists call "the Jews and crusaders." Formed by Osama bin Laden in the 1980s to bring together Arabs and other Muslims fighting in **Afghanistan** against the Soviet occupation, al Qai'da's goal is to establish a pan-Islamic state throughout the world by overthrowing "non-Islamic" regimes and expelling Westerners and non-Muslims from Muslim countries.

Its long-term strategy calls for the use of force as a preferred method. Al Qai'da has been implicated in numerous terrorists acts, such as the 1993 bombings of the World Trade Center in New York City, the assassination plot against Pope John Paul II in 1994, the plan to hijack American commercial airliners over the Pacific in 1995, the bombings of U.S. embassies in Africa in August 1998, the attack on the USS *Cole* on 12 October 1999, the **terrorist attacks of 11 September 2001**, and the bombings of two synagogues in Istanbul, Turkey, on 15 November 2003.

AMERICAN INTELLIGENCE COMMAND (AIC). Established in the summer of 1942 by the **Military Intelligence Division** (MID), AIC was an effort to establish a series of intelligence-gathering networks in

Latin America. Run by the American defense attachés attached to U.S. embassies in the western hemisphere during **World War II**, AIC ran into numerous problems and points of conflict with **Special Intelligence Service** (SIS) agents of the **Federal Bureau of Investigation** (FBI). These jurisdictional disputes continued throughout the war and were only addressed by the establishment of the **Central Intelligence Group** (CIG) in 1946.

AMES, ALDRICH (1941–). Aldrich Ames was a mid-level employee of the **Central Intelligence Agency** (CIA) who was arrested in 1994 for spying for the Russians. Ames entered CIA duty in 1967 as a case officer, working primarily against the **Soviet Union**. He later was transferred to counterintelligence duties against Soviet targets. According to his own statements, Ames began providing information to the Soviets in April 1985 and continued these activities even after the Soviet Union collapsed in 1991. According to damage assessments, Ames provided Moscow the largest amount of secret information in the history of American intelligence, including the identities of eleven assets of the CIA and the **Federal Bureau of Investigation** (FBI) inside the Soviet Union who were reporting on Soviet activities and who were promptly executed when identified.

In August 1985, Ames was selected as one of the CIA officers to debrief defector **Vitaly Yurchenko**. Ames reportedly told his handlers at the Soviet Embassy in Washington everything Yurchenko was telling his interrogators. Both the CIA and the FBI became suspicious of Ames's activities in the mid-1980s and began clandestinely searching his home, intercepting his communications, and conducting physical surveillance in order to develop evidence of his treachery, a process that took over eight years. The FBI arrested Ames on 21 February 1994.

ANGLETON, JAMES J. (1917–1987). James J. Angleton headed the Counterintelligence Staff of the **Central Intelligence Agency** (CIA) from 1954 until his forced retirement by **Director of Central Intelligence** (DCI) **William E. Colby** in 1974. Angleton had earlier served in the **Office of Strategic Services** (OSS) and from late 1944 had been in charge of OSS **counterintelligence** operations in Italy. He met and became friends with **Harold ("Kim") Philby**, British

MI-6 officer and **Soviet** agent, during a stay in England in 1943. His personal and professional relationship with Philby continued when Philby later became the Secret Intelligence Service (SIS) liaison with the CIA and the **Federal Bureau of Investigation** (FBI) in Washington. His close friendhip with Philby colored Angleton's judgments about the British officer, probably delaying the identification of Philby as a Soviet penetration agent.

Once Philby's treachery became known, Angleton became obsessed with the notion of further penetrations of the CIA, particularly after the defection of **Anatoly Golitsyn** from the **KGB** in 1961. In fact, Angleton came to believe that most of the CIA's assets and contacts were KGB-controlled and that **defectors** were actually Russian agents sent to the West to spread **disinformation**. Angleton subsequently engaged in a "mole hunt" that targeted numerous innocent CIA officers, ruining many careers. Angleton's excesses led DCI Colby to force Angleton into retirement in 1974.

ARBENZ GUZMAN, JACOBO (1913–1971). Democratically elected president of Guatemala between 1950 and and 1954. An agrarian reformer, Arbenz instituted various projects to confiscate unusued land for distribution to peasants. He also threatened to nationalize the holdings of the United Fruit Company, in which many American politicians and prominent individuals held stock. President **Dwight D. Eisenhower** condemned the Arbenz government as a "communist dictatorship" and authorized the **Central Intelligence Agency** (CIA) to conduct a **covert action** to oust Arbenz. The CIA employed a combination of **propaganda** and **paramilitary** forces to whip up opposition to the Arbenz regime and force him out of office. Toppling Arbenz and his government ushered in decades of dictatorhips and numerous human rights violations of genocidal proportions. *See also* SUCCESS (OPERATION).

ARMS CONTROL. Arms control refers to the diplomatic efforts by both the United States and the **Soviet Union** during the **Cold War** to establish limits on the quantitative and qualitative aspects of nuclear weapon stocks or to reduce their numbers on a reciprocal basis. The **Limited Nuclear Test Ban Treaty** (LNTBT), for example, was negotiated in the 1960s to restrict nuclear tests to underground experimental conditions.

In addition, arms control efforts have focused on disarming various regions of the globe—Antartica, for example—and space, such as the Outer Space Treaty, from nuclear weapons. American intelligence has had a vital role in these efforts of supporting American arms control negotiators with intelligence information and monitoring and verifying compliance with the resulting treaties. *See also* ARMS CONTROL AND DISARMAMENT AGENCY; ARMS CONTROL INTELLIGENCE STAFF.

ARMS CONTROL AND DISARMAMENT AGENCY (ACDA). Established as an independent agency by the Arms Control and Disarmamant Act of 26 September 1961, ACDA was the leading organizational unit for formulating U.S. policy on **arms control** and disarmament issues and for U.S. participation in international negotiations over such issues. Executive Order 11044, dated 20 August 1962, also endowed ACDA's director with the authority to coordinate policy planning for diplomatic negotiations. As such, ACDA was deeply involved in all major arms control agreements, such as the **Strategic Arms Limitation Talks** (SALT) I and II. ACDA also supported efforts to prevent missile and weapons proliferation by fully participating in two of the **National Security Council's** (NSC's) **interagency working groups** (IWGs), one on nonproliferation and export controls and the other on arms control.

Although not a formal member of the **intelligence community** (IC), ACDA was an active member of various interagency intelligence committees working on verification issues and to ensure that U.S. policy initiatives were based on accurate intelligence information. ACDA ceased to be an independent agency on 1 April 1999 and was integrated into the **Department of State**.

ARMS CONTROL INTELLIGENCE STAFF (ACIS). Formerly attached to the Office of the **Director of Central Intelligence** (DCI), ACIS, now a part of the **Directorate of Intelligence** (DI) in the **Central Intelligence Agency** (CIA), supports all American **arms control** negotiations and provides advice on verification and compliance issues. Tasking for ACIS at one time came from the Intelligence Resources Division of the **Arms Control and Disarmament Agency** (ACDA), but now tasking primarily comes from the **Department of**

State and elements of the White House, such as the **National Security Council** (NSC). ACIS remains the principal coordinating mechanism for requirements on arms control intelligence issues.

ARMY INTELLIGENCE. *See* ARMY INTELLIGENCE AND SECURITY COMMAND.

ARMY INTELLIGENCE AGENCY (AINTA). *See* ARMY INTELLIGENCE AND SECURITY COMMAND.

ARMY INTELLIGENCE AND SECURITY COMMAND (INSCOM). Established on 1 January 1977, INSCOM is responsible for fielding intelligence assets in support of combat commanders. It provides **threat assessments** as well as training for contingency operations that range from war fighting to peacekeeping operations.

INSCOM originally combined the **Army Security Agency** (ASA), the Army Intelligence Agency (AINTA), and the various intelligence production agencies falling under the army chief of staff. The Army Security Agency was the latest successor to the War Department's Cipher Bureau within the **Military Intelligence Division** (MID), in which **Herbert O. Yardley**, a pioneer in American **cryptology**, had played an important role. Its immediate successor, the Army **Signals Intelligence Corps**, broke the **Purple** cipher system that carried the most secret Japanese diplomatic messages. On 15 September 1945, the U.S. Army Security Agency (USASE) came into being to conduct army **signals intelligence** (SIGINT) and communications security (COMSEC) until its incorporation into INSCOM in 1977.

The Army Intelligence Agency had its genesis in **World War I counterintelligence** operations within the United States. It evolved into the **Counter Intelligence Corps** (CIC) after the Japanese attack on **Pearl Harbor** on 7 December 1941, with its personnel functioning as plainclothes investigators on the home front and abroad. In 1961, the CIC was folded into the Intelligence Corps, which gathered **positive intelligence** in addition to conducting counterintelligence. On 1 July 1965, the **Department of Defense** (DOD) disbanded the CIC and established the Army Intelligence Command (USAINTC), which, over time, acquired **human intelligence** (HUMINT), **imagery intelligence** (IMINT), counterintelligence, and other capabilities. The Defense

Investigative Service (DIS) in 1971 absorbed USAINTC, abandoning some intelligence activities and focusing more on conducting personnel investigations in the United States.

ARMY INTELLIGENCE SUPPORT ACTIVITY (USAISA). The Army Intelligence Support Activity was established in 1980 to provide assistance to a possible second mission to rescue the American hostages in **Iran**. When the rescue mission did not materialize, USAISA, known as "the activity," received a formal charter on 5 July 1983 to provide military operational support for the army, other **Department of Defense** (DOD) components, and non-DOD agencies; **human intelligence** (HUMINT) and **signals intelligence** (SIGINT) collection in support of the army, **Joint Chiefs of Staff** (JCS), and DOD contingency and wartime operations; and clandestine HUMINT and SIGINT collection in response to high-priority or quick-reaction requirements. It also acquired limited authority to engage in **special activities** pursuant to a **presidential finding** that assigned the missions to the Defense Department and specifically tasked the army and USAISA. Over its lifetime, USAISA conducted operations in Egypt, **Iran**, Iraq, Italy, Jordan, Lebanon, Morocco, Nigeria, Saudi Arabia, Somalia, Sudan, Syria, and approximately 10 Latin American countries. USAISA grew in the decade of the 1980s in personnel, scope of its missions, and the areas of the world where it operated. However, the secrecy surrounding the work of USAISA, as well as the perception that USAISA was not under effective military control, sparked calls to disband the organization, which came about on 1 April 1989. Its component parts eventually found their way into the Army Special Operations Command.

ARMY SECURITY AGENCY (ASA). *See* NATIONAL SECURITY AGENCY.

ARNOLD, BENEDICT (1741–1801). A hero of the Revolutionary War prior to his treason, Benedict Arnold was recruited by his wife, Peggy Shippen, to spy for the British. He did so probably because he felt slighted by his comrades and the Continental Congress over issues of military rank, seniority, and pay. Arnold likely was already in the employ of the British by 1779, corresponding with the British commander over the possible capture of West Point in New York. When American forces captured a courier—Major John Andre—with correspondence implicating Arnold, he defected to the British, receiving a substantial reward for his defection in the form of pay, land, and a pension. The British, who distrusted Arnold, refused to give him a military commission, and he died in London in 1801 in relative obscurity. Benedict Arnold's name has become a euphemism for treason in the United States.

ASPIN/BROWN COMMISSION. *See* COMMISSION ON THE ROLES AND CAPABILITIES OF THE UNITED STATES INTELLIGENCE COMMUNITY.

ASSASSINATIONS. The **Hughes-Ryan Amendment** of 1974 was the first piece of legislation to ban political assassinations by the **Central Intelligence Agency** (CIA), which had been implicated in such schemes as **Operation Mongoose** against **Cuba's Fidel Castro** and the overthrow and death of Chilean president **Salvador Allende** in 1973. President **Jimmy Carter's Executive Order** (EO) **12036** extended the ban to the rest of the U.S. government. **Executive Order 12333,** which still is in effect, reaffirmed EO 12036's application. The ban is still in effect, although the **USA PATRIOT Act** and other legislation passed in the aftermath of the **terrorist attacks of 11 September 2001** now allow the president to authorize the assassination of terrorists and other select individuals on a case-by-case basis.

ASSISTANT TO THE PRESIDENT FOR NATIONAL SECURITY AFFAIRS (APNSA). Commonly referred to as the national security advisor, the APNSA advises the president on national security matters and heads the **National Security Council** (NSC) staff.

ASSOCIATION OF FORMER INTELLIGENCE OFFICERS (AFIO). Established in 1975 by retired and former intelligence officers, AFIO is a nonprofit educational organization, promoting understanding of the role of intelligence in American national security and foreign policy. It also provides a forum in which former intelligence professionals can exchange ideas and make their expertise available to the corporate and private sectors. The association's central office is located in Arlington, Virginia, which has a small cadre of professional staffers. Much of its work, however, is carried out by volunteers in various chapters around the country.

– B –

BASIC INTELLIGENCE. Basic intelligence refers to descriptive data about a country, region, or issue. It involves not only data about a country's geography, topography, population, political structures, resources, and capabilities, but also information about its history, culture, and social composition. Intelligence analysts and policymakers often employ the usually unclassified basic intelligence as contextual information or for background purposes.

BAY OF PIGS INVASION. The Bay of Pigs invasion, code-named **Operation Zapata**, was an ill-fated incursion into **Cuba** by exiles trained by the **Central Intelligence Agency** (CIA) in April 1961. The purpose of the invasion was to encourage a popular uprising on the island against the regime of **Fidel Castro**, who had come to power in 1959. However, the operation failed totally, largely because of inadequate preparations, insufficient political backing, faulty assumptions about what the Cuban population thought of the Castro regime and what it might do in the wake of the invasion, and "reckless" expert opinion about its outcome. President **John F. Kennedy** was compelled to accept responsibility for the failure and ransom the captured exiles by paying $10 million in medical supplies to Cuba. In addition, the failure prompted the Kennedy administration to seek alternative ways of ousting Castro, one of which was **Operation Mongoose**. However, the Bay of Pigs debacle convinced President Kennedy that force and **covert action** should be applied only as a last resort.

BERLIN TUNNEL. *See* GOLD (OPERATION).

BLACK CHAMBER. The cryptologic arm of the **Military Intelligence Division** (MID), the Black Chamber was established immediately after **World War I** and operated out of a townhouse in New York City under commercial **cover**. As part of the MID, it was officially known as MI-8, for Military Intelligence–8, and was actually a joint operation between the army and the **Department of State** to break the diplomatic codes of several different nations. Cryptologists of the Black Chamber were responsible for breaking Japan's "**Purple**" codes in 1919. The intercepted communications gave the United States an enormous advantage in diplomatic negotiations and strategic matters. For example, one set of decrypts were used by U.S. secretary of state Charles Evans Hughes to improve his diplomatic position during the Washington Naval Conference of 1921–1922. He was actually reading Japanese diplomatic traffic on Tokyo's negotiating positions every day before he went into the bargaining sessions. Despite its apparent usefulness, the State Department closed down the Black Chamber in 1929, although the army **Signals Intelligence Corps** continued cryptologic work in secret. *See also* CRYPTOLOGY; YARDLEY, HERBERT O.

BLACK PROPAGANDA. *See* PROPAGANDA.

BLAKE, GEORGE (1922–). George Blake was a British intelligence officer who spied for the **Soviet Union** in the 1950s. Blake became involved with intelligence work during **World War II**, first as a courier for Dutch resistance in Nazi-occupied Holland, but he escaped to Britain in 1942, joining the British navy. After the war, Britain's Secret Intelligence Service (SIS) recruited Blake into its ranks and sent him for a short time to West Germany to run agents in the Soviet zone. In the late 1940s, SIS sent Blake to Korea, where he was captured by North Korean forces on 24 June 1950. During his incarceration, he became a communist.

North Korea repatriated Blake in 1953, and SIS assigned him to work on intercepted Soviet communications. In 1955, Blake was assigned to Berlin to recruit Soviet officers, and while there, he gave the Soviets the names of British intelligence officers. He also gave Moscow operational details, including those of **Operation Gold**, the Berlin tunnel caper. On his return to Britain in 1959, Blake came under suspicion from tips provided by a **defector** and was eventually arrested for espionage. He received a 42-year jail sentence in 1961. However, he escaped from prison on 22 October 1966 and fled to the Soviet Union.

BNL AFFAIR. The Banca Nazionale del Lavoro (BNL) affair in 1989 centered on charges that the Department of Justice and the **Central Intelligence Agency** (CIA) covered up the channeling of military assistance to Iraq by the administration of President **George H. W. Bush** prior to the 1991 Persian Gulf War. BNL's Atlanta branch was alleged to have engineered billions of dollars in unauthorized loans to Iraq and other nations. There were also charges that the same branch laundered CIA money to enable it to finance **covert actions** outside of channels. Congressional investigations and court testimony showed some illegal activity by BNL managers but were unable to establish any links to the CIA or covert actions.

BOARD OF NATIONAL ESTIMATES. Established on 1 December 1950, the Board of National Estimates was the first formal intelligence entity to seek to produce coordinated **national intelligence estimates** (NIEs). Specifically, the board was charged with initiating and directing the production of the national estimates, evaluating current intelligence circulated by the **Central Intelligence Agency** (CIA) outside the agency, and assisting the **director of central intelligence** (DCI) in the coordination of intelligence relating to national security and in providing for its appropriate dissemination. The board over the years evolved into the present-day **National Intelligence Council** (NIC). *See also* OFFICE OF NATIONAL ESTIMATES.

BOLAND AMENDMENTS. The Boland amendments were a series of congressional amendments that sought to define the relationship between the **Central Intelligence Agency** (CIA) and the Nicaraguan **Contra** rebels. Named after Congressman Edward P. Boland (D-MA), the first Boland Amendment was enacted in the wake of a series of CIA-sponsored sabotage acts in 1982 against the ruling **Sandinista** regime in Nicaragua, about which the Congress had no knowledge and to which it had not given consent. The so-called Boland I amendment prohibited the CIA and the **Department of Defense** (DOD) from providing military support to the Contras in order to overthrow the Sandinista regime. Boland II, enacted in October 1984, prohibited the CIA from any contact with the Contra rebels. Boland III, passed in December 1985, authorized the CIA to provide the Contra rebels with communications equipment and to exchange intelligence. *See also* NATIONAL SECURITY DECISION DIRECTIVE 17.

BOLAND, EDWARD P. (1911–2001). Democratic congressional representative from Massachusetts, Congressman Boland was instrumental in the enactment of various prohibitions against giving assistance to the Nicaraguan **Contra** rebels in the early 1980s. Representative Boland, elected to the House of Representatives in 1952, was also the first chairman of the **House Permanent Select Committee on Intelligence** (HPSCI) from 1977 until 1985. *See also* BOLAND AMENDMENTS.

BOREN, DAVID L. (1941–). David L. Boren was U.S. senator from Oklahoma between 1980 and 1994. Prior to his election to the Senate, Boren, a Yale graduate and a Rhodes Scholar, served as governor of Oklahoma from 1975 until 1979. In the Senate, Boren served on the Senate Finance and Agriculture Committees as well as chairman of the **Senate Select Committee on Intelligence** (SSCI), the principal committee in the Senate overseeing the activities of U.S. intelligence. Prior to leaving Congress, Boren authored the National Security Education Act of 1992, which established the **National Security Education Program** (NSEP), a grants and scholarship program to promote the study of foreign languages, area studies, and national security issues. He is currently the president of the University of Oklahoma.

BOYD, BELLE (1843–1900). A Confederate spy during the American **Civil War**, Belle Boyd is credited with supplying General Stonewall Jackson with intelligence on the strength and disposition of Union forces around Front Royal, Virginia, in 1862. Although imprisoned and released several times, Belle Boyd undertook many risky assignments, one of which was to act as a Confederate courier to England in 1864. The war ended before she could return, and so she stayed in England to establish a stage career. Boyd eventually came back to the United States to pursue her career in the theater.

BRILLIANT PEBBLES. Brilliant Pebbles was successor to the **Strategic Defense Initiative** (SDI), first proposed by President **Ronald Reagan**, in 1984. Brilliant Pebbles, originally conceived in a series of 1986 war games by Edward Teller, the father of the American hydrogen bomb, was designed to thwart a **Soviet** nuclear strike by intercepting the missiles before they reached American soil. The initial plan called for space- and ground-based interceptors and sensors as well as a battle management system. Later on, a new Brilliant Pebbles design replaced space-based interceptors with an early warning and tracking system in support of thousands of small space-based miniature computers and sensors—therefore the title "brilliant"—each capable of autonomous interception of enemy missiles that traveled within range. This change supposedly was to make the system less vulnerable to enemy antisatellite weapons. Brilliant Pebbles gave way to theater-level antimissile defense proposals during the **William J. Clinton** administration in the 1990s and the land-based missile defense initiative of the **George W. Bush** White House in 2001 and 2002.

BRITISH SECURITY COORDINATION. *See* STEPHENSON, WILLIAM SAMUEL.

BROWSER, MARY E. (Dates of birth and death unknown). Mary E. Browser was born a slave and worked on the John van Lew plantation. In 1851, **Elizabeth van Lew** freed her and the other family slaves and sent Mary Browser to school in Philadelphia. During the **Civil War**, Elizabeth van Lew recruited Mary Browser as a spy by planting her as a maid in the home of Confederate president Jefferson Davis. Browser read war dispatches as she dusted furniture and traveled to the van Lew mansion at night to report her information. Her intelligence was sent directly to General Ulysses S. Grant, greatly enhancing the Union's conduct of the war. Mary Browser probably was the highest placed agent of any of the spies during the Civil War.

BUCHANAN, JAMES (1791–1868). Fifteenth president of the United States between 1857 and 1861.

BUREAU OF INTELLIGENCE AND RESEARCH (INR). The State Department's INR, established in 1946, is an all-source agency that engages in political, economic, and military intelligence analysis. The INR does not have a collection capability of its own but is a consumer of raw intelligence from other U.S. intelligence agencies as well as of diplomatic reports from U.S. embassies abroad. Its principal customer is the secretary of state and his senior advisors, but INR products are distributed to a wider audience outside the **Department of State**. As a vital member of the **intelligence community** (IC), the

INR participates in the drafting and production of **national intelligence estimates** (NIEs). It also serves as the focal point within the Department of State for all policy issues and activities involving the intelligence community. The INR uses the "Morning Summary" as the medium for keeping the secretary of state abreast of current developments around the globe.

BUREAU OF INVESTIGATION. *See* FEDERAL BUREAU OF INVESTIGATION.

BUREAU OF NARCOTICS AND DANGEROUS DRUGS (BNDD). *See* DRUG ENFORCEMENT ADMINISTRATION.

BUSH, GEORGE HERBERT W. (1924–). The 41st president of the United States between 20 January 1989 and 20 January 1993, and the eleventh **director of central intelligence** (DCI) between 30 January 1976 and 20 January 1977. George H. W. Bush became interested in politics in the early 1950s, first serving two terms as congressman from Texas and then running unsuccessfully for the U.S. Senate. He also served in various high-level appointive positions that thrust him into the national political limelight: U.S. ambassador to the United Nations (UN), chairman of the Republican National Committee, director of central intelligence for 12 months between 1976 and 1977, and chief of the U.S. Liaison Office in the **People's Republic of China** (PRC). In 1980, George H. W. Bush campaigned for the Republican nomination for president, and when he lost, President **Ronald Reagan** chose Bush as his vice president. In 1988, candidate Bush won the Republican nomination and the general election and served one term in the White House, between 1989 and 1993. George H. W. Bush's presidency saw the end of the **Cold War**, the dissolution of the **Soviet Union**, and the successful conduct of the 1991 Persian Gulf War, which ousted Saddam Hussein's Iraqi forces from Kuwait. In the 1992 general election, President Bush lost to Democratic candidate **William J. Clinton** because of a faltering economy and general discontent at home. He is the father of **George W. Bush**.

BUSH, GEORGE W. (1946–). Forty-third president of the United States between January 2001 and January 2009. A former governor of Texas, President Bush came into office vowing to support a stronger political and economic relationship with Latin America but to focus less on "nation building" and small-scale military commitments. He also pledged to build a missile shield to protect the United States from tactical nuclear weapons. In pursuit of his objectives, he pulled the United States out of the Kyoto Protocol, which sought to regulate global warming, and the 1972 Anti-Ballistic Missile Treaty (ABM). Because of his conservative social beliefs, he also cut off funding for the United Nations Population Fund.

President Bush had the misfortune to be in the White House when the **terrorist attacks of 11 September 2001** took place. Consequently, he organized a coalition to send military forces into **Afghanistan** to oust the Taliban regime that had supported the perpetrators of the attacks. On the pretext that Iraqi strongman Saddam Hussein possessed weapons of mass destruction and had links to international terrorism, President Bush launched a war against Iraq in March 2003 that alienated the United States from its allies and split the American public on the issue.

– C –

CAMP DAVID ACCORDS. Brokered by the United States, the Camp David Accords were two agreements signed in 1978 between Egypt and Israel over issues that had provoked several wars between the two countries. The first agreement focused on the Sinai Peninsula, a territory belonging to Egypt that had been occupied by Israeli forces as a result of the 1973 Yom Kippur War. This agreement also provided for peace between Egypt and Israel, to include Egypt's recognition of Israel and the establishment of relations between the two countries. The second agreement focused on arrangements for autonomy of the West Bank and the Gaza Strip.

CARTER, JAMES EARL, JR. (1924–). The 39th president of the United States, serving between 1977 and 1981. A former naval officer with training in nuclear matters, President Carter entered Georgia politics in 1962, eventually becoming governor of the state in 1970. He began pursuing presidential ambitions in 1974, defeating incumbent president **Gerald R. Ford** in 1976.

President Carter championed human rights during his presidency, which frequently brought him into conflict with the **Soviet Union**. His approach, however, earned him several foreign policy achievements, the most important of which are the Panama Canal treaties in 1977, the **Camp David Accords** in 1978, the treaty of peace between Israel and Egypt in 1978, and the establishment of full diplomatic relations with the **People's Republic of China** (PRC), a move that built upon the work of his predecessors. Carter also concluded the negotiations for the **Strategic Arms Limitation Talks** (SALT) II with the Soviet Union.

Despite these achievements, President Carter's presidency also experienced some serious foreign policy setbacks. The **Sandinista** regime came to power in Nicaragua in 1979, and the Soviet invasion of **Afghanistan** in 1979, which U.S. intelligence failed to foresee, caused the suspension of plans to ratify the SALT II pact. Moscow's move into Afghanistan also prompted President Carter to issue a trade embargo for the Soviet Union and to boycott the 1980 Moscow Summer Olympic Games.

U.S. intelligence also failed to anticipate the 1979 Iranian revolution because it lacked human assets in **Iran** who could have given American intelligence the necessary information. **Director of Central Intelligence** (DCI) **Stansfield Turner** had previously fired a significant portion of clandestine operatives of the **Central Intelligence Agency** (CIA) because he believed that **national technical means**, especially the use of satellites, made **human intelligence** (HUMINT) less important for the U.S. intelligence effort. DCI Turner undoubtedly was also responding to the intense criticism of the American spy machine in the mid-1970s for engaging in illegal activities. The last year of Carter's presidency was dominated by developments in Iran, especially the issue of the Americans who were taken hostage by Islamic militants who had ousted the regime of Shah Reza Pehlevi in 1979 and had occupied the U.S. Embassy in Tehran.

After his defeat by Republican presidential candidate **Ronald Reagan** in 1980, President Carter returned to his peanut farm in Georgia and, in 1982, founded the Carter Center at Emory University in Atlanta. He has since engaged in numerous conflict-mediation efforts around the globe and served as the personal envoy of several presidents in the 1980s and 1990s. *See also* EAGLE CLAW (OPERATION).

CASE OFFICER. Case officers are intelligence officials sent abroad under **cover** to recruit spies—foreign officials with access to the needed information—and acquire intelligence information. Case officers form the backbone of **human intelligence** (HUMINT) collection. In the U.S. government, most case officers are within the ranks of the **Directorate of Operations** (DO) in the **Central Intelligence Agency** (CIA), although the **Defense HUMINT Service** (DH) and some other parts of the **Department of Defense** (DOD) also employ case officers.

CASEY, WILLIAM JOSEPH (1913–1987). Director of central intelligence (DCI) during the administration of **Ronald Reagan** and a controversial figure in the **Iran-Contra Affair** during the 1980s. Although a former member of the **Office of Strategic Services** (OSS) during **World War II**, Casey became a successful tax lawyer after the war and later served in several senior positions in the administrations of Presidents **Richard M. Nixon** and **Gerald R. Ford**, including chairman of the Securities and Exchange Commission (1973–1974) and head of the Export-Import Bank (1975). In the 1970s, he also served as a member of a presidential commission investigating U.S. intelligence and on the **President's Foreign Intelligence Advisory Board** (PFIAB) until President **Jimmy Carter** abolished it on the grounds that its members were too enamored of **covert actions**.

A conservative Republican, Casey was President Ronald Reagan's campaign chairman. Upon President Reagan's election, Casey tried to get the position of secretary of defense, but President Reagan, considering Casey's OSS experience, felt he needed him to revitalize U.S. intelligence. DCI Casey was responsible for an aggressive expansion of the clandestine service, which had been decimated by his predecessor, **Stansfield Turner**. Casey presided over a 25 percent increase in the **intelligence budget**, whipped the intelligence estimative process into shape, attempted to establish a healthy balance between **human intelligence** and technical intelligence collection, improved competitive analysis, extended CIA's mandate to study such new issues as drug trafficking and **terrorism**, and established the first **fusion center**—the **Counterterrorism Center** (CTC)—in 1986. DCI Casey was also a central figure in the complex sequence of covert activities that became part of the Iran-Contra Affair. He suffered a stroke in 1986 and died the next year without revealing the details of his involvement in the events.

CASTRO, FIDEL (1926–). Fidel Castro has been the revolutionary leader of **Cuba** since ousting the regime of Fulgencio Batista in 1959. A trained lawyer, Castro campaigned for a parliamentary seat in 1952, but his political ambitions fell victim to Batista's coup d'etat against President Carlos Prio Socarras. Opposing Batista, Castro began his revolutionary activities in 1953 by leading an armed attack on 26 July against military barracks. He was caught and spent time in jail until 1955. On his release, Castro went to Mexico and organized the 26th of July Revolutionary Movement, which soon began attacks against the Batista regime from its stronghold in the Sierra Maestra mountains. The rebellion succeeded in ousting Batista on 1 January 1959.

The United States initially recognized the Castro regime, but relations quickly cooled when Castro began cozying up to the **Soviet Union** in 1960. The U.S. government initiated a series of **covert actions** to oust the Castro regime, the most famous of which was the disastrous **Bay of Pigs invasion** in 1961. The U.S. also undertook assassination attempts against Castro as part of **Operation Mongoose**. The American moves probably had the effect of moving Castro closer to the Soviet Union. *See also* CUBAN MISSILE CRISIS; KENNEDY, JOHN F.

CENTER FOR THE STUDY OF INTELLIGENCE (CSI). Founded in 1974 within the **Central Intelligence Agency** (CIA), the CSI's mission is to provide contextual information to key CIA leaders, to write the authoritative history of the CIA, and to promote the public's understanding of the role of intelligence in national security. In support of this mission, the CSI regularly hosts conferences and publishes historical studies on various intelligence topics, including its in-house series Studies in Intelligence. The CSI includes the CIA History Staff, the CIA Museum, and the Historical Intelligence Collection in the CIA library.

CENTRAL IMAGERY OFFICE (CIO). The CIO was established on 6 May 1992 by both the **Department of Defense** (DOD) and **director of central intelligence directives** (DCIDs) to provide imagery to the Defense Department, combat commanders, the **Central Intelligence**

Agency (CIA), and other agencies; advise the secretary of defense and the **director of central intelligence** (DCI) regarding future imagery requirements; and evaluate the performance of imagery components. The CIO, working closely with the **National Reconnaissance Office** (NRO), also established imagery architectures, set interoperability standards, and supported research and development. On 1 October 1996, the CIO was merged with the Defense Mapping Agency (DMA) and the Defense Dissemination Program Office (DDPO) to establish the **National Imagery and Mapping Agency** (NIMA), which in 2003 became the **National Geospatial-Intelligence Agency** (NGA). *See also* COMMITTEE ON IMAGERY REQUIREMENTS AND EXPLOITATION.

CENTRAL INTELLIGENCE AGENCY (CIA). Established by the **National Security Act of 1947**, the CIA is an independent government agency whose principal task is to warn American leaders of strategic threats to the nation. To do this, the CIA engages in three types of activities: intelligence collection and **intelligence analysis**, **counterintelligence**, and **covert action**. While the first two activities have not been controversial, covert actions have generated much public debate and controversy, contributing to public perceptions that the CIA is in the business only of attempting assassinations of political leaders and overthrowing governments.

While the CIA has the mandate to conduct covert actions, its primary work is the collection and analysis of intelligence information and the production of intelligence products that are disseminated to intelligence consumers. As one of the three all-source intelligence agencies in the **intelligence community** (IC), the CIA receives intelligence information from other U.S. intelligence agencies and foreign intelligence organizations. It also collects intelligence on its own through **espionage** activities abroad. In fact, the CIA coordinates all U.S. espionage activities, or **human intelligence** (HUMINT), including espionage conducted by elements of the **Department of Defense** (DOD), although a plan under consideration in late 2004 by the **George W. Bush** administration would transfer some of the CIA's espionage responsibilities to the Department of Defense, possibly the **Defense HUMINT Service** (DH). Intelligence collection results in intelligence analysis and the production of **current** and **long-term** finished **intelligence**, such as the **senior executive intelligence brief**

(SEIB), the **president's daily brief** (PDB), and **national intelligence estimates** (NIEs).

The CIA's counterintelligence activities are meant to protect the nation's secrets, undermine the effectiveness of hostile intelligence services, and guard the nation against foreign espionage and sabotage. The conduct of counterintelligence is shared with the **Federal Bureau of Investigation** (FBI)—a law enforcement agency—but the CIA has domestic counterintelligence responsibilities only in regards to its employees. The FBI performs the bulk of counterintelligence work within the United States. The military commands have counterintelligence responsibilities on military bases and installations abroad. Other U.S. intelligence agencies conduct counterintelligence for themselves, but also have to harmonize this activity closely with their sister agencies. Counterintelligence requires a good deal of coordination and cooperation among the agencies charged with counterintelligence duties, but such cooperation between the FBI and the CIA has been spotty at best, as illustrated by the postmortem investigations of the **Aldrich Ames** and the **Robert Hannsen** espionage cases.

Covert actions, or special activities, technically are not intelligence but employ intelligence resources in support of American foreign policy objectives in a way that hides or disguises government sponsorship. Most proposals for covert action originate outside the CIA, either within the policy frameworks of the **Department of State** and the Defense Department or with the **National Security Council** (NSC). Presidential orders require the CIA to manage and implement covert actions, unless the president deems another agency more suitable. The designated agencies, usually with the CIA in the lead, employ a variety of secret techniques to conduct covert actions, such as **propaganda**, political and economic actions, and **paramilitary** activities.

CENTRAL INTELLIGENCE AGENCY ACT OF 1949. The Central Intelligence Agency (CIA) Act of 1949 provides special administrative authorities and responsibilities for the **Central Intelligence Agency** (CIA) and the **director of central intelligence** (DCI). Specifically, the act, as amended, permits the CIA to use confidential fiscal and administrative procedures, such as spending money by voucher; exempts it from many of the usual limitations on the use of federal funds; and frees the CIA from having to disclose its "organization, functions, officials, titles, salaries, or numbers of personnel employed." The act also provides that CIA funds could be hidden in the budgets of other departments and then transferred to the agency without regard to the restrictions placed on the initial appropriation. As such, the act contributes to the legal basis for CIA secrecy over its activities and **intelligence budgets**. *See also* INTELLIGENCE OVERSIGHT.

CENTRAL INTELLIGENCE AGENCY INFORMATION ACT. The Central Intelligence Agency Information Act, signed by President **Ronald Reagan** on 15 October 1984, amended the **National Security Act of 1947** to relieve the **Central Intelligence Agency** (CIA) of the necessity of searching for and reviewing records in its "operational" files, thereby protecting the CIA from **Freedom of Information Act** (FOIA) requests about its operations and security processes. The CIA must still apply **Executive Order 12356** and other appropriate regulations to records and materials not covered by this act. Such records include the final intelligence products that are directed to national policymakers as well as administrative and other "nonoperational" files.

CENTRAL INTELLIGENCE GROUP (CIG). Established on 22 January 1946 as part of the **National Intelligence Authority** (NIA), which was to make intelligence policy while the CIG was to implement it. The CIG was also charged with coordinating information produced by America's various intelligence agencies in the aftermath of **World War II**—most of them military—and was dependent on the defense establishment and the **Department of State** for its budget. At this early stage in the development of America's postwar intelligence apparatus, the CIG's principal work was the preparation of an intelligence summary for the president.

In March 1946, army, navy, and air force intelligence were directed to cooperate with the CIG to prepare an evaluation of **Soviet** military capabilities, but the military refused to give the CIG any information. As a result, General **Hoyt Vandenberg**, the **director of central intelligence** (DCI) at the time, sought and won permission for the CIG to generate its own intelligence. DCI Vandenberg also won the right to collect intelligence in Latin America, which until then had been performed by the **Federal Bureau of Investigation** (FBI), and to organize the Office of Special Operations (OSO), which combined the old **Office of Strategic Services** (OSS) **espionage** and **counterintelligence** operations that had been transferred to the War Department when the OSS was abolished in 1945. Despite these gains, CIG's efforts remained disorganized, and disaffection with the American intelligence effort probably contributed to the establishment of the **Central Intelligence Agency** (CIA) in 1947. *See also* NATIONAL SECURITY ACT OF 1947.

CHALET (SYSTEM). *See* VORTEX.

CHAOS (OPERATION). A joint **Central Intelligence Agency** (CIA) and **Federal Bureau of Investigation** (FBI) operation initiated during the administration of President **Lyndon B. Johnson** to determine whether or not the **Vietnam** antiwar movement was manipulated or financially supported from abroad. Both agencies opened files on many Americans, which, in the CIA's case, was a violation of its mandate. Even though the operation found no foreign links, it lasted well into the administration of President **Richard M. Nixon**. *See also* COINTELPRO.

CHEKA. The All Russian Extraordinary Commission for Combating Counterrevolution and Sabotage, or Cheka, was formed in December 1917 by Vladimir I. Lenin and entrusted to a corps of international revolutionaries. By 1921, Cheka had grown to a cadre of more than 250,000 men and women, and by the mid-1930s, although renamed several times, it had become the largest secret service in world history. Prior to **World War II**, Cheka was known as NKVD, which stood for the People's Commissariat of Internal Affairs, the predecessor to the **KGB**, the Committee on State Security. *See also* SOVIET UNION.

CHIEF OF STATION (COS). The chief of station is the most senior official of the **Central Intelligence Agency** (CIA) appointed to supervise and manage the CIA station and its activities in a foreign country. The COS is a key advisor to the ambassador and is usually a member of the ambassador's country team. As a senior CIA case officer, the COS is normally under **cover**, but he may be "declared" to the host government for **intelligence liaison** purposes.

CHILE. *See* ALLENDE, SALVADOR; NATIONAL SECURITY DE-CISION MEMORANDUM 93; NIXON, RICHARD M.; PINOCHET, AUGUSTO.

CHIN, LARRY WU-TAI (1918–1986). An American of Chinese ancestry and former employee of the **Central Intelligence Agency** (CIA), Larry Wu-Tai Chin was arrested in 1985 for spying for the **People's Republic of China** (PRC). Born in Beijing, Chin was recruited by communist intelligence agents while a college student in the early 1940s. Later he became a naturalized U.S. citizen, worked for the U.S. Army Liaison Office in China in 1943, and joined the CIA in 1952. He worked for the CIA's **Foreign Broadcast Information Service** (FBIS) and allegedly provided Beijing classified documents and photographs. Chin retired in 1981 at 63, was arrested on 22 November 1985, and was charged with carrying out a 33-year **espionage** career. At his trial in 1986, Chin admitted spying for the PRC for 11 years. Following his conviction, he committed suicide on 21 February 1986.

CHINA, PEOPLE'S REPUBLIC OF (PRC). Founded as a communist state in 1949, the PRC is now one of the major players in the international politics of the post-9/11 world. Not officially recognized by the United States until the early 1970s, the PRC supported its ideological cousins, the North Koreans, during the **Korean War** and the North Vietnamese during the **Vietnam War**. In April 1970, APNSA **Henry A. Kissinger** established a secret intelligence relationship with Beijing by presenting it **communications intelligence** (COMINT) and satellite **imagery intelligence** (IMINT) on Soviet forces along China's border. The United States and the PRC established formal diplomatic relations in the late 1970s, and the intelligence relationship expanded to include, in addition to intelligence sharing, assistance in developing the PRC's own signals and imagery intelligence capabilities. In exchange, the United States acquired **signals intelligence** (SIGINT) sites in western China to eavesdrop on Soviet communications.

Occasional incidents have tended to mar the growing intelligence relationship. One such incident was the forcing down of an American **P-3C Orion aircraft** in international airspace in 2002 after it collided with a Chinese fighter. Yet, the U.S.-PRC intelligence relationship has continued unabated and now encompasses counterterrorism as a liaison issue. *See also* CHIN, LARRY WU-TAI.

CHURCH COMMITTEE. Officially known as the Senate **Select Committee to Study Governmental Operations with Respect to Intelligence Activities**, the Church Committee was established in 1975 to conduct wide-ranging investigations of U.S. intelligence agencies in the post-**Watergate** period. Named after its chairman Idaho senator **Frank Church**, the committee took public and private testimony from hundreds of people; collected volumes of files from the **Federal Bureau of Investigation** (FBI), **Central Intelligence Agency** (CIA), **National Security Agency** (NSA), Internal Revenue Service (IRS), and many other federal agencies; and issued 14 reports in 1975 and 1976. Church Committee reports specifically focused on U.S. attempts to assassinate foreign leaders, such as **Cuba's Fidel Castro**; the Congo's **Patrice Lumumba**; the Dominican Republic's **Rafael Trujillo**; South Vietnam's Ngo Dinh Diem; and Rene Schneider, commander in chief of the Chilean army, who opposed a military coup against **Salvador Allende**. In its final report in 1976, the Church Committee endorsed President **Gerald R. Ford's** ban, through **Executive Order 11905**, on government-sanctioned assassinations. The Church Committee in 1976 evolved into the **Senate Select Committee on Intelligence** (SSCI). *See also* INTELLIGENCE OVERSIGHT; SENATE RESOLUTION 400.

CHURCH, FRANK FORRESTER (1924–1984). Frank Church was the Democratic senator from Idaho who in 1975 chaired the Senate **Select Committee to Study Governmental Operations with Respect to Intelligence Activities**. His committee publicly revealed plots by the **Central Intelligence Agency** (CIA) to assassinate world leaders, a coup against **Chile's** Marxist president **Salvador Allende**, and **covert actions** against radical groups in the United States. He became famous for calling the CIA a "rogue elephant" in the belief that the agency acted from the 1950s through the 1970s independently of any **oversight** by the executive or legislative branches. He later retracted the allegation because his committee found no evidence to support the charge that the CIA acted without orders. His committee made 100 recommendations including curbing illegal wiretaps, mail opening, break-ins, surveillance, harassment of political dissidents, **assassination** plots against foreign leaders, and campaigns to smear civil rights activists. *See also* CHURCH COMMITTEE.

CIVIL AIR TRANSPORT (CAT). A **proprietary** of the **Central Intelligence Agency** (CIA) that secretly transported weapons and other materials in support of the agency's clandestine and **covert actions** during the 1940s and 1950s. In 1947, American generals Claire Chennault, the wartime commander of the **Flying Tigers**, and Whitey Willaumer inaugurated a small airline, NCRRA Air Transport, in postwar China. After a year of hauling United Nations (UN) cargo, they received a commercial contract and changed the name of the airline to Civil Air Transport (CAT), operating throughout China on a commercial basis. CAT was deeply involved in the Chinese civil war, evacuating more than 100,000 people from the city of Mukden in Manchuria and supplying the wounded during the battle of Hshuchow. When the communists came to power in 1949, CAT withdrew to Taiwan and shortly after was acquired by the CIA.

Subsequently CAT began operating in conjunction with **Air America**. CAT carried CIA cargo during the **Korean War**, delivered weapons to anticommunist elements in Burma, and supported guerrilla operations on the Chinese mainland and Manchuria. CAT flew supply missions to the French at Dien Bien Phu in 1954, supported **Operation Success** in Guatemala in 1954, assisted a CIA covert operation in Indonesia in 1958, and was involved in supporting the abortive **Bay of Pigs invasion** in 1961.

CIVIL WAR. The American Civil War began long before the first shots were fired on Fort Sumter, South Carolina, on 12 April 1981. The industrial North and the agricultural South had been drifting apart over economic issues and the slavery question for quite a while. On 20 December 1860, the North-South split came to a head when South Carolina seceded from the Union, followed by Mississippi, Florida, Alabama, Georgia, Louisiana, and Texas within two months. The secessionist states established the Confederate States of America on 9 February 1861. **Abraham Lincoln** was sworn in as the 16th president of the United States on 4 March 1981, presiding over the conduct of the four-and-a-half-year war. The war ended with the Confederate surrender on 9 April 1985.

During the war, each side attempted to develop intelligence capabilities. **Allan Pinkerton** took it upon himself to try organizing a Union intelligence effort, without much success. The **Secret Service Bureau** began with little fanfare and ended with no success. What came to be effective intelligence for the Union was little more than private intelligence services established by federal officers to serve their own units. The South had a more organized intelligence capability in the form of the **Confederate Secret Service**, which existed for much of the war. However, there is little information to suggest that it contributed significantly to the Southern cause. Individual espionage missions probably did more than organized efforts to contribute to each side's war effort. *See also* CUSHMAN, PAULINE; EDMONDS, EMMA; GREENHOW, ROSE O'NEAL; VAN LEW, ELIZABETH.

CLASSIFIED INFORMATION PROCEDURES ACT (CIPA). The Classified Information Procedures Act, enacted on 15 October 1980, governs the use of classified information in criminal proceedings. The CIPA tries to balance the right of a criminal defendant to access relevant information with the right of the government to know in advance the damage that might accrue if classified information were revealed during the course of a trial. The act was passed after some former intelligence officers, brought up on criminal charges for official and nonofficial activities, began demanding the use of classified materials during the conduct of their legal defense.

CLINTON, WILLIAM JEFFERSON (1946–). Forty-second president of the United States between 1993 and 2001. President Clinton, like President **Jimmy Carter**, campaigned as a Washington outsider and defeated incumbent president **George H. W. Bush** over economic issues. Clinton was a beneficiary of the end of the **Cold War**, which allowed him to cut back on government spending, including intelligence, as part of the "peace dividend." However, the end of the Cold War also thrust President Clinton into new and unchartered foreign policy waters that compelled him, in his second term, to boost spending on defense and intelligence.

During his two terms as president, Clinton successfully dispatched peacekeeping forces to war-torn Bosnia, bombed Iraq when Saddam Hussein stopped United Nations (UN) inspections for evidence of weapons of mass destruction, lobbed a cruise missile at **al Qai'da** terrorist hideouts in **Afghanistan**, and conducted a coalition war against Serbian forces in Kosovo. He also became a global proponent for democracy, an expanded **North Atlantic Treaty Organization** (NATO), more open international trade, and a worldwide campaign against drug trafficking.

COAST GUARD. The nation's premier maritime agency, the Coast Guard is an amalgam of five historical federal units that over time have come to be united under the Coast Guard umbrella: the Revenue Cutter Service, the Lighthouse Service, the Steamboat Inspection Service, the Bureau of Navigation, and the Lifesaving Service.

The Coast Guard has traditionally performed two roles in wartime. The first has been to augment the navy with men and cutters. The second has been to undertake special missions, including the enforcement of boating safety regulations, search and rescue, maintenance of aids to navigation, enforcement of merchant marine safety regulations, environmental protection, enforcement of customs, fisheries, and immigration laws, and port safety. In wartime, the Coast Guard performs port security, ship escort, and transport duty as part of the U.S. Navy. In peacetime, the Coast Guard is part of the **Department of Homeland Security** (DHS) and an independent member of the **intelligence community** (IC).

COBRA DANE (SYSTEM). A phased-array radar deployed in 1977 that was intended to acquire precise data on the system characteristics of **Soviet** ballistic missile weapons. Located on the northwestern section of Alaska's Shemya Island, the radar, the responsibility of **air force intelligence, surveillance, and reconnaissance** is part of the Integrated Tactical Warning and Attack Assessment network. It can track a basketball-size object at a range of 2,000 miles. It can also track up to 300 incoming warheads and up to 200 satellites. COBRA DANE also has a space-object tracking and identification mission, providing warning of all Earth-impact objects, including ballistic missiles on the United States. As such, it is an integral part of the **Measurement and Signature Intelligence** (MASINT) technique of intelligence collection.

COINTELPRO (OPERATION). COINTELPRO is the **Federal Bureau of Investigation** (FBI) acronym for a series of **covert action**

programs directed against domestic groups from mid-1956 until 1971. In these programs, the FBI went beyond the collection of intelligence and conducted clandestine operations to "disrupt" and "neutralize" target groups and individuals within the United States.

The origins of COINTELPRO were in the Bureau's jurisdiction to investigate hostile foreign intelligence activities on American soil. In 1956, the FBI decided that a formal **counterintelligence** program, coordinated from headquarters, would be an effective weapon in the fight against the American Communist Party and its sympathizers within the United States. The Bureau's covert action programs were aimed at five perceived domestic threats: the Communist Party of the United States (1956–1971); the Socialist Workers Party (1961–1969); white hate groups (1964–1971); black nationalist hate groups (1967–1971); and the New Left (1968–1971). COINTELPRO activities against these groups comprised 2,370 separate counterintelligence actions, including many "dirty tricks," among which were such actions as mailing anonymous letters to a member's spouse accusing the target of infidelity; using informants to raise controversial issues at meetings in order to cause dissent; falsely labeling a group member as an informant; encouraging street warfare between violent groups; contacting an employer to get a target fired; notifying state and local authorities of a target's criminal law violations; and using the Internal Revenue Services (IRS) to audit a professor in order to audit political dissidents. In the politically charged atmosphere of the **Vietnam War**, during which there was near paranoia about the government's actions against its own people, the FBI decided to discontinue COINTELPRO. The program came to an end on 27 April 1971.

COLBY, WILLIAM E. (1920–1996). Tenth **director of central intelligence** (DCI), serving between 4 September 1973 and 30 January 1976. Colby was a Princeton graduate who served in the **Office of Strategic Services** (OSS) during **World War II** and earned a law degree from Columbia in 1949. He joined the **Office of Policy Coordination** (OPC) in 1950, serving tours in Italy and South Vietnam. He was **chief of station** (COS) in Vietnam in 1960 and, later, Director of Civil Operations and Rural Development Support, which was the pacification program that included **Operation PHOENIX**. He later became **deputy director of central intelligence** (DDCI) under DCI **Richard Helms**.

At the time of his appointment as DCI in 1973, Colby was under pressure to make major changes in the **Central Intelligence Agency** (CIA). Consequently, on 7 September 1973, Colby sent President **Richard M. Nixon** an ambitious set of proposed DCI objectives to improve the intelligence product. Colby's most significant innovations were to abolish the **Office of National Estimates** (ONE) and to establish the **national intelligence officer** (NIO) system under the **National Intelligence Council** (NIC). In his first three months as DCI, Colby also established an Office of Political Research (OPR) in the CIA's **Directorate of Intelligence** (DI) to provide in-depth intelligence support to top-level decision makers, revitalized strategic warning capabilities, created "Alert Memorandums" for key policymakers, and ordered postmortems prepared on the **intelligence community's** (IC's) performance in various crises.

DCI Colby also faced a series of unexpected crises as soon as he took office. His tenure began with the CIA's failure to warn U.S. policymakers of the outbreak of the Yom Kippur War in October 1973. The CIA and intelligence community also failed to warn of the ensuing oil crisis brought on by the Organization of Petroleum Exporting States (OPEC).

Colby spent much of his tenure as DCI trying to deflect criticism of U.S. intelligence with regard to alleged illegal activities, especially the overthrow and death of Chilean president **Salvador Allende**. As a way of thwarting efforts to dismantle the CIA, Colby completed a study of CIA wrongdoing since its inception and shared these "Family Jewels" with the Congress, thus earning him the enmity of American intelligence professionals. Colby died under mysterious circumstances in 1996.

COLDFEET (OPERATION). Initiated in May 1961 on a trial basis, the operation sought to drop agents onto an abandoned **Soviet** ice drift station, designated NP8, in order to explore it and exploit intelligence information about Soviet intentions. The U.S. Navy dropped two **Central Intelligence Agency** (CIA) contract employees by parachute on the station and retrieved them later by using the **Skyhook system**. Assessments of the operation later confirmed the practicality of parachute-drop and aerial-retrieval techniques to investigate otherwise inaccessible areas.

COLD WAR. A term coined by American journalist H. B. Swope and made popular by Walter Lippman, the Cold War refers to the state of neither war nor peace between the Western and Eastern blocs after **World War II.** The two bloc leaders, the United States and the **Soviet Union**, spent most of the Cold War in adversarial diplomacy, interspersed by periods of détente, although they did come close to armed confrontation on several occasions, including during the **Cuban Missile Crisis** in 1962, the Arab-Israeli conflict in 1973, and the **Soviet war scare** in the early 1980s.

Several themes dominated the Cold War between the East and the West. One, the contest over Germany gave rise to two Berlin crises, one in the 1948–1949 period and the other during 1958–1962. It also led to the establishment of rival military alliances, first the **North Atlantic Treaty Organization** (NATO) on 4 April 1949 and then the **Warsaw Pact** on 1 May 1955. Two, the American policy determination to limit Soviet expansion through a policy of "**containment**" and Soviet efforts to frustrate the policy defined the conduct of much of the Cold War. Three, the ideological conflict was played out through surrogates in Korea in the early 1950s, in Hungary and Czechoslovakia in the mid 1950s, in **Cuba** beginning in 1960, in Vietnam in the 1960s and 1970s, and in **Afghanistan**, Central America, and Africa in the 1980s. Four, there was the occasional drive for accommodation that included the development of a whole body of international law based on **arms control** treaties to reduce tensions, establish a record of confidence-building measures, and set the stage for collaborative efforts in such areas as space exploration, antiterrorism, environmental protection, and international rule making. Five, the Cold War was fought largely in the shadows, in a silent and secret intelligence war to ferret out secrets and gain advantage over each other in a game of one-upmanship over nuclear capabilities and political influence. *See also* KENNAN, GEORGE; NATIONAL SECURITY COUNCIL 68.

COMMISSION ON CIA ACTIVITIES WITHIN THE UNITED STATES. *See* ROCKEFELLER COMMISSION.

COMMISSION ON THE INTELLIGENCE CAPABILITIES OF THE UNITED STATES REGARDING WEAPONS OF MASS DESTRUCTION. Established by Executive Order 13328 on 6 February 2004, the presidential commission evaluated the performance of the U.S. **intelligence community** (IC) in forecasting threats to the United States from countries thought to possess weapons of mass destruction (WMD) programs. The administration of President **George W. Bush** had used Iraq's purported possession of weapons systems as justification for launching a war in the spring of 2003 to oust Saddam Hussein and destroy his WMD capabilities.

The commission's report, released on 31 March 2005, found the intelligence community to have been "dead wrong" in virtually all its prewar judgments about Iraq's weapons of mass destruction. It also concluded that the United States knew "disturbingly little about the programs and even less about the intentions of many of America's dangerous adversaries," including **Iran** and North Korea. The report asserted that the spy agencies were disorganized and fragmented, even after the changes instituted in the aftermath of the **9/11 Commission's** report in the fall of 2004 and the enactment of the **Intelligence Reform and Terrorism Prevention Act** in January 2005.

The commission made 74 recommendations, the most important of which are giving the new **director of national intelligence** (DNI) greater powers over the intelligence agencies, including their budgets, programs, personnel, and priorities; setting up a National Security Service within the **Federal Bureau of Investigation** (FBI) to address counterterrorism and **counterintelligence** issues; establishing a National Counterproliferation Center to combat the spread of weapons; creating a new office within the **Central Intelligence Agency** (CIA) to **coordinate** intelligence among the different agencies; training more intelligence agents; and revamping the **president's daily brief** (PDB) to include more divergent views and alternative analyses.

On the day of the report's release, President Bush publicly said that he shared the commission's assessment that U.S. intelligence "needed fundamental change," but did not indicate which, if any, of the recommendations he would consider implementing. U.S. intelligence agencies have a solid record of fiercely opposing any change proposed from outside the community.

COMMISSION ON THE ROLES AND CAPABILITIES OF THE UNITED STATES INTELLIGENCE COMMUNITY. Also known as the Aspin/Brown Commission, the congressionally mandated body began its work in 1995 with the charge to review "the efficacy and appropriateness" of U.S. intelligence activities in the global environment of the post–**Cold War** period. The commission released its report on 1 March 1996, titled "Preparing for the 21st Century: An Appraisal of U.S. Intelligence," which examined the entire range of intelligence issues, such as the size of the **intelligence community** (IC), collection capabilities, organizations, overall structure, management, analysis, and oversight. The report also addressed the proposal to give the **director of central intelligence** (DCI) direct line control of the major **Department of Defense** (DOD) intelligence agencies—the **National Security Agency** (NSA), the **National Reconnaissance Office** (NRO), and the **National Imagery and Mapping Agency** (NIMA). In 1996, Congress passed legislation providing the DCI with greater power to coordinate the IC but declined to give him direct control.

COMMITTEE OF SECRET CORRESPONDENCE. Created on 29 November 1775, the Committee on Secret Correspondence carried out intelligence activities for the Continental Congress, corresponded with agents, and established precedents for secrecy in its operations. The committee included numerous well-known Revolutionary War figures, including **Benjamin Franklin** and James Lovell, the latter becoming Congress's expert on codes and ciphers, thereby earning him the sobriquet of "the father of American **cryptology**."

The committee employed secret agents abroad, conducted **covert actions**, devised codes and ciphers, funded **propaganda** activities, authorized the opening of private mail, acquired foreign publications for analysis, and established a courier system.

On 17 April 1777, the Committee of Secret Correspondence was renamed the Committee of Foreign Affairs, but kept its intelligence function. Matters of diplomacy were conducted by other committees or by the Congress as a whole. With the creation of a Department of Foreign Affairs—the forerunner of the **Department of State**—on 10 January 1781, correspondence "for the purpose of obtaining the most extensive and useful information relative to foreign affairs" was shifted to the new body, whose secretary was empowered to correspond "with all other persons from whom he may expect to receive useful information." *See also* HOUSE INTERNATIONAL RELATIONS COMMITTEE; SONS OF LIBERTY.

COMMITTEE ON IMAGERY REQUIREMENTS AND EX-PLOITATION (COMIREX). Established on 1 July 1967 as a sub-committee of the National Foreign Intelligence Board (NFIB), COMIREX replaced the Committee on Overhead Reconnaissance (COMOR) to coordinate imagery collection requirements in the United States government. The establishment of COMIREX reflected the increasing use of imaging capabilities of overhead collection systems, including satellites. COMIREX was designed to set priorities for the imagery needs of competing **intelligence community** (IC) agencies, including the **Central Intelligence Agency** (CIA), the **Defense Intelligence Agency** (DIA), and the military services. COMIREX was absorbed by the **Central Imagery Office** (CIO) in May 1992. *See also* NATIONAL IMAGERY AND MAPPING AGENCY.

COMMITTEE ON OVERHEAD RECONNAISSANCE (COMOR). *See* COMMITTEE ON IMAGERY REQUIREMENTS AND EX-PLOITATION.

COMMUNICATIONS INTELLIGENCE (COMINT). *See* SIG-NALS INTELLIGENCE.

COMMUNITY MANAGEMENT STAFF (CMS). Established in 1992 and headed by the executive director for intelligence community affairs (EXDIR/ICA), CMS superceded the **Intelligence Community Staff** (ICS) in providing assistance to the **director of central intelligence** (DCI) in coordinating and managing the **intelligence community** (IC). Specifically, CMS now supports the **director of national intelligence** (DNI) as the focal point for IC management of the **National Foreign Intelligence Program** (NFIP), program assessment and evaluation, and the management of collection requirements.

COMPARTMENTATION. Compartmentation refers to the segregation of information into discrete categories, with access to such information restricted on the "need to know" basis. Compartmentation of intelligence information usually occurs along lines corresponding to specific intelligence collection disciplines, such as **signals intelligence** (SIGINT) and **human intelligence** (HUMINT), with further compartmentation within each discipline to reflect particular programs or systems. Only individuals who have the need to know about the systems or programs and have received clearances for them are allowed access to the information. *See also* SPECIAL COMPARTMENTED INTELLIGENCE FACILITY.

COMPREHENSIVE TEST BAN TREATY (CTBT). Negotiated with the **Soviet Union** between 1994 and 1996, the treaty commits the parties to a total ban on nuclear explosions. To enforce this stipulation, the treaty establishes a global network of 321 internationally maintained monitoring stations to detect clandestine explosions and provides for on-site challenge inspections in cases of doubt. As such, the CTBT extends the limits imposed by the 1963 **Limited Nuclear Test Ban Treaty's** (LNTBT's) prohibitions on atmospheric, undersea, and outer-space testing. Over 165 countries have signed and over 90 have ratified the CTBT, but, according to its provisions, the treaty can come into force only when it is ratified by all nuclear capable states—a total of 44 countries. To date, the treaty lacks ratifications from nearly a dozen of those countries. The role of U.S. intelligence would be in verifying compliance with the terms of the treaty.

The United States has failed to ratify the CTBT, arguing that, in the aftermath of the **terrorist attacks of 11 September 2001**, the U.S. may develop new tactical nuclear weapons, whose efficacy can only be assured through testing. The administration of President **George W. Bush**, moreover, has expressed little confidence that the treaty will actually thwart nuclear proliferation. Proponents of the treaty, on the other hand, argue that its implementation would curtail advances in nuclear weaponry; limit the development of more advanced weapons by countries vying to develop nuclear weapons technology; and establish an international norm against testing that would reinforce the provisions of the **Nonproliferation Treaty** (NPT).

CONDOR (OPERATION). A network of Latin American secret police agencies that in the mid- to late 1970s coordinated attacks against their political opponents around the world. The plan called for the regime of **Augusto Pinochet** in Chile, along with other military governments in the region, to assassinate subversives, politicians, and prominent figures both within the national borders of the southern cone countries and abroad. On 21 September 1976, a bomb planted by agents of the Chilean secret police exploded under the car of Pinochet's leading critic in the United States, Orlando Letelier, killing him and his American colleague, Ronni Moffitt. Until the **terrorist attacks of 11 September 2001**, the Letelier-Moffitt **assassination** was considered the most egregious act of international terrorism ever committed in Washington, D.C.

CONFEDERATE SECRET SERVICE. The secessionist Confederate States of America (CSA) had at least two intelligence organizations, the first being the **Secret Service Bureau**, organized in 1862 as part of the CSA Signal Corps. The head of the bureau, Maj. William Norris, eventually coordinated the activities of dozens of **espionage** and counterespionage agents who operated along the "Secret Line," an underground link between Richmond and the Washington-Baltimore region. In time, Norris and his assistant, Captain Charles Cawood, sought to extend this network of intelligence outlets as far north as Canada. Arguably the most effective military intelligence establishment of the war, Norris's bureau directed all espionage activity along the Potomac River, supervised the passage of agents to and from enemy lines, and forwarded dispatches from the Confederate War and State Departments to contacts abroad. A second Confederate secret-service unit was organized early in 1864. A prototype commando outfit, it was attached to the Torpedo Bureau of Brig. Gen. Gabriel J. Rains, but was neither as large nor as well administered as the agency headed by Major Norris.

CONGRESS FOR CULTURAL FREEDOM. Considered to be one of the more daring and effective **Cold War covert actions** by the **Central Intelligence Agency** (CIA). Initiated as a conference of intellectuals in West Berlin in June 1950, the congress published literary and political journals and hosted dozens of conferences bringing together some of the most eminent Western thinkers. Its purpose was to demonstrate that communism, despite its rhetoric, was an enemy of art and thought. By doing so, it sought to negate communism's appeal among artists and intellectuals, and, at the same time, to undermine the communist claim to moral superiority. The work of the congress was an integral part of the CIA's strategy of promoting the noncommunist Left. The CIA's sponsorship of the Congress for Cultural Freedom became publicly known in 1967, effectively ending this covert operation.

CONTAINMENT POLICY. Containment refers to the foreign policy strategy of the United States in the early years of the **Cold War**. The policy was first laid out in **George F. Kennan's** famous long telegram. It was then made public in 1947 in his anonymous *Foreign Affairs* article "The Sources of Soviet Conduct," better known as the X article.

Kennan argued that the primary goal of the United States should be to prevent the spread of communism by "containing" it within its borders. The **Truman Doctrine** incorporated containment as one of its key principles. This led to American support for regimes, some of them quite authoritarian and repressive, around the world to block the spread of communism. After the disaster of the **Vietnam War**, Kennan asserted that his ideas had been misinterpreted and that he never advocated military intervention, merely economic support.

CONTRAS (*contrarevolucionario*). The Contras were the armed opponents of **Nicaragua**'s revolutionary **Sandinista** government following the July 1979 overthrow of Anastasio Somoza Debayle and the ending of the Somoza family's 43-year rule. The label was commonly used by the press in the United States to cover a range of disparate groups.

The Contras comprised remnants of Somoza's national guard, disaffected former Sandinistas, and various Amerindian groups that were alienated by the Sandinista modernization efforts. They were considered terrorists by the Sandinistas, and many of their attacks targeted civilians.

The United States played a key role in the development of the Contra alliance following President **Ronald Reagan's** assumption of the presidency in January 1981. Accusing the Sandinistas of importing Cuban-style communism and aiding leftist guerrillas in El Salvador, President Reagan on 23 November 1981 signed the top-secret **National Security Decision Directive 17** (NSDD-17), giving the **Central Intelligence Agency** (CIA) the authority to recruit and support the Contras.

The Contra alliance came to an end in the 1984–1985 time frame, with each of the alliance partners making their own deal with the Sandinista regime. The ceasefire of 23 March 1988, under Costa Rican leadership, effectively brought the Contra War to an end. *See also* BOLAND AMENDMENTS; IRAN-CONTRA AFFAIR; *NICARA-GUA V. UNITED STATES*.

COORDINATION. Coordination is the process of acquiring interagency agreement on judgments, assessments, and other intelligence products intended for policymakers. Virtually all intelligence agencies coordinate their judgments and evaluations internally. The **Central Intelligence Agency** (CIA) is required by law to coordinate its analytic products with select members of the **intelligence community** (IC) as well. In addition, all estimative products undergo a coordination process overseen by **national intelligence officers** (NIOs). The theoretical basis for coordination is that the **director of national intelligence** (DNI) must present a unified and common judgment to senior officials.

COPELAND, MILES (1913–1991). A former **Central Intelligence Agency** (CIA) covert operative in the Middle East, who in 1949 orchestrated a coup d'etat in Damascus, Syria, that was supposedly to bring democracy to Syrian politics. Copeland later claimed to have planned a deception operation during the Suez Crisis of 1956, but his claim of involvement is in dispute. However, he was an advisor to President Gamel Abdul Nasser in Egypt before leaving the CIA for good in 1957 to become an oil company executive. He is now better known for his many books, most of which extol his own exploits as a CIA operative. *See also* RAINBOW (OPERATION).

CORONA (SYSTEM). CORONA refers to the first operational space photo reconnaissance satellite, approved by President **Dwight D. Eisenhower** in February 1958. CORONA satellites were designed to take pictures in space of the **Soviet** Bloc countries and return the photographic film to earth for processing. The **intelligence community** (IC) used the designator **Keyhole** (KH), followed by a number— KH-1, KH-2, KH-3, KH-4, KH-4A, and KH-4B—to indicate the specific CORONA version.

    CORONA spacecraft were built from 1959 to 1972 by Lockheed Space Systems under **Central Intelligence Agency** (CIA) and air force contracts spanning 145 launches. CORONA cameras were developed by **Itek** and used Eastman Kodak film. Resolution in early flight years was in the range of 35 to 40 feet. By 1972, CORONA delivered resolutions of 6 to 10 feet.

The CORONA program ended with a launch on 25 May 1972. President **William J. Clinton** signed an executive order on 22 February 1995 directing the declassification of CORONA imagery as well as its later iterations, ARGON and LANYARD. The order provided for the declassification of more than 860,000 images of the earth's surface, collected between 1960 and 1972.

Recently released **national intelligence estimates** (NIEs) reveal that CORONA covered virtually all Soviet military developments and provided superb verification capabilities for the **Strategic Arms Limitation Talks** (SALT) I treaty, including its antiballistic missile (ABM) provisions. It also allowed coverage of **People's Republic of China** (PRC) missile-launching sites.

COUNTERINTELLIGENCE (CI). Counterintelligence is the analytic and operational process of identifying and neutralizing foreign intelligence activities against the United States. Counterintelligence has three facets: the physical security of information, from guarding buildings to **compartmenting** information on the "need to know" basis; identifying and catching American citizens who spy for foreign governments; and identifying foreign agents working against U.S. interests and either turning them into double agents or prosecuting them for **espionage**. Although responsibility for counterintelligence in the **intelligence community** (IC) is shared between the **Federal Bureau of Investigation** (FBI) at home and the **Central Intelligence Agency** (CIA) abroad, virtually all American intelligence elements engage to some degree in counterintelligence activities. Congress has also mandated that the IC work to identify and help American companies neutralize **industrial espionage** perpetrated against them. *See also* NATIONAL COUNTERINTELLIGENCE EXECUTIVE; NEGATIVE INTELLIGENCE.

COUNTERINTELLIGENCE CENTER (CIC). Established on 1 April 1988 by **William H. Webster**, the **director of central intelligence** (DCI), the CIC was the second **fusion center** created to bring greater coherence to a specific intelligence activity. Housed within the **Directorate of Operations** (DO) of the **Central Intelligence Agency** (CIA), the CIC brings together representatives of different agencies of the **intelligence community** (IC), including analysts, to plan, coordinate, and manage effective **counterintelligence** activities within the United States and the intelligence community. It also provides the CIA a venue for dealing with other intelligence agencies and foreign liaison services over counterintelligence matters. The CIC consolidated the Counterintelligence Staff, the Foreign Intelligence Capabilities Unit (established in 1983 to uncover attempts by foreign intelligence agencies to manage perceptions of U.S. intelligence), elements of the DO's Office of Security, and other intelligence community elements.

COUNTER INTELLIGENCE CORPS (CIC). Established in 1942 as part of the army, the CIC played a significant intelligence role during **World War II** and the first decade of the **Cold War**. The CIC's mission was to detect treason, sedition, subversive activity, or disaffection among service personnel. In addition, it sought to detect, prevent, or neutralize **espionage** or sabotage within the army or directed against the army. During the war, the CIC recruited over 50,000 informants within the ranks of the army, most of whom produced reports on the activities of their fellow soldiers. This activity soon became politically controversial and prompted the army to curtail the CIC's domestic work.

The CIC also deployed operatives at all command levels to support tactical operations. These detachments identified Nazi sleeper agents and investigated suspected civilians and enemy personnel. CIC elements operated independently of **army intelligence** units. Former secretary of state **Henry A. Kissinger** was a special CIC agent.

At the end of the war, the CIC assumed new responsibilities. It served as the army's chief agency in occupied Austria, Germany, and Italy, rounding up individuals with Nazi affiliations. The CIC also got involved in handling problems associated with displaced persons as well as black market activities. In fact, between 1945 and 1950, the CIC possessed greater resources than those allotted to the **Office of Strategic Services** (OSS) during the war or to the **Central Intelligence Group** (CIG) in 1946. The CIC's part in fighting the nascent **Cold War** was to recruit former Nazis to provide **positive intelligence** on Soviet targets. During the first 15 years of the Cold War, CIC units were dispersed throughout the world in America's expanding overseas commitments as part of the **containment policy**. The CIC was so dominant an entity that, throughout the 1950s, it tried to reconcile its intelligence mission abroad with that of the **Central Intelligence Agency** (CIA) in order to avoid duplication and recruitment of the same assets. Despite its early prominence, the CIC was disbanded in 1961 and its assets merged into the newly formed army intelligence. *See also* GEHLEN ORGANIZATION.

COUNTERMEASURES. Countermeasures are actions taken by governments and their agencies to thwart the activities of hostile intelligence services. Countermeasures may include **denial/deception operations** or remedial actions that would stymie the adversary's intrusions. In intelligence terms, countermeasures comprise both offensive and defensive **counterintelligence** actions.

COUNTERTERRORISM CENTER (CTC). Established in 1986 by **Director of Central Intelligence** (DCI) **William J. Casey,** the CTC was a response to criticism that the U.S. government did not aggressively operate to disrupt **terrorist** activities. Organizationally, the CTC is located within the **Central Intelligence Agency's** (CIA's) **Directorate of Operations** (DO), intended to combat international terrorist threats. A 1990 **director of central intelligence directive** (DCID) gave the CTC an analytic capability by creating an Interagency Intelligence Committee on Terrorism (IICT) under the direction of the Community Counterterrorism Board (CCB), both designed to produce such analytic products as coordinated terrorism alerts and advisories for a government-wide audience. In 1995 and 1998, President **William J. Clinton** issued a series of directives that further defined terrorism as a crime and set up procedures to apprehend and punish terrorists worldwide. In 1997, the CCB established a Terrorism Warning Group to get warnings of impending terrorist attacks quickly to senior military and civilian policymakers. After the **terrorist attacks of 11 September 2001**, the analytic functions of the CTC were gradually integrated into the **Terrorism Threat Integration Center** (TTIC) and then into the **National Counterterrorism Center**, established in 2005. *See also* NATIONAL COUNTERTERRORISM CENTER.

COVER. Cover refers to the guise employed by intelligence officers and installations to disassociate themselves from intelligence activities. The U.S. government uses three types of cover. Official cover associates the intelligence officer with a government entity other than an intelligence agency. Nonofficial cover refers to an association with a commercial entity. Diversified cover is a combination of official and nonofficial cover that gives the intelligence officer flexibility to undertake intelligence operations. *See also* CASE OFFICER.

COVERT ACTION. A covert action is a secret government program in pursuit of foreign policy objectives by influencing events abroad in ways unattributable to the U.S. government. Covert action has long been a foreign policy tool in the repertoire of options available to U.S. presidents, even before the passage of the **National Security Act of 1947**, which set up the outlines of present-day U.S. intelligence. In the early days of the Republic, covert operations played significant roles in the country's territorial expansion in North America and in overcoming adversaries in the wars of the 19th century. The 1947 act made covert action an essential part of the American intelligence repertoire by granting the **National Security Council** (NSC) the authority to direct "special activities" from time to time. Various successes in the 1950s thrust covert action into the forefront of American intelligence methods, but the spectacular failures of the 1960s soured the public's support of such actions. In the 1970s, the White House and Congress imposed restrictions and procedural mechanisms on the conduct of covert operations, most of which remain in effect to this day. *See also* AJAX (OPERATION); ASSASSINATIONS; BAY OF PIGS INVASION; COVERT ACTION PLANNING GROUP; EXECUTIVE ORDER 12333; FINDING; 5412 SPECIAL GROUP; 40 COMMITTEE; HUGHES-RYAN AMENDMENT; MONGOOSE (OPERATION); OVERSIGHT; SUCCESS (OPERATION); 303 COMMITTEE.

COVERT ACTION PLANNING GROUP (CAPG). The CAPG is an entity within the **Central Intelligence Agency** (CIA) that prepares and reviews covert action **findings**. Composed of the CIA's associate deputy director of operations (DDO), senior CIA staff chiefs, and those individuals within the CIA with substantive responsibility for the proposed covert action finding and its implementation, the CAPG may stop covert action proposals if it deems them unfeasible, inappropriate, illegal, or contrary to American principles. *See also* COVERT ACTION REVIEW GROUP.

COVERT ACTION REVIEW GROUP (CARG). This **Central Intelligence Agency** (CIA) committee is comprised of senior CIA officials, including the deputy director of operations (DDO), who review **covert action** plans, pursuant to a **finding**, prepared by the **Covert Action Planning Group** (CAPG). The CARG has the authority to put a stop to a planned covert operation for any number of reasons, including impracticality, expense, adverse publicity, or possible damage to U.S. foreign relations.

CRATEOLOGY. Crateology refers to the science of determining the contents of a box or a crate from its attributes. Developed by U.S. intelligence in the 1950s, the methodology helps to interpret obscure markings on crates and determine their contents from their shapes and sizes. U.S. intelligence had determined during the **Cold War** that **Warsaw Pact** countries, and especially the **Soviet Union**, used the same kind of crates to ship known types of military equipment, such as aircraft wings or missiles. By identifying the type of crate and its markings, intelligence analysts could then make reasonable judgments about the crate's contents. Because of the possibility of deception and the uncertainty associated with such judgments, however, intelligence analysts almost certainly tried to corroborate the information from other sources, such as **human intelligence** (HUMINT) assets. Crateology is a subfield of the **Measurement and Signature Intelligence** (MASINT) collection system.

CRYPTOLOGY. Cryptology is the science of designing communications codes and of finding the appropriate keys for decoding foreign communications, both of which have been, and are, central to intelligence work. Specially trained cryptologists seek to design unbreakable codes while also searching for the formulas that might give them clues in deciphering foreign messages. Cryptology is one of the oldest intelligence techniques, a discipline now practiced and managed by the **National Security Agency** (NSA) in the U.S. government.

Among the more notable successes in this are were the **Purple** decryptions of Japanese communications in the late 1930s and the **VENONA Operation** against the Soviet spies in the United States during the 1940s and 1950s.

CUBA. Liberated from Spanish colonial occupation by American forces during the **Spanish-American War of 1898**, Cuba has occupied a special position in American foreign policy because of its location in the Caribbean and proximity to the United States. Since **Fidel Castro** came to power in 1959, successive presidents have attempted to use American intelligence resources to influence developments in Cuba through such methods as fomenting insurrection in the country and trying to **assassinate** Castro himself. In addition, Cuba played an infamous role during the **Cold War**, as the country over which the two superpowers—the United States and the **Soviet Union**—nearly clashed with nuclear weapons. *See also* BAY OF PIGS INVASION; CUBAN MISSILE CRISIS; MONGOOSE (OPERATION).

CUBAN MISSILE CRISIS. The Cuban Missile Crisis was a confrontation between the United States and the **Soviet Union** over the placement of Soviet medium-range nuclear missiles in **Cuba**. On 16 October 1962, the **Central Intelligence Agency** (CIA) informed President **John F. Kennedy** that **U-2** aerial reconnaissance photos revealed Soviet missiles had been secretly moved into **Cuba**. The CIA's **National Photographic Interpretation Center** (NPIC) had discovered the missiles, which it deemed capable of striking the United States, on 14 October 1962, and corroborating intelligence was received from a Cuban refugee on 20 September 1962 that he had seen a Russian missile on a truck in Cuba that matched the characteristics of a Soviet medium-range missile. On 27 October 1962, President Kennedy went on nationwide television and announced a "quarantine" of the island nation. President Kennedy's action intensified fears that a full-scale nuclear war with the Soviet Union was possible, especially if Soviet ships on their way to Cuba defied the quarantine.

At the same time, the Cubans shot down a U-2 aircraft over Cuba, and agents of the **Federal Bureau of Investigation** (FBI) reported that Soviet diplomats were burning documents in anticipation of a rupture in relations. With each incident, the United States and the Soviet Union moved closer to nuclear confrontation. However, after intense diplomatic exchanges, Moscow backed down on 29 October 1962 and agreed to remove its missiles from Cuba, in exchange for an American pledge not to invade the island nation and to dismantle American Jupiter missiles that were stationed in Turkey.

CULPER SPY RING. *See* TALLMADGE, BENJAMIN; WASHING-TON, GEORGE.

CURRENT INTELLIGENCE. Current intelligence is processed and analyzed intelligence information on daily or ongoing international matters. Because of its emphasis on the current aspects of world affairs, current intelligence is highly perishable and must be delivered to the consumers in a timely manner. Moreover, policymakers tend to prefer current intelligence to **long-term intelligence** because it is immediate and more relevant to their daily needs. The **president's daily brief** (PDB) and the **senior executive intelligence brief** (SEIB) are among the dozens of current intelligence publications available to intelligence consumers.

CURRENT MANAGEMENT ACCOUNT (CMA). The current management account is the part of the **National Foreign Intelligence Program** (NFIP) that funds current intelligence activities. *See also* INTELLIGENCE BUDGETS.

CUSHMAN, PAULINE (1833–1893). A Union spy during the American **Civil War**, Cushman provided intelligence information to the federal **Secret Service Bureau** and military intelligence in Louisville, Kentucky, and Nashville, Tennessee. On a mission behind Confederate lines, she was captured and sentenced to death, but was left behind when the Union army forced the Confederates to withdraw. After the war, President **Abraham Lincoln** bestowed on her the honorary rank of major. Pauline Cushman later traveled around the country, touting her exploits as a Union spy.

– D –

DCI CRIME AND NARCOTICS CENTER (CNC). Established in April 1989 by **Director of Central Intelligence** (DCI) **William H.**

Webster, the CNC is a **fusion center** intended to monitor and produce intelligence information about international trafficking in illegal drugs and international organized crime. Although the drug trade had become a national concern as early as the 1970s, international crime came to the forefront of national concern only with the end of the **Cold War** and the dissolution of the **Soviet Union**. Because of the connection between illegal drug trafficking and international crime, the CNC, in addition to gathering and analyzing intelligence, has a mandate to assist and work with law enforcement agencies.

DCI ENVIRONMENTAL CENTER (DEC). The DEC is a **fusion center** established in 1997 by **Director of Central Intelligence** (DCI) **John M. Deutch** as the focal point for all **intelligence community** (IC) activities related to environmental issues. Housed in the **Central Intelligence Agency's** (CIA's) **Directorate of Intelligence** (DI), the DEC's mission is to assess transboundary environmental crime; support environmental treaty negotiations and assess foreign environmental policies; evaluate the role of environmental issues in regional instability and conflict; support the international environmental efforts of other U.S. government agencies; and provide environmental data to nondefense agencies. The DEC also provides data to the environmental community.

DCI NONPROLIFERATION CENTER (NPC). Established on 17 September 1991 within the **Central Intelligence Agency's** (CIA's) **Directorate of Intelligence** (DI), the Center's mission was to track the worldwide development and acquisition of production technology, designs, components, or complete military systems in the areas of weapons of mass destruction and advanced conventional weaponry. It also provided support to proliferation-related monitoring and compliance activities, including United Nations (UN) inspection teams. In April 1992, DCI **Robert M. Gates** raised NPC's stature by making it a DCI **fusion center**. On 25 March 1993, DCI **R. James Woolsey Jr.** designated the director of the NPC as his special assistant for nonproliferation. DCI Woolsey also broadened the NPC's mission, assigning it principal responsibility for ensuring the **coordination** of **intelligence community** (IC) proliferation-related analysis and support to the policy, export licensing, law-enforcement, military, and operations communities. After the **terrorist attacks of 11 September 2001**, the NPC was integrated into the DCI Weapons Intelligence, Nonproliferation, and Arms Control Center, housed in the CIA's Directorate of Intelligence. In 2005, President George W. Bush established the National Counterproliferation Center, absorbing the functions of the NPC.

DEEP BLUE (OPERATION). Deep Blue is the code name for a navy tactical group established after the **terrorist attacks of 11 September 2001** to conduct research on new weapons systems, intelligence sensors, and operational tactics and procedures to be used in the antiterror fight. The team, put together in 2002, assesses innovative ideas for effectively linking intelligence and combat operations, such as improving forward staging capabilities or linking navy's SEAL teams with regular navy functions, as well as improving naval battle operations against terrorists. *See also* TACTICAL INTELLIGENCE AND RELATED ACTIVITIES.

DEFECTOR. A defector is an individual, usually a highly placed official of a government, who flees his country, switches allegiance, and agrees to give the government of his new country intelligence information about the country and the government from which he has fled. For example, **Edward Lee Howard**, an employee of the **Central Intelligence Agency** (CIA), defected to the **USSR**, and **Vitaly Yurchenko** defected to the United States, both in the 1980s.

DEFENSE ADVANCED RESEARCH PROJECTS AGENCY (DARPA). The Defense Advanced Research Projects Agency was established in 1958 as the first U.S. response to the Soviet launching of **Sputnik**. Since that time, the DARPA's mission has been to assure that the U.S. maintains a lead in applying state-of-the-art technology for military capabilities and to prevent technological surprise from its adversaries.

The DARPA's original operating philosophy has changed over the years in three ways. First, the DARPA has entered the commercial marketplace in a way that assures the Defense Department's long-term interests. Second, in the past decade, the DARPA has pioneered revolutionary research and development practices by leading the way in adopting innovative trade and contracting arrangements. Third, since the **Goldwater-Nichols Act of 1986**, the DARPA has focused considerable attention on resolving problems associated with greater "jointness" among the services.

DEFENSE ATTACHÉS. As military officers posted to U.S. embassies abroad, defense attachés have the responsibility of collecting and reporting intelligence on foreign military developments. Defense attachés are generally known as "open spies" and are an integral part of the **Defense HUMINT Service** (DH), which consolidates military **espionage** activities. Defense attachés also represent the **Department of Defense** (DOD) and the military services abroad, administer military assistance programs and foreign military sales, and advise U.S. ambassadors on military and political-military issues.

DEFENSE HUMINT SERVICE (DH). Established on 2 November 1993 within the **Defense Intelligence Agency** (DIA), the Defense HUMINT Service consolidates the **human intelligence** (HUMINT) activities of the military services under one umbrella organization. As such, it engages in **espionage** and other clandestine activities in support of military missions. The Defense HUMINT Service is now referred to by the designation DH, to differentiate it from the **Department of Homeland Security** (DHS), which was established in 2002. The DH is funded out of a consolidated HUMINT budget within the **General Defense Intelligence Program** (GDIP), which is part of the **National Foreign Intelligence Program** (NFIP) under the nominal control of the **director of national intelligence** (DNI). The DH is now under the joint purview of the deputy secretary of defense and assistant secretary of defense for command, control, communications, computers, and intelligence. The **George W. Bush** White House began considering a plan in late 2004 to give the DH greater espionage responsibilities, possibly at the expense of the **Central Intelligence Agency** (CIA).

DEFENSE INTELLIGENCE AGENCY (DIA). Established in 1961 by Secretary of Defense Robert McNamara, DIA is an all-source intelligence agency supporting the **Joint Chiefs of Staff** (JCS). As a member of the **intelligence community** (IC), its mission is to provide strategic military intelligence affecting national defense. Its defense intelligence officers (DIOs) act in a similar capacity within the **Department of Defense** (DOD) as the **national intelligence officers** (NIOs) do within the **National Intelligence Council** (NIC). DIOs formulate, design, prepare, draft, and coordinate defense estimative products. They also represent the interests of the DIA at the appropriate **coordination** meetings of **national intelligence estimates** (NIEs) prepared by the NIC. The DIA operates the **Joint Military Intelligence College** (JMIC) and runs the defense attaché program. The **George W. Bush** administration began considering a plan in late 2004 to create a Joint Intelligence Operational Command within the Defense Department, which would increase the organizational power of intelligence and possibly replace the DIA.

DEFENSE INTELLIGENCE COLLEGE (DIC). *See* JOINT MILITARY INTELLIGENCE COLLEGE.

DEFENSE INTELLIGECE SCHOOL (DIS). *See* JOINT MILITARY INTELLIGENCE COLLEGE.

DEFENSE SECURITY SERVICE (DSS). The Defense Security Service, formerly known as the Defense Investigative Service (DIS), conducts personnel security investigations and provides industrial security products and services as well as comprehensive security education and training to the Defense Department and other government entities. Although not a formal member of the **intelligence community** (IC), the DSS works closely with IC agencies to provide counterintelligence services.

DENIAL/DECEPTION OPERATIONS. These are clandestine operations intended to deny information or access to hostile governments and their agents or to deceive them into false scenarios.

DEPARTMENT OF DEFENSE (DOD). A central military organization authorized by Congress in 1947 and officially established in 1949. At the end of **World War II**, U.S. policymakers decided that a central military organization was needed at the national and major commands levels. In 1947, through the **National Security Act**, Congress created the civilian position of secretary of defense, as well as the **National Military Authority**, to provide centralized civilian direction to the military apparatus. It also established the air force as its own department and subordinated all military services to the new secretary. In 1949, a further effort to centralize authority resulted in an amendment to the original act that made the new agency an executive department, renamed it the Department of Defense, and withdrew the cabinet-level status of the three military secretaries.

Five units within the Department of Defense collect intelligence information. The **National Security Agency** (NSA) collects, processes, and reports **signals intelligence** (SIGINT). The **Defense Intelligence Agency** (DIA) oversees an all-source collection effort to ensure that current and future Department of Defense military requirements are met. The **National Reconnaissance Office** (NRO) manages the government's space-borne reconnaissance system. The Defense Airborne Reconnaissance Office (DARO) operates the Defense Department's airborne reconnaissance program, including manned and unmanned aircraft and their ground processing stations. Finally, each of the military services maintains its own collection efforts within its areas of specialization.

DEPARTMENT OF HOMELAND SECURITY (DHS). Established by the Department of Homeland Security Act of 2002, the DHS is the executive agency with a mandate to protect the security of the American homeland by preventing terrorist attacks within the United States, reducing the country's vulnerabilities to attack, and minimizing the damage from natural disasters and attacks within the country. The DHS incorporated 23 federal entities that previously were scattered throughout the government.

The department is organized around five directorates. The Border and Transportation Security directorate brings under one roof all domestic agencies that deal with perimeter and transportation security, including the Customs Service, the Transportation Security Administration (TSA), and parts of the former Immigration and Naturalization Service (INS). The Emergency Preparedness and Response directorate oversees training for disaster readiness and coordinates the government's response. The Science and Technology directorate employs scientific and technological techniques to oversee defensive methods and **countermeasures**. The Information Analysis and Infrastructure Protection directorate analyzes intelligence information received from other **intelligence community** (IC) agencies and prepares **threat assessments** intended for the secretary and other senior policymakers. The Management directorate provides overall guidance and direction to the entire department.

In addition to the directorates, the DHS also incorporates several agencies that remain quasi-autonomous within the department, reporting directly to the secretary. Along with some obscure offices, the **Coast Guard**, a member of the intelligence community, and the **Secret Service**, formerly part of the Treasury Department, fall in this category.

DEPARTMENT OF STATE. The Department of State, America's diplomatic service, was established on 15 September 1789 upon the passage of "An Act to provide for the safe keeping of the Acts, Records, and Seal of the United States, and for other purposes." This law allowed the department to assume some domestic responsibilities that its predecessor, the Department of Foreign Affairs, did not have. The first secretary of state, Thomas Jefferson, was appointed in 1789, and since then there have been 63 more.

The secretary of state is a statutory member of the **National Security Council** (NSC), which sets intelligence policy through its interagency mechanisms. The State Department's **Bureau of Intelligence and Research** (INR) is a member of the **intelligence community** (IC) and provides intelligence support to the secretary and other elements of the diplomatic service. *See also* MORNING SUMMARY.

DEPUTIES COMMITTEE. The National Security Council's Deputies Committee (NSC/DC) serves as the senior subcabinet interagency forum for consideration of policy issues affecting national security. The NSC/DC can prescribe and review the work of the **National Security Council** (NSC) interagency groups and ensures that issues being brought before the NSC/PC or the NSC have been properly analyzed and prepared for decision.

The NSC/DC has as its regular members the deputies and undersecretaries of the relevant executive departments, including the **deputy director of central intelligence** (DDCI) and the vice chairman of the **Joint Chiefs of Staff** (JCS). The **assistant to the president for national security affairs** (APNSA) usually chairs the Deputies Committee, which focuses on immediate problems. While the deputies have occasionally met to consider long-term policy matters, such sessions are unusual. They focus largely on producing options that can be acted on in a relatively short period.

DEPUTY DIRECTOR OF CENTRAL INTELLIGENCE (DDCI). The DDCI was second in command of the **intelligence community** (IC) until 2005 and was appointed by the **director of central intelligence** (DCI) and confirmed by the Senate. Under the terms of the **National Security Act of 1947** and various other enabling legislation, both the DCI and DDCI could be civilians, but only one could be a serving military officer. *See also* Appendix B.

DESERT ONE. Desert One was the U.S. government designation for that part of the Iranian desert that was to be used by the U.S. military to rescue the American hostages in Tehran in 1980. *See also* EAGLE CLAW (OPERATION).

DEUTCH, JOHN MARK (1938–). Seventeenth **director of central intelligence** (DCI) between 10 May 1995 and 15 December 1996. John M. Deutch has served in significant government and academic posts throughout his career. Prior to becoming DCI, he was deputy secretary of defense from March 1994 until March 1995 and undersecretary of defense for acquisitions and technology from March 1993 until March 1994.

In addition, John Deutch served in a number of positions in the Department of Energy (DOE) from 1977 until 1980 and on many commissions during several presidential administrations: the President's Nuclear Safety Oversight Committee (1980–1981); the President's Commission on Strategic Forces (1983); the White House Science Council (1985–1989); the President's Committee of Advisors on Science and Technology (1997–2001); the President's Intelligence Advisory Board (1990–1993); the President's Commission on Aviation Safety and Security (1996); the Commission on Reducing and Protecting Government Secrecy (1996); and the Commission to Assess the Organization of the Federal Government to Combat the Proliferation of Weapons of Mass Destruction (chairman, 1998–1999). After leaving his DCI post in 1996, Deutch became embroiled in a controversy over his alleged cavalier attitude toward security by keeping classified information on a nonsecure computer at home. After an investigation, **George J. Tenet**, Deutch's successor as DCI, revoked his security clearances.

DIPLOMATIC BAG. A diplomatic bag is a term used to describe shipping containers that have diplomatic immunity from search or seizure. The diplomatic bag need not be an actual bag. The Vienna Convention on Diplomatic Relations (1961) ensures that diplomats and their official belongings are given safe passage in transit or in the host country.

DIPLOMATIC IMMUNITY. Diplomatic immunity, as defined by the Vienna Convention on Diplomatic Relations (1961), allows designated diplomats to engage in their official duties without interference from the host government to which they are accredited. The home country can waive immunity if it so desires, but this tends only to happen when the individual has committed a serious crime, unconnected with the diplomatic role, or has witnessed such a crime. Alternatively, the home country may decide to prosecute the individual. Even though diplomats are exempt from host country laws, they may be expelled for "actions inconsistent with their diplomatic status" (spying), smuggling, child custody law violations, and even murder in a few cases.

DIPLOMATIC SECURITY. Security within the **Department of State** was formally established in 1916 under Secretary of State Robert Lansing. In 1918, Congress passed legislation requiring passports for Americans traveling abroad and visas for aliens wishing to enter the United States, and responsibility for enforcing the new law fell on the State Department's security office. At this time, diplomatic security also protected distinguished visitors to the United States. During **World War I**, the State Department also acquired responsibility for incarcerating and exchanging diplomatic officials of enemy powers and assisting in screening people repatriated from enemy-controlled areas, a job it also undertook during **World War II**.

After the war, reorganization enabled the State Department's security office to maintain bureaus and to station U.S. Marines at U.S. embassies abroad. With the rise of the **terrorist** threat against U.S. interests in the 1980s, the State Department established the Bureau of Diplomatic Security (DS) and the Diplomatic Security Service (DSS) on 4 November 1985. The Diplomatic Courier Service joined the new Bureau at this time. The DS acquired the Rewards for Justice Program in 1992, in which the State Department pays for information to resolve acts of international terrorism against Americans. The DS also conducts criminal and personnel security investigations and provides protective services to distinguished dignitaries visiting the United States.

DIRECTORATE OF INTELLIGENCE (DI). The DI is the analytic arm of the **Central Intelligence Agency** (CIA), processing and analyzing intelligence information and producing intelligence assessments and other products for policymakers. Successor to the **Office of Research and Analysis** (ORA), the DI was renamed **National Foreign Assessment Center** (NFAC) in 1978, but **Director of Central Intelligence** (DCI) **William J. Casey** in 1981 reverted to using its original designation.

The DI's analytic functions are organized along both functional and regional lines. Analysts receive intelligence information from all available sources in the **intelligence community** (IC) and draft intelligence assessments and estimates that correspond to the requirements set by national decision makers. The DI's products include **current intelligence** items, such as the **senior executive intelligence brief** (SEIB) and the **president's daily brief** (PDB), and **long-term intelligence**, such as intelligence memorandums. DI analysts also participate in the estimative process under the guidance and direction of the **National Intelligence Council** (NIC).

DIRECTORATE OF OPERATIONS (DO). The clandestine arm of the **Central Intelligence Agency** (CIA), the DO's mission is to collect **human intelligence** (HUMINT), conduct **counterintelligence** (CI) abroad, and carry out **covert actions** as authorized by the president. Formerly known as the **Directorate of Plans** (DP), the DO came into existence in 1973 when **James Schlesinger**, the **director of central intelligence** (DCI), renamed the organization in order to make the CIA appear more open about its activities.

The DO's **case officers** as well as its covert operatives in the past have had an almost fanatical zeal in carrying out their missions. Because of the DO's specialized and politically sensitive work, the DO has also tended toward insularity, cutting itself off from outsiders, including from other components of the CIA. These twin cultural precepts at times have prompted DO officers to overstep the bounds of propriety and legality, culminating in sensational revelations and embarrassing scandals, such as rogue operations involving assassination attempts and overthrow of governments. *See also* DIRECTORATE OF INTELLIGENCE; OFFICE OF POLICY COORDINATION.

DIRECTORATE OF PLANS (DP). The **Central Intelligence Agency** (CIA) in August 1952 consolidated the activities of the **Office of Policy Coordination** (OPC) and the **Office of Secret Operations** (OSO) by establishing the Directorate of Plans. The DP's mission was to engage in **espionage**, **counterintelligence**, and **covert actions**. The DP was renamed the **Directorate of Operations** (DO) in 1973.

DIRECTOR OF CENTRAL INTELLIGENCE (DCI). Until 2005, the nominal head of the **intelligence community** (IC), the position of the DCI was established in January 1946 for coordinating—not directing—American intelligence activities. This thrust did not change much over the years, although the White House and Congress occasionally bolstered the DCI's authorities in coordinating U.S. intelligence.

The DCI's responsibilities evolved over the years to include three functions. First, he put together, submitted, and controlled the **National Foreign Intelligence Program** (NFIP) budget—the IC budget—although a substantial portion of it went to **Department of Defense** (DOD) intelligence elements. Second, the DCI had authority to coordinate **counterintelligence** programs of all intelligence community agencies. Third, the DCI had the responsibility to ensure the **protection of sources and methods**, which enabled him to establish standard rules and regulations governing access to intelligence installations, personnel, and information.

These three responsibilities—submitting a community budget, conducting counterintelligence, and protecting sources and methods—were the only ones the DCI exercises in his statutory role as head of the intelligence community. Even in these tasks, the DCI was only able to exercise soft power techniques like persuasion and influence. To overcome this deficiency, the typical DCI had to bring to his office attributes that would enable him better to manage the community—a personal relationship and access to the president, the skills of an excellent negotiator, and the patience of a mediator.

Some DCIs, such as **Allen W. Dulles**, brought such qualities to their job to great effect. Most, however, lacked in these qualities and therefore were less successful in wielding their community hat. Because the heads of IC agencies—except the CIA—reported directly to their policy principals, the DCI's relative position in the White House pecking order also came into play in the bureaucratic politics of the intelligence community. This was especially so regarding the Pentagon's intelligence units, over which the secretary of defense retained complete control. From time to time, a particular secretary of defense would give lip service to allowing the DCI greater authority over the defense-related intelligence organizations, but no defense secretary to date has relinquished any significant amount of power to the DCI. Under the terms of the **Intelligence Reform and Terrorism Prevention Act** of 2004, the DCI is now only the director of the **Central Intelligence Agency** (CIA). *See also* Appendix A; BUSH, GEORGE H. W.; CASEY, WILLIAM J.; COLBY, WILLIAM E.; DEUTCH, JOHN M.; GATES, ROBERT M.; GOSS, PORTER; HELMS, RICHARD M.; HILLENKOETTER, ROSCOE; McCONE, JOHN A.; RABORN, WILLIAM F., JR.; SCHLESINGER, JAMES R.; SMITH, WALTER BEDELL; SOUERS, SIDNEY; TENET, GEORGE J.; TURNER, STANSFIELD; VANDENBERG, HOYT; WEBSTER, WILLIAM H.; WOOLSEY, R. JAMES, JR.

DIRECTOR OF CENTRAL INTELLIGENCE DIRECTIVES (DCIDs). DCIDs are instructions to the **intelligence community** (IC) agencies on implementing the decisions of the president and the **National Security Council** (NSC). The DCI's staff transforms presidential directives (PDs) emanating from the NSC to DCIDs, providing guidance on myriad issues ranging from security classification and handling of classified information to personnel issues governing hiring, firing, retention, and retirement. DCIDs remain in force until supplanted by other DCIDs.

DIRECTOR OF NATIONAL INTELLIGENCE (DNI). A position long considered essential for overcoming the parochial interests and the turf wars of the intelligence agencies in the **intelligence community** (IC), the office of the DNI was established by the **Intelligence Reform and Terrorism Prevention Act** of December 2004. The **9/11 Commission** report, issued in July 2004, and the families of the victims of the **terrorist attacks of 11 September 2001** considered a strong DNI the central ingredient in reforming American intelligence to respond to future terrorist attacks. Legislation creating the DNI as chief of the **National Intelligence Authority** (NIA) and providing for antiterror immigration and law enforcement measures quickly wound through the congressional process in the fall of 2004 but bogged down in conference committee. Ensuing recalcitrance by congressional defenders of the **Department of Defense's** (DOD's) intelligence prerogatives produced a compromise that made the DNI substantially weaker than that sought by the 9/11 Commission report.

For example, under the new law, the DNI will have a say in hiring the heads of the intelligence agencies but will have no authority to fire them. The DNI can move money from one agency to another to meet needs, but always within strict limits. Under the law, the DNI has only limited authority to reprogram funds and transfer personnel from the Defense Department, while the department still keeps control over its massive intelligence agencies as well as 30 percent of intelligence moneys. While the legislation puts the new national intelligence chief in the position of commanding the attention of agency heads—the DNI, under the law, is supposed to develop and determine their budgets, although he is only empowered to monitor the implementation and execution of intelligence spending—greater intelligence coherence and effectiveness certainly are not assured by this legislation. Instead, the new position constitutes an additional bureaucratic layer, now separating the titular head of U.S. intelligence from collectors and analysts who reside within the agencies. The **director of central intelligence** (DCI) remains the head of the **Central Intelligence Agency** (CIA).

DISINFORMATION. *See* PROPAGANDA.

DONOVAN, WILLIAM JOSEPH (1883–1959). William Donovan was the legendary chief of the **Office of Strategic Services** (OSS) during **World War II**. Donovan had been a New York City lawyer and a classmate of President **Franklin D. Roosevelt**, who appointed Donovan as coordinator of information (COI) in 1941 and, subsequently, as OSS chief in 1942.

Donovan made a name for himself as early as 1912 when he formed and led a troop of cavalry of the New York State Militia (a forerunner of the National Guard) that in 1916 served on the Mexican border in the Pancho Villa campaign. During **World War I**, he distinguished himself on the battlefield in France, and by the end of the war, he had received three Purple Hearts and the Distinguished Service Cross.

After the war, he resumed his law practice, becoming the U.S. attorney for the western district of New York, and became famous for his energetic enforcement of prohibition. He also ran for public office several times, all unsuccessfully, but he served in the Justice Department's Antitrust Division until the beginning of **World War II**.

At the start of the war, President Roosevelt sent Donovan to Europe to collect information, and, in 1941, named him COI. This made Donovan the first overall chief of the United States **intelligence community** (IC), which at the time was fragmented into army, navy, **Federal Bureau of Investigation** (FBI), **Department of State**, and other interests. The FBI retained its independence and control of intelligence in South America, at the insistence of FBI director **J. Edgar Hoover**.

The COI organization became the OSS in 1942, and Donovan returned to active duty in his former rank of colonel, being promoted to major general by the end of the war. OSS responsibility included **espionage** and sabotage operations in Europe and in parts in Asia, but not in Latin America or the Philippines.

Roosevelt's death weakened Donovan's position, which depended on his personal connection to the president. President **Harry S. Truman**, who distrusted intelligence generally, dissolved the OSS at the end of the war. For his service in the war, Donovan received the Distinguished Service Medal and reverted to his lifelong role as a lawyer by becoming special assistant to the chief prosecutor at the Nuremberg Tribunal. At the conclusion of the Nuremberg trials, Donovan returned to his Wall Street law firm.

DRUG ENFORCEMENT ADMINISTRATION (DEA). The Premier U.S. government antidrug law enforcement agency, the DEA was established in 1973 as successor to the Bureau of Narcotics and Dangerous Drugs (BNDD). BNDD's operations were largely ineffective due to intense rivalry with several other bureaus in the Department of Justice focusing on drug issues as well as with the U.S. Customs Service. The DEA's mission now includes the enforcement of controlled substances laws and regulations and investigating and preparing criminal prosecutions of those who violate laws on controlled substances at both national and international levels. The purpose of the DEA, moreover, is to provide a focal point for coordinating federal drug enforcement efforts with those of the state and local authorities, as well as with international police entities.

The DEA is not a member of the **intelligence community** (IC) but clearly has intelligence responsibilities in the counterdrug effort. Therefore, the DEA relies heavily on the IC agencies for its strategic intelligence needs and exchanges appropriate intelligence information with its intelligence community counterparts.

DULLES, ALLEN WELSH (1893–1969). The fifth **director of central intelligence** (DCI) from 1953 until 1961 and the first civilian DCI since the establishment of the U.S. intelligence apparatus in 1947. As such, Dulles presided over many of America's early **covert actions**, some of which were later to haunt United States foreign policy.

A scion of a politically connected family, Allen Dulles entered the foreign service in 1916. During **World War I**, he was stationed in Berne, Switzerland, where the Russian revolutionary Vladimir I. Lenin supposedly tried to approach him to elicit American help. Dulles reportedly put off Lenin's request for a meeting, an incident that Dulles often recounted in his later years. At the end of World War I, Allen Dulles served on the staff of the American delegation to the Paris Peace Conference and then was posted to the **Department of State** in Washington, D.C. In 1926, he left the government for a law practice but joined the **Office of Strategic Services** (OSS) when **World War II** broke out. He returned to Berne, Switzerland, from where he operated a spy ring inside Nazi Germany. After the war, Dulles returned to his law practice but remained active in intelligence matters by helping draft the **National Security Act of 1947**. DCI **Walter Bedell Smith** recruited Allen Dulles in 1951 to be **deputy director of central intelligence** (DDCI), and, in 1953, Dulles succeeded Smith as DCI.

Dulles's accomplishments during his tenure included the overthrow of President **Jacobo Arbenz Guzman** in Guatemala, the building of the **Berlin Tunnel** to eavesdrop on Soviet military communications, the development of the **U-2** spy airplane, and the acquisition of Soviet Premier **Nikita S. Khrushchev's secret speech** to the Twentieth Party Congress. Dulles resigned in 1961 in the wake of the disastrous **Bay of Pigs invasion** in **Cuba**. However, during his eight years as the head of U.S. intelligence, Allen Dulles and his brother, Secretary of State John Foster Dulles, exerted enormous influence over U.S. foreign policy, helping shape America's approach to the rest of the **Cold War**.

– E –

EAGLE CLAW (OPERATION). Operation Eagle Claw was a military operation to rescue the American hostages from the U.S. Embassy in Tehran, **Iran**, on 24 April 1980. Planned as Operation Rice Bowl, the **covert action** was designed as a complex two-night mission with a small staging site established inside Iran, called **Desert One**, that provided a base for the transport planes and helicopters for the actual rescue operation. The plan called for using helicopters to evacuate the hostages, who would then be brought to an air base outside of Tehran and flown out of the country. The role of the **Central Intelligence Agency** (CIA) was primarily in support, as former **Air America** specialists provided logistics. In addition, the CIA's paramilitary staff furnished and installed navigational devices at Desert One.

The action aborted when a helicopter collided with an air force plane at Desert One. Postmortem evaluations showed that the operation failed because the various services worked independently of each other and did not coordinate their actions. As a result of this failure, the Pentagon established the U.S. Special Operations Command (USSOCOM) in 1988 to overcome fragmentation and get the military services to work closer together by inducing them to engage in joint operations, an effort that was mandated by the **Goldwater-Nichols Act of 1986**. The hostages were released after 444 days of captivity on 20 January 1981, the day that President **Jimmy Carter** left office.

ECONOMIC ESPIONAGE ACT OF 1996. Signed by President **William J. Clinton** on 11 October 1996, this amendment to the **National Security Act of 1947** makes it a crime to wrongfully copy or otherwise control trade secrets, if done with the intent either to benefit a foreign government, instrumentality, or agent or to disadvantage the rightful owner of the trade secret and for the purpose of benefiting another person. Congress passed the law because economic **espionage** conducted against the United States had become a national priority after the end of the **Cold War**, and various sectors of the American business community believed the law regarding corporate trade secrets was inadequate and did not address new economic realities. In studying the matter, the **Federal Bureau of Investigation** (FBI) found that in the early 1990s, over 100 countries had financed operations to acquire U.S. technology, and 57 of them had used **covert methods** against U.S. corporations. To counter the threat, the FBI listed a roster of countries spying against American companies on its **National Security Threat List** (NSTL). To bolster the effort against **industrial espionage**, the Clinton administration also established the **National Counterintelligence Executive** (NCIX), intended to coordinate intelligence, **counterintelligence**, and law enforcement agencies in their attempts to prevent foreign economic espionage.

ECONOMIC INTELLIGENCE. Economic intelligence refers to basic information about a country's economic output, trade relations, and infrastructure. *See also* ECONOMIC ESPIONAGE ACT OF 1996; INDUSTRIAL ESPIONAGE.

EDMONDS, EMMA (1841–1898). Purported to be a Union spy during the American **Civil War**, Emma Edmonds masqueraded as a male, with the alias Frank Thompson, to enlist in the Union army in 1861. She subsequently claimed to have been recruited by General George B. McClellan to conduct **espionage** against the Confederacy. However, **Allan Pinkerton**, McClellan's espionage chief, does not mention her at all in his writings, thereby casting doubt on Emma Edmonds's claims to have spied for McClellan. That she was also Private Frank Thompson, however, is substantiated by the fact that Congress awarded her a pension in 1886, and she was admitted to a Civil War veterans association as its only female member.

EISENHOWER, DWIGHT D. (1890–1969). Thirty-fourth president of the United States between 1953 and 1961. President Eisenhower came to office with vast experience in military affairs and enormous public support. A former president of Columbia University, Eisenhower's foreign policy focused on easing the strains of the **Cold War** while keeping the country militarily strong. He argued strongly for proliferating nuclear energy in his "atoms for peace" initiative and providing a semblance of transparency in Soviet-American relations in his "open skies" proposal.

In conjunction with his moderate policies, President Eisenhower presided over the dramatic expansion of the U.S. **intelligence community** (IC). During his tenure as president, the **Central Intelligence**

Agency (CIA) overthrew Iranian prime minister Mohammad Mossadegh in 1953 and President **Jacobo Arbenz Guzman** of Guatemala in 1954. The CIA also launched a series of daring covert operations in the 1950s, such as **Operation Gold** and **Operation Genetrix**, which embroiled the United States in international controversy. President Eisenhower gave permission for the development and deployment of the **U-2** spy plane, one of which was shot down over the **Soviet Union** on 1 May 1960, effectively canceling a planned summit with Soviet leader **Nikita S. Khrushchev**. In addition, President Eisenhower authorized covert operations against **Fidel Castro** of **Cuba**, who came to power in 1959. Finally, President Eisenhower approved expedited plans for the space race by establishing the National Aeronautics and Space Administration (NASA) and gave the green light for the development and deployment of America's first spy satellite, **CORONA**.

ELECTRONIC INTELLIGENCE (ELINT). *See* SIGNALS INTELLIGENCE.

EL PASO INTELLIGENCE CENTER (EPIC). The El Paso Intelligence Center, so named for its location in El Paso, Texas, is a clearinghouse for tactical intelligence and the collection, analysis, and dissemination of information related to worldwide drug movement and alien smuggling. In 1973, with increasing drug activity along the Southwest border, the **Drug Enforcement Administration** (DEA) found that the DEA, the Customs Service, the **Federal Bureau of Investigation** (FBI), and the Federal Aviation Administration (FAA) collected intelligence information, but that there was no central coordination of this information. The DEA and Immigration and Naturalization Service (INS) were also collecting information on the smuggling of aliens and guns. In 1974, the Department of Justice recommended establishing a regional intelligence center to collect and disseminate information relating to drug, illegal alien, and weapons smuggling and to support field enforcement agencies throughout the country. As a result, the El Paso Intelligence Center was established in 1974 to provide **tactical intelligence** to federal, state, and local law enforcement agencies on a national scale. Staffed by representatives of the DEA and **Department of Homeland Secu-**

rity (DHS) professionals, EPIC has since expanded into a national drug intelligence center supporting U.S. law enforcement entities that focus on worldwide drug smuggling.

ENIGMA. Enigma was a cipher machine used by Nazi Germany in the interwar years and during **World War II**. Originally designed by Dr. Arthur Scherbius to protect business secrets, the Nazi government employed it in military and diplomatic communications. The Polish government initially broke the German cipher in 1932, but the Germans redesigned the machine to produce a large number of combinations (around 150 million million million) and, therefore, considered it unbreakable. The British navy acquired an Enigma machine during the early stages of the war and was able to break its secrets. The intercepts derived from Enigma were given the code name ULTRA. Experts credit turning the tide of the war against Germany to breaking the secrets of the Enigma machine.

ESPIONAGE. *See* HUMAN INTELLIGENCE.

ESTIMATIVE INTELLIGENCE. Estimative intelligence is a category of **intelligence analysis** that attempts to project probable future developments and their implications for U.S. interests. In essence, estimative intelligence comprises judgments about a region, country, or issue covering the near future, perhaps up to a year. The **national intelligence estimates** (NIEs) produced by the **National Intelligence Council** (NIC) are the principal, but not the only, estimative products of American intelligence.

EXECUTIVE ORDER (EO) 11905. Issued on 18 February 1976, EO 11905 enhanced the position of the **director of central intelligence** (DCI) in the White House hierarchy and named the DCI chair of the Committee on Foreign Intelligence of the **National Security Council** (NSC). It also replaced the **Forty (40) Committee** with an **Operations Advisory Group** composed of cabinet-level officials to review and approve **covert actions**. Finally, EO 11905 created the **Intelligence Oversight Board** (IOB), composed of three private individuals, to review the propriety and legality of intelligence activities. *See also* PRESIDENT'S FOREIGN INTELLIGENCE ADVISORY BOARD.

EXECUTIVE ORDER (EO) 12036. Issued by President **Jimmy Carter** on 24 January 1978, Executive Order 12036 attempted to give greater coherence to American intelligence activities. In addition to establishing coordinating mechanisms for U.S. **counterintelligence**, EO 12036 redefined **special activities**—covert actions—and expanded the prohibition against **assassination** to include all parts of the U.S. government. Moreover, the order gave the **director of central intelligence** (DCI) full responsibility for the national intelligence effort and made the president, cabinet officers, and other senior officials accountable for U.S. covert actions. EO 12036 was superceded by **Executive Order 12333** in 1981.

EXECUTIVE ORDER (EO) 12331. Issued on 20 October 1981 by President **Ronald Reagan**, EO 12331 reestablished the **President's Foreign Intelligence Advisory Board** (PFIAB), which President **Jimmy Carter** abolished in 1977. *See also* EXECUTIVE ORDER 12537.

EXECUTIVE ORDER (EO) 12333. Issued by President **Ronald Reagan** on 4 December 1981, the order identifies the individual agencies of the U.S. **intelligence community** (IC), specifies their authorities and specific responsibilities, and codifies the constraints imposed on U.S. intelligence activities, including **covert actions**. EO 12333 is still in force and, together with the **National Security Act of 1947** (as amended), constitutes the legal basis for U.S. intelligence activities.

EXECUTIVE ORDER (EO) 12356. Issued on 2 April 1982, Executive Order 12356 provides for a uniform system of classifying, declassifying, and safeguarding national security information. According to the order, information may not be classified unless its disclosure reasonably could be expected to cause damage to the national security.

EXECUTIVE ORDER (EO) 12537. Issued by President **Ronald Reagan** on 28 October 1985, EO 12537 superceded **Executive Order 12331**, which had reestablished the **President's Foreign Intelligence Advisory Board** (PFIAB) after President **Jimmy Carter** disbanded it in 1977. EO 12537 streamlined the PFIAB within the Executive Office of the President of the White House. Under the terms of the order, the PFIAB was to consist of no more than 14 members chosen from among trustworthy and distinguished citizens outside the government who qualified based on achievement, experience, and independence. The board was empowered to assess the quality, quantity, and adequacy of intelligence collection, of analysis and estimates, of **counterintelligence**, and other intelligence activities. In addition, the executive order authorized the board to review, on a continual basis, the performance of all agencies of the Federal government engaged in the collection, evaluation, or production of intelligence or the execution of intelligence policy. Furthermore, the order empowered the board to assess the adequacy of management, personnel, and organization in the intelligence agencies and report its findings to the president and advise him concerning the objectives, conduct, management, and coordination of the various activities of the agencies of the **intelligence community** (IC). Finally, the executive order gave PFIAB the authority to advise and make recommendations to the **director of central intelligence** (DCI) and the intelligence community on ways to achieve increased effectiveness in meeting national intelligence needs. *See also* EXECUTIVE ORDER 12863.

EXECUTIVE ORDER (EO) 12863. Issued by President **William J. Clinton** on 13 September 1993, EO 12863 superceded **EO 12537** by reaffirming the role of the **President's Foreign Intelligence Advisory Board** (PFIAB) in U.S. intelligence; increased its membership from 14 to 16 renowned and influential experts; and made the heretofore independent **Intelligence Oversight Board** (IOB) a standing committee of the PFIAB. *See also* EXECUTIVE ORDER 12331.

EXECUTIVE ORDER (EO) 12958. Issued by President **William J. Clinton** on 17 April 1995, EO 12958 prescribed a uniform system for classifying, safeguarding, and declassifying national security information. The executive order established the Information Security Oversight Office to regulate the government's security classification system. It also instructed all federal agencies to release records that were 25 years old or older. *See also* EXECUTIVE ORDER 13292.

EXECUTIVE ORDER (EO) 13292. Issued by President **George W. Bush** on 25 March 2003, EO 13292 amends **Executive Order 12958**

by exempting some types of information, such as that on international **terrorism** and weapons of mass destruction, from the provisions of EO 12958, in effect tightening up security classification.

EXECUTIVE ORDER (EO) 13376. Issued by President **George W. Bush** on 18 April 2005, EO 13376 replaced the **director of central intelligence** (DCI) with the **director of national intelligence** (DNI) on the **President's Foreign Intelligence Advisory Board** (PFIAB). The DNI, whose position was established by the **Intelligence Reform and Terrorism Prevention Act of 2004**, oversees the **intelligence community** (IC), a responsibility that had belonged to the DCI since 1946.

– F –

FAMILY JEWELS. "Family Jewels" refers to a compilation of **Central Intelligence Agency** (CIA) illegal activities, first commissioned by **Director of Central Intelligence** (DCI) **James Schlesinger** in 1973 and made public by his successor, DCI **William Colby**, later that year. There is reason to believe that by making public the compendium of CIA misdeeds, Colby felt he would be helping to forestall any damaging congressional action against the CIA—an agency in which he had spent most of his adult life—and reinvigorate American intelligence by "coming clean." The revelations, however, sparked public outcry against the intelligence establishment and ushered in a period of intense scrutiny, culminating in the investigations of the **Rockefeller Commission** and the **Church** and **Pike Committees** in Congress.

FEATURE (OPERATION). Feature was a **Central Intelligence Agency** (CIA) **covert action**, ordered by Secretary of State **Henry A. Kissinger** in late 1975 to provide material assistance to Angolan rebels fighting against the **Soviet** and **Cuban**-backed government. Although approving lethal assistance in the form of weapons, the **40 Committee** forbade the CIA from sending advisors to Angola. Congress voted in 1976 to terminate the operation.

FEDERAL BUREAU OF INVESTIGATION (FBI). The FBI is the premier federal law enforcement agency of the U.S. government and, as such, is legally prohibited from engaging in foreign intelligence activities. However, its **counterintelligence** unit is a formal member of the **intelligence community** (IC).

The FBI originated from a force of special agents created in 1908 during the presidency of Theodore Roosevelt. Initially called the Bureau of Investigation, it primarily investigated violations of laws involving national banking, bankruptcy, naturalization, antitrust, **espionage**, and land fraud. The Mann Act of June 1910 expanded the Bureau's jurisdiction into investigating transportation of women across state lines for immoral purposes. At the same time, the Bureau of Investigation established field offices around the country, each with a special agent in charge who was responsible to headquarters in Washington.

With U.S. entry into **World War I** in April 1917, the Bureau acquired new counterespionage responsibilities as well as jurisdiction in selective service, sabotage, and enemy alien cases. In July 1919, with the passage of the National Motor Vehicle Theft Act, the Bureau received additional responsibilities for investigating thefts of motor vehicles across state lines.

The Bureau's specific jurisdictions prevented it from taking the lead in antigangster and prohibition actions during the gangster era of 1921–1933. Yet, its stature continued to increase as it employed creative legal means against such groups as the Ku Klux Klan and some gangsters.

On 10 May 1924, **J. Edgar Hoover** assumed the directorship of the Bureau, a position he occupied for the next 50 years. Hoover immediately set about imposing professional standards for the organization and initiated a rigorous public relations program that kept the Bureau, and later the FBI, in the public limelight as battling evil forces. He also established an identification unit that encouraged state and local law enforcement officials to contribute to a nationwide fingerprint and identification data bank.

On 1 July 1931, the Bureau was renamed the United States Bureau of Investigation, which in 1935 was changed to the Federal Bureau of Investigation. In the run-up to **World War II**, the FBI assumed expanded responsibilities in investigating sabotage, subversion, and espionage, as well as collecting intelligence in Latin America. With the establishment of the **Central Intelligence Agency** (CIA) in 1947, a move that FBI Director Hoover vehemently opposed, the FBI lost its intelligence collection responsibilities in Latin America but retained its jurisdiction over counterintelligence within the United States. In this context, the FBI engaged in **covert activities** against domestic dissident groups during the **Vietnam War**, as in **Operation COIN-TELPRO**, and became embroiled in the **Watergate scandal** as well as the congressional investigations of the mid-1970s. J. Edgar Hoover died on 2 May 1972, ushering in a period of instability for the FBI.

In 1982, FBI Director **William H. Webster** expanded FBI jurisdiction over **terrorism**, the illicit narcotics trade, and white-collar crime. With the end of the **Cold War** in 1991, the FBI established the **National Security Threat List** (NSTL), changing its approach from defending against hostile intelligence services to protecting U.S. information technologies. The list included a compendium of new threats, including proliferation of weapons of mass destruction, the loss of critical technologies, and the improper collection of trade secrets and proprietary information. Counterterrorism jumped to the forefront of the list with the first terrorist attack on the World Trade Center in 1993 and the Oklahoma City bombing in 1995. Internal crime also rose high on the list as a national security threat.

The terrorist attacks of 11 September 2001 called into question the strict separation of intelligence and law enforcement functions that had existed since 1947. The **USA PATRIOT Act** and similar antiterror tools enacted in the aftermath of 9/11 now blur the separation between intelligence and law enforcement by promoting cooperation between foreign intelligence agencies and the law enforcement community, including the state and local levels. Indeed, the FBI now contains the National Security Service, established by Executive Order in 2005, to strengthen the bureau's intelligence capabilities. *See also* SPECIAL INTELLIGENCE SERVICE.

FEDORA. Fedora was the code name given to a **Soviet** citizen, Aleksei Isidorovich Kulak, who spied for the **Federal Bureau of Investigation** (FBI) during the 1960s. Fedora actually was a **KGB case officer** in New York with the **cover** of consultant to the United Nations Scientific Committee on the Effects of Atomic Radiation. In March 1962, Fedora offered his services to the FBI, and the Bureau so prized and so jealously protected Fedora's information that it hid Fedora's, as well as another FBI informant, Top Hat's, existence from the **Central**

Intelligence Agency (CIA) for much of 1962. FBI Director **J. Edgar Hoover** bypassed CIA **counterintelligence** chief **James J. Angleton** and sent reports straight to President **John F. Kennedy**.

However, the FBI brought the CIA into the loop by 1963, especially because the FBI had to provide Fedora and Top Hat "feed material," doctored or low-grade intelligence, to keep their KGB handlers satisfied. But the very nature of Fedora's approach to the FBI had caused suspicion, and the double agents failed to receive the full trust of the FBI and CIA, so much so that Angleton to the end of his life believed Fedora to be a Soviet disinformation agent.

FINANCIAL CRIMES ENFORCEMENT NETWORK (FinCEN). As reflected in its name, the Financial Crimes Enforcement Network is a network bringing people and information together to fight the complex problem of money laundering. Since its creation in 1990, FinCEN has worked to maximize information sharing among law enforcement agencies and its other partners in the regulatory and financial communities.

FinCEN's mission is to support law enforcement investigative efforts and foster interagency and global cooperation against domestic and international financial crimes and to provide U.S. policymakers with strategic analyses of domestic and worldwide money laundering developments, trends, and patterns. To accomplish this, FinCEN collects, analyzes, and shares information and implements the Bank Secrecy Act and other Treasury authorities through technological assistance. The organization consists of approximately 200 employees, the majority of whom are intelligence professionals, specialists from the financial industry, and technology experts. In addition, there are approximately 40 long-term detailers from 20 different law enforcement and regulatory agencies.

FINDING. A finding is a presidential authorization for a **covert action**. First mandated by the 1974 **Hughes-Ryan Amendment**, findings are now an essential part of the intelligence landscape. A typical finding originates in the policy channels of the **National Security Council** (NSC) or the **Department of Defense** (DOD) and winds its way through the planning and review process in the **Central Intelligence Agency** (CIA). A covert action proposal may be modified or scrapped at any time in the process, including at the level of the **director of**

central intelligence (DCI), who must ultimately sign off on any such proposal. Once approved by all relevant parties, the president signs the finding. The **Intelligence Authorization Act of 1991** legislated that findings must be approved prior to the commencement of a covert operation and must be in writing. In addition, various other legal instruments, such as the **Intelligence Oversight Act of 1980**, stipulate that the CIA—responsible for all aspects of covert actions—must notify the congressional **oversight** committees of a finding in "a timely manner," understood to mean in advance of the covert action, unless the president directs the CIA not to do so for identifiable national security reasons. *See also* INTELLIGENCE OVERSIGHT.

5412 SPECIAL GROUP. The group was a committee of the **National Security Council** (NSC) that reviewed and authorized **covert actions** during the administrations of Presidents **Dwight D. Eisenhower** and **John F. Kennedy**. The establishment of the committee was the result of a series of National Security Council directives (NSCDs). On 15 March 1954, the NSC issued NSC Directive 5412— hence the "5412" Special Group designation—reaffirming the responsibility of the **Central Intelligence Agency** (CIA) to conduct covert actions, defining the nature of such covert operations, and describing the process of coordinating the proposals. NSC Directive 5412/1, dated 12 March 1955, designated the CIA's Planning Coordination Group as the body responsible for coordinating covert operations. NSC Directive 5412/2, dated 28 December 1955, established the 5412 Special Group as the executive body to review and approve covert action programs. The committee normally was composed of the **national security advisor**, representatives of the secretary of defense and secretary of state, the chairman of the **Joint Chiefs of Staff** (JCS), and others. *See also* 40 COMMITTEE; 303 COMMITTEE.

FLYING TIGERS. Officially known as the American Volunteer Group (AVG), the Flying Tigers were a small group of American airmen who, at the beginning of **World War II**, flew missions against Japanese forces under the flag of nationalist China. The formation of the volunteer group was at the behest of President **Franklin D. Roosevelt** who, in March 1941, decided secretly to assist the struggling Chinese government against invading Japanese forces. President

Roosevelt approved $25 million for China to purchase Tomahawk aircraft and signed a secret order in April 1941 allowing military personnel to resign from the services to join the AVG. The AVG flyers were said to be so ferocious that Chinese newspapers began calling them the "Flying Tigers," after the teeth markings on the noses of the Tomahawk aircraft. The AVG disbanded on 4 July 1942 so that its flyers could rejoin the military services for the American war effort.

FORD, GERALD RUDOLPH (1913–). Thirty-eighth president of the United States between 1974 and 1977. Vice President Ford assumed the presidency when President **Richard Nixon** resigned on 9 August 1974 in the aftermath of the **Watergate scandal.** A long-term congressman from Michigan, Ford was elected to the U.S. House of Representatives in 1949 and stayed there until he was named vice president on 6 December 1973. With a reputation for openness, integrity, and loyalty to the Republican Party, Ford set a record of supporting large defense expenditures and led the opposition to President **Lyndon B. Johnson's** Great Society social programs.

Upon President Nixon's resignation, newly inaugurated President Ford pledged to follow the Nixon foreign policy and pardoned the former president. During his administration, Ford largely focused on domestic issues, seeking to address inflation arising from spikes in oil prices in the aftermath of the 1973 OPEC oil embargo and to curb the ensuing recession by proposing tax cuts, reduced social spending, and heavy taxation of imported oil.

Watergate and other events raised many questions regarding the intelligence activities carried out by federal agencies such as the **Central Intelligence Agency** (CIA) and the **Federal Bureau of Investigation** (FBI). Both houses of Congress investigated the agencies. In February 1976, President Ford proposed a sweeping reform of intelligence-gathering activities built around three components: limitations on the domestic activities of U. S. agencies engaged in foreign intelligence; an organizational restructuring of various agencies to bring them into compliance with new restrictions; and better procedures to protect classified information dealing with intelligence sources and methods. Most of President Ford's recommendations were put into effect by executive order. In May 1976, the Senate created a new **Senate Select Intelligence Committee** (SSCI) to have broad legislative authority over the CIA, the FBI, and other components of the federal intelligence community. President Ford ran for reelection in 1976 but lost to challenger **Jimmy Carter.**

FOREIGN AGENTS REGISTRATION ACT (FARA) OF 1938. The Foreign Agents Registration Act, as amended in 1966, is a disclosure statute aimed at "agents of foreign principals." The act requires such agents to register with the Department of Justice and disclose their affiliations, methods, and funding sources.

From its passage in 1938 until the 1966 amendments, the FARA was focused on propagandists. The original act included a fairly broad definition of the term agent and a single felony penalty for the most serious transgressions. It was used in the **World War II** era to prosecute some 23 criminal cases successfully. The Department of Justice assumed responsibility for the administration of the act from the **Department of State** in 1942. In 1966, the FARA was significantly amended to focus on the integrity of the United States government decision-making process by emphasizing agents seeking economic or political advantage for their clients. The amendments required any person engaged in "political activities" as an agent on behalf of a foreign principal to register. This is substantially narrower than the original act, which did not require that the activities be "for or on behalf of" the foreign principal.

FOREIGN BROADCAST INFORMATION SERVICE (FBIS). In 1940, the Federal Communications Commission created the Foreign Broadcast Information Division to take on the task of monitoring the radio broadcasts in key foreign countries. In 1942, this function was transferred to the U.S. Army, where it remained until it was transferred to the **Central Intelligence Group** (CIG) in 1946. The FBIS became part of the **Central Intelligence Agency** (CIA) when it was established on 18 September 1947. As part of the CIA's Directorate of Science and Technology (DS&T), the FBIS maintains stations around the world to pick up radio and television broadcasts and monitors the print media. Its translators transform the raw materials into publications usable by American decision makers and other consumers.

FOREIGN INTELLIGENCE SURVEILLANCE ACT (FISA) of 1978. FISA is legislation that authorizes the United States government to set up procedures for allowing electronic monitoring, within the United States, of individuals for foreign intelligence purposes. In 1968, the Omnibus Crime Control and Safe Streets Act contained provisions for authorizing the government to use electronic monitoring against criminal activities. However, it failed to answer the question of whether or not the government is required to obtain court authorization for electronic monitoring conducted for the collection of information regarding threats to national security, not for criminal investigations. FISA filled this gap by requiring court approval before the government engaged in electronic surveillance (as well as physical searches) for foreign intelligence purposes. To do this, the act established the **Foreign Intelligence Surveillance Court**, consisting of U.S. District Court judges designated by the chief justice of the U.S. Supreme Court.

An application for a FISA warrant need only state facts supporting probable cause to believe that the target of the intercept or search is a foreign power, or an agent of a foreign power, and that the facilities to be monitored or searched are being used, or are about to be used, by a foreign power, or an agent of a foreign power, and to certify that the purpose of the surveillance is to obtain foreign intelligence information. The **USA PATRIOT Act** of 2002 modified this requirement by allowing certification that a "significant" (but not sole) purpose of the surveillance would be for foreign intelligence purposes. To show that a person is an agent of a foreign power, the government need only demonstrate that the subject is an officer or employee of a foreign power or acts on the foreign power's behalf; or knowingly engages in clandestine intelligence-gathering activities that may involve a violation of U.S. criminal statutes; or knowingly engages in sabotage, international **terrorism**, or in the preparation of these activities on behalf of a foreign power.

FOREIGN INTELLIGENCE SURVEILLANCE COURT. A special court established by the **Foreign Intelligence Surveillance Act (FISA) of 1978** to review government applications for national security electronic monitoring and searches and to issue warrants with appropriate limitations. If the FISA Court denies an application for an order authorizing a national security wiretap or search, the matter is referred under seal to the FISA Court of Review, comprised of three federal judges selected by the chief justice of the U.S. Supreme Court. The court of review determines whether the application was properly denied. Its decision can be appealed directly to the U.S. Supreme Court.

40 COMMITTEE. This **National Security Council** (NSC) committee was established during the presidency of **Richard M. Nixon** to review and approve **covert action** proposals. The committee was composed of the **national security advisor**, representatives of the secretary of defense and secretary of state, the chairman of the **Joint Chiefs of Staff** (JCS), and the attorney general. **Henry A. Kissinger**, the national security advisor and secretary of state during the Nixon administration, chaired the committee. *See also* 5412 SPECIAL GROUP; 303 COMMITTEE.

FRANKLIN, BENJAMIN (1706–1790). One of the most famous founding fathers and, after President **George Washington**, the best known American intelligence operative during and after the Revolutionary War. A writer, publisher, scientist, and politician, Franklin served in various positions in pre- and postrevolutionary America. In 1753, he was appointed postmaster general of the colonies by the British government and then was sent by the Pennsylvania assembly to London to act as its agent. He returned to America in 1775 and joined the Second Continental Congress, where he served on the committee to draft the Declaration of Independence.

Congress in December 1776 sent Franklin to France to secure French aid for the Revolution. Franklin, with a strong reputation in France, did much to gain French recognition of the new republic in 1778. He also helped to direct U.S. naval operations and was a successful agent for the United States in Europe—the sole one after suspicions and quarrels caused Congress to annul the powers of the other American commissioners. In 1781, Franklin was chosen as one of the American diplomats to negotiate peace with Great Britain and laid the groundwork for the 1783 Treaty of Paris, in which Great Britain officially recognized the breakaway republic.

FREEDOM OF INFORMATION ACT (FOIA) OF 1966. The FOIA was the first law to establish a legal right of access to government information and allowing individuals to request access to government information about themselves or public issues. Under the terms of the act, government agencies must release that information in a timely fashion if they have it, unless the information falls within a narrow set of exceptions. The law requires government agencies to search their records, examine documents for information that may not be released (such as classified data), and release the remaining information to the requestor. In 1996, Congress passed the "Electronic Freedom of Information Amendments" to the law that incorporated digital and other electronic data in the act's coverage. Since the enactment of the FOIA in 1966, the number of requests has virtually exploded, such that most government agencies now have substantial backlogs. According to a 2003 report by the Government Accounting Office (GAO), only the **Central Intelligence Agency** (CIA) has made steady progress each year since 1998 in reducing its backlog of pending cases.

FSB (FEDERAL'NAYA SLUZHBA BEZOPASNOSTI). The FSB is the federal security service of the Russian Federation and a successor to the **Soviet KGB**. The FSB is responsible largely for domestic security and intelligence while its sister agency, the **SVRR**, focuses on external intelligence.

FUBELT (OPERATION). FUBELT was a secret **Central Intelligence Agency** (CIA) program to block the election of **Salvador Allende** as president of **Chile** in 1970. In the run-up to the election, the CIA employed **propaganda**, **disinformation**, and scare tactics in its attempt to persuade Chileans not to vote for the Social Democrats and Allende. It also spent over $2 million to prop up the Christian Democrats. In addition, FUBELT envisaged a possible coup in the event of Allende's election. Coup planning included contacting like-minded Chilean military officers, providing them weapons, conducting propaganda to create the political conditions for a coup, and taking actions to destabilize Chile's economy. Even so, FUBELT failed to bring down President Allende. Operation FUBELT was supplanted by **National Security Decision Memorandum 93**, issued by the **National Security Council** (NSC), in November 1970.

FU GO (OPERATION). *See* GENETRIX.

FUSION CENTERS. Fusion centers are interdisciplinary and interagency units established to address specific intelligence issues. The first fusion center was the **Counterterrorism Center** (CTC), set up in 1986 to bring together government assets to combat international terrorism. Successive **directors of central intelligence** (DCIs) since then have established nearly a dozen fusion centers focusing on such issues as nonproliferation, counter narcotics, **counterintelligence**, the environment, **arms control**, and the like. Some of the centers are analytic, in that they focus on producing intelligence assessments. Others are operational, engaged in designing and conducting operations against targets. Although personnel from relevant **intelligence community** (IC) agencies staff the centers, most are located within the **Central Intelligence Agency** (CIA) and rely on CIA information and beneficence for their activities. *See also* ARMS CONTROL INTELLIGENCE STAFF; COUNTERINTELLIGENCE CENTER; DCI CRIME AND NARCOTICS CENTER; DCI ENVIRONMENTAL CENTER; DCI NONPROLIFERATION CENTER.

– G –

GATES, ROBERT M. (1943–). Fifteenth **director of central intelligence** (DCI), serving between 6 November 1991 and 20 January 1993. Robert M. Gates, the first DCI from the analytic ranks of the **Central Intelligence Agency** (CIA) and an expert on the **Soviet Union**, assumed office at a time of great change in global politics. Following DCI **William J. Casey's** resignation in 1987, President **Ronald Reagan** had nominated Gates as DCI, but questions about his role as Casey's deputy in the **Iran-Contra Affair** forced Gates to withdraw his nomination. Four years later, President **George H. W. Bush** again nominated Gates, to succeed DCI **William H. Webster**. This time, Gates faced charges that he had politicized intelligence estimates to conform more closely to his own worldviews and to those of the Republican president he had served. After committing himself to unbiased and objective intelligence analysis and to a more forward-looking and open CIA, Gates received the Senate's confirmation.

DCI Gates realized that the CIA needed to prove itself to an American public that now questioned both its necessity and its highly secretive culture. He therefore quickly established a multitude of **intelligence community** (IC) and CIA task forces to improve performance. These included interagency task forces on **imagery intelligence** (IMINT) and **human intelligence** (HUMINT) collection and **national intelligence estimates** (NIEs) as well as on **coordination** of various activities within the IC. DCI Gates also set up CIA task forces to expand human intelligence capabilities, improve support for military operations, provide near-real-time intelligence to senior policymakers, and raise the quality of intelligence publications. In addition, he announced CIA task forces to improve internal communication, increase openness, and address concerns about real or perceived politicized intelligence.

By February 1992, DCI Gates had already adopted many of the proposals of his task forces. He took dramatic steps to make the CIA more open to the public and the media, increased contacts with academia, and instituted a more extensive declassification program of CIA records.

GEHLEN ORGANIZATION. Named after General Reinhardt Gehlen, who headed German army intelligence activities against the **Soviet Union** during **World War II**. Gehlen had amassed enormous amounts of documentary information about the Soviet Union, which he volunteered to turn over to the United States after the war, providing he and his colleagues were not prosecuted as part of the denazification process. In fact, Gehlen successfully negotiated with the Americans to allow him and his staff—known as the Gehlen Organization—to continue intelligence activities against the Soviets. At its zenith, the Gehlen Organization employed over 4,000 people, mainly former army and *SS* officers, and had nearly that many agents inside the USSR. Western intelligence services, however, believed the Gehlen Organization to be thoroughly penetrated by Soviet intelligence. Yet, Gehlen participated in **Operation Gold**, the Berlin tunnel caper in 1956. That year, West Germany's new intelligence organization, the BND (Bundesnachrichttendienst), absorbed the Gehlen Organization, with Gehlen remaining chief of the BND until his retirement in 1968. *See also* WISNER, FRANK G.

GENERAL DEFENSE INTELLIGENCE PROGRAM (GDIP). The GDIP is an intelligence budget specifically funding the activities of the **Defense Intelligence Agency** (DIA) and related programs. It is managed by the assistant secretary of defense for command, control, communications, computers, and intelligence and is authorized by Defense Department Directive 3305.5, dated 9 May 1986. It includes all non–**signals intelligence** (SIGINT), nonreconnaissance defense intelligence programs. Specifically, the GDIP includes activities relating to general military intelligence production, defense **imagery intelligence** (IMINT) collection and processing, defense **human intelligence** (HUMINT) collection programs under the auspices of the **Defense HUMINT Service** (DH), nuclear monitoring, research and development procurement, support of commanders in the field, general military support, and scientific and technical intelligence production. The GDIP, together with the Consolidated Cryptologic Program (CCP), form the Consolidated Defense Intelligence Program, a key part of the **National Foreign Intelligence Program** (NFIP). *See also* JOINT MILITARY INTELLIGENCE PROGRAM; TACTICAL INTELLIGENCE AND RELATED ACTIVITIES.

GENETRIX (OPERATION). Operation Genetrix was an air force **covert action**, approved on 27 December 1955, that sought to secure **photographic intelligence** (PHOTINT) about the **Soviet Union**, Eastern Europe, and the **People's Republic of China** (PRC) by floating camera-carrying reconnaissance balloons across their territories. Genetrix had its origins in wartime Japan's attempts, through its **Operation Fu Go**, to use the winds to launch bomb-carrying balloons across the Pacific and drop them on U.S. territory. The Japanese program had only limited success, tying down some American fighter planes but achieving little of note otherwise. Britain had a similar program during the war, code-named OUTWARD, that targeted the Nazi power grid. The British program scored some notable successes, one of which short-circuited the Leipzig power grid and caused the destruction of a power plant.

Genetrix sought to use the same concept to acquire photographic intelligence, but the project encountered several technical problems in camera design and recovery techniques. The air force launched 516 balloons during the short life span of the program, but many drifted off course, some were shot down by hostile aircraft, and some descended too soon. The air force recovered only 46 balloons, of which four had malfunctioning cameras and eight produced photography of little intelligence value. Only 34 balloons succeeded in obtaining useful photographs.

In addition to the low rate of success, Genetrix caused an international outcry, not only from targeted countries but also from international aviation authorities, who asserted that the balloons posed a danger to civilian aircraft. The outcry also put the nascent **U-2** project in jeopardy. Furthermore, the Soviet Union collected several balloons, cameras, and transmitters and put them on display in Moscow for the international press. This Soviet propaganda coup convinced President **Dwight D. Eisenhower** to discontinue the program on 7 February 1956.

GEOSPATIAL INTELLIGENCE (GEOINT). Geospatial intelligence is animated renditions of **imagery intelligence** (IMINT) and geospatial data, which allow users to visualize inaccessible terrain. Managed by the **National Geospatial-Intelligence Agency** (NGA), such products reportedly have helped solve long-standing border disputes, such as those between Peru and Ecuador and Israel and South Lebanon. They have also supported peace treaties, aided disaster relief efforts, developed safer commercial flight charts, and remapped the world.

GLOBAL HAWK (SYSTEM). Global Hawk is a high altitude, long endurance **unmanned aerial vehicle** (UAV) that provides military field commanders with high resolution, near-real-time **imagery intelligence** (IMINT) of ground targets. The program is funded by the Defense Airborne Reconnaissance Office (DARO) and managed by the **Defense Advanced Research Projects Agency** (DARPA) and the air force.

GOLD (OPERATION). Operation Gold was a daring **Cold War espionage** operation in the mid-1950s, in which American and British intelligence agents tunneled half a mile into East Berlin and set up a listening post to intercept Russian and East German military communications. **Director of Central Intelligence** (DCI) **Allen W. Dulles** called the tunnel operation "one of the most valuable and daring projects ever undertaken." However, **George Blake**, a British intelligence officer who was on the **KGB's** payroll, probably passed details of the operation to the Soviet KGB. This suggests that the Soviets were aware of the entire operation even before it started and were possibly feeding the Western intelligence services false information. Reports also indicate that the Soviets used transmissions into the tunnel to reassure the West that Moscow did not intend to launch a first-strike nuclear attack. Moscow finally dug up the tunnel in 1961, not long before the British identified George Blake as a Soviet agent.

GOLDWATER-NICHOLS ACT OF 1986. The Goldwater-Nichols Department of Defense Reorganization Act of 1986 reorganized and streamlined the entire American military establishment. The act elevated the role of the **Joint Chiefs of Staff** (JCS) chairman by designating him, not the entire JCS as a corporate body, the principal advisor to the president, the secretary of state, and the **National Security Council** (NSC). The legislation specifically spelled out the national security chain of command as running from the president to the secretary of defense to the field commanders in chief, taking the JCS out of the equation. The act also strengthened the powers of the unified and specified commanders and placed emphasis on "joint" military operations. Many experts, including the commander of American forces during the 1991 Persian Gulf War, General Norman Schwarzkopf, credit "jointness" for the speed and success of the war.

GOLITSYN, ANATOLY (1926–). Golitsyn was a **Soviet KGB** major who defected to the United States in December 1961. During his debriefing, he claimed that all Western intelligence services were penetrated and that the KGB and **GRU** would send false **defectors** to the West to spread **disinformation**. Golitsyn also claimed that the problems plaguing the Soviet Union in the late 1980s were part of a deception campaign, aimed at lulling the West into complacency. *See also* ANGLETON, JAMES J.

GORDIEVSKY, OLEG (1938–). Oleg Gordievsky was a former **KGB** officer who defected to the United States in 1985. Gordievsky was employed by the KGB from 1962 to 1985, spending nine years at the Moscow Center (1963–1965 and 1970–1972) and as resident in Copenhagen (1965–1970), where he organized KGB illegal operations. From 1973 until his defection, he worked on political intelligence in Denmark and then became KGB resident in the United Kingdom.

GOSS, PORTER (1938–). Porter Goss has been **director of central intelligence** (DCI) since 22 September 2004. President **George W. Bush** named Goss DCI in August 2004 amid uncertainty and vigorous debate over the future of U.S. intelligence in the aftermath of the **9/11 Commission** report.

Goss spent 16 years in Congress, eight of those as chair of the **House Permanent Select Committee on Intelligence** (HPSCI), during which he investigated intelligence failures in the 1990s and the **terrorist attacks of 11 September 2001**. Porter Goss champions better and enhanced **human intelligence** (HUMINT) collection and is an advocate of a reasoned and gradual reform of the **intelligence community** (IC).

A former **army intelligence** officer from 1960 until 1962, Porter Goss joined the **Directorate of Operations** (DO) of the **Central Intelligence Agency** (CIA) in 1962 and conducted clandestine operations for over 10 years. Upon leaving the CIA in 1972, he embarked on a career in local Florida politics until his election to the House of Representatives in 1988.

GRAY PROPAGANDA. *See* PROPAGANDA.

GREENHOW, ROSE O'NEAL (1817–1864). A Confederate spy during the American **Civil War**, Rose Greenhow was a Washington, D.C., socialite who elicited intelligence information from Union officials and officers. Her intelligence contributions are sketchy and were probably short-lived, but some experts give her credit for providing intelligence that enabled Confederate forces to win at the Battle of First Bull Run. **Allan Pinkerton** caught and imprisoned her at the beginning of the war, releasing her in mid-1862. Rose O'Neal Greenhow drowned in August 1864 while returning from a European trip.

GRU (GLAVNOYE RAZVEDYVATELNOYE UPRAULENYE). The GRU is the principal intelligence unit of the Russian armed forces. Established in 1920 by Leon Trotsky during the Russian civil war, the GRU was first subordinate to the **KGB** even though the GRU was the intelligence arm of the Soviet General Staff. Over time, the GRU evolved to have its own intelligence collection networks abroad but was required to share its information with the KGB. **Rudolph Abel**, a Soviet spy in the United States during the 1950s, worked for the GRU.

Although the Soviet KGB broke up into its foreign and domestic component parts upon the dissolution of the **Soviet Union** in 1991, the GRU continues today virtually unchanged from its Soviet days. According to various sources, GRU now is a cohesive, highly efficient, and professional military organization, with far greater resources for collecting foreign intelligence than its civilian counterparts.

GULF OF TONKIN RESOLUTION. The Gulf of Tonkin Resolution was a congressional bill passed on 7 August 1964, authorizing the president to use armed force to repel North Vietnamese attacks on American military vessels in the Gulf of Tonkin in the South China Sea. The **Lyndon B. Johnson** White House used the resolution to justify air attacks over North Vietnam and, eventually, to escalate American involvement in the **Vietnam War**. Critics suggest that the resolution's premise, that North Vietnamese gunboats attacked American naval ships, was really a hoax to justify American military involvement and that there were no such attacks.

GUZMAN, JACOBO ARBENZ. *See* ARBENZ GUZMAN, JACOBO.

– H –

HALE, NATHAN (1755–1776). Nathan Hale probably was the first American to die at the hands of the enemy for spying for his country. A Yale graduate and a schoolteacher, Hale joined the Continental Army's 19th Continental Regiment during the siege of Boston. In 1776, he was promoted to captain and was selected by Lieutenant Colonel Thomas Knowlton to lead a company of rangers. When the British forced the Americans to retreat from Long Island to Manhattan, General **George Washington** asked for volunteers to infiltrate behind British lines to gather intelligence information. The only volunteer to step forward was Nathan Hale, an unlikely spy, with no training in **espionage**, no **cover** story, and no disguise. Yet, Hale slipped behind enemy lines and managed to collect the information General Washington needed but was captured by the British as he attempted to return to his own lines. British general William Howe ordered that he be hanged. On 22 September 1776, Hale was brought before the gallows where he reportedly uttered his famous final words: "I only regret that I have but one life to lose for my country." A statue of Nathan Hale is now located in front of **Central Intelligence Agency** (CIA) headquarters, inscribed with his statement.

HALL, VIRGINIA (1906–1982). The first female agent of the **Office of Strategic Services** (OSS), Virginia Hall was the unlikeliest spy. Born in Baltimore, Maryland, she had long wanted to enter America's foreign service but was turned down because she was a woman missing a leg that she had lost in a hunting incident in Turkey. When **World War II** came, she enlisted with the British **Special Operations Executive** (SOE), for whom she organized a spy network in Vichy France and liaised with the French underground. Her daring escapades brought her to the attention of both the German Gestapo—the Germans referred to her as the woman with a limp—and the American OSS. However, her tradecraft was such that she eluded the Germans and helped coordinate airdrops in support of the Allied landings in Normandy on 6 June 1944. Both the British and American governments awarded her their countries' highest decorations after the war. Virginia Hall joined the **Central Intelligence Agency** (CIA) in 1947 and retired in 1966.

HANSSEN, PHILIP (ROBERT) (1945–). Robert Hanssen, a senior special agent of the **Federal Bureau of Investigation** (FBI) with more than 27 years of experience, was arrested in February 2001 on charges of spying for the **Soviet Union** and its successor, Russia. According to postmortem damage assessments, Hanssen provided the Russians with more than 6,000 pages of highly classified documentary material, and he compromised numerous human sources and technical operations of extraordinary importance and value. Hanssen spied for the Russians from 1979 until his arrest, and he received more than $600,000 in cash and diamonds for his **espionage**. To date, he is the highest-ranking FBI special agent to have committed espionage. Hanssen pled guilty on 6 July 6 2001 to 15 counts of espionage and conspiracy charges and was sentenced to life in prison without parole on 10 May 2002.

HARRIMAN, WILLIAM AVERELL (1891–1986). A presidential advisor from **Franklin D. Roosevelt** to **Ronald Reagan**, Averell

Harriman was one of the most influential public figures during the **Cold War**. Heir to the Union Pacific Railroad fortune, he joined his father's company in 1915 and became chairman of the board in 1932. At the same time, he was involved in other ventures in banking, shipbuilding, and international finance.

Averell Harriman was one of the first Americans to seek business opportunities in the **Soviet Union**. President Franklin D. Roosevelt sent him to Moscow in 1941, first as a minister and later as ambassador, a post he held until 1946. Harriman served briefly as ambassador to the United Kingdom in 1946 but was called back to the United States to serve as President **Harry S. Truman's** secretary of commerce and worked on the Marshall Plan. He later served as **national security advisor** during the **Korean War**.

A member of the Democratic Party, Averell Harriman was elected governor of New York in 1954 and served in that capacity until 1959. Harriman tried twice, unsuccessfully, to become the Democratic Party nominee for president, in 1952 and 1956. When President **John F. Kennedy** came to office in 1961, he appointed Harriman as undersecretary of state as well as the negotiator of the **Limited Nuclear Test Ban Treaty** (LNTBT) in 1963. President **Lyndon B. Johnson** appointed him ambassador at large for Southeast Asian affairs in 1965, a position in which he traveled around the world eliciting support for the U.S. position on the **Vietnam War**. He also served as chief U.S. negotiator when preliminary peace talks opened in France between the United States and North Vietnam in 1968. President **Richard M. Nixon** removed Harriman as negotiator in the Paris peace talks because he had criticized the manner in which the Nixon White House handled both the war and the peace talks. Harriman, however, returned to government service in 1978 when he was appointed the senior member of the U.S. delegation to the United Nations (UN) General Assembly's Special Session on Disarmament.

HELMS, RICHARD McGARRAH (1913–2002). Director of central intelligence (DCI) from 1966 until 1973. Helms, a former member of the **Office of Strategic Services** (OSS) during **World War II**, entered the **Central Intelligence Agency** (CIA) when it was established in 1947 and worked in the clandestine ranks until the mid-1960s. He headed CIA clandestine operations during the **Bay of Pigs invasion**

and, falling into disfavor with the administration of President **John F. Kennedy**, was sent to Vietnam to oversee the overthrow of South Vietnamese president Ngo Dinh Diem. President **Lyndon B. Johnson** chose Helms to be **deputy director of central intelligence** (DDCI) in 1965 and DCI in 1966. The **Richard M. Nixon** White House kept him in that position when it came into office in 1969. Helms successfully distanced the CIA from the **Watergate scandal**, prompting President Nixon to consider Helms disloyal—President Nixon fired Helms in 1973—and to name him to be U.S. Ambassador to **Iran**, where he served until 1976. In 1977, Helms was convicted of two misdemeanor counts of lying to Congress over what he knew about the overthrow of **Salvador Allende** in **Chile** and received a suspended two-year sentence. He later became an international consultant, specializing in trade with the Middle East.

HEUER, RICHARDS, JR. Richards J. Heuer Jr. is arguably the leading authority on the psychology of intelligence analysis. First recruited into the **Central Intelligence Agency** (CIA) in 1951, Heuer spent 24 years in the **Directorate of Operations** (DO). In 1975, he moved to the **Directorate of Intelligence** (DI) where he worked on analytic methods until his retirement in 1979. He now consults on security matters.

HILLENKOETTER, REAR ADMIRAL ROSCOE (1897–1982). The third **director of central intelligence (DCI)**, serving from 1 May 1947 until 7 October 1950. A former **navy intelligence** officer in the Pacific, Hillenkoetter presided over the transformation of the **intelligence community** (IC) by the passage of the **National Security Act of 1947**. He also faced the complex intelligence problems posed by the start of the **Cold War**. Hillenkoetter's short tenure as DCI was unremarkable. He left his position as DCI in 1950 to command cruisers off Korea.

HISS, ALGER (1904–1996). Alger Hiss was a **Department of State** official during **World War II** who was charged and convicted of spying for the **Soviet Union** in the early 1950s. Trained as a lawyer, Hiss' early career included a stint in the Agriculture Department and, later, as point man for the legal defense of the constitutionality of the

New Deal programs. He also spent about a year working as special assistant to the attorney general in the Department of Justice.

In 1935, Hiss joined the State Department where he worked on legal issues pertaining to trade agreements. In 1941, he became the department's political advisor on Far Eastern affairs and, in 1944, was in charge of the Dumbarton Oaks Conference, which formally drew up the United Nations Charter.

Hiss left the government in 1946 to become head of the Carnegie Endowment for International Peace. In 1948, the House Un-American Activities Committee (HUAC) alleged that Hiss was a secret communist. When Hiss denied the charges, he was prosecuted for perjury. The first trial ended in a hung jury but the second trial convicted him, and Hiss spent more than three years in jail. Once out of jail, he sought vindication but could begin the process only in the 1970s when documents newly released to him indicated **Federal Bureau of Investigation** (FBI) complicity in withholding evidence that would have cleared Hiss. He died on 15 November 1996 without vindication. *See also* HUMAN INTELLIGENCE; McCARTHY ERA.

HISTORICAL REVIEW PROGRAMS. Mandated by **Executive Order 12958** and other similar directives, historical review programs review classified documents for declassification and eventual release to the public. Virtually all intelligence agencies have such programs. The Office of Information Management in the **Central Intelligence Agency** (CIA), for example, oversees the agency's document declassification plans. To implement the program, the CIA employs a three-prong strategy. First, it supports the **Department of State's** *Foreign Relations of the United States* series, which attempts to be a thorough, accurate, and reliable documentary history of major U.S. foreign policy decisions and activities. Second, it reviews and, when appropriate, declassifies materials that are 25 years old or older. Third, it contributes directly to the scholarly literature on the CIA and intelligence by reviewing and declassifying selected **national intelligence estimates** (NIEs), articles from the agency's in-house journal, *Studies in Intelligence*, and other records and documents, some of which are published in anthologies in conjunction with specific issue-oriented academic conferences.

HISTORY (OPERATION). Following the overthrow of Guatemalan president **Jacobo Arbenz Guzman** by the **Central Intelligence Agency** (CIA) in June 1954, the agency launched a follow-up operation to gather and exploit the documents of the Guatemalan Communist Party. Operation History apparently collected a large number of records—more than 150,000 documents, not including government records—making it, according to declassified U.S. government records, the greatest cache of documents ever left behind by a Communist Party, at least in quantitative terms. In addition, experts say that, aside from efforts to overthrow **Cuba's Fidel Castro** in the early 1960s, Operation History has been the covert operation most written about during the **Cold War**. *See also* SUCCESS (OPERATION).

HOMELAND SECURITY ACT OF 2002. The Homeland Security Act of 2002, signed into law on 25 November 2002, established the **Department of Homeland Security** (DHS) to prevent **terrorist** attacks within the United States, reduce the United States' vulnerability to terrorism, minimize the damages from attacks that occur, and help to recover from any attacks. The new department's primary responsibilities include: analyzing information and protecting infrastructure; developing countermeasures against chemical, biological, radiological, and nuclear attacks; securing U.S. borders and transportation systems; organizing emergency preparedness and response efforts; and coordinating counterterrorism activities with other federal agencies, state and local governments, and the private sector. The DHS incorporates over 30 existing federal agencies or portions of agencies. Each of these agencies continues to be responsible for carrying out its other, non-homeland-security functions.

HOMELAND SECURITY COUNCIL. *See* PRESIDENT'S HOMELAND SECURITY ADVISORY COUNCIL.

HONEYMAN, JOHN (1729?–1822?). One of **George Washington's** most effective operatives during the Revolutionary War. Honeyman, who lived in Griggstown, New Jersey, posed as a Loyalist but was in fact a Patriot spy. He is supposed to have alerted George Washington to the lack of discipline among the British-allied Hessian troops in Trenton. He also spread **disinformation** by assuring the Hessian commander that the American forces across the river in Pennsylvania were demoralized and in retreat from their defeat in New York City. An unassuming and humble man, Honeyman received a pension after the war and lived to be 93 years old.

HOOVER, J. EDGAR (1895–1972). J. Edgar Hoover was the legendary and long-serving director of the **Federal Bureau of Investigation** (FBI). First appointed director of the **Bureau of Investigation** in 1924, Hoover brought his legal and prosecutorial expertise to the Bureau, honed by his controversial role in the "Palmer Raids" against suspected communists and anarchists in 1919. As the national police chief, Hoover upgraded the Bureau's technological investigative techniques, improved training, presided over the name change to FBI in 1935, and prosecuted notorious gangsters with a zeal that made him a national hero.

He also vigorously pursued added responsibilities for the FBI in law enforcement and foreign intelligence. During the administration of **Franklin D. Roosevelt**, Hoover won the right to investigate foreign **espionage** in the United States and to collect intelligence in Latin America. He also began a fervent drive against members of the American Communist Party and left-leaning intellectuals. Hoover secretly amassed files on friends and foes alike, a practice that gave him enormous influence in Washington until his death in 1972.

Hoover vehemently opposed the establishment of the **Central Intelligence Agency** (CIA) in 1947, a position that soured his relationships with successive **directors of central intelligence** (DCIs). During the 1950s, Hoover's anticommunist sentiments led him wholeheartedly to support the **McCarthy** hearings that purported to seek and root out communists in the federal government and elsewhere. Under his leadership, the FBI also investigated prominent individuals Hoover thought held dangerous political views. At the same time, he virtually ignored organized crime, and his investigations into political corruption were mainly used as a means to gain political control over powerful politicians. In the 1960s, Hoover became even more controversial for his opposition to the civil rights movement and the administration of President **John F. Kennedy**. His reputation declined in later years following revelations of vendettas against civil rights leaders and widespread illegal FBI activities. *See also* COINTELPRO; SPECIAL INTELLIGENCE SERVICE.

HOUSE ARMED SERVICES COMMITTEE. Established by the Legislative Reorganization Act of 1946, the House Armed Services Committee has served as the principal authorization committee for defense agencies and national security issues in the House of Representatives. Less well known than its Senate counterpart, the committee held some oversight responsibilities over intelligence matters until 1977, when the House of Representatives established the **House Permanent Select Committee on Intelligence** (HPSCI). The committee's oversight responsibilities now are conducted within the context of the annual defense authorization bill. This legislation covers the **Department of Defense** (DOD) as well as a significant portion of the annual operating budget of the Department of Energy (DOE). *See also* SENATE ARMED SERVICES COMMITTEE.

HOUSE INTERNATIONAL RELATIONS COMMITTEE. A standing committee of the House of Representatives. The House International Relations Committee shares jurisdiction with other committees on foreign policy and national security matters. It is the primary house committee overseeing U.S. foreign relations, principally through its power to authorize foreign economic and military assistance.

The committee evolved from the **Committee of Secret Correspondence** established in 1775. In 1777, a name change to the Committee for Foreign Affairs suggested the committee's additional responsibilities for the new nation's foreign affairs. With the new federal constitution, approved in 1789, however, foreign affairs powers shifted to the Senate and the executive branch, leaving the house committee without much authority. In 1822, the House of Representatives made the Committee on Foreign Affairs a standing committee, with jurisdiction over U.S. foreign relations. In 1885, the committee gained authority to report germane appropriations measures, a power it lost to the House Appropriations Committee in 1920.

The committee changed its name yet again at the end of the **Cold War** to reflect new realities in global politics. Its jurisdiction now covers declaration of war and neutrality, military intervention abroad, foreign commercial relations, payments to international organizations, acquisition of official property abroad, protection of American citizens abroad, and foreign relations generally.

HOUSE PERMANENT SELECT COMMITTEE ON INTELLI- GENCE (HPSCI). The HPSCI is the intelligence **oversight** committee in the House of Representatives that reviews the operations of intelligence agencies, authorizes intelligence activities, and seeks to ensure that intelligence resources are expanded appropriately and in a lawful manner. The HPSCI was established in 1977 in the aftermath of the **Pike Committee** hearings in the mid-1970s into the activities of U.S. intelligence, particularly the **Central Intelligence Agency** (CIA). According to its enabling legislation, the HPSCI is composed of no more than 18 members, of whom not more than 10 can be of the same political party. In addition, the committee must include at least one member from the Committee on Appropriations, Committee on Armed Services, Committee on International Relations, and Committee on the Judiciary. The HPSCI's mandate covers all intelligence and intelligence-related activities (IRA) of the U.S. government, including those that fall outside the purview of the **intelligence community** (IC). *See also* SELECT COMMITTEE ON INTELLIGENCE TO IN- VESTIGATE ALLEGATIONS OF ILLEGAL OR IMPROPER AC- TIVITIES OF FEDERAL INTELLIGENCE AGENCIES; SENATE SELECT COMMITTEE ON INTELLIGENCE; RULE X.

HOWARD, EDWARD LEE (1952–2002). Edward Lee Howard was an operative of the **Central Intelligence Agency** (CIA) who resigned in 1983 and was identified in 1985 by **defector Vitaly Yurchenko** as a Soviet spy. Subsequent investigations showed that Howard had met Soviet intelligence officers in Austria in 1984 to receive payment for revealing the identities of U.S. intelligence assets in Moscow. Howard, slated to go to Moscow as a **case officer** after joining the CIA, was trained in operational tradecraft and thus eluded **Federal Bureau of Investigation** (FBI) surveillance. He fled the United States in 1986 and escaped to the **Soviet Union**. Moscow granted Howard asylum on 7 August 1986. Howard died in Moscow on 12 July 2002 as a result of a fall in his home.

HUGHES-RYAN AMENDMENT. An amendment to the 1961 Foreign Assistance Act that banned **assassinations** by the **Central Intelligence Agency** (CIA). It also prohibited the use of appropriated funds for **covert actions** unless and until the president found that each such operation was important to national security and submitted this "**finding**" to the appropriate congressional committees. The amendment was incorporated into **Executive Order** (EO) **12333** and was later superceded by the **Intelligence Authorization Act of 1991**.

HUMAN INTELLIGENCE (HUMINT). Also known as espionage, HUMINT is the collection of intelligence information from human sources, such as spies, émigrés, and defectors. The **Central Intelligence Agency** (CIA) is the principal entity in the **intelligence community** (IC) engaging in HUMINT collection, although other organizations, such as the **Defense HUMINT Service** (DH), also collect intelligence using human sources. In addition, many consider diplomatic reporting to be human source reporting, although it is normally not included in the definition of HUMINT. *See also* TASK FORCE 157.

– I –

IMAGERY INTELLIGENCE (IMINT). Imagery intelligence is the use and exploitation of images of target areas taken by platforms like satellites, **unmanned aerial vehicles** (UAVs), and manned spy airplanes, such as the **U-2**. Prior to the development of digital imaging, the platforms collected information by taking photographs, and so the discipline was then known as **photographic intelligence (PHOTINT)**.

INDIGO. *See* LACROSSE.

INDUSTRIAL ESPIONAGE. Industrial espionage is spying conducted for commercial, not national security, purposes. Both government and private organizations engage in such conduct. At its most innocent, the term applies to such competitive intelligence activities as examining corporate publications, websites, patent filings, and the like to determine the activities of a firm. At the other extreme, it can involve bribery, blackmail, technological surveillance, and even occasional violence. Governments seek industrial secrets, for example, to determine the terms of a government contract.

The United States government has steadfastly denied engaging in industrial espionage. It has, however, acknowledged its role in

economic intelligence (different from industrial espionage), such as gathering information on a country's industrial output, gross domestic product, and trade practices. For the United States, industrial espionage poses a legal dilemma, in that stealing the secrets of a foreign company in order to divulge them to an American company would mean favoring one American firm over other American commercial interests. In addition, U.S. corporations oppose such espionage because, they claim, they can do it themselves more effectively than the U.S. government can. When U.S. intelligence agencies come across industrial information, they turn it over to the Department of Commerce, which, in turn, publishes the materials openly for use by all American corporations.

INMAN, BOBBY RAY (1931–). Deputy director of central intelligence (DDCI) from 12 February 1981 until 10 June 1982. Inman joined the Naval Reserve in 1951 and was commissioned an ensign in 1952. In a naval career spanning 31 years, Inman spent 19 years as an analyst in the **Office of Naval Intelligence** (ONI); served on an aircraft carrier, two cruisers, and a destroyer; and worked in a variety of onshore assignments. Inman was named chief of the ONI in 1974 and vice director of the **Defense Intelligence Agency** (DIA) in 1976. In 1977, he became the director of the supersecret **National Security Agency** (NSA) and served four years in that capacity until he was named DDCI in 1981. In 1982, he became the first naval intelligence specialist to earn the rank of four-star admiral. In the **intelligence community** (IC), he was known as one of the nation's finest intelligence officers. Since leaving the navy, Inman has been involved in business ventures, serving on a variety of corporate boards and acting as an advisor to three presidents, the **Department of State**, and the Congress.

IN-Q-TEL. Established in February 1999, In-Q-Tel is a private, nonprofit enterprise funded by the **Central Intelligence Agency** (CIA). Its mission is to identify and invest in cutting-edge technology solutions that serve U.S. national security interests. Working from an evolving strategic blueprint that defines the agency's most pressing technology needs, In-Q-Tel connects with entrepreneurs, established companies, universities, researchers, and venture capitalists to develop technologies that enhance intelligence capabilities. Although In-Q-Tel is a private company that works exclusively for the CIA and the **intelligence community** (IC), it does not belong to any intelligence agency.

INQUIRY. A secret organization created by President Woodrow Wilson in September 1917 to analyze and evaluate the war aims, including territorial demands, of the belligerents in **World War I**. The Inquiry also had the mandate to document the geographic, ethnic, economic, and legal bases for the demands of the parties to the war and to identify the various options that might be acceptable to the parties for resolving these claims. Although not a formal intelligence organization, it acted as one by receiving intelligence information from the **Department of State**, the **Military Intelligence Division** (MID), and other parts of the U.S. government. It also established **intelligence liaison** relationships with British and French intelligence, from which the Inquiry received valuable information. President Wilson wanted its existence to stay secret in order to prevent the implication of an imminent end to hostilities. The Inquiry's studies and evaluations contributed to the development of President Wilson's 14-point peace proposals. The Inquiry was disbanded at the conclusion of the peace negotiations.

INTELLIGENCE ANALYSIS. Intelligence analysis is the systematic processing of intelligence information in order to establish facts and derive significant judgments about a country, region, or issue. Analysis constitutes a critical step in the **intelligence cycle**, where intelligence analysts evaluate intelligence information from a variety of different classified and open sources and produce judgments on key intelligence and national security issues that are of importance to policymakers. These assessments take the form of either **current intelligence** or **long-term intelligence**, including **national intelligence estimates** (NIEs), which then are disseminated to mid-level and senior government officials.

INTELLIGENCE AUTHORIZATION ACT OF 1991. This act replaces the 1974 **Hughes-Ryan Amendment** in the area of **intelligence oversight** of **covert actions**. It stipulates that the president is the final approving authority for covert action programs, that he so designates by signing a "**finding**," and that he affirms that the programs are in support of identifiable policy objectives. The finding must list all U.S. government agencies that have a role to play in the program, as well as any "third party" foreign governments. The U.S. government cannot use covert action programs to influence U.S. political processes, media, policies, or public opinion. Finally, no part of a covert action program can violate the Constitution or any federal laws in force.

INTELLIGENCE BUDGETS. *See* JOINT MILITARY INTELLIGENCE PROGRAM; NATIONAL FOREIGN INTELLIGENCE PROGRAM; TACTICAL INTELLIGENCE AND RELATED ACTIVITIES.

INTELLIGENCE COMMUNITY (IC). The U.S. intelligence community is now comprised of 15 agencies, 14 of which belong to specific policy departments. The agencies of the **Department of Defense** (DOD) are the **Defense Intelligence Agency** (DIA); the **National Security Agency** (NSA); **army intelligence**; **Office of Naval Intelligence** (ONI); **air force intelligence, surveillance, and reconnaissance; marine corps intelligence**; the **National Reconnaissance Office** (NRO); and the **National Geospatial-Intelligence Agency** (NGA). The intelligence offices of the Departments of Treasury and Energy and **Department of Homeland Security** (DHS) are also members. The **Coast Guard**—which is within the DHS—the **counterintelligence** component of the **Federal Bureau of Investigation** (FBI), and the State Department's **Bureau of Intelligence and Research** (INR) are official members of the intelligence community. The **Central Intelligence Agency** (CIA) is the only member of the IC that is independent of a policy department; the CIA reports directly to the president of the United States through the **National Security Council** (NSC). Prior to the **National Security Act of 1947**, the IC existed informally as a conglomeration of existing agencies. However, with the passage of the 1947 act, the IC became a legal entity and grew from a handful to the 15 competing and highly fractious entities they are today, under the nominal control of the **director of central intelligence** (DCI).

INTELLIGENCE COMMUNITY STAFF (ICS). The Intelligence Community Staff was the **director of central intelligence**'s (DCI's) instrument for **coordinating** and managing the **intelligence community** (IC). The ICS was reconstituted as the **Community Management Staff** (CMS) in 1992.

INTELLIGENCE COMMUNITY (IC) 21 REPORT. Commissioned by the members of the **House Permanent Select Committee on Intelligence** (HPSCI) in 1997, IC 21 was a staff study of the entire American intelligence apparatus, ranging from issues like the appropriate structural arrangements to an examination of all collection disciplines and their impact on intelligence performance. While identifying specific dysfunctions in each area, IC 21's most important finding was the lack of collection synergy and structural integration in the **intelligence community** (IC).

INTELLIGENCE CYCLE. The intelligence cycle refers to the specific steps in the intelligence process. The **Central Intelligence Agency** (CIA) identifies five steps in the process. Planning and direction come from policymakers in the form of requirements or needs. Collection, the second step, is the acquisition of intelligence information by secret or open means. Processing, the third step, converts collected information into a suitable form for **intelligence analysis**. Analysis is the transformation of information into intelligence through the systematic evaluation, integration, and interpretation of data and the preparation of intelligence products. Dissemination, the final step, is the delivery of the intelligence products to policymakers.

INTELLIGENCE IDENTITIES ACT OF 1982. This law imposes a 10-year prison term on anyone knowingly disclosing the identity of a covert intelligence officer. The act is applicable only when the identified person has served in a covert capacity abroad or in a post involving foreign **counterintelligence** at least five years under a **cover** intended to shield that identity. Congress enacted the law after several disgruntled former intelligence officers published exposes that disclosed the identities of officers of the **Central Intelligence Agency** (CIA) and other agencies in the 1970s.

INTELLIGENCE LIAISON. Intelligence agencies often establish and maintain liaison relationships with their counterparts in other countries. These relationships serve several purposes, the most important of which is to share intelligence information and thereby supplement each other's collection capabilities. Occasionally, they liaise to cement ties between their countries. Frequently, they establish intelligence liaisons in order to discern each other's activities.

The intensity of a liaison relationship for U.S. intelligence agencies depends in large measure on whether or not the United States maintains a formal defense arrangement with the country in question. Where there is no formal defense relationship, intelligence liaison is issue specific and sporadic. Where a formal defense relationship exists, such as an alliance treaty or a friendship pact, the intelligence liaison relationship tends to be close. However, even in this context, there are gradations of closeness, and intelligence relationships often depend on additional factors, such as the degree of "friendship," like the "special relationship" between the United States and the United Kingdom.

INTELLIGENCE OVERSIGHT. Intelligence oversight refers to the authorities ascribed to external entities to review and authorize intelligence programs, appropriate funds for them, and investigate, evaluate, and audit intelligence activities. Intelligence oversight also refers to the accountability of intelligence agencies for their actions. While the concept refers both to executive and legislative oversight, it is generally associated with the activities of congressional oversight committees.

The history of modern American intelligence is replete with executive oversight but little by way of legislative oversight. From the enactment of the **National Security Act of 1947** onward, various executive bodies have exercised considerable oversight. The **National Security Council** (NSC), its **covert action** review committees, and other entities like the **United States Intelligence Board** (USIB) and its successor, the **President's Foreign Intelligence Advisory Board** (PFIAB), have maintained significant executive control over intelligence agencies.

Until the late 1970s, however, legislative oversight was confined to occasional meetings between the **director of central intelligence** (DCI) and chairmen of the congressional authorizing committees, such as the Armed Services Committees, which had jurisdiction over intelligence. In response to past misdeeds, identified in the "**Family Jewels**" document and congressional investigations, Congress established the **Senate Select Committee on Intelligence** (SSCI) in 1976 and the **House Permanent Select Committee on Intelligence** (HPSCI) in 1977 for the purpose of permanently and regularly conducting oversight of U.S. intelligence activities. The armed services, foreign relations, and appropriations committees in both chambers also asserted some jurisdiction.

Since the late 1970s, legislative oversight has been both rigorous and ongoing, prompting some intelligence officers to complain of congressional "micromanagement." Former DCI **Robert M. Gates** has asserted that reporting requirements now place U.S. intelligence, especially the **Central Intelligence Agency** (CIA), halfway between the White House and Congress. In addition to providing information about their activities to executive bodies, intelligence agencies now report on a regular basis to Congress. They do so through oral briefings, testimonies, and myriad intelligence products, which routinely find their way to the oversight committees. As such, Congress now serves in the dual roles of overseer and consumer of intelligence. *See also* INTELLIGENCE OVERSIGHT ACT OF 1980; INTELLIGENCE OVERSIGHT BOARD; ROCKEFELLER COMMISSION.

INTELLIGENCE OVERSIGHT ACT OF 1980. A congressional attempt to firm up legislative **oversight** of **covert actions** in the wake of the revelations in the 1970s, the act provided that the heads of intelligence agencies would keep the oversight committees "fully and currently informed" of their activities including "any significant anticipated intelligence activity." The legislation also established detailed ground rules for reporting covert actions to Congress and limited the number of congressional committees receiving notice of covert actions to the two **intelligence oversight** committees. Prior to the passage of the act, intelligence agencies reported to more than eight congressional committees, including those overseeing foreign relations and the defense establishment.

INTELLIGENCE OVERSIGHT BOARD (IOB). The Intelligence Oversight Board was established in 1976 to review and oversee the activities and programs of U.S. intelligence agencies and assess their legality, efficiency, and effectiveness. Executive Order (EO) 12334, issued on 4 December 1981 by President **Ronald Reagan**, placed the IOB within the Executive Office of the President and gave the board its legal authorities. In 1993, the IOB was made a standing committee of the **President's Foreign Intelligence Advisory Board** (PFIAB), with four members of the PFIAB appointed by its chairman. Executive Order (EO) 13301, issued by President **George W. Bush** on 14 May 2003, increased the IOB's membership to five. The IOB conducts independent **oversight** investigations as required and reviews the oversight practices and procedures of the inspectors general and general counsels of intelligence agencies.

INTELLIGENCE REFORM AND TERRORISM PREVENTION ACT. Passed by Congress in December 2004, the legislation reorganized the **intelligence community** (IC) by creating the position of the **director of national intelligence** (DNI) and transferring some significant powers to him from the **director of central intelligence** (DCI) and the secretary of defense. Specifically the law created the **National Intelligence Authority** (NIA)—akin to the one created in January 1946 to oversee the activities of the **Central Intelligence Group** (CIG)—and placed the DNI at its head. It established a civil liberties board to monitor government counterterrorism agencies for violations of civil and privacy rights and an Analytic Review Unit within the ombudsman's office to review the estimative and analytic process. The law also mandated a unified network for information sharing among federal, state, and local agencies and the private sector. Moreover, it included provisions for adding border patrol agents; installing cameras in baggage-handling areas of airports; increasing cargo inspections; taking measures designed to secure borders transportation and critical infrastructure; and promoting outreach to the Muslim world in order stem **terrorist** recruiting and improve the image of the United States.

INTERAGENCY WORKING GROUPS (IWGs). IWGs are committees of the **National Security Council** (NSC) that coordinate implementation of decisions made at the higher levels of the NSC. Some IWGs are permanent and some are ad hoc. Under the supervision of the NSC's **Deputies Committee**, IWGs are organized both along issues of national importance—for example, on proliferation issues—and along regional lines, to correspond to important national security and foreign policy areas. Usually staffed at the assistant secretary level, each IWG includes those departments and agencies that have an interest in the issue of country of concern.

INTERDEPARTMENTAL INTELLIGENCE COMMITTEE (IIC). An executive directive, dated on 26 June 1939, consolidated responsibility for **espionage, counterintelligence**, and sabotage matters in the hands of the **Federal Bureau of Investigation** (FBI) and the military intelligence services. The directive also established the IIC to **coordinate** and oversee these intelligence activities. By doing so, President **Franklin D. Roosevelt** probably hoped to bring order to the chaos that had thus far marked the U.S. government's response to internal espionage threats. Despite the onset of war in Europe, IIC members fought jurisdictional conflicts over their mandates, including over **covert action**, which none of them wanted to take on. To overcome their disputes, the IIC as a corporate body proposed an interdepartmental and independent foreign intelligence organization, but President Roosevelt instead ordered on 26 June 1940 that foreign intelligence gathering be split between the FBI in the western hemisphere and the military services in the rest of the world. The IIC continued to operate throughout **World War II,** becoming redundant with the establishment of the **Central Intelligence Group** (CIG) in January 1946.

INTERNAL SECURITY ACT OF 1950. The Internal Security Act, or McCarran Act, of 1950, named after Nevada senator Pat McCarran, required communist and communist-front organizations to register with the attorney general. It also stipulated that members of these groups could not become citizens, and those who already were citizens of the United States could be denaturalized.

President **Harry S. Truman,** who had imposed the loyalty order on federal employees in 1947, intially vetoed the legislation, but Congress overrode the veto. The Senate Internal Security Subcommittee, working closely with **J. Edgar Hoover's Federal Bureau of Investigation** (FBI), conducted hearings for the next 27 years.

One of the more controversial provisions of the McCarran Act was its authorization of concentration camps "for emergency situations." Gradually, the U.S. Supreme Court ruled portions of the act to be unconstitutional, and the court repealed the legislation completely in 1990.

IRAN. A key country in the Middle East, possessing vast oil reserves and strategically located between the Fertile Crescent and the Indian subcontinent, Iran was a focal point of competition between the United States and the **Soviet Union** during the **Cold War**. American intelligence restored the pro-American shah to his throne in 1953 and trained his security service, **SAVAK**, which sparked intense opposition to American policies among many influential Iranians. The shah's heavy-handed approach to his own people produced intense hatred of the Iranian monarch and culminated in the Islamic revolution in 1979, which ousted the shah and transformed Iran into a radical Islamic republic. *See also* AJAX (OPERATION); DESERT ONE; IRAN-CONTRA AFFAIR.

IRAN-CONTRA AFFAIR. The Iran-Contra Affair was a political scandal that took place from mid-1985 until the early months of 1988. The scandal involved a two-stage **covert action** run out of the **National Security Council** (NSC), first, to sell weapons to **Iran** in exchange for exerting its influence on the terrorist group holding American hostages in Lebanon, and, second, using the profits from the weapons sale to secretly fund the **Contra** rebels in **Nicaragua**.

The operation became a messy scandal for a number of reasons. One, the administration of President **Ronald Reagan** had previously announced publicly that it would not negotiate with terrorists nor trade weapons for hostages. Two, the U.S. Congress had already terminated lethal and nonlethal funds for the Contras, who were allegedly involved in human rights violations in their fight against the **Sandinistas**. And three, the covert operation was directed by the NSC, in contravention of U.S. law, which requires the **Central Intelligence Agency** (CIA), not the NSC, to conduct American covert actions. The scandal resulted in a series of highly visible prosecutions of administration officials, including members of the NSC and the CIA, and marred President Reagan's second term.

ITEK. A technical contractor for sophisticated satellite reconnaissance cameras employed in **CORONA** from 1957 until 1965. The **Central Intelligence Agency** (CIA) was Itek's principal consumer, such that by 1963, Itek's classified operations produced 57 percent of the firm's sales and accounted for 75 perecent of its pretax income. This dependence on a single consumer eventually stripped Itek of its competitive advantage and thrust the company into financial difficulties. In 1965, Itek's leadership decided to withdraw from its CIA contracts, and Itek did not receive any subsequent CIA contract after its decision to pull out of its CIA commitments. In the 1966–1967 period, Itek made some gadgets for the space program. It also continued to build CORONA satellites until the program's end in 1972. Litton Industries bought the firm in the early 1980s. *See also* IN-Q-TEL.

IVY BELLS (OPERATION). Ivy Bells was a joint navy–**National Security Agency** (NSA) operation initiated in the 1970s to tap into **Soviet** communications in the Sea of Oskotsk in the Pacific. The action involved stealthy U.S. submarines entering the denied area and placing wraparound, nonpenetrating pods around the undersea cable carrying highly classified Soviet communications. The pods were designed to fall off in the event the Soviets raised the cable. U.S submarines would return every six to eight weeks to collect the recordings in the pods. The tapes were then delivered to the NSA for processing and distribution to military and civilian consumers.

The operation came to an end in 1981 when Soviet authorities discovered the pods. A postmortem investigation revealed that Ronald Pelton, an NSA employee, had sold the secret to the Soviets. Considered one of the more successful intelligence gathering operation of the **Cold War**, Ivy Bells provided U.S. intelligence with significant information on Soviet military operations in the Pacific.

– J –

JENNIFER (PROJECT). Jennifer was a secret **Central Intelligence Agency** (CIA) effort to raise a sunken Soviet submarine from the Pacific seabed in the summer of 1974. The Soviet submarine had sunk on 11 April 1968, and the Soviets had been unable to raise their sunken vessel. **Henry A. Kissinger**, national security advisor, approved the plan to raise the wreckage. A special ship, the *Glomar Explorer,* was built by a mining company owned by billionaire Howard Hughes. On 12 August 1974, the *Glomar Explorer* and a submersible barge used a large mechanical claw to recover about half of the submarine, along with some weapons and the remains of several sailors. The operation gave the United States valuable information about the design of soviet nuclear submarines and their capabilities. The U.S. government gave the Soviet sailors full military honors and returned their remains to the **Soviet Union** when the operation became public. *See also* COVERT ACTION.

JEREMIAH COMMISSION. Director of Central Intelligence (DCI) **George J. Tenet** in the summer of 1998 asked Admiral David Jeremiah to investigate the performance of the **intelligence community** (IC) in assessing India's nuclear tests, which had taken place in May 1998 to the surprise of the IC. The commission found that the work of intelligence analysts was based on faulty assumptions, which were not examined; information was too compartmented to be usefully integrated; there was inadequate utilization of existing collection resources; policymakers paid little attention to intelligence requirements; and intelligence structures and jurisdictions continued to be ambiguous. However, the commission did acknowledge the fact that the Indian tests posed difficult collection problems, largely because India went to great lengths to hide its preparations, and only a few Indian leaders were aware of the test plans.

JOHNSON, LYNDON BAINES (1908–1973). The 36th president of the United States between 1963 and 1969. Lyndon B. Johnson rose to prominence in 1960 when Democratic Party candidate **John F. Kennedy** chose Johnson as his vice president. Until then, Lyndon B. Johnson had represented Texas in Congress. When President Kennedy was assassinated on 22 November 1963, Vice President Johnson was sworn in as president.

Initially, President Johnson focused on domestic issues, vowing to continue President Kennedy's legacy. In 1964, after being elected by the widest margin of votes in American history, he put forth a civil rights bill and a tax cut and urged the nation to build a "great society." This new program became Johnson's centerpiece for Congress in January 1965, with new initiatives in education, urban renewal, conservation, antipoverty, and voting rights. He also succeeded in passing the 1965 Medicare amendment to the Social Security Act.

His foreign policy initiatives were less popular and successful. Despite efforts to end communist aggression and achieve a settlement in Vietnam, President Johnson used the 1964 **Gulf of Tonkin Resolution** as a pretext to escalate American military involvement to the point that, by 1968, there were more than a half-million American soldiers in Southeast Asia. By that year, moreover, the American public had become highly fractious over the **Vietnam War**. Consequently, President Johnson startled the world in 1968 by withdrawing as candidate for reelection in order to pursue peace but did not live to see the success of the Vietnam negotiations. He died of a heart attack at his Texas ranch on 22 January 1973.

JOINT CHIEFS OF STAFF (JCS). The Joint Chiefs of Staff is an organization that combines the chiefs of the military services. Its chairman serves as advisor to the president, secretary of defense, and the **National Security Council** (NSC) on military matters. The chairman of the JCS acquired this highly political role as a result of the 1986 **Goldwater-Nichols Act**.

During **World War II**, the JCS acted as a combined command for theater and area commanders. However, the **National Security Act of 1947** made the JCS an advisory, not command, institution. Yet, a 1948 agreement allowed the JCS to serve limited command responsibilities. Congress abolished this authority in a 1953 amendment to the National Security Act. Goldwater-Nichols reaffirmed the exclusion of the JCS from command responsibilities by asserting that the chain of command runs from the president to the secretary of defense and from the secretary of defense to the commander of the combatant command. The chairman of the JCS may transmit communications to the commanders of the combatant commands from the president and secretary of defense but does not exercise military command over any combatant forces.

Goldwater-Nichols also created the position of vice chairman of the Joint Chiefs of Staff, who performs such duties as the JCS chairman may prescribe. By law, he is the second ranking member of the armed forces and replaces the chairman in his absence or disability. Although the vice chairman was not originally included as a member of the JCS, the National Defense Authorization Act of 1992 made him a full voting member of the JCS.

The military service chiefs play a somewhat ambiguous but dual role in the process. As members of the JCS, they offer advice to the president, the secretary of defense, and the NSC. As the chiefs of the military services, they are responsible to the secretaries of their military departments for management of the services. The service chiefs serve for four years. By custom, the vice chiefs of the services act for their chiefs in most matters having to do with day-to-day operation of the services. The duties of the service chiefs as members of JCS take precedence over all their other duties.

The JCS chairman has a staff, called the Joint Staff, that assists in providing strategic direction of the combatant forces and their operation under unified command, and for their integration into a "joint" force. The Joint Staff is composed of approximately equal numbers of officers from the army, navy, marine, and air force personnel. In practice, the marines make up about 20 percent of the number allocated to the navy. The director of the Joint Staff has authority to review and approve issues when there is no dispute among the services, when the issue does not warrant JCS attention, when the proposed action conforms to policy, or when the issue has not been raised by a JCS member.

JOINT INTELLIGENCE COMMITTEE (JIC). One of the least known of U.S. intelligence organizations that emerged during **World War II**, the JIC survived well into the late 1950s despite the reorganization of U.S. intelligence in 1947 and the establishment of the **Central Intelligence Agency** (CIA). Officially established on 11 February 1942, the JIC, like its British cousin, produced intelligence reports for the **Joint Chiefs of Staff** (JCS) and "higher authorities" of the United States. Reporting to the JCS's Joint Planning Staff, this agency initially contained representation from the coordinator of information (COI)—predecessor to the **Office of Strategic Services** (OSS)—although there was concern that civilian representation in a military organization would set a dangerous precedent. The **Federal Bureau of Investigation** (FBI) and its director, **J. Edgar Hoover**, were specifically excluded from sitting on the JIC.

The JIC's wartime charter called for it to furnish **current intelligence** for use by the JCS, but it did succeed in producing **national intelligence estimates** (NIEs) as well. The JIC's Joint Intelligence Staff drafted all the memorandums, summaries, and, eventually, intelligence estimates for JCS approval. The JIC produced a significant number of intelligence estimates and policy papers during the war and the early postwar period. According to one report, the JIC completed 16 major intelligence estimates and 27 policy papers between 15 June and 9 August 1945. It drafted assessments and estimates on the **Soviet** threat, including specific analyses of Soviet air power, missiles, nuclear war planning, and economic outlook. One of the JIC's policy papers, JIC 397, anticipated **National Security Council 68** by laying out the emerging Soviet strategic and conventional military threat in stark and clear terms.

Yet, the JIC never did manage to acquire sufficient influence to compete with the nascent **intelligence community** (IC). Duplicating some of the CIA's work, for example, made it suspect in the eyes of the new civilian intelligence professionals. Its critics also maintained that the JIC was a cumbersome bureaucracy that reflected the ongoing rivalries of the military services. Although the JIC was disbanded in 1958, retrospective evaluations show that it produced studies of "national" scope that provided significant contributions to military, and sometimes national, decision making.

JOINT INTELLIGENCE INQUIRY. On 14 February 2002, the House of Representatives and the Senate **intelligence oversight** committees announced the establishment of an unprecedented joint inquiry into the **terrorist attacks of 11 September 2001**. The inquiry's original mandate was to determine why the **intelligence community** (IC) did not learn of the attacks at their planning stages and to recommend reform. The joint inquiry held public and secret hearings and produced a report that identified deficiencies in the intelligence process and recommended structural reforms. The families of the 9/11 victims, however, charged a whitewash, which gave greater credence to calls for an independent commission to investigate the terrorist attacks. *See also* NATIONAL COMMISSION ON TERRORIST ATTACKS UPON THE UNITED STATES.

JOINT MILITARY INTELLIGENCE COLLEGE (JMIC). The JMIC is the intelligence school of the **Department of Defense** (DOD), providing professional military education in intelligence, national security, and regional issues. First established in 1962 as the **Defense Intelligence School**, it consolidated existing army and navy academic programs in strategic intelligence. In 1980, Congress authorized the school to award the Master of Science of Strategic Intelligence (MSSI) degree. In 1981, the Commission on Higher Education of the Middle States Association of Colleges and Schools accredited the school. That same year, the Defense Department rechartered the institution as the **Defense Intelligence College** (DIC), placing additional emphasis on its research mission.

Renamed the Joint Military Intelligence College in 1993, the JMIC offers a highly diverse curriculum. It also sponsors research and publication opportunities for students and faculty, attracts noteworthy individuals as distinguished speakers, and provides field trips to key intelligence activities. Its students come from throughout the **intelligence community** (IC), including the Coast Guard and other federal civilian agencies, and participate in field exercises and simulations in partnership with their peers at the military staff and war colleges. The JMIC's campus is located on Bolling Air Force Base in Washington, D.C., but it also provides off-campus programs at various intelligence agencies.

JOINT MILITARY INTELLIGENCE PROGRAM (JMIP). Established in 1995, the JMIP is one of three intelligence budgets of the U.S. government, consolidating all defense-wide intelligence programs under navy executive authority, so long as they involve more than one defense component. As such, the JMIP incorporates three major aggregations: The Defense Cryptologic Program (DCP), the Defense Imagery and Mapping Program (DIMAP), and the Defense General Intelligence and Applications Program (DGIAP). Prior to 1995, these and other similar defense intelligence programs were within the **tactical intelligence and related activities** (TIARA) budget, but defense planners established the JMIP to centralize planning, management, coordination, and oversight of defense-wide programs and to produce greater effectiveness in defense-related intelligence activities. The JMIP allocations increased to around $7 billion in fiscal year 2002, but defense planners expect a steady decline to about $4.2 billion in fiscal year 2005. *See also* GENERAL DEFENSE INTELLIGENCE PROGRAM; NATIONAL FOREIGN INTELLIGENCE PROGRAM.

– K –

KENNAN, GEORGE F. (1904–). Renowned American diplomat and historian, George F. Kennan was the architect of the **containment policy**, first enunciated during the administration of **Harry S. Truman**. Specifically, Kennan advocated a strategy of patient, long-term "containment" of the **Soviet Union** and a simultaneous all-out effort to establish a stable balance of power by rebuilding Western Europe and Japan. While in Moscow, he set down his views in a diplomatic cable to Washington, which *Foreign Affairs* published under the pseudonym "X." In accordance with his philosophy, Kennan played a major role in both the Marshall Plan and the rebuilding of Japan as well as overall U.S. strategy toward the Soviet Union. He also espoused giving the **Central Intelligence Agency** (CIA) a **covert action** capability, something he later came to regret.

Over time, Kennan became increasingly skeptical about the direction of U.S. foreign policy. In his view, U.S. foreign policy suffered from confusion, ignorance, narcissism, escapism, and irresponsibility. His disillusionment compelled him to leave the **Department of State** in the early 1950s to join Princeton University's Institute for Advanced Study and write and speak about American foreign policy and the deleterious effects of the arms race. With the end of the **Cold War**, Kennan argued that the United States should limit its foreign policy to maintaining its alliances with Western Europe and Japan and to addressing domestic problems.

KENNEDY, JOHN F. (1917–1963). The 35th president of the United States between 1961 and 1963. John F. Kennedy, the scion of a politically connected New England family, entered politics after **World War II** as senator and served in that capacity until becoming Democratic Party candidate for president in 1960. Voters in the 1960 presidential election chose Kennedy, a relatively unknown politician with impeccable connections, over Republican challenger **Richard M. Nixon** because they distrusted Nixon, not because they endorsed Kennedy.

President Kennedy brought in young political entrepreneurs with new ideas to run his administration, and they infused a sense of energy, renewal, and dynamism into American politics. The Kennedy administration championed civil rights, space exploration, and economic progress for everyone. President Kennedy's foreign policy initiatives, however, were more tumultuous than his more successful domestic programs. He assumed a confrontational approach with the **Soviet Union**, authorized the **Bay of Pigs invasion**, began America's long and painful involvement in the **Vietnam War**, sanctioned **Fidel Castro's** ouster and **assassination** as part of **Operation Mongoose**, and presided over the near-calamitous **Cuban Missile Crisis** in October 1962. President Kennedy was assassinated on 22 November 1963 in Dallas, Texas. He was succeeded by his vice president, **Lyndon B. Johnson**, the same day.

KENT, SHERMAN (1903–1986). The legendary pioneer in analysis and **estimative intelligence** and chair of the **Board of National Estimates** from 1957 until 1967. Kent, a professor of history at Yale University, joined the Research and Analysis Branch of the **Office of Strategic Services** (OSS) in 1941. He showed uncommon talent in applying rigorous scholarship to producing intelligence and persuading academicians to work in teams, meet tight deadlines, and satisfy the needs of action-oriented policy consumers. At the end of **World War II**, Kent wrote his seminal book, *Strategic Intelligence for World Policy*, prior to returning to Yale in 1947. In 1949, however, **Director of Central Intelligence** (DCI) **Walter Bedell Smith** recruited Kent into the **Central Intelligence Agency** (CIA) and appointed him to the **Office of National Estimates** (ONE). Because Kent's genius lay in his recognition that scholarship had to adapt to the policy world—not the other way around—he eventually became director of the ONE and chair of the Board of National Estimates. Kent retired from the CIA in 1967. *See also* NATIONAL INTELLIGENCE ESTIMATE.

KEYHOLE (KH). The designation Keyhole refers to the entire range of unarmed U.S. satellites operated by the **Central Intelligence Agency** (CIA) from 1960 onward. The early KH satellites used photographic film on spools that were ejected and returned to earth in capsules. KH-11, deployed on 19 December 1976, was the first U.S. satellite to provide real-time digital telephoto television signals, but it was also a **signals intelligence** (SIGINT) platform. The United States has developed more recent versions of KH as well as other more sophisticated and capable satellites, but KH-11 is still in use. *See also* CORONA.

KGB (Komitet Gosdarstvennoi Bezopasnotsi/Committee on State Security). The political and security police of the former **Soviet Union**, the KGB was established in 1954 to guard Soviet borders, conduct **espionage** and **counterintelligence**, protect Soviet officials, suppress political dissidence, and maintain its own independent armed forces. It evolved from the secret police of the early Stalinist era into a highly autonomous and centralized organization that, by the 1960s, had become firmly established as the security watchdog of the Community Party of the Soviet Union. At its peak, the KGB also was the largest secret police and espionage organization in the world. It became so influential in Soviet politics that several of its directors moved on to become premiers of the Soviet Union. Russian president Vladimir V. Putin is a former head of the KGB. Upon the dissolution of the Soviet Union in 1991, KGB's far-flung operations were consolidated into two separate agencies—the **FSB**, Russia's domestic federal security service and the **SVRR**, Russia's external intelligence agency. *See also* GRU.

KHRUSHCHEV, NIKITA SERGEYEVICH (1894–1971). Nikita S. Khrushchev was the Soviet Communist Party chairman from 1954 until 1964. He rose to prominence by unquestioningly supporting **Josef Stalin**'s bloody purges in the 1930s that consolidated his political power. Although a peasant by birth, Khrushchev rose quickly to become Moscow Communist Party chief in 1935. During **World War II**, he was head of the Ukrainian Communist Party, and after the war, became a top advisor to Stalin.

Stalin died in 1953 and, after a power struggle, Khrushchev emerged as the new leader of the **Soviet Union**. He immediately set out to remake the Soviet system by undoing Stalin's excesses. In a 1956 secret speech to the 20th congress of the Communist Party, Khrushchev denounced Stalin for his crimes and proposed reforms, which gave Soviet citizens hope for the future and emboldened East Europeans to strive for independence. However, Khrushchev's moderation did not include toleration of dissent. Soviet forces brutally crushed the Hungarian revolt in 1956, and Khrushchev made sure that Soviet client states knew the limits of his benevolence.

In his relations with the West, Khrushchev advocated "peaceful co-existence" but presided over a series of crises that marred East-West relations—the downing of **Francis Gary Powers's U-2** spy craft in May 1960, the building of the Berlin wall in 1961, and the **Cuban Missile Crisis** in 1962. His internal reforms and external accommodations alienated the more conservative elements of the Soviet Communist Party, who ousted Khrushchev from power in 1964.

KHRUSHCHEV'S SECRET SPEECH. Soviet premier **Nikita S. Khrushchev** delivered a secret speech before the Twentieth Congress of the Communist Party in February 1956. In the speech, Khrushchev detailed the crimes of **Josef Stalin**, his predecessor. The Soviet government maintained strict secrecy over its contents, although the **Central Intelligence Agency** (CIA) acquired a copy of the speech, probably from the Israeli intelligence agency Mossad, had it translated and printed by the Department of State, and then leaked it to the *New York Times.* By doing so, the CIA hoped to foment discontent in East European countries occupied by Soviet forces and to boost the chances of its **Red Sox/Red Cap covert action** to foster rebellion in Soviet-occupied East European countries by the end of 1959.

KISSINGER, HENRY A. (1923–). Dr. Henry A. Kissinger was the 56th secretary of state of the United States from 1973 to 1977 while also serving as **assistant to the president for national security affairs** (APNSA), a position he filled from 1969 until 1975.

Born in Germany, Dr. Kissinger came to the United States in 1938 and was naturalized a citizen in 1943. From 1943 to 1946, he served in the **Counter Intelligence Corps** (CIC) and from 1946 to 1949 was a captain in the military intelligence reserve. He attended Harvard University, earning MA and PhD degrees in 1952 and 1954, respectively. From 1954 until 1971, he was a member of the faculty of Harvard University, both in the Department of Government and at the Center for International Affairs, and headed various centers, task forces, and projects during this time. Kissinger took a leave of absence from Harvard between 1969 and 1971 to serve in the **Richard M. Nixon** administration and subsequently became a highly controversial figure in American foreign policy.

As architect of President Nixon's **Vietnam War** policy of negotiating through strength, Kissinger presided over the heavy bombing of

North Vietnam, the incursion into Cambodia, and the peace negotiations in Paris. He also authorized various controversial covert operations in Chile, Angola, and elsewhere. Despite his closeness to President Nixon, Kissinger was not implicated in the **Watergate scandal**. President **Gerald R. Ford** retained him as secretary of state upon President Nixon's resignation in August 1974. After leaving government in 1975, Dr. Kissinger founded Kissinger Associates, an international consulting firm, of which he is chairman. *See also* FEATURE (OPERATION); FUBELT (OPERATION); NATIONAL SECURITY DECISION MEMORANDUM 93.

KOREAN WAR. The Korean War began with North Korea's surprise invasion of its southern neighbor on 25 June 1950; a truce was signed on 27 July 1953. The conflict had its origins in the deal between the United States and the **Soviet Union** at the end of **World War II**, in which Korea, a colony of Japan until the war's end, was split between the Soviet controlled part north of the 38th parallel and the American-controlled south. The war was also the first proxy war between the United States and the Soviet Union in the nascent **Cold War**.

For U.S. intelligence, the Korean War constituted an embarrassing intelligence failure. The **Central Intelligence Agency** (CIA) not only failed to forecast the North Korean invasion but also the entry of the **People's Republic of China** (PRC) into the war on 19 October 1950. The CIA had warned American policymakers in 1949 that a North Korean attack was "probable" if the United States withdrew troops from South Korea, but many in the policy community, including the **Department of Defense** (DOD), attributed the warnings to the CIA's pessimism and dismissed them. After the attack, President **Harry S. Truman** replaced **Director of Central Intelligence** (DCI) **Roscoe Hillenkoetter** with **General Walter Bedell Smith**, who promptly reorganized the CIA for greater efficiency and established its analytic capability. *See also* OFFICE OF NATIONAL ESTIMATES.

– L –

LACROSSE. A project to develop a space-based imaging radar satellite was initiated in late 1976 by **Director of Central Intelligence**

(DCI) **George H. W. Bush**. This effort led to the successful test of the INDIGO prototype imaging radar satellite in January 1982. Although the decision to proceed with an operational system was controversial, development of the Lacrosse system was approved in 1983. Later known as **VEGA**, this set of intelligence satellites carry imaging radar that can penetrate cloud cover.

The distinguishing features of the design of the Lacrosse satellite include a very large radar antenna and solar panels to provide electrical power for the radar transmitter and a resolution of better than one meter, which presumably is adequate for the identification and tracking of major military units such as tanks or missile transporter vehicles.

The first version of Lacrosse was launched on 2 December 1988 by the Space Shuttle; Lacrosse 2 was launched on 8 March 1991; and Lacrosse 3 was launched in the fall of 1997, replacing Lacrosse 1. *See also* CORONA; KEYHOLE.

LANDSAT. Landsat is a satellite of the National Aeronautics and Space Administration (NASA) that was launched on 23 July 1972 to conduct a detailed survey of the earth's surface. The first Landsat originally was called the Earth Resources Technology Satellite (ERTS), but there are now at least seven later versions of the satellite in use. The satellites monitor important natural processes and human land use such as vegetation growth, deforestation, agriculture, coastal and river erosion, snow accumulation and fresh-water reservoir replenishment, and urbanization. In addition, the United States Geological Survey (USGS) uses Landsat data to spot the amount and condition of dry biomass on the ground, which are potential sources for feeding wildfires that can threaten humans, animals, and natural resources. Farmers and land managers use Landsat data to help increase crop yields and cut costs while reducing environmental pollution.

LANGER, WILLIAM L. (1896–1977). William L. Langer was the founder of the **Office of National Estimates** (ONE) in the **Central Intelligence Agency** (CIA) in 1950 and the chief of research and analysis in the **Office of Strategic Services** (OSS) during **World War II**. A Harvard historian by profession, Langer also was the author of several books on U.S. foreign policy just prior to and during the war. In 1950, he took a leave of absence from Harvard to organize the ONE, which he headed until leaving government in 1952. Langer served a brief period as a member of the **President's Foreign Intelligence Advisory Board** (PFIAB) in 1961, but he remained at Harvard until his death in 1977.

LANSDALE, EDWARD G. (1908–1987). Covert operative, military officer, and **Cold War** counterinsurgency specialist, Edward G. Lansdale had colorful and lengthy careers in both the military and intelligence in the formative years of the cold war. His dual career began in **World War II** when he worked simultaneously for the **Office of Strategic Services** (OSS) and **army intelligence**. After the war, the air force (to which he had transferred) loaned him to the **Office of Policy Coordination** (OPC), which became part of the **Central Intelligence Agency** (CIA) in 1952. Although he was never an employee of the CIA, Lansdale often worked on its behalf as an air force officer.

During the early decades of the Cold War, he became legendary for identifying and funding effective noncommunist alternative leaders, engineering psychological warfare (PSYWAR) operations in North Vietnam, and channeling U.S. support to the new Republic of South Vietnam and its president. Under President **John F. Kennedy**, Lansdale was put in charge of **Operation Mongoose**, which involved attempts to eliminate **Fidel Castro** and disrupt the economy of communist **Cuba**. Lansdale's exploits provided the backdrop for two fictional charaters: Alden Pyle in Graham Greene's *The Quiet American* (1955) and Col. Edwin B. Hillandale in William J. Lederer and Eugene Burdick's *The Ugly American* (1958). Lansdale retired from active duty as a major general in 1963.

LEWIS AND CLARK EXPEDITION. On 28 February 1803, Congress approved President Thomas Jefferson's request for an appropriation to fund the Corps of Discovery to explore the American Northwest. President Jefferson chose his secretary, Meriwether Lewis, and Lewis's friend, William Clark, to lead the expedition. Although billed as a voyage of exploration, the Lewis and Clark expedition was an intelligence mission to collect **basic intelligence** information about the lands acquired under the Louisiana Purchase, announced on 4 July 1803. The expedition, comprised of nearly 50 men, set off from St. Louis, Missouri, on 14 May 1803 and traveled thousands of miles through the Great Plains, up the Missouri and Yellowstone Rivers, and into the Columbia River basin until it reached the Pacific coast in December 1805. On the way, Lewis and Clark recorded their observations about the lay of the land and the Native Americans who inhabited it. The Corps of Discovery returned to St. Louis on 23 September 1806. The explorers submitted their report to President Jefferson later that year.

LIBERTY INCIDENT. Israeli fighter planes and torpedo boats attacked the U.S. Navy spy ship USS *Liberty* on 8 June 1967 while the ship was gathering **electronic intelligence** (ELINT) off the coast of Egypt and Israel during the Six-Day War. By the end of the attack, 34 U.S. sailors were dead and 171 injured. Israel subsequently claimed that the attack was a mistake caused by misidentification of the *Liberty* as an Egyptian vessel. Rear Admiral Isaac Kidd was directed to put together a panel of inquiry that in a short time concluded that the *Liberty* incident was in fact a case of mistaken identity.

The findings of the panel, however, were controversial. According to some experts, the ruling was entirely political, especially since Admiral Kidd was ordered by President **Lyndon Johnson** and Defense Secretary Robert McNamara to conclude that the attack was indeed a mistake. The critics of the panel's decision suggest that Israel wanted to stop the *Liberty* from spying on its military during the Six-Day War.

LIMITED NUCLEAR TEST BAN TREATY (LNTBT). Formally known as the Treaty Banning Nuclear Weapons Tests in the Atmosphere, in Outer Space, and Under Water, the treaty was opened for signature on 5 August 1963 and entered into force on 10 October 1963. The LNTBT was one of the earliest **arms control** agreements of the **Cold War**, initiated by President **Dwight D. Eisenhower** in October 1958 and concluded by President **John F. Kennedy** in August 1963. The treaty sought to limit nuclear weapons testing to identifiable and verifiable areas of the earth's surface by excluding atmospheric, space, and oceanic testing as permissible venues. The role of U.S. intelligence was to monitor nuclear tests in order to determine compliance with the terms of the treaty.

LINCOLN, ABRAHAM (1809–1865). The 16th president of the United States between 1861 and 1865. President Lincoln apparently saw the need for intelligence during the **Civil War** but did not seek to establish it within the federal government. The Confederate side went further by actively putting together a variety of units, including the **Confederate Secret Service**, to carry out operations against the North. The plot to **assassinate** President Lincoln allegedly was carried out by Southern intelligence operatives.

LONG-TERM INTELLIGENCE. Long-term intelligence refers to in-depth research projects on a region, country, or issue that may not necessarily have current importance but may contribute to understanding the intelligence problem or to developing future policy options.

LUMUMBA, PATRICE EMERY (1925–1961). Patrice Lumumba was the first prime minister of the Democratic Republic of the Congo. In 1959 Belgium announced a plan to grant the Congo its independence over a five-year period, and Lumumba's political party won a convincing majority despite his incarceration at the time. A 1960 conference in Belgium agreed to bring independence forward to June with elections in May. Lumumba formed the first government on 23 June 1960, with Lumumba as prime minister and Joseph Kasavubu as president.

Yet, the province of Katanga, with Belgian support, declared a separate independence under Moise Tshombe in June 1960, plunging the Congo into civil war. To counter what he considered to be Western manipulation, Lumumba sought **Soviet** aid, setting in motion Western actions to remove him from office. On 14 September 1960, a coup d'etat, headed by Colonel Joseph Mobutu, later to be known as Mobutu Sese Seko, ousted Lumumba and arrested him on 1 December 1960. Mobutu declared that Lumumba would be tried for inciting the army to rebellion and other crimes.

On 17 January 1961, Lumumba was moved to a prison and was executed two months later, along with his two aides. On February 2002, the Belgian government admitted to "an irrefutable portion of responsibility in the events that led to the death of Lumumba." In July 2002, released documents showed that the **Central Intelligence Agency** (CIA) had played a role in Lumumba's **assassination**, aiding his opponents with money and political support, and in the case of Mobutu, with weapons and military training.

– M –

MAGIC. *See* PURPLE.

MARINE CORPS INTELLIGENCE. According to the Marine Corps, its intelligence mission is to provide commanders at every level with seamless, tailored, timely, and mission-critical **tactical intelligence** and to ensure this intelligence is integrated into the operational planning process. Two-thirds of all intelligence marines serve in the operating forces, with the majority assigned to the staffs and units of tactical commands.

The Marine Corps director of intelligence (DIRINT) is the commandant's principal intelligence staff officer and the functional manager for intelligence, **counterintelligence**, and **cryptologic** matters. Through his staff within the intelligence department at Marine Corps headquarters, DIRINT allocates resources and manpower to develop and maintain specific expertise in the areas of human and technical reconnaissance and surveillance, general military/naval intelligence duties, **human intelligence** (HUMINT), counterintelligence, **imagery intelligence** (IMINT), **signals intelligence** (SIGINT), and tactical exploitation of national capabilities.

The Marine Corps Intelligence Activity (MCIA) is the service production center and is collocated with the navy's National Maritime Intelligence Center (NMIC). The MCIA provides Marine Corps headquarters with threat assessments, estimates, and intelligence for service planning and decision making. It also provides combat planners with threat data and other intelligence support for doctrine and force structure development, systems and equipment acquisition, war gaming, and training and education. It is fully integrated into the **Department of Defense** (DOD) intelligence production program and is tasked with expeditionary warfare intelligence to support all, not just Marine Corps, decision makers.

MAYAGUEZ INCIDENT. The Mayaguez incident refers to the seizing of an U.S. merchant ship on 12 May 1975 by Khmer Rouge gunboats in international waters off Cambodia. A rescue operation on 15 May 1975, including the landing of marines, succeeded in freeing the ship. However, the Americans sustained at least 40 killed and 50 wounded. The Cambodian Khmer Rouge government, possibly on appeal by the government of the **People's Republic of China** (PRC), released the crew, who were brought out of Cambodia by the rescuers. The reasons for the ship's capture and subsequent release of the crew have baffled researchers.

McCARTHY ERA. The McCarthy era refers to the years between 1950 and 1954 when Wisconsin senator Joseph McCarthy zealously sought to unmask communist infiltration of the U.S. government. The stage for the McCarthy Era was set as early as 1940, when the Alien Registration Act made it illegal for anyone in the United States to advocate, abet, or teach the overthrow of the government. The law also required all alien residents over 14 years of age living in the country to file a statement of personal and occupational status as well as a record of their political beliefs. The main objective of the Act was to undermine the American Communist Party and other left-wing political groups in the United States. Politicians soon settled on the House Un-American Activities Committee (HUAC), set up in 1938 to investigate unpatriotic behavior, as the best venue to enforce the Alien Registration Act.

After **World War II**, the HUAC began investigating intellectuals, artists, and movie stars, a task assumed by Senator McCarthy in February 1950 when he became chairman of the committee. With the communist takeover in China in 1949 and the onset of the **Korean War** in 1950, the American public felt genuinely frightened by the possibilities of internal subversion. However, McCarthy went further and began attacking government officials as communist infiltrators. For the next two years, Senator McCarthy investigated government agencies and a large number of people about their political past. Some of these people lost their jobs, mostly because of the implication associated with being investigated. This witch hunt and hysteria became known as McCarthyism.

When McCarthy started alleging communist infiltration of the military and the intelligence services, the White House began having doubts about McCarthy's investigations and sought ways to discredit him. The televised hearings also showed McCarthy, according to one newspaper column of the time, to be "evil and unmatched in malice." The Senate passed a motion of censure against Senator McCarthy on

2 December 1954, after which McCarthy lost his power base and his podium for his anticommunist harangues.

McCONE, JOHN ALEX (1902–1991). Named **director of central intelligence** (DCI) on 29 November 1961, about six months after the **Bay of Pigs** fiasco, John A. McCone brought an engineering background and a hands-on management style to his position as DCI.

As an outsider, McCone quickly began asserting his authority by pressuring the White House to reaffirm the DCI's role as the president's principal foreign intelligence advisor and coordinator of the entire U.S. intelligence effort. He also reorganized the **Central Intelligence Agency** (CIA) by, first, establishing a new Directorate of Research (which a year later became the Directorate of Science and Technology) on 19 February 1962, and, second, elevating the comptroller's position and later moving the comptroller as well as those of general counsel, legislative counsel, and audit staff into the Office of the DCI. He also created the position of executive director, who now actually runs and directs the CIA on a day-to-day basis.

DCI McCone, moreover, placed **Operation Mongoose** under a **National Security Council** (NSC) oversight group to prevent what he termed "reckless" activity. As DCI and former chairman of the Atomic Energy Commission (AEC), McCone also took an active part in the committee of senior administration officials that prepared policy recommendations on **arms control** issues. Finally, he undertook several reforms to improve the quality of intelligence products and make intelligence useful to the policymaker.

McCURDY PLAN. The McCurdy Plan refers to legislation proposed in 1992 by Congressman David McCurdy, Democrat from Oklahoma (and simultaneously by Senator **David Boren** of Oklahoma) to reorganize the **intelligence community** (IC). The proposals would have created a director of national intelligence (DNI) removed from the **Central Intelligence Agency** (CIA); reduced the CIA to a **human intelligence** (HUMINT) organization; established a new office for national intelligence analysis; created a national imagery agency responsible for all phases of imagery activity (which actually occurred with the establishment of the **National Imagery and Mapping Agency** [NIMA] in 1996); assigned equivalent responsibilities in the

SIGINT area to the **National Security Agency** (NSA); and eliminated the **National Reconnaissance Office** (NRO). The intelligence community agencies and the secretary of defense opposed the proposals, effectively killing the plan.

MEASUREMENT AND SIGNATURE INTELLIGENCE (MASINT). The newest collection discipline in the repertoire of U.S. intelligence, MASINT is a compendium of techniques rather than an identifiable intelligence collection methodology. The **Department of Defense** (DOD) Instruction Number 5105.58 officially defines MASINT as technically derived intelligence—excluding **signals intelligence** (SIGINT) and traditional **imagery intelligence** (IMINT)—that, when collected, processed, and analyzed results in intelligence that locates, tracks, identifies, or describes the signatures (distinctive characteristics) of fixed or dynamic target sources. MASINT includes the use of ground-based radars; acoustic, seismic, and magnetic geophysical sensors; satellite-based infrared, optical, nuclear radiation, and radio-frequency sensors; remote detection of effluents, debris, and particulate materials; and multi- and hyperspectral imagery. MASINT falls under the guidance of the **director of central intelligence** (DCI) but actually is managed by the Central MASINT Office within the Department of Defense, which provides services to the entire **intelligence community** (IC) on behalf of the DCI.

MEXICAN SPY COMPANY. Also known as the Dominguez Mexican Company, the Mexican spy company was a group of Mexican citizens who offered their services to United States military forces during the Mexican-American War (1846–1848). Headed by Manuel Dominguez, the spy company provided the Americans with information on Mexican military plans and protected American supply lines and communications. Contrary to the popularly held belief that the spy company's members were deserters, historians agree that members of the spy company worked for the Americans because they thought Mexican leaders were corrupt and had abused their power. *See also* TAYLOR, ZACHARY.

MILITARY INTELLIGENCE DIVISION (MID). First established in 1885, the Military Intelligence Division became part of the army general staff established on 26 August 1918 to oversee intelligence production and **counterintelligence** activities. Prior to that date, the army had an assistant chief of staff, G-2, who was charged with intelligence matters. A larger organization, the Military Intelligence Branch (MIB), was organized on 9 February 1918, assuming functions formerly exercised by the military intelligence section of the general staff. All these intelligence units became part of the MID, and the MID was designated G-2 on 16 August 1921.

The Military Intelligence Service (MIS) was established as the operating arm of the MID on 9 March 1942, and on 19 April 1947, the MID and the MIS were incorporated into the Military Intelligence Service. On 27 December 1955, the Pentagon leadership transformed the MIS into the assistant chief of staff for intelligence. On 1 May 1987, this intelligence position received a promotion in rank and was incorporated into the Office of the Deputy Chief of Staff for Intelligence.

MILITARY INTELLIGENCE SERVICE (MIS). *See* MILITARY INTELLIGENCE DIVISION.

MILSTAR (SYSTEM). Milstar is a series of advanced U.S. military communications satellites. The original Milstar program, initiated in the early 1980s, was designed to provide secure communications for strategic and tactical military forces during a nuclear conflict. The first set of satellites was launched in 1995, with replacements following into space beginning in 1999. The latest iterations have improved the original design.

Milstar is the most advanced military communications satellite system to date. The operational Milstar satellite constellation consists of five satellites positioned around the earth in geosynchronous orbits, which are linked to highly mobile ground terminals installed on ships, submarines, vehicles, and aircraft. Because the system is mobile and geographically dispersed, planners believe Milstar can survive a nuclear conflict.

MKULTRA (OPERATION). Operation MKULTRA was a joint **Central Intelligence Agency** (CIA) and **Department of Defense** (DOD) program, initiated in April 1953 to determine the usefulness of mind-control techniques, particularly of drugs, on human behavior by conducting experiments on witting and unwitting participants. The program originated in 1950 and was motivated by Soviet, Chinese, and North Korean use of mind control and brainwashing techniques.

The program was controversial from the start. After the death of an unwitting person (Frank Olson, an army scientist who was given LSD in 1953 and committed suicide a week later), an internal CIA investigation warned that such experimentation was dangerous. Ten years later, a 1963 inspector general report recommended termination of unwitting testing; however, deputy director for plans (DDP) **Richard M. Helms** continued to advocate covert testing on the grounds that the Soviet Union was making strides in this area. Once Richard Helms became **director of central intelligence** (DCI), he was compelled to end unwitting testing on the grounds that it was morally questionable and it risked embarrassing the CIA.

MKULTRA was the subject of investigation by the **Rockefeller Commission** in 1975, the Senate **Church Committee** in 1976, and other entities. The CIA told the Church Committee that MKULTRA involved human experimentation using every research "avenue" listed in the MKULTRA document except for radiation. The CIA also noted that most of the MKULTRA records were deliberately destroyed in 1973 by the order of DCI Helms. In early September 1994, the CIA found a document that asserted that it had explored radiation on humans directly.

Following revelations of MKULTRA and other unethical CIA practices, President **Gerald R. Ford** issued the first executive order on intelligence activities in 1976, which, among other matters, prohibited experimentation with drugs on human subjects, except with informed consent; in writing and witnessed by a disinterested third party; and in accordance with the guidelines issued by the National Commission for the Protection of Human Subjects for Biomedical and Behavioral Research. Subsequent executive orders by Presidents **Jimmy Carter** and **Ronald Reagan** expanded the directive to apply to all human experimentations. Successive DCIs have issued internal guidelines for implementing the executive orders.

MONGOOSE (OPERATION). Operation Mongoose was a **Central Intelligence Agency** (CIA) **covert action** program in 1961–1962 to undermine and overthrow the **Fidel Castro** regime in **Cuba**. First proposed in May 1961, President **John F. Kennedy** authorized the operation in November 1961 under the policy direction of the **5412 Special Group** of the **National Security Council** (NSC). President Kennedy designated General **Edward G. Lansdale**, who had implemented **Operation Gold** in the mid-1950s, to act as chief of operations. Operation Mongoose included a series of disparate but related activities, including **paramilitary** actions, sabotage, and political **propaganda**. President Kennedy terminated Operation Mongoose after the **Cuban Missile Crisis** in October 1962.

MORNING SUMMARY. The morning summary is the **current intelligence** publication of the **Bureau of Intelligence and Research** (INR) in the **Department of State**. INR **coordinates** the summary within the State Department and delivers it to the secretary of state five times a week.

MOUNTAIN (OPERATION). A **covert** program initiated by the **Central Intelligence Agency** (CIA) in the late 1950s and continued well into the 1960s in conjunction with Israel's Mossad to employ its excellent contacts to mount intelligence gathering and influence operations in the Third World. As part of the program, the CIA used Israeli **proprietary companies**, such as the Reynolds Construction Company, to build intelligence communications facilities in **Iran**, Turkey, and Ethiopia. In the 1960s, moreover, the CIA extended the program into other areas of Africa where **Soviet** anticolonial **propaganda** had given it an advantage over the United States. Israel sent agricultural advisors, irrigation specialists, and other experts to African nations to promote economic development, but the CIA and Mossad also provided weapons and internal security training when some African leaders expressed interest in them. Such arrangements provided American and Israeli intelligence excellent opportunities for intelligence gathering. The Israeli proprietary company Zimex Aviation, for example, sold Libyan strongman Muammar Qaddafi an airplane whose crew was comprised entirely of Israeli and American agents. A similar operation was set in place when Ugandan dictator Idi Amin purchased a whole fleet of aircraft from Zimex.

MUJAHIDEEN, AFGHAN. The Afghan mujahideen were loosely allied Islamic and nationalist groups brought together by the common goal of ousting Soviet military forces that had invaded Afghanistan in December 1979. In April 1978, left-leaning Afghan military officers overthrew the centrist government and handed power to two Marxist political parties, the Khalq ("Masses") and Parcham ("Flag"), which together had formed the People's Democratic Party of Afghanistan. Having little popular support, the new government forged close ties with the **Soviet Union**, launched ruthless purges of all domestic opposition, and began extensive land and social reforms that were bitterly resented by the devoutly Muslim and largely anticommunist population.

Muslim tribal-based insurgencies arose against the government, and these uprisings, along with internal fighting and coups between the Khalq and Parcham factions, prompted the invasion of the country by about 30,000 Soviet troops in December 1979 with the aim of propping up the client state. The Soviets initially left the suppression of the rebels to the Afghan army, which was unable to contain the resistance. The war quickly settled down into a stalemate, with about 100,000 Soviet troops controlling the cities, large towns, and major garrisons and the mujahideen roaming relatively freely throughout the countryside. The Soviet military tried to eliminate the mujahideen's civilian support by bombing and depopulating the rural areas, but this tactic sparked a massive flight from the countryside; by 1982 some 2.8 million Afghans had sought asylum in Pakistan, and another 1.5 million had fled to **Iran**.

The mujahideen were eventually able to neutralize Soviet air power through the use of shoulder-fired Stinger antiaircraft missiles supplied by the **Central Intelligence Agency** (CIA). In 1988 the United States, Pakistan, Afghanistan, and the Soviet Union signed an agreement for the withdrawal of Soviet troops and the return of Afghanistan to nonaligned status.

In April 1992, various rebel groups, together with disaffected government troops, stormed the capital of Kabul and ousted the communist president Mohammad Najibullah. A new transitional government, sponsored by various rebel factions, proclaimed an Islamic republic. The extreme Islamist Taliban came to power, and they were in turn ousted by a coalition of U.S.-led military force in 2002. *See also* AL QAI'DA; COVERT ACTION.

MULLIGAN, HERCULES (1740–1825). Hercules Mulligan was a New York City tailor who catered to British officers and thereby collected intelligence information for General **George Washington**. Mulligan also had access to British secrets through British officers billeted in his house. He is credited with informing George Washington of British plans to move into Delaware in April 1777 and with supplying information that helped foil at least two British assassination and capture plots against General Washington.

– N –

NATIONAL COMMISSION ON TERRORIST ATTACKS UPON THE UNITED STATES. Also known as the 9/11 Commission, this independent bipartisan group was established by Congress in 2002 to investigate the events of and circumstances surrounding the **terrorist attacks of 11 September 2001**. The panel heard from members of the administrations of President **William J. Clinton** and President **George W. Bush**, New York City emergency personnel, and victims' families. The commission's final report was released on 22 July 2004. It recommended some important reforms of American intelligence, including the appointment of a national intelligence director and the establishment of a **National Counterterrorism Center** (NCC).

NATIONAL COUNTERINTELLIGENCE EXECUTIVE (NCIX). Established on 1 May 2001 by **presidential decision directive** (PDD) 75, the NCIX has had the mandate to serve as the substantive leader of national-level **counterintelligence** activities. The NCIX coordinates and supports the critical counterintelligence missions of the United States government. It conducts counterintelligence activities to protect the political, economic, and military interests of the United States, including the technology of U.S. business and industry from foreign **espionage**.

NATIONAL COUNTERTERRORISM CENTER (NCC). The NCC was established by President **George W. Bush** on 27 August 2004 as a response to the criticism levied against the George W. Bush administration by the **9/11 Commission**, which investigated the **terrorist attacks of 11 September 2001**. According to the executive order creating the center, the NCC is to be the primary organization within the U.S. government for analyzing and integrating intelligence information pertaining to **terrorism** and counterterrorism. In addition, the NCC is to conduct strategic counterterrorism operational planning by integrating all instruments of national power. It can assign, but not direct, operational responsibilities to lead agencies, and in doing so, the center is to ensure that all agencies have access to and receive needed intelligence to accomplish assigned activities. Finally, the NCC is to serve as the central information repository on all known and suspected terrorists and international terror groups. Accordingly, the executive order charges the NCC with preparing the daily terrorism report for the president and senior officials. The NCC's director now reports to the **director of national intelligence** (DNI). *See also* TERRORISM THREAT INTEGRATION CENTER.

NATIONAL DRUG INTELLIGENCE CENTER (NDIC). Established in 1993 as the nation's principal center for strategic domestic counternarcotics intelligence. A component of the Department of Justice, the NDIC supports national policymakers and law enforcement leaders by producing **threat assessments** based on **open-source intelligence** (OSINT) information from the **intelligence community** (IC) as well as from state and local law enforcement sources. Its assessments focus both on global drug trafficking and on drug trends within each state of the United States. While the bulk of its work centers on narcotics trafficking, the NDIC also provides threat assessments on ancillary issues, such as gang violence.

NATIONAL FOREIGN ASSESSMENT CENTER (NFAC). The **Directorate of Intelligence** (DI) of the **Central Intelligence Agency** (CIA) was renamed in 1978 as NFAC in order to become the analytic arm of the **intelligence community** (IC) and to distance analysis somewhat from the criticisms leveled against U.S. intelligence in the late 1970s. During its short existence, NFAC carried out analytic functions but also absorbed some community-wide organizations like the **Arms Control Intelligence Staff** (ACIS) and the Technology Transfer Assessment Center (TTAC). In 1981, newly appointed **Director of Central Intelligence** (DCI) **William J. Casey** reorganized NFAC into interdisciplinary regional offices and reverted to using its previous designation as **Directorate of Intelligence**.

NATIONAL FOREIGN INTELLIGENCE BOARD (NFIB). *See* COMMITTEE ON IMAGERY REQUIREMENTS AND EXPLOITATION.

NATIONAL FOREIGN INTELLIGENCE PROGRAM (NFIP). One of the three U.S. intelligence budgets, NFIP represents the resources of the **intelligence community** (IC) nominally controlled by the **director of national intelligence** (DNI). NFIP funds national-level, government-wide intelligence programs, such as the Consolidated Cryptologic Program (CCP), which pays for the activities of the **National Security Agency** (NSA) and other **signals intelligence** (SIGINT) programs of other community agencies, and the **General Defense Intelligence Program** (GDIP), which funds the **Defense Intelligence Agency** (DIA). It also includes the **current management account** (CMA), which finances current intelligence operations. The bulk of NFIP pays for **Department of Defense** (DOD) intelligence programs, which, together with the portion allotted to the **Central Intelligence Agency** (CIA), constitute over 95 percent of NFIP moneys. The intelligence components of the civilian agencies represented in the intelligence community absorb less than 5 percent of NFIP. *See also* JOINT MILITARY INTELLIGENCE PROGRAM; TACTICAL INTELLIGENCE AND RELATED ACTIVITIES.

NATIONAL GEOSPATIAL-INTELLIGENCE AGENCY (NGA). Established in November 2003, the NGA replaced the **National Imagery and Mapping Agency** (NIMA) by incorporating **geospatial intelligence**, GEOINT, into its imagery and mapping capabilities. NIMA had been established only in 1996 by consolidating the Defense Mapping Agency (DMA), the **Central Imagery Office** (CIO), the **National Photographic Interpretation Center** (NPIC), the imagery exploitation unit of the **Defense Intelligence Agency** (DIA), and other similar agencies. However, the need to employ geospatial information—complete visualization of geographically referenced areas on the earth—induced **Department of Defense** (DOD) managers to expand NIMA's original jurisdiction. In addition to providing geospatial intelligence, the NGA now manages **imagery intelligence**, or IMINT, in the U.S. government by setting imagery priorities, levying imagery requirements, and analyzing imagery for national customers. Even though it is part of the Defense Department, the NGA serves the entire intelligence community and provides combat support to the military. The secretary of defense and the **director of national intelligence** (DNI) share the management of the NGA, although the DCI retains "tasking" authority over national imagery systems and has a large say over the appointment of the NGA director.

NATIONAL IMAGERY AND MAPPING AGENCY (NIMA). The U.S. National Imagery and Mapping Agency (NIMA) was established 1 October 1996 by the National Imagery and Mapping Agency Act of 1996. NIMA centralized **imagery intelligence** (IMINT) and mapping requirements by incorporating the **National Photographic Interpretation Center** (NPIC), the **Central Imagery Office** (CIO), the Defense Mapping Agency (DMA), the Defense Dissemination Program Office (DDPO), and the imagery capabilities of the **National Reconnaissance Office** (NRO), the **Defense Intelligence Agency** (DIA), and the Defense Airborne Reconnaissance Office (DARO). As such, it merged imagery, maps, charts, and environmental data to produce **geospatial intelligence** (GEOINT). NIMA's products supported a variety of military, civil, and international needs. Under the terms of the 2004 Defense Authorization Bill, NIMA became the **National Geospatial-Intelligence Agency** (NGA) on 24 November 2003. Geospatial intelligence has been employed for a variety of intelligence and civilian purposes, including the monitoring and enforcement of peace treaties.

NATIONAL INFRASTRUCTURE PROTECTION CENTER (NIPC). An interagency center, NIPC was created in 1998 by **Presidential Decision Directive** (PDD) 63 to serve as a focal point for U.S. government efforts to warn about and respond to cyber attacks against the nation's critical infrastructure. These infrastructures include telecommunications and information, energy, banking and finance, transportation, government operations, and emergency services. PDD 63 envisaged NIPC as providing **threat assessments**, warning, vulnerability and law enforcement investigations, and national response. Initially, NIPC was located at the **Federal Bureau of Investigation** (FBI) but was later incorporated into the **Department of Homeland Security** (DHS) upon its establishment in 2002.

NATIONAL INTELLIGENCE AUTHORITY (NIA). Established by presidential directive (PD) on 22 January 1946, the NIA provided executive **oversight** of the **Central Intelligence Group** (CIG), headed by the **director of central intelligence** (DCI). The NIA's members were the secretaries of state, war, navy, and the president's military advisor. An additional directive, dated 8 July 1946, gave the DCI the authority to coordinate intelligence information without actually giving him significant control over existing intelligence agencies or budgetary powers. New intelligence arrangements created by the 1947 **National Security Act** superceded the National Intelligence Authority.

The **Intelligence Reform and Terrorism Prevention Act** of 2004 also created a National Intelligence Authority and placed the newly established **director of national intelligence** (DNI) as its leader. This NIA included all the agencies of the **intelligence community** (IC) except for the **tactical intelligence** organizations of the **Department of Defense** (DOD).

NATIONAL INTELLIGENCE COLLECTION BOARD (NICB). Established on 12 June 1995 as part of the **Community Management Staff** (CMS), the National Intelligence Collection Board, composed of senior officials representing the intelligence collection disciplines and the principal **intelligence community** (IC) production officers, manages the overall intelligence collection requirements process, ensures **coordination** among the major collection disciplines, and evaluates performance in satisfying consumer needs for information. To ensure responsiveness to the current and anticipated information needs of intelligence consumers, the board acts as a forum for integrating the efforts of the separate collection disciplines and issuing guidance to collectors, as appropriate. The board is chaired by the executive director for intelligence community affairs (EXDIR/ICA) or his designee and occasionally meets in subgroups and committees.

NATIONAL INTELLIGENCE COUNCIL (NIC). The NIC is the successor to the **Office of National Estimates** (ONE), which was established in 1950 to produce **national intelligence estimates** (NIEs). **Director of Central Intelligence** (DCI) **William Colby** disbanded the ONE in September 1973 and established the NIC system, comprised of **national intelligence officers** (NIOs) with substantive expertise in their areas of concern. The NIC now has six regional and six issue NIOs who commission and oversee the drafting, production, and dissemination of NIEs under the authority of the **director of national intelligence** (DNI).

NATIONAL INTELLIGENCE DAILY (NID). The NID was the **Central Intelligence Agency's** (CIA's) daily intelligence report to senior- and mid-level government officials from the mid-1960s until the mid-1990s. *See also* SENIOR EXECUTIVE INTELLIGENCE BRIEF.

NATIONAL INTELLIGENCE DIGEST. The National Intelligence Digest was the **Central Intelligence Agency's** (CIA's) daily report to senior- and mid-level government officials during the 1950s and 1960s. *See also* NATIONAL INTELLIGENCE DAILY; SENIOR EXECUTIVE INTELLIGENCE BRIEF.

NATIONAL INTELLIGENCE ESTIMATE (NIE). National intelligence estimates are forward-looking official judgments of the **intelligence community** (IC) on a specific issue, country, or region that address the consequences of various policy options. The **National Intelligence Council** (NIC) has the responsibility to commission and produce NIEs. The NIC's **national intelligence officers** (NIOs) either draft and produce the NIEs themselves or commission them from analysts in the intelligence community. Once drafted, NIOs take charge of **coordinating** the estimate among all the relevant IC agencies, so that the estimate results in community, rather than specific agency, judgments. NIOs attempt to arrive at a consensus, but dissenting views find their way either into the text or into footnotes. The **director of national intelligence** (DNI) signs the coordinated and finished NIE after approval by the **President's Foreign Intelligence Advisory Board** (PFIAB).

NATIONAL INTELLIGENCE OFFICER (NIO). NIOs are senior officials of the **intelligence community** (IC), academia, or business who are chosen for their expertise in substantive areas of importance to U.S. intelligence Now appointed by the **director of national intelligence** (DNI), NIOs comprise the **National Intelligence Council** (NIC), which is responsible for the production of **national intelligence estimates** (NIEs). *See also* COLBY, WILLIAM.

NATIONAL INTELLIGENCE PRODUCTION BOARD (NIPB). Established in 1979, the NIPB now operates under the **National Intelligence Council** (NIC) and is chaired by an associate director of central intelligence. In addition to advising the **director of national intelligence** (DNI) on all production matters, it oversees several **intelligence community** (IC) programs that focus on minimizing unnecessary duplication of effort and maximizing efforts to meet consumer needs. The NIPB consists of the heads of the intelligence community's analytic and production organizations or other appropriate designees. It is the senior intelligence community advisory forum for achieving consensus on analysis and production issues.

NATIONAL MILITARY AUTHORITY. *See* DEPARTMENT OF DEFENSE; INTELLIGENCE REFORM AND TERRORISM PREVENTION ACT.

NATIONAL PHOTOGRAPHIC INTERPRETATION CENTER (NPIC). The NPIC was a joint **Central Intelligence Agency** (CIA) and **Department of Defense** (DOD) unit that analyzed photographic and **imagery intelligence** (IMINT) and produced reports and other products for national-level customers, including the military. First established in 1953 as the Photographic Intelligence Division within the CIA, the unit merged in 1958 with a statistical analysis group to form the Photographic Interpretation Center (PIC). The **National Security Council** (NSC) transformed the PIC into the NPIC in 1961 by requiring it to serve all national-level customers, including those outside the CIA. The CIA's Office of Imagery Analysis continued to serve CIA's needs and often duplicated and competed with the NPIC. The **National Imagery and Mapping Agency** (NIMA) absorbed the NPIC in 1996. Imagery interpretation is now within the jurisdiction of the **National Geospatial-Intelligence Agency** (NGA).

NATIONAL RECONNAISSANCE OFFICE (NRO). The NRO is the manager of America's airborne and space reconnaissance programs. The NRO now contracts for, builds, controls, and uses the hardware that goes into airborne and space reconnaissance. It also constructs and uses sensors for the exploitation of intelligence information from emissions of factories, nuclear power plants, nuclear explosions, and the like, and from foreign military equipment (materiel exploitation). In addition, the NRO manages satellite systems designed to intercept communications from space, a field known as Space SIGINT. As the agency that contracts for and operates vastly expensive satellite and other hardware systems, the NRO probably spends the bulk of the intelligence community's financial resources.

The NRO was established on 25 August 1960 after the White House, the **Central Intelligence Agency** (CIA), the air force, and the **Department of Defense** (DOD) agreed to joint responsibilities for satellite reconnaissance. This agreement was in response to recommendations from a Defense Department panel that such an organization was in the national security interest of the United States, particularly after the 1 May 1960 downing of the **U-2** spy plane piloted by **Francis Gary Powers** over the **Soviet Union.** The decision to form a "national" agency was intended to ensure that the interests of all parties, including the military and civilian intelligence communities, were taken into account. By 1961, the CIA and the air force had established a working relationship for overhead reconnaissance systems through a central administrative office, whose director reported to the secretary of defense but accepted intelligence requirements through the **United States Intelligence Board** (USIB). By informal agreement, the air force provided launchers, bases, and recovery capability for reconnaissance systems, while the CIA was responsible for research, development, contracting, and security.

This arrangement proved unsatisfactory, since it gave the CIA the bigger say in deploying particular systems. Ensuing intense negotiations over control of the NRO resulted in another agreement in 1965 that created a three-person executive committee (EXCOM) to administer overhead reconnaissance. Its members included the **director of central intelligence** (DCI), an assistant secretary of defense, and the president's scientific advisor. The EXCOM reported to the secretary of defense, who was assigned primary administrative authority for overhead reconnaissance systems.

This arrangement recognized the DCI's authority as head of the community to establish collection requirements and to process and utilize data generated by overhead reconnaissance. In the event of disagreements, the DCI could appeal to the president. The agreement represented a compromise that provided substantive recognition of the DCI's national intelligence responsibility.

This arrangement has worked relatively well but has not addressed the bureaucratic competition over technical collection systems. The NRO is actually a federation of intelligence and military organizations that maintain their separate identities and loosely cooperate in the common task of exploiting imagery and other information derived from its collection systems. Because the NRO spends large sums of money on physical assets, each organization eagerly and jealously guards its access to its portion of the reconnaissance pie.

The NRO's existence was a closely held secret for much of its lifetime. In 1994, the White House made public the existence of the NRO, but the organization remains, along with the **National Security Agency** (NSA), one of the least known of the intelligence community agencies.

NATIONAL RESETTLEMENT OPERATIONS CENTER (NROC). A part of the **Central Intelligence Agency** (CIA) that handles defector resettlements.

NATIONAL SECURITY ACT OF 1947. Considered to be the foundation legislation for U.S. intelligence, the 1947 National Security Act created the **Central Intelligence Agency** (CIA) under the authority of the **National Security Council** (NSC), which it also created. It also combined the war and navy departments along with the newly independent air force into a single bureaucratic unit, the **National Military Authority**, and provided for the position of a civilian secretary of defense. It provided for unified military commands but prohibited the merger of the military services into a single force. As amended in 1949, it created the **Department of Defense** (DOD) and institutionalized the **Joint Chiefs of Staff** (JCS).

NATIONAL SECURITY ACT OF 1959. Enacted on 29 May 1959, the legislation allowed the **National Security Agency** (NSA) to provide employment incentives, without regard to the civil service laws, in order to encourage the hiring of scientifically and technically capable individuals. Congress passed the act in the wake of the launching of the **Soviet Sputnik** satellite, which alarmed the U.S. government that the United States was falling behind in technical and scientific education. In order to enable the NSA to compete effectively with the private sector, the act authorized the secretary of defense to set the pay of certain officers in the NSA commensurate with private sector standards.

NATIONAL SECURITY ASSISTANT. *See* ASSISTANT TO THE PRESIDENT FOR NATIONAL SECURITY AFFAIRS.

NATIONAL SECURITY AGENCY (NSA). Established in November 1952, the NSA, America's **cryptologic** organization, manages **signals intelligence** (SIGINT) programs, ensures the safety and confidentiality of government communications, and employs sophisticated technology to break the codes and encryption systems of foreign governments.

The NSA's early work led to the first predecessors of the modern computer and pioneered efforts in flexible storage media, such as the tape cassette. Its research in semiconductors has made the NSA a world leader in many technological fields. As a cryptologic organization, the NSA employs mathematicians, who design American cipher systems and decode adversaries' systems. To remain at the cutting edge of technology, the NSA runs the National Cryptologic School, which trains cryptologists in the latest developments. According to the NSA, the school not only provides unique training for the its workforce, but also serves as a training resource for the entire **Department of Defense** (DOD). It also sends its employees for further education at America's top universities as well as the war colleges.

NATIONAL SECURITY COUNCIL (NSC). Established by the **National Security Act of 1947**, the NSC is at the center of the foreign policy **coordination** system. The act stipulated that the NSC serve as an advisory body under the leadership of the president, with the vice president and secretaries of state and defense as its statutory members. It was to coordinate foreign and defense policy and reconcile diplomatic and military requirements. This mandate over the years gave way to the view that the NSC existed to serve the president alone. In its nearly 60 years of existence, the NSC also has evolved from a body intended to foster collegiality among departments to an elaborate organization that the president could use to manage and control competing agencies.

The NSC organization encompasses the NSC staff, headed by the **assistant to the president for national security affairs** (APNSA), commonly referred to as the national security advisor. The role of the NSC advisor has likewise expanded from advisory to a critical member of the president's foreign and national security policy team.

Historically, the NSC's importance has varied with the amount of attention each president has given it. The **Department of State** dominated President **Harry S. Truman's** NSC, while the military took center stage in President **Dwight D. Eisenhower's** NSC. President **John F. Kennedy**, who preferred interpersonal groups for policymaking, permitted the NSC advisor to take the leading role in coordinating policy but largely ignored the rest of the NSC in policy matters, a course President **Lyndon B. Johnson** pursued with greater vigor than had President Kennedy.

Under Presidents **Richard M. Nixon** and **Gerald R. Ford, Henry A. Kissinger's** expanded NSC acquired a great deal of influence. Dr. Kissinger kept the important issues for himself and devolved the less important to the Department of State and **Department of Defense** (DOD). He also fed President Nixon's desire for formal written expositions rather than interpersonal groupings. Dr. Kissinger at first attempted to restore the separation between policymaking and implementation but eventually found himself personally performing both roles.

Under President **Jimmy Carter**, the national security advisor became a principal source of foreign affairs ideas and the NSC staff was recruited and managed with that in view. The Department of State took the lead and provided institutional memory and served as operations coordinator. The **Ronald Reagan** administration, on the other hand, emphasized a collegial approach to government decision making and allowed the White House chief of staff to supercede the national security advisor in coordinating national security and foreign policy.

President **George H. W. Bush** brought his own considerable foreign policy experience to the NSC, reorganized the council to include a **Principals Committee, Deputies Committee**, and eight **Policy Coordinating Committees**. The NSC played an effective role during such major developments as the collapse of the **Soviet Union**, the unification of Germany, and the deployment of American troops in Iraq and Panama.

The **William J. Clinton** administration continued to emphasize a collegial approach within the NSC on national security matters. The NSC membership was expanded to include the secretary of the treasury, the U.S. representative to the United Nations, the newly created assistant to the president for economic policy, the president's chief of staff, and the national security advisor. President **George W. Bush** continued this emphasis and relied on the NSC structure even more during the difficult years of his administration.

For 60 years, presidents have sought to use the NSC system to integrate foreign and defense policies in order to preserve the nation's security and advance its interests abroad. Recurrent structural modifications over the years have reflected presidential management style, changing requirements, and personal relationships.

NATIONAL SECURITY COUNCIL DIRECTIVE (NSCD) 4-A. Issued in December 1947, the directive assigned responsibility for **covert action** in the emerging **Cold War** to the **Central Intelligence Agency** (CIA), which had been established the previous September. President **Harry S. Truman** and his **national security advisors** had become alarmed over Soviet **psychological warfare** (PSYWAR) operations and, to counter the threat, issued the directive to establish, for the first time in U.S. history, a covert action capability during peacetime. NSCD 4-A made the **director of central intelligence** (DCI) responsible for psychological warfare actions against the nascent **Soviet** threat. However, opposition to the entire idea of psychological operations, led by the **Department of State**, sparked a government-wide debate and led to the issuance of **National Security Council Directive 10/2**, which superceded NSCD 4-A in June 1948.

NATIONAL SECURITY COUNCIL DIRECTIVE (NSCD) 10/2. Issued on 18 June 1948, NSC 10/2 created the semiautonomous **Office of Policy Coordination** (OPC) within the **Central Intelligence Agency** (CIA) to conduct U.S. **covert actions**. It replaced the emphasis on **psychological warfare** (PSYWAR) with the broader concept of covert actions, to include **propaganda**, economic warfare, preventive direct action such as sabotage and demolition, subversion against hostile states, and support of indigenous anticommunist elements in threatened countries. The directive required that covert action be run by the OPC under the guidance, in peacetime, of the **Department of State**, and, in wartime, of the **Department of Defense** (DOD). In addition, NSC 10/2 outlined a convoluted chain of command, nominally under the leadership of **National Security Council** (NSC), State Department, and CIA officials.

In practice, however, **George F. Kennan**, director of the State Department's Policy Planning Staff and, later, the author of the **containment policy**, dominated meetings, claiming that political warfare is essentially an instrument of foreign policy and any office conducting it should function as an agent of the State Department and the military. **Director of Central Intelligence** (DCI) **Roscoe Hillenkoetter** acceded to this view, so long as he was informed of all important projects and decisions. According to some experts, NSC 10/2 was essentially a treaty between the secretaries of state and defense that gave the OPC two competing masters. **National Security Council 68** (NSC 68) eventually superceded NSC 10/2.

NATIONAL SECURITY COUNCIL 68 (NSC 68). NSC 68 was a **National Security Council** (NSC) document produced in April 1950 that defined the course of American foreign policy during the **Cold War**. President **Harry S. Truman** asked for an intensive examination of Soviet military capabilities and intentions in the immediate aftermath of the communist takeover of China and the Soviet test of its atomic bomb in the fall of 1949. The resulting study compared the two powers—the United States and the **Soviet Union**—from military, economic, political, and psychological standpoints. The study defined American national interests largely in moral terms, arguing that America's strategic objectives were morally worthy. However, it identified Soviet interests primarily as retaining and solidifying absolute power, both in the Soviet Union itself and in its satellite countries. It asserted that the Cold War was a real war and envisaged the contest between the U.S. and the **USSR** as one of ideas, in which American fundamental values must dominate. This could be done, according to the document, by enhancing American military readiness and taking actions to foster fundamental change in the nature of the Soviet System. Nuclear war being unacceptable, it advocated a variety of actions to boost American security at home and through bilateral and multilateral negotiations. It also advocated undermining Soviet state power structures by implementing an affirmative program of diplomacy, **covert action**, and military actions. *See also* CONTAINMENT POLICY.

NATIONAL SECURITY DECISION DIRECTIVE (NSDD). NSDDs were policy instructions and guidance issued to the foreign policy and national security agencies during the **Ronald Reagan** administration. *See also* NATIONAL SECURITY DIRECTIVE; NATIONAL SECURITY PRESIDENTIAL DIRECTIVE; PRESIDENTIAL DECISION DIRECTIVE.

NATIONAL SECURITY DECISION DIRECTIVE (NSDD) 17.
Dated 4 January 1982, NSDD 17 gave the **Central Intelligence Agency** (CIA) approval to provide military assistance to the Nicaraguan **Contra** rebels. It also authorized economic support to Central American and Caribbean countries in order to counter "the actions by **Cuba**, Nicaragua, and others to introduce into Central America heavy weapons, troops from outside the region, trained subversives, or arms and military supplies for insurgents." *See also* BOLAND AMENDMENTS.

NATIONAL SECURITY DECISION MEMORANDUM (NSDM) 93. A classified document issued by the **National Security Council** (NSC) in November 1970, titled "Policy Toward Chile," that supplanted **Operation FUBELT**. The document called for maximum pressure on President **Salvador Allende** and his government to prevent its consolidation by isolating, weakening, and destabilizing Chile until the country became ungovernable. It also envisaged intense economic destabilization and diplomatic efforts to turn other Latin American countries against Chile. An annex to the document provided for **Central Intelligence Agency** (CIA) intervention, specifically by using the newspaper *El Mercurio* to conduct a massive **propaganda** campaign. NSDM 93 became part of Track I, which called for a destabilization campaign. Track II, developed a few years later, envisaged the overthrow of the Allende government. *See also* KISSINGER, HENRY A.

NATIONAL SECURITY DIRECTIVE (NSD). NSDs were policy instructions and guidance issued to foreign policy and national security agencies during the administration of **George H. W. Bush**. *See also* NATIONAL SECURITY DECISION DIRECTIVE; NATIONAL SECURITY PRESIDENTIAL DIRECTIVE; PRESIDENTIAL DECISION DIRECTIVE.

NATIONAL SECURITY EDUCATION PROGRAM (NSEP). The National Security Education Program (NSEP) was initiated by Senator **David L. Boren's** National Security Education Act of 1991. The act created the National Security Education Board to oversee a trust fund in the U.S. Treasury to provide resources for scholarships, fellowships, and grants. The rationale was to develop a national capacity by educating

U.S. citizens to understand foreign cultures, strengthen U.S. economic competitiveness, and enhance international cooperation and security. The NSEP was designed to provide American students with the resources and encouragement they need to acquire skills and experience in countries and areas of the world crucial to the future security of the U.S.

NATIONAL SECURITY PRESIDENTIAL DIRECTIVE (NSPD). NSPDs were the policy instruments for conveying presidential decisions and guidance to the foreign policy and national security agencies during the administration of **George W. Bush**. President Bush also initiated the homeland security presidential directive (HSPD), which serves the same role in the homeland security area. Although classified, brief synopses of the NSPDs are available to the public. *See also* NATIONAL SECURITY DECISION DIRECTIVE; NATIONAL SECURITY DIRECTIVE; PRESIDENTIAL DECISION DIRECTIVE.

NATIONAL SECURITY THREAT LIST (NSTL). The **Federal Bureau of Investigation** (FBI) established the National Security Threat List in 1991 to set out the bureau's foreign **counterintelligence** mission. It includes national security issues as well as a classified list of foreign powers that pose a strategic intelligence threat to U.S. security interests.

By creating the National Security Threat List, the FBI changed its approach from defending against hostile intelligence agencies to protecting U.S. information and technologies. It identified all countries—not just hostile intelligence services—that pose a continuing and serious intelligence threat to the United States. It also defined expanded threat issues, including the proliferation of chemical, biological, and nuclear weapons; the loss of critical technologies; and the improper collection of trade secrets and proprietary information. This portion of the list was developed in concert with the **intelligence community** (IC).

NATIONAL TECHNICAL INFORMATION SERVICE (NTIS). The National Technical Information Service, part of the Department of Commerce, produces and disseminates information about economic and ancillary issues important to U.S. national security. Covering a broad range of subject matter, its reports bridge the gap between the government and the private sector. In the national security area, the NTIS publishes reports on a variety of technical subjects and disseminates the unclassified publications of intelligence agencies.

NATIONAL TECHNICAL MEANS. "National technical means" refers to the aggregate of technological methodologies for collecting intelligence information. Examples of national technical means are: intercepting diplomatic communications (**signals intelligence**— SIGINT), imaging target areas of the earth from orbiting satellites (**imagery intelligence**—IMINT), and analyzing emissions from smoke stacks (**Measurement and Signature Intelligence**— MASINT). National technical means also includes the collection of intelligence by means of sensors.

NAVY INTELLIGENCE. *See* OFFICE OF NAVAL INTELLIGENCE.

NEGATIVE INTELLIGENCE. Negative intelligence is information for countering a threat or manipulating foreign events. Negative intelligence may include **propaganda**, **counterintelligence**, forgery, and **denial/deception operations**.

NEGROPONTE, JOHN D. (1939–). John D. Negroponte was appointed in February 2005 by President **George W. Bush** to be America's first **director of national intelligence** (DNI). The position of the DNI was created by the **Intelligence Reform and Terrorism Prevention Act**, passed by Congress in December 2004, at the insistence of the families of the victims of the 9/11 terrorist attacks and the independent **9/11 Commission** that investigated those attacks. The position was established to unify America's sprawling **intelligence community** (IC) of 15 agencies and to provide them greater incentives to cooperate with one another in the fight against **terrorism** and other significant threats against the United States. Negroponte brings substantial expertise in the political maneuverings of the U.S. government but little intelligence experience to his new assignment.

DNI Negroponte is a career American diplomat, having spent nearly 40 years in America's foreign service. His last assignment was as Ambassador to Iraq, when the United States transferred sovereignty to the Iraqi government in spring 2004. His long career included service as U.S. Ambassador to the United Nations, Philippines, Mexico, and Honduras, but in between official assignments, he also had occasion to work in the private sector and as deputy national security advisor during the administration of **William J. Clinton**. Negroponte began his foreign service career in the early 1960s, serving in Hong Kong and Vietnam, later becoming a key advisor to **National Security Advisor Henry A. Kissinger**, with whom he eventually clashed during the Paris peace negotiations over the insufficient protections provided to the beleaguered government of South Vietnam.

NICARAGUA. *See* CONTRAS; IRAN-CONTRA AFFAIR; NEGRO-PONTE, JOHN D.; *NICARAGUA v. UNITED STATES.*

NICARAGUA v. UNITED STATES. During the administration of **Ronald Reagan** in the 1980s, the United States actively supported the **Contra** insurgency against the leftist **Sandinista** regime in Nicaragua. As part of its support, President Reagan authorized the **Central Intelligence Agency** (CIA) to assist the Contras and conduct covert operations against the Sandinistas. Nicaragua brought charges against the United States before the International Court of Justice (ICJ) in The Hague, Netherlands, claiming substantial injury from the covert operations. The Reagan administration in turn invoked its right not to be a party to the suit and revoked U.S. acceptance of the optional clause, first with regard to lawsuits on Central America and later for any and all disputes. The United States also refused to appear before the court during the final hearings on the merits and never recognized the ICJ rulings as binding.

The United States maintained that security issues are nonjusticiable and that Nicaragua never properly accepted the optional clause. The U.S. delegation also filed an affirmative defense for its activities in Nicaragua under the theory of collective self-defense. The ICJ, however, rejected this argument and refused to review countercomplaints filed by both the United States and El Salvador regarding Nicaraguan violations of international law in the form of active Sandinista support for Salvadoran rebels. It awarded Nicaragua an unspecified but potentially tremendous level of damages, estimated to be as large as $17 billion.

Subsequently, the United States viewed the ICJ with active hostility and distrust and has never reinstated its acceptance of the optional clause. After the civil war, Nicaragua formally withdrew its ICJ case in 1991, thereby abandoning all claims to the judgment. It did so only under intense pressure from the **George H. W. Bush** administration, which made future U.S. aid to Nicaragua contingent on renunciation of the case. *See also* NATIONAL SECURITY DECISION DIRECTIVE 17.

NICHOLSON, HAROLD (1950–). Harold Nicholson was an officer of the **Central Intelligence Agency** (CIA) arrested by the **Federal Bureau of Investigation** (FBI) on 16 November 1996 for spying for Russia. Nicholson is reputed to be the highest ranking CIA officer charged with **espionage** to date. During the period of his espionage, he passed a wide range of highly classified information to Russia, including biographic information on every CIA case officer trained between 1994 and 1996 and highly sensitive **counterintelligence** information that included a summary report of interviews with **Aldrich Ames**, another CIA employee who spied for the Russians. He also compromised the identities of U.S. and foreign businesspeople who provided information to the CIA.

According to investigators, he "hacked" into the CIA computer system and provided the Russians with every secret that he could steal. Nicholson received approximately $120,000 from Russian intelligence. On 3 March 1997, Nicholson pleaded guilty, admitting he had been a Russian spy. On 6 June 1997, he was sentenced to 23 years and seven months, a much reduced sentence because of his cooperation with the investigators regarding the material he had compromised.

9/11 ATTACKS. *See* TERRORIST ATTACKS OF 11 SEPTEMBER 2001.

9/11 COMMISSION. *See* NATIONAL COMMISSION ON TERRORIST ATTACKS UPON THE UNITED STATES.

NIXON, RICHARD MILHOUS (1913–1994). The 34th president of the United States between 1969 and 1974. A controversial politician for most of his life, President Nixon was the first chief executive to resign from office because of a scandal. A conservative politician and vice president to President **Dwight D. Eisenhower**, President Nixon was almost obsessive about world stability. To that end, he established relations with the **People's Republic of China** (PRC) and sought to reduce tensions with the **Soviet Union**. His summit meetings with Soviet leader Leonid I. Brezhnev produced a treaty to limit strategic nuclear weapons. He pursued peace negotiations to end the **Vietnam War**, and, in January 1973, he announced an accord with North Vietnam to end American involvement in Indochina. Moreover, his secretary of state, **Henry A. Kissinger**, negotiated disengagement agreements in 1974 between Israel and its opponents, Egypt and Syria, arising out of the 1973 war.

After the 1972 election, the Nixon administration was embroiled in the **Watergate scandal**, stemming from a break-in at the offices of the Democratic National Committee during the 1972 campaign. The break-in was traced to officials of the Committee to Reelect the President. A number of administration officials resigned; some were later convicted of offenses connected with efforts to cover up the affair. President Nixon denied any personal involvement, but the courts forced him to yield tape recordings that indicated that he had, in fact, tried to divert the investigation. Faced with what seemed almost certain impeachment, President Nixon announced on 8 August 1974 that he would resign the next day to begin "that process of healing which is so desperately needed in America." His resignation allowed Vice President **Gerald R. Ford** to assume the presidency.

NONPROLIFERATION TREATY (NPT). The NPT was an **arms control** agreement negotiated in the late 1960s to prevent the spread of nuclear weapons and weapons technology, to promote cooperation in the peaceful uses of nuclear energy, and to foster an environment for nuclear disarmament. The NPT remains the only international agreement committed to disarming nonnuclear states. Opened for signature in 1968, the treaty went into force on 5 March 1970, and to date over 185 nations have signed the pact.

The NPT provides for two categories of states. Nuclear weapons states—the United States, Russia, the **People's Republic of China** (PRC), France, and the United Kingdom—commit themselves not to spread nuclear weapons or weapons technology to states that do not possess them. Nonnuclear weapons states commit themselves to forego developing or acquiring nuclear weapons. The treaty also tasks the International Atomic Energy Agency (IAEA) with the inspection of nonnuclear states' nuclear facilities and establishes safeguards for the transfer of fissionable materials between nuclear weapons states and nonnuclear weapons states. Nonnuclear states retain the right to research, develop, and use nuclear energy for nonweapons purposes. Finally, the NPT commits the nuclear weapons states to end the nuclear arms race and to seek a treaty on general and complete disarmament under strict and effective international control.

The NPT envisaged a review 25 years after coming into force. Signatory parties met on 11 May 1995 and agreed to extend the treaty indefinitely despite charges by some nonnuclear weapons states that the treaty creates a discriminatory regime that works to the detriment of nonpossessing states. The role of U.S. intelligence concerning the NPT is limited to verifying compliance with its provisions.

NORTH ATLANTIC TREATY ORGANIZATION (NATO). Established by treaty on 4 April 1949, NATO was designed to be a collective defense arrangement to counter perceived **Soviet** expansionist goals in Europe at the beginning of the **Cold War**. NATO's founding states were: Belgium, Canada, Denmark, France, Iceland, Italy, Luxembourg, the Netherlands, Norway, Portugal, the United Kingdom, and the United States. Four more states joined NATO in subsequent years: Greece (1952), Turkey (1952), Germany (1955), and Spain (1982). During the 40 years of East-West confrontation, NATO also evolved into a club of democratic states.

Following the end of the Cold War, 10 East European states, most former members of the **Warsaw Pact**, joined NATO: the Czech Republic (1999), Poland (1999), Hungary (1999), Estonia (2004), Lithuania (2004), Latvia (2004), Romania (2004), Slovakia (2004), Slovenia (2004), and Bulgaria (2004).

NORTH, OLIVER LAURENCE (1943–). Oliver North, a Marine Corps lieutenant colonel, acquired notoriety in the mid-1980s for his role in the **Iran-Contra Affair**. North, at the time a staff member of the **National Security Council** (NSC), directed a network of former military and intelligence officials and businesspeople in the resupply of the **Contra** rebels in Nicaragua. He was also implicated in the sale of weapons to **Iran** to raise the money for assistance to the Contras. The operations, conducted outside the normal **covert action** channels of the **Central Intelligence Agency** (CIA) in contravention of the law, had their own personnel, equipment, communications, and secret bank accounts. North was convicted in 1989 on criminal charges for his role in the affair, but his conviction later was overturned because the prosecution at the trial had used congressional testimony that had received immunity. North has since had a career as a talk-show host and conservative columnist. In 1994 he ran unsuccessfully for the U.S. senate, from Virginia.

– O –

OCTOBER SURPRISE. The October surprise refers to allegations in the early 1980s that **William Casey**, Republican presidential candidate **Ronald Reagan's** campaign chief in 1980, worked to delay the release of the American hostages held by Islamic militants in **Iran** in order to prevent Democratic presidential candidate **Jimmy Carter** from arranging a release in October 1980, just prior to the general election. However, there appears to be no evidence to corroborate the charges, which remain unproven. William Casey went on to become President Reagan's **director of central intelligence** (DCI).

OFFICE OF INTELLIGENCE (DEPARTMENT OF ENERGY). The Department of Energy's (DOE) Office of Intelligence is the **intelligence community's** (IC's) premier intelligence resource in nuclear weapons and nonproliferation technologies, energy security, nuclear safety, and nuclear waste disposal. DOE's Office of Intelligence also taps the DOE's national laboratories to provide timely analytic assessments to the national policy community, as well as specialized technological applications and operational support to the intelligence, law enforcement, and military communities.

Regulating nuclear energy dates back to the Manhattan Project, which produced the first atomic bomb. The DOE's predecessor, the Atomic Energy Commission (AEC), initially provided specialized analysis of the nascent atomic weapons program of the **Soviet Union**. By the 1970s, that program—like the functions of the old AEC—had come to reside within the DOE.

OFFICE OF INTELLIGENCE SUPPORT (TREASURY DEPARTMENT). The Treasury Department's Office of Intelligence Support openly collects financial and monetary data from around the globe and subjects this information to analysis for government and business consumers. Treasury intelligence, a member of the **intelligence community** (IC), also seeks intelligence information about technology transfers and the spread of weapons technology. As such, it is an important element in identifying money flows, collecting trade information, ferreting out money laundering schemes, and distributing licensing data.

OFFICE OF NATIONAL ESTIMATES (ONE). Established by **Director of Central Intelligence** (DCI) **Walter Bedell Smith** in 1950, the ONE's mandate was to produce and disseminate **national intelligence estimates** (NIEs). DCI **William Colby** disbanded the ONE and created the **National Intelligence Council** (NIC) system in September 1973.

OFFICE OF NAVAL INTELLIGENCE (ONI). America's premier source for maritime intelligence, the ONI employs civilian and military personnel around the world in support of navy operational commanders and war fighters. The ONI is also the nation's oldest continuously operating intelligence service. Located in the Federal Center in Suitland, Maryland, the National Maritime Intelligence Center (NMIC) is the home and nerve center of the ONI. The NMIC also supports the **Coast Guard** Intelligence Coordination Center, the Naval Information Warfare Activity, and the Marine Corps Intelligence Activity (MCIA).

The ONI was established on 23 March 1882 to seek and report on global maritime technological developments. Naval attachés and military affairs officers soon began a systematic collection of technical information about foreign governments and their naval advancements. Reports of foreign technology advances circulated between the various bureaus of the navy, stimulating new interest in naval matters.

During the **Spanish-American War of 1898**, the ONI provided vital information about Spanish fleet capabilities as well as details about harbor defenses that had great value in shaping naval strategy. By the time the nation entered **World War I** in 1917, the ONI was the recognized authority on technical information to help improve fleet capabilities. While the ONI had few responsibilities in war planning, it took on new responsibilities for all aspects of physical security for installations, security checks for navy personnel, censorship, and ferreting out spies and saboteurs. Following the war, the navy was scaled down, but the primary duties for the collecting, evaluating, and disseminating of information were retained on a temporary basis. The Chief of Naval Operations in 1929 made these functions permanent.

As the world slid into another world war, the ONI assumed responsibilities in disseminating decrypted Japanese materials. The decoding function was controlled by navy's Office of Communication, but the translation, evaluation, and dissemination fell to the ONI. The two functions eventually were combined into one unit. Breaking the Japanese naval code was a major breakthrough, but it did not come in time to prevent the surprise attack on the fleet in **Pearl Harbor** on the morning of 7 December 1941. The navy did use the Japanese intercepts to score a major victory at Midway in June 1942. Despite demobilization and downsizing following **World War II**, the ONI continued to play an important role in the **Cold War** and after, from Korea all the way to the invasion of Iraq in 2004.

OFFICE OF POLICY COORDINATION (OPC). Established on 1 September 1948 by **National Security Council Directive 10/2**, a directive of the **National Security Council** (NSC) issued on 18 June 1948, the OPC was given responsibility for organizing and managing **covert actions**. NSC 10/2 specified that the OPC, although within the bureaucratic structure of the **Central Intelligence Agency** (CIA), was to take its guidance from the **Department of State** in peacetime and the **Department of Defense** (DOD) in wartime. The OPC's relatively autonomous existence continued until 1950, when the arrangement was modified to ensure that policy guidance came through the **director of central intelligence** (DCI). NSC 10/5, issued in October 1951, reaffirmed the CIA's covert action mandate, thereby placing the OPC squarely within the CIA, and expanded the CIA's authority over guerrilla warfare. The OPC merged with the CIA's Office of Special Operations (OSO) in 1952 to form the **Directorate of Plans** (DP), predecessor of the **Directorate of Operations** (DO).

OFFICE OF RESEARCH AND ANALYSIS (ORA). Predecessor of the **Directorate of Intelligence** (DI) in the **Central Intelligence Agency** (CIA), the ORA was established in the early 1950s to produce and disseminate intelligence analyses to mid- and senior-level decision makers.

OFFICE OF STRATEGIC SERVICES (OSS). Established on 13 June 1942 to replace the coordinator of information (COI), the OSS was America's wartime intelligence and sabotage organization. Headed by **William J. Donovan**, the OSS was placed under the jurisdiction of the **Joint Chiefs of Staff** (JCS), and its personnel came from all the branches of the armed forces as well as civilians. "Wild Bill" Donovan was not too keen on intelligence analyses but wanted the OSS to support military operations in the field by providing research, **propaganda**, and commando support.

OSS "cloak and dagger" operations focused on actions behind enemy lines as well as liaison with the underground in Nazi-occupied countries. Despite Donovan's preoccupation with the action-oriented part of the OSS, some of the most valuable work was done by the research and analysis (R&A) section, which was headed by Harvard historian **William L. Langer**.

Even in wartime, **coordination** of intelligence remained a problem in Washington. The **Pearl Harbor** disaster underscored the problems with interservice cooperation. The army and navy **signals intelligence** (SIGINT) organizations barely cooperated, jealously guarding their reports and their access to President **Franklin D. Roosevelt**. They also prevented intelligence analysts from reading signals intelligence at all. Outside the White House, no one collated and analyzed the totality of the intelligence data collected by the U.S. government. This lack of government-wide coordination limited the success of intelligence analysis and prompted efforts to reform the intelligence establishment after the war. The OSS was disbanded in 1945. In 1946, many of its functions were transferred to the **Central Intelligence Group** (CIG), and, in 1947, to the **Central Intelligence Agency** (CIA).

OPEN-SOURCE INTELLIGENCE (OSINT). OSINT is intelligence information collected from overt sources, such as newspapers, books, journals, and similar publications. Because it is widely available, OSINT is easy to collect but often difficult to use. For one thing, the sheer volume of open-source information makes it difficult to separate the wheat from the chaff. For another, intelligence analysts, accustomed as they are to relying on classified sources, are suspicious of the reliability of open-source materials. During the **Cold War**, only about 20 percent of intelligence information about the **Soviet Union** came from open sources. Following the Cold War, over 80 percent of intelligence information about Russia has come from open sources.

OPERATION AJAX. *See* AJAX (OPERATION).

OPERATION CHAOS. *See* CHAOS (OPERATION).

OPERATION COLDFEET. *See* COLDFEET (OPERATION).

OPERATION CONDOR. *See* CONDOR (OPERATION).

OPERATION DEEP BLUE. *See* DEEP BLUE (OPERATION).

OPERATION EAGLE CLAW. *See* EAGLE CLAW (OPERATION).

OPERATION FEATURE. *See* FEATURE (OPERATION).

OPERATION FUBELT. *See* FUBELT (OPERATION).

OPERATION FU GO. *See* GENETRIX (OPERATION).

OPERATION GENETRIX. *See* GENETRIX (OPERATION).

OPERATION GOLD. *See* GOLD (OPERATION).

OPERATION HISTORY. *See* HISTORY (OPERATION).

OPERATION IVY BELLS. *See* IVY BELLS (OPERATION).

OPERATION MKULTRA. *See* MKULTRA (OPERATION).

OPERATION MONGOOSE. *See* MONGOOSE (OPERATION).

OPERATION MOUNTAIN. *See* MOUNTAIN (OPERATION).

OPERATION PHOENIX. *See* PHOENIX (OPERATION).

OPERATION RAINBOW. *See* RAINBOW (OPERATION).

OPERATION RED SOX/RED CAP. *See* RED SOX/RED CAP (OPERATION).

OPERATION SENIOR BOWL. *See* TAGBOARD (OPERATION).

OPERATION SHAMROCK. *See* SHAMROCK (OPERATION).

OPERATION STAR GATE. *See* STAR GATE (OPERATION).

OPERATION SUCCESS. *See* SUCCESS (OPERATION).

OPERATION TAGBOARD. *See* TAGBOARD (OPERATION).

OPERATION TROPIC. *See* TROPIC (OPERATION).

OPERATION TRUST. *See* TRUST (OPERATION).

OPERATION VEIL. *See* VEIL (OPERATION).

OPERATION VENONA. *See* VENONA (OPERATION).

OPERATION WINTELPRO. *See* WINTELPRO (OPERATION).

OPERATION WINTER HARVEST. *See* WINTER HARVEST (OPERATION).

OPERATION ZAPATA. *See* BAY OF PIGS INVASION.

OPERATIONS ADVISORY GROUP. Established by President **Gerald R. Ford's** Executive Order 11905, dated 18 February 1976, the Operations Advisory Group of the **National Security Council** (NSC) was set up to review and approve **covert action** programs. The group replaced President **Richard M. Nixon's 40 Committee**, which had engaged in similar functions since 1969.

OVERSIGHT. *See* INTELLIGENCE OVERSIGHT.

– P –

PARAMILITARY OPERATIONS. *See* COVERT ACTION.

PEARL HARBOR. The harbor in Hawaii, which is home base for the U.S. Pacific fleet, has the dubious distinction of being the place where Japanese military forces launched an attack on the United States on 7 December 1941. The name of the base, moreover, has come to be synonymous with surprise attack. Experts consider the event the first major American intelligence failure that fueled the reorganization of the national security apparatus after **World War II** and sparked the creation of the **Central Intelligence Agency** (CIA) in 1947. As a result of the attack, the United States declared war on Japan on 8 December 1941.

In a postmortem assessment, a special commission appointed by President **Franklin D. Roosevelt** accused the army and navy commanders at Hawaii of dereliction of duty in a report on 24 January 1942. However, a congressional committee, formed in September 1945, absolved the army and navy commanders in a formal report on 16 July 1946, but censured the War Department as well as the Department of the Navy.

PENKOVSKY, OLEG VLADIMIROVICH (1919–1963). Oleg V. Penkovsky possibly was the most important spy for the United States in the **Soviet Union** during the **Cold War**. A Soviet **GRU** officer and mole within the Soviet High Command, Penkovsky provided information that revealed that Soviet missile capabilities were inferior to those of the United States and that Soviet premier **Nikita S. Khrushchev** was bluffing when he threatened nuclear war during the 1962 **Cuban Missile Crisis**. Moreover, Penkovsky's information gave the **Central Intelligence Agency** (CIA) a good idea of the time it would take to make Soviet nuclear missiles in Cuba operational. Intelligence experts consider Penkovsky's information to have been so critical during the crisis that they have dubbed him "the spy who saved the world." Penkovsky also revealed that Moscow could not put pressure on Berlin during the Berlin Crisis of 1961.

Penkovsky was arrested on 22 October 1962, while the Cuban Missile Crisis was under way. He was tried on charges of **espionage** and was convicted. Soviet authorities executed him in May 1963.

PHILBY, HAROLD (KIM) (1912–1988). The privileged son of a British diplomat, Harold "Kim" Philby became one of the most famous spies of the 20th century when he defected to the **Soviet Union** in 1963, after a career in British intelligence. A student at Cambridge in the 1930s, Philby was drawn to Marxist ideas and was an associate of what came to be known as "The Cambridge Spies"—Guy Burgess, Donald Maclean, and Anthony Blunt. Burgess, Maclean, and Philby were apparently recruited in the 1930s to be Soviet spies, possibly by Blunt. In the 1940s they began working for Britain's Secret Intelligence Service (SIS), quickly rising in the ranks, and in the early 1950s, Philby became the liaison officer in Washington with the **Central Intelligence Agency** (CIA) and the **Federal Bureau of Investigation** (FBI). In 1951, Philby fell under suspicion and was recalled to London. There he successfully resisted interrogation. When the SIS refused to reinstate him, he went to the Lebanon as a freelance intelligence agent, under **cover** as a journalist.

In 1963, defector **Anatoly Golitsyn** named Philby as a Soviet agent, and a fellow SIS officer went to Beirut to persuade him to confess to his work for the **KGB**. Instead, Philby boarded a Soviet freighter and fled to Moscow, where he spent the rest of his life.

PHOENIX (OPERATION). The Phoenix operation was a counterinsurgency project undertaken by the **Central Intelligence Agency** (CIA) and the army during the **Vietnam War** to identify and root out the secret communist guerrilla infrastructure in South Vietnam. The operation called for the Americans to provide training, advice, weapons, and money to the South Vietnamese forces. It also authorized the Americans to help the South Vietnamese identify communists and communist sympathizers, who would then be neutralized by the South Vietnamese authorities. However, the operation quickly soured as indiscriminate raids were launched, villagers were rounded up and tortured, and those thought to be communists quickly executed.

PHOTOGRAPHIC INTELLIGENCE (PHOTINT). *See* IMAGERY INTELLIGENCE.

PIKE COMMITTEE. *See* SELECT COMMITTEE ON INTELLIGENCE TO INVESTIGATE ALLEGATIONS OF ILLEGAL OR IMPROPER ACTIVITIES OF FEDERAL INTELLIGENCE AGENCIES.

PINKERTON, ALLAN (1810–1884). Allan Pinkerton was an American detective and a pioneer of U.S. intelligence during the **Civil War**. Born in Glasgow, Scotland, Pinkerton immigrated to the United States in 1842, settled in Chicago, and opened a detective agency in 1850 that evolved into his famous National Detective Agency in 1852. He provided security for many of the railroad companies that were laying track to the American West in the 1840s and 1850s. At the beginning of the Civil War, Pinkerton claimed to have unearthed an assassination plot against President **Abraham Lincoln**.

During the war, Pinkerton offered to set up an intelligence service for the Union side, but nothing came of his proposal. Union general George McClellan subsequently asked Pinkerton to set up a private intelligence service to spy on the Confederacy, and Pinkerton did so. Although he considered himself a master-spy and was fond of extolling his own intelligence virtues, Pinkerton's intelligence often was inaccurate and many of his agents proved to be failures. However, he had some successes in unearthing Confederate **espionage**. For example, he is credited with catching Confederate spy **Rose O'Neal Greenhow**.

When General McClellan was relieved of command in 1862, Pinkerton returned to his detective business, providing security for the railroads. Some experts believe that Pinkerton developed the **Secret Service** out of his own organization, under the assumed name of Major E. J. Alien, but there is contradictory evidence on this score.

After a stroke in 1869, Pinkerton left the management of his detective agency to his sons and focused on writing several books, which extolled his achievements as an intelligence master sleuth.

PINOCHET, AUGUSTO (1915–). General Augusto Jose Ramon Pinochet Ugarte was the head of the military government that ruled Chile from 1973 until 1990. Pinochet came to power with the ouster of President **Salvador Allende** on 11 September 1973 and quickly consolidated power by organizing a military junta, which proclaimed Pinochet president on 27 June 1974. Pinochet's government instituted market-oriented economic policies and set out systematically to repress its political opponents though mass arrests and murders. No one really knows how many people "disappeared" for opposing the Pinochet government, but estimates run into several thousand. Despite repression, opposition to the Pinochet government during the 1980s grew to such an extent that Pinochet was compelled to schedule a plebiscite on 5 October 1988, which went against his government. The general left the presidency on 11 March 1990 but continued as the commander in chief of the army. In 1998, while traveling abroad, Pinochet was arrested on a Spanish warrant of torturing Spanish citizens, but the British court refused to extradite him on humanitarian grounds. Pinochet returned to Chile, and on 20 July 2004, a Chilean court began an investigation into the origins of Pinochet's funds for fraud, misappropriation of official money, and bribery.

PLAUSIBLE DENIAL. Plausible denial refers to a **cover** story employed to deflect attribution from the United States government, especially the president, for covert intelligence activities. Prior to the imposition of the **finding** requirement, most **covert actions** contained elements of plausible deniability. However, the finding process, which requires the president to certify over his signature that the covert action is in the national interest of the United States, has made plausible denial redundant. Covert action programs must still maintain secrecy, but findings now attribute covert operations directly to the president.

PLOUGHSHARES (PROGRAM). The Ploughshares program was intended to explore the nonmilitary uses of explosive nuclear devices.

Approved by the Atomic Energy Commission (AEC) on 27 June 1957, the program sought to explore Canada's Athabasca oil sands (Oil Sands Project) by using nuclear detonations below ground, but disagreements between the United States and Canada eventually killed the project. The nuclear testing moratorium from 1958 until 1961 also slowed the program down, but the U.S. detonated 35 nuclear devices between December 1961 and May 1973. One such detonation, on 10 December 1967, was targeted at the stimulation of low productivity, low permeability gas fields (Project Gasbuggy). Other projects, such as the exploitation of oil shale, never got off the ground. The U.S. government discontinued the program in 1975. Overall, the Ploughshares program did not yield any significant results in terms of developing alternative sources of petroleum and other fossil fuels.

POLICY COORDINATING COMMITTEES. Policy coordinating committees were the **National Security Council's** (NSC's) **interagency working groups** (IWGs) during the presidency of **George H. W. Bush**. Policy Coordinating Committees assumed regional and functional responsibilities in place of the multiple interagency groups of the **Ronald Reagan** era. NSC policy papers were named national security review papers (NSRs) and **national security directives** (NSDs) to distinguish them from the Reagan era documentation. Presidents **William J. Clinton** and **George W. Bush** have continued the use of policy coordinating committees in their NSCs. The committees coordinate the implementation of policy decided at the NSC's higher levels. *See also* DEPUTIES COMMITTEE; NATIONAL SECURITY COUNCIL; PRINCIPALS COMMITTEE.

POLLARD, JONATHAN (1954–). A **navy intelligence** analyst, Pollard was convicted and sentenced to life imprisonment on 4 March 1987 for spying for Israel. Pollard reportedly began his **espionage** activities in 1982 out of the belief that the U.S. government was not doing enough to support the government of Israel. He leaked thousands of pages of classified information to the Israelis, later claiming that he provided only information he believed was vital to Israeli security and was being withheld by the United States—data on Soviet arms shipments to Syria, Iraqi and Syrian chemical weapons, the Pakistani nuclear bomb project, and Libyan air defense systems.

Initially, the Israeli government denied knowing of or employing Jonathan Pollard. Subsequently, the Israelis apologized for the affair and asserted that the operation was unauthorized. Repeated appeals to the president of the United States by some Jewish groups for a pardon or clemency have consistently been turned down.

POLYGRAPH. Commonly known as the lie detector, polygraph testing is widely used in the **intelligence community** (IC) to screen employees, to establish eligibility for access to classified intelligence information, and for general **counterintelligence** purposes. The **Central Intelligence Agency** (CIA) in particular uses the polygraph to test any candidate for employment and retest personnel as a condition for continued employment. The polygraph is also used as a tool in the investigation of unauthorized disclosures of classified information and other offenses as well as in law enforcement for specific purposes.

The polygraph machine is designed to record physiological changes resulting from telling a lie. However, because physical changes caused by emotional factors, such as feelings of guilt, are similar to those caused by lies, American courts have ruled that the results of a polygraph are unacceptable in legal cases. In addition, the National Research Council has found that lie detectors are too unreliable to be used in screening for national security purposes. For instance, some Americans who have spied for foreign nations—such as the CIA's **Aldrich Ames** and the **Federal Bureau of Investigation's** (FBI's) **Robert Hanssen**—did so with relative impunity after passing repeated polygraph examinations focusing on counterintelligence issues designed to ferret them out. However, the polygraph machine continues to be useful as a deterrent and a method of intimidation.

The Employee Polygraph Protection Act of 1988 prohibits much, but not all, preemployment private sector polygraph testing. Testing of employees is permitted to solve an employer's "economic loss." There are exceptions for guards, armored car personnel, and those who handle drugs and narcotics. The EPPA does not affect testing for attorneys or local, state, or federal agencies.

POPOV, DUSKO (1912–1981). Dusko Popov was a **World War II** German spy who also worked for British intelligence. *See also* TRICYCLE AFFAIR.

POPOV, PIOTR. Not much is known about Lieutenant Colonel Piotr Popov, except that he was a Soviet **GRU** officer who in 1953 offered to spy for the **Central Intelligence Agency** (CIA). He told the CIA everything he knew about the GRU and its operations, especially in running illegal agents. Soviet authorities arrested and executed Popov in 1958.

POSITIVE INTELLIGENCE. Positive intelligence is **espionage** intended to acquire intelligence information and may include **human intelligence** (HUMINT) collection, maps, photographs, ciphers, codes, and translations.

POSSE COMITATUS ACT. The Posse Comitatus Act, passed in 1878 after the end of Reconstruction, was intended to prohibit federal troops from supervising elections in former Confederate states. It generally prohibits federal military personnel and units from acting in a law enforcement capacity within the country, except where expressly authorized by the Constitution or Congress. The original act only referred to the army, but the air force was added in 1956, and the navy and marines have been included by regulation of the **Department of Defense** (DOD).

There are a number of exceptions to the act. These include national guard units while under the authority of the governor when used pursuant to the federal authority to quell domestic violence. In December 1981, Congress passed additional laws clarifying permissible military assistance to civilian law enforcement agencies—including the **Coast Guard**—especially in combating drug smuggling into the United States. Posse Comitatus clarifications emphasize supportive and technical assistance (e.g., use of facilities, vessels, aircraft, intelligence, tech aid, surveillance, etc.) while generally prohibiting direct participation of Defense Department personnel in law enforcement (e.g., search, seizure, and arrests). For example, Coast Guard law enforcement detachments (LEDETS) serve aboard naval vessels and perform the actual boarding of interdicted suspect drug smuggling vessels and, if need be, arrest their crews.

The **George W. Bush** administration sought changes to the law after the **terrorist attacks of 11 September 2001** to give the federal government authority to use the national guard in emergencies, currently a power reserved to governors, or to use the military for civilian defense, including enforcing quarantines in case of a biological weapons attack.

POWERS, FRANCIS GARY (1929–1977). Francis Gary Powers was the air force pilot who flew the **U-2** aircraft that was shot down over the **Soviet Union** on 1 May 1960. The incident soured Soviet-American relations, prompting the cancellation of a presidential summit meeting. Soviet authorities put Powers on trial for **espionage**, convicted him, and sentenced him to 10 years confinement, three in prison and seven at hard labor. Powers was exchanged for Soviet spymaster **Rudolph Abel** on 10 February 1962. Following his return to the United States, Francis Gary Powers wrote his memoirs and worked as a pilot for a Los Angeles television station. He died in 1977 in a helicopter crash.

PREDATOR (PROGRAM). A medium altitude **unmanned aerial vehicle** (UAV) that uses a variety of sensors to gather **tactical intelligence**, such as the number of tanks, vehicles, and troops. The drone's electro-optical sensors provide high-resolution images. It also carries infrared sensors that can track heat sources; high-tech synthetic aperture radar (SAR) that can penetrate bad weather or nighttime; and live video that can be transmitted to ground stations in real time.

PRESIDENTIAL DECISION DIRECTIVE (PDD). In the administration of President **William J. Clinton**, the presidential decision directives were equivalent to the **national security decision directives** (NSDDs) of the **Ronald Reagan** administration and the **national security directives** (NSDs) of the **George H. W. Bush** administration. While the number of PDDs issued by President Clinton remains a secret, his administration probably issued more than 70 such directives. PDDs were instructions and guidance to federal agencies on implementing administration policy. *See also* NATIONAL SECURITY PRESIDENTIAL DIRECTIVE.

PRESIDENTIAL DIRECTIVE (PD). Presidential orders during the administration of President **Jimmy Carter**. President Carter issued at least 54 PDs during his tenure.

PRESIDENTIAL FINDING. *See* FINDING.

PRESIDENTIAL REVIEW DIRECTIVE (PRD). For President **William J. Clinton**, presidential review directives (PRDs) were the equivalent of the nation security study memoranda of the **Ronald Reagan** administration and the national security reviews (NSRs) of the **George H. W. Bush** administration.

PRESIDENTIAL REVIEW MEMORANDA (PRM). PRMs were the presidential national security studies during the administration of President **Jimmy Carter**.

PRESIDENTIAL SUPPORT STAFF. The Presidential Support Staff replaced the **President's Daily Brief** (PDB) **Staff** in 1994 as the unit within the **Central Intelligence Agency** (CIA) that prepared and delivered the president's daily brief and provided briefings to a presidentially determined list of senior government officials on the contents of the PDB.

PRESIDENT'S ANALYTIC SUPPORT STAFF. The President's Analytic Support Staff replaced the **Presidential Support Staff** after the **terrorist attacks of 11 September 2001**. This **Central Intelligence Agency** (CIA) unit continues to prepare and deliver the **president's daily brief** (PDB) and to provide briefings to a presidentially determined list of senior government officials on the contents of the PDB.

PRESIDENT'S BOARD OF CONSULTANTS ON FOREIGN INTELLIGENCE ACTIVITIES. *See* PRESIDENT'S FOREIGN INTELLIGENCE ADVISORY BOARD; UNITED STATES INTELLIGENCE BOARD.

PRESIDENT'S DAILY BRIEF (PDB). A **current intelligence** publication, the PDB is a loose-leaf notebook that serves as a kind of briefing book containing about a dozen items on developments around the world and on broad trends abroad. Initiated under this name in 1964, the PDB is published six days a week—except on Sundays—is highly classified, and has a very small distribution, generally determined by the president. *See also* SENIOR EXECUTIVE INTELLIGENCE BRIEF.

PRESIDENT'S DAILY BRIEFING. This is the intelligence briefing the president and his advisors receive along with the **president's daily brief** (PDB). The president determines who will receive the briefings, along with the PDB. At a minimum, the vice president, the secretary of state, the secretary of defense, and the **national security advisor** receive such briefings.

PRESIDENT'S DAILY BRIEF (PDB) STAFF. Established in 1964, the PDB Staff within the **Central Intelligence Agency** (CIA) prepared and delivered the **president's daily brief** (PDB) and provided briefings to a presidentially determined list of senior government officials on the contents of the PDB. *See also* PRESIDENT'S ANALYTIC SUPPORT STAFF; PRESIDENTIAL SUPPORT STAFF.

PRESIDENT'S FOREIGN INTELLIGENCE ADVISORY BOARD (PFIAB). Established in 1956 by President **Dwight D. Eisenhower** as the President's Board of Consultants on Foreign Intelligence Activities to head off closer congressional scrutiny of intelligence. It acquired its current title under President **John F. Kennedy** and has served each president since then, with the exception of President **Jimmy Carter**, who abolished it in 1977. President **Ronald Reagan** reinstated the PFIAB by issuing **Executive Order 12331** on 20 October 1981.

The PFIAB was and is a nonpartisan entity of 14 renown individuals providing the president expert advice on the conduct of U.S. intelligence activities. Since its inception, it has also occasionally served as an executive oversight body concerning the quality and adequacy of intelligence collection, of analysis and estimates, of counterintelligence, and of other intelligence activities. The PFIAB has frequently sought to streamline the organization of U.S. intelligence and ensure the development and deployment of major intelligence programs.

In the late 1950s, the PFIAB focused more on scientific and technological challenges and was probably instrumental in the development of the **U-2** aircraft. More recently, it has tackled major intelligence management issues and has had an important role in approving **national intelligence estimates** (NIEs) bound for senior leadership. The PFIAB absorbed the **Intelligence Oversight Board** (IOB) in the late 1990s and thereby acquired the authority also to advise the president on the legality of foreign intelligence activities. *See also* EXECUTIVE ORDER 12537.

PRESIDENT'S HOMELAND SECURITY ADVISORY COUNCIL (PHSAC). Created on 19 March 2002 by executive order, the PHSAC, also known as the Homeland Security Council, is comprised of no more than 21 members appointed by the president from the government and the private sector to advise him on homeland security matters. Specifically, the council was established to provide advice on a national homeland security strategy, evaluate counterterrorism measures, and make recommendations on improving coordination among federal, state, local, and private entities. *See also* NATIONAL SECURITY COUNCIL.

PRESIDENT'S INTELLIGENCE CHECK LIST (PICL). Predecessor to the **president's daily brief** (PDB), the PICL was a publication inaugurated during the administration of President **John. F. Kennedy** to keep the president informed of current international developments. The **Central Intelligence Agency** (CIA), which produced the publication, designed it in card format to fit in the president's breast pocket so that he could consult it as he chose. The card, printed virtually on a daily basis, was delivered to the president as part of his daily briefing. Known informally as the "pickle," those who worked on its production in the CIA liked to claim that they worked in the "pickle factory." President **Lyndon B. Johnson** discontinued the PICL in 1964 and asked the CIA to produce a readable document more suitable to his tastes. The result was the PDB.

PRESIDENT'S SPECIAL REVIEW BOARD. *See* TOWER COMMISSION.

PRINCIPALS COMMITTEE. The **National Security Council** (NSC) principals committee was established by President **George H. W. Bush** and continued with some modification by President **William J. Clinton** as the senior interagency forum for the consideration of policy issues affecting national security. President **George W. Bush** has continued the use of the principals committee.

The function of the principals committee is to review, coordinate, and monitor the development and implementation of national security policy. According to the NSC's website, the Principals Committee, as a flexible instrument, is intended to be "a forum available to cabinet-level officials to meet to discuss and resolve issues not requiring the President's participation." The **national security advisor** chairs the Principals Committee. Its members, along with the national security advisor, include the secretary of state, the secretary of defense, the U.S. representative to the United Nations (UN), the **director of national intelligence** (DNI), the chairman of the **Joint Chiefs of Staff** (JCS), the assistant to the president for economic policy, and the assistant to the vice president for national security. President George W. Bush also includes the secretary of the **Department of Homeland Security** (DHS) in the principals committee.

The secretary of the treasury, the attorney general, and other heads of departments and agencies are invited as needed. The secretaries of energy and commerce, or their deputies, are routinely invited to Principals Committee meetings involving proliferation and nuclear related issues. Other members of the White House staff, including the president's chief of staff, the Director of the Office of Management and Budget (OMB), and the deputy assistant to the president for national security affairs (APNSA), may also attend, depending on the agenda.

PROJECT JENNIFER. *See* JENNIFER (PROJECT).

PROJECT RODRIGUISTA. *See* RODRIGUISTA (PROJECT).

PROJECT SAFEHAVEN. *See* SAFEHAVEN (PROJECT).

PROPAGANDA. Refers to dissemination of information intended to further one's cause or damage the adversary. Numerous U.S. agencies, including the **Department of Defense** (DOD), engage in propaganda activities, but, in the lexicon of U.S. intelligence, propaganda is part of **covert action** programs of the **Central Intelligence Agency** (CIA). Propaganda activities range from white propaganda—broadcasting news about the United States by **Voice of America** (VOA), for example—to black propaganda, which is the spreading of disinformation. Gray propaganda falls somewhere in between the two and includes broadcast activities intended to cast the United States in a positive light. During the **Cold War**, U.S. propaganda focused on exposing the dark side of communism and warning of its dangers. It also sought to win the hearts and minds of various publics toward the West by focusing on freedoms and democratic principles. Entities like **Radio Free Europe** (RFE) and **Radio Liberty** (RL) were covert efforts to influence opinion behind the iron curtain. U.S. agencies like the **United**

States Information Agency (USIA) employed a variety of open techniques—cultural exchanges, newspapers, newsreels, libraries, and the like—to disseminate favorable information about the United States. Propaganda activities continue to be integral parts of open and covert government propaganda activities. *See also* UNITED STATES INFORMATION AGENCY; RADIO MARTI; RADIO SAWA.

PROPRIETARY COMPANY. Proprietaries are front organizations covertly owned by the **Central Intelligence Agency** (CIA) to carry out **special activities** and other **covert actions**. These seemingly private commercial or nonprofit entities have facilitated and provided **cover** for clandestine operations.

Historically, there have been two types of proprietaries. Operating companies actually served the general public and even generated income; nonoperating companies appeared to be doing business but actually performed services exclusively for the CIA. Among the more prominent proprietaries were the International Armaments Corporation (Interarmco) and the **Civil Air Transport** (CAT), which operated out of Taiwan and was organized as a Delaware corporation in the 1950s. The CIA expanded its holdings to include **Air America** (which operated in Southeast Asia and grew huge with the American involvement in Vietnam), Air Asia (a major repair and maintenance facility based in Taiwan), **Southern Air Transport** (SAT), acquired in 1963, and Intermountain Aviation (a parking, repair, and maintenance facility and "charter service" operating from a private airfield near Tucson, Arizona).

Because these proprietaries in some cases have been highly profitable, legitimate carriers have complained of unfair competition. Although the CIA continues to own proprietaries for covert action, it divested itself of most of its air proprietaries by 1975.

PROTECTING SOURCES AND METHODS. The protection of sources and methods is the justification for the classifying and **compartmenting** of intelligence information. What is secret about intelligence is the identities of information sources and the methods employed to acquire information. Intelligence officers must protect their sources, virtually at all costs, because without them, they have no intelligence information. They must also obfuscate their intelligence methods in order to thwart **denial/deception operations**.

PSEUDONYM. An internal designation used by an officer of the **Central Intelligence Agency** (CIA) to refer to himself in communications. CIA officers use their pseudonyms to sign cables sent back to headquarters and are sometimes referred to by their pseudonyms in internal discussions. Pseudonyms are not employed during operations. *See also* ALIAS.

PSYCHOLOGICAL WARFARE (PSYWAR). The **Department of Defense** (DOD) defines psychological warfare as the planned use of **propaganda** and other psychological actions with the primary purpose of influencing the opinions, emotions, attitudes, and behavior of hostile foreign groups in such a way as to support the achievement of national objectives. Because psychological warfare intends to manipulate the adversary's fears and desires, it is often confused with propaganda. PSYWAR includes such activities as distributing leaflets, beaming carefully scripted radio or television messages, placing a particular strategy in a specific perspective to elicit a particular response (such as "shock and awe" in the 2003 Iraq War), renaming cities and other places when captured, and **terrorism.**

P-3C ORION AIRCRAFT. This airplane is an airborne intelligence collection platform used by the U.S. Navy. The aircraft is equipped with radar and an electro-optic camera system for both live video and radar images of the tactical situation on the ground and has the ability to stay aloft for 10 to 12 hours without refueling. The Orion can operate in all weather, day or night. A downlink to ground stations provides instant access to intelligence gathered during a mission. The **People's Republic of China** (PRC) forced down an Orion aircraft in international airspace off its coast in 2002 after it collided with a Chinese fighter.

PUEBLO INCIDENT. The North Koreans seized the lightly armed U.S. naval vessel, the USS *Pueblo*, on 23 January 1968. A spy ship, the *Pueblo* was tracking maritime activity and intercepting electronic messages when North Korean gunboats attacked. Commander Lloyd M. Bucher thought the ship was ill equipped to respond to the North Korean assault and so surrendered the ship without destroying classified materials. The *Pueblo* was the first U.S. ship since the War of 1812 to surrender. North Korea imprisoned commander Bucher and

82 crewmembers aboard and subjected them to 11 months of interrogation and torture. After forced confessions and an apology from the U.S. government, later repudiated, North Korea released the prisoners on 23 December 1968.

The decision to surrender the ship without resistance led to a naval inquiry that recommended the court martial of commander Bucher, but the secretary of the navy overruled the board. However, the incident prompted the navy to undertake a modernization program to reinforce armaments on intelligence ships and to provide them with destruct systems, secret weapons, and rapid scuttling devices. The navy also reexamined and improved operational doctrine as well as communications between command-and-control forces.

PURPLE. Purple was the American designation for the Japanese code used to encode diplomatic and military communications prior to **World War II**. The U.S. government gave the acronym MAGIC to intercepted and decoded messages from Purple. The first successful Purple decoded message was sent to Washington in August 1940, but the government encountered legal problems because the Federal Communications Act of 1934 prohibited wiretaps and the interception of messages between the U.S. and other countries. Because of this law, American cable companies initially refused to hand over messages but eventually agreed to limited cooperation. *See also* CRYPTOLOGY; SHAMROCK (OPERATION).

– R –

RABORN, WILLIAM, JR. (1905–1990). Seventh **director of central intelligence** (DCI) between 28 April 1965 and 30 June 1966. A U.S. Naval Academy graduate, Admiral Raborn made substantial contributions to the U.S. Navy prior to his appointment as DCI. During **World War II**, he commanded a gunnery school and after the war was assigned to command ships. In December 1955, Admiral Raborn was put in charge of the development of the Polaris, a submarine-launched ballistic missile (SLBM) weapons system. Subsequently, he managed the development of various missiles, guidance systems, and launches for the navy. In 1962, he became deputy chief of naval operations and retired from the navy in 1963. Throughout his career,

Admiral Raborn had the reputation for getting along with people during stressful situations and for his management abilities.

President **Lyndon B. Johnson** appointed Admiral Raborn to be DCI because he thought that the admiral's standing in Congress would facilitate the mission of the **Central Intelligence Agency** (CIA). His short tenure as DCI, however, did little to endear the CIA to President Johnson, who continued to ignore the agency's analytic assessments that the **Vietnam War** could not be won. On leaving his DCI post in June 1966, Admiral Raborn became a senior manager of Aerojet General in California and later headed his own consulting firm until his full retirement in 1986.

RADARSAT. Launched on 4 November 1995, RADARSAT is a Canadian satellite that is occasionally used by the U.S. Air Force for imaging purposes. The satellite has a synthetic aperture radar (SAR) sensor onboard, which is capable of imaging the earth regardless of time of day or cloud, haze, or smoke over an area. Because different applications require different imaging modes, RADARSAT gives users tremendous flexibility in choosing the type of SAR data most suitable for their application.

RADIO FREE EUROPE/RADIO LIBERTY (RFE/RL). Radio Free Europe/Radio Liberty were covert **propaganda** programs of the **Central Intelligence Agency** (CIA) during the **Cold War**. Radio Free Europe went on the air in 1950, beaming a prodemocracy, anticommunist messages to Poland, Czechoslovakia, Hungary, Romania, and Bulgaria. The CIA also founded RFE's sister station, Radio Liberty, which broadcast similar messages to the **Soviet Union** in both Russian and the languages of the non-Russian peoples.

Managers of RFE/RL approached their propaganda tasks with finesse and sensitivity. They did not laud American popular culture or the American way of life, and any comparisons were limited to Western Europe. The stations focused instead on such issues as the ills of agricultural collectivization, the persecution of religion, the suppression of culture, party purges, and the like. Indeed, each station, staffed by exiles from East European countries and the Soviet Union, functioned much like the press of a democratic opposition movement. In fact, the stations became so well known and respected, some Polish leaders later asserted that the stations played an important role in bringing down at least three

Polish Communist Party leaders and were instrumental in sustaining the Solidarity trade union in Poland when it was forced underground by martial law in 1981. During Romanian strongman Nicolae Ceausescu's time, RFE was Romania's most popular source of news.

American isolationists in the 1970s tried to shut down the radio stations, claiming that they were relics of the Cold War and served no useful purpose other than to goad the Soviet Union and its puppet regimes in Eastern Europe. This attempt at closing the stations failed, but the management of RFE/RL eventually was transferred from the CIA to an independent agency. When communism collapsed in 1991 and the exiled RFE/RL journalists visited their native lands—some for the first time in 40 years—they were greeted as conquering heroes. RFE/RL were officially closed down on 28 November 2003 as a cost-saving measure.

RADIO MARTI. On 23 September 1981, President **Ronald Reagan** announced plans to establish a radio station to transmit news reports to **Cuba**. Despite controversy and occasional attempts to disband the station, Radio Marti continues its broadcasts as part of the Voice of America (VOA). *See also* TELEVISION MARTI.

RADIO SAWA. After the **terrorist attacks of 11 September 2001**, the administration of President **George W. Bush** created the position of undersecretary of state for public diplomacy in the **Department of State**. This office launched Radio Sawa on 23 March 2002, which is currently broadcasting on FM transmitters in Amman, Jordan; Kuwait City, Kuwait; and in the United Arab Emirates cities of Abu Dhabi and Dubai. It also transmits from Cyprus to Egypt, Lebanon, and Syria. According to various polls, however, listeners consider the radio to be American **propaganda** and reject its political messages outright.

RAINBOW (OPERATION). Operation Rainbow was a purported covert deception campaign during the 1956 Suez Crisis to convince oil-producing Arab states that the United States was on the verge of overcoming its dependence on their oil and thereby affecting the future expectations of producing countries. According to former **Central Intelligence Agency** (CIA) operative **Miles Copeland**, the deception was supposed to involve a fake experimental facility secluded in the western United States as well as fake operations to support the ruse. Copeland claimed that the plan was discarded when experts demonstrated that, even under the most optimistic scenarios, the U.S. would still be dependent on Middle Eastern oil. The nature, substance, and veracity of Operation Rainbow is in dispute, largely because of Copeland's tendency to exaggerate his stories. Some experts, however, have found evidence to support his claim.

RC-135 RIVET JOINT AIRCRAFT. This aircraft is an airborne intelligence platform used by the air force to eavesdrop on radio conversations or pick up signals from radars. The airplane flies some distance from the target, employs an array of sensors to collect the intelligence, and then sends warnings about the location of threatening forces. The aircraft has been used to great effect in peacekeeping and contingency operations, such as the 1999 war in Kosovo.

REAGAN, RONALD (1911–2004). The 40th president of the United States between 1981 and 1989. A Liberal Democrat in his youth, President Reagan joined the Republican Party in 1962 and began to champion conservative causes, enthusiastically endorsing presidential candidate Barry Goldwater in 1964. In the California gubernatorial election of 1966, he defeated incumbent governor, Edmund G. "Pat" Brown, and served two terms (1967–1975) as governor. President Reagan also unsuccessfully ran twice, in 1968 and 1976, for the Republican presidential nomination but lost to **Richard M. Nixon** and **Gerald R. Ford**, respectively. In 1980, with the help of his friend, **William J. Casey**, Ronald Reagan won his party's nomination for president and went on to defeat incumbent president **Jimmy Carter**.

Ronald Reagan advocated a balanced budget to combat inflation and pursued supply-side economic programs of tax and nondefense budget cuts through Congress. Adopting a hard-line stance against the **Soviet Union** and other communist countries, President Reagan advocated and presided over an escalation of military spending, which included his 1983 proposal for a space-based defense system known as the **Strategic Defense Initiative** (SDI).

During his two terms as president, Ronald Reagan was keenly interested in strengthening U.S. intelligence capabilities. He installed William Casey, a veteran of the **Office of the Strategic Service** (OSS), as **director of central intelligence** (DCI), issued **Executive Order 12333** on 4 December 1981, approved various anti-Soviet

covert actions in Africa and elsewhere, and launched a covert war in Nicaragua to unseat the **Sandinista** regime that had come to power in 1979.

During his second term, President Reagan began softening his anti-Soviet stance—in his first term, he had branded the Soviet Union the "evil empire"—in response to Soviet leader Mikhail Gorbachev's initiatives to open up the Soviet Union. The two leaders met four times between 1985 and 1987, when they concluded the Intermediate Nuclear Force (INF) Missile Treaty, which not only sharply reduced medium-range nuclear forces but also sought to eliminate an entire class of weapon system.

President Reagan's second term, however, was marred by the **Iran-Contra Affair**, which broke in late 1986 and involved the White House's complicity in the illegal diversion of profits from arms-for-hostage deals with **Iran** to the **Contra** guerrillas fighting the Sandinistas in Nicaragua.

RED CELL. The Red Cell is a unit of the **Central Intelligence Agency** (CIA) established after the **terrorist attacks of 11 September 2001** to engage in the analysis of low probability, high-risk alternative scenarios. The Red Cell is comprised of analysts from the **Directorate of Intelligence** (DI), although the unit is organizationally located in the Office of the **Director of National Intelligence** (DNI), not within the organizational structure of the CIA.

RED SOX/RED CAP (OPERATION). A **covert action** designed by **Frank Wisner**, the **Central Intelligence Agency's** (CIA) deputy director for plans (DDP), to foment rebellion by the East Europeans in the late 1950s against the Soviet occupiers. According to the plan, once the rebellions sufficiently weakened Soviet forces, **North Atlantic Treaty Organization** (NATO) troops were then to be sent in as peacekeepers to conduct democratic elections. However, the whole plan began to come apart when the CIA was ordered not to assist in the Hungarian revolt of 1956, thus bringing the operation's legitimacy and usefulness into question. President **Dwight D. Eisenhower** eventually terminated the program in the late 1950s.

ROCKEFELLER COMMISSION. Formally known as the president's Commission on CIA Activities within the United States, the Rockefeller Commission, headed by former Vice President Nelson A. Rockefeller, was established by Executive Order 11828 on 4 January 1975. It mandate was to determine whether the **Central Intelligence Agency** (CIA) conducted domestic surveillance and other illegal activities within the United States in the period 1947–1975. It was also to conduct a narrower study of issues relating to the assassination of President **John F. Kennedy**.

The commission's report, issued on 6 June 1975, found that the CIA had engaged in illegal domestic acts, such as infiltrating dissident groups, opening private mail, testing drugs on unknowing citizens, and subjecting foreign **defectors** to physical abuse and prolonged confinement. The report did not delve into the assassination of President Kennedy, prompting critics to allege a "white wash" of the matter. The Rockefeller Commission's work set the stage for the congressional investigations of the CIA, first by the **Church Committee** in the Senate and then by the **Pike Committee** in the House of Representatives. *See also* ANGLETON, JAMES J.; COINTELPRO (OPERATION); MKULTRA (OPERATION).

RODRIGUISTA (PROJECT). A **Soviet covert action** operation in support of the Chilean Communist Party to enable it to pursue an underground armed struggle against the regime of **Augusto Pinochet** during the early 1980s. The operation was supervised by the International Department of the Central Committee of the Soviet Communist Party, the **KGB**, and the **GRU**. The project's goals were to develop an underground network for pursuing an armed struggle to depose the repressive regime, to train Chileans in Eastern Europe and the Soviet Union in the doctrine and techniques of armed struggle, and to infiltrate these individuals back inside the country to direct the struggle. Specifically, the Soviet Union trained Chilean Communist Party members in underground activities and covert intelligence gathering techniques, provided forged documents and passports, gave financial assistance, and prepared "foreign comrades" in various paramilitary activities, including weapons training and explosives. The operation ended toward the end of the 1980s when the Chilean Communist Party renounced armed struggle against Pinochet. *See also* ALLENDE, SALVADOR; FUBELT (OPERATION); NATIONAL SECURITY DECISION MEMORANDUM 93.

ROOSEVELT, FRANKLIN D. (1882–1945). The 32nd president of the United States between 1933 and 1945. A wartime leader, President Roosevelt set the stage for the establishment of the contemporary U.S. **intelligence community** (IC). A lawyer by training, Roosevelt entered state politics in 1910, but in 1913, President Woodrow Wilson appointed him his assistant secretary of the navy, a position FDR held until 1920. His popularity convinced Democratic Party leaders to field him as a vice presidential candidate, but Warren Harding, the Republican candidate, won the presidency.

In 1921, Franklin D. Roosevelt contracted polio, which affected his legs. Yet, he pursued his political ambitions, first serving as governor of New York beginning in 1928 and then running for the presidency in 1932. His activism and personal charm, and the effects of the deepening depression, helped elect him to the presidency by a wide margin of votes.

President Roosevelt's many contributions to the nation included numerous New Deal laws, such as social security, direct relief to the poor, the works projects administration, and the like. In addition, he led the nation into and through **World War II**, during which he established the position of coordinator of information (COI), which in 1942 evolved into the **Office of Strategic Services** (OSS). His wartime strategy was to create a "grand alliance" against the Axis powers through the "Declaration of the United Nations" on 1 January 1942, in which all nations fighting the Axis agreed not to make a separate peace and pledged themselves to a peacekeeping organization in victory. President Roosevelt died in office on 12 April 1945 from a massive stroke.

ROSENBERG CASE. *See* VENONA.

RULE X. A rule of the House of Representatives that in 1977 established the **House Permanent Select Committee on Intelligence** (HPSCI), articulated its structure, and defined its authorities as an entity overseeing U.S. intelligence agencies and activities. Under the rule, the committee is restricted to no more than 18 members, of which no more than 10 may be from the same political party. The committee's membership, moreover, must include at least one member from the Committee on Appropriations, the Committee on Armed Services, the Committee on International Relations, and the Committee on the Judiciary. The HPSCI evolved from the **Pike Commit-**

tee, which in the mid-1970s investigated the activities of U.S. intelligence, particularly the **Central Intelligence Agency** (CIA).

Under Rule X, the HPSCI performs an annual review of the intelligence budget submitted by the president and prepares legislation authorizing appropriations for the various civilian and military agencies and departments comprising the **intelligence community** (IC). These entities include the CIA, the **Defense Intelligence Agency** (DIA), the **National Security Agency** (NSA), the **National Geospatial-Intelligence Agency** (NGA), the **National Reconnaissance Office** (NRO), as well as the intelligence-related components of the **Department of State**, the **Federal Bureau of Investigation** (FBI), the Department of the Treasury, the Department of Energy (DOE), and the **Department of Homeland Security** (DHS). The committee makes recommendations to the House Committee on Armed Services on authorizations for the intelligence-related components of the army, navy, air force, and marines. The committee also conducts periodic investigations, audits, and inspections of intelligence activities and programs.

In February 2002, the HPSCI and the **Senate Select Committee on Intelligence** (SSCI) agreed to conduct a joint inquiry into the failures of U.S. intelligence to anticipate the **terrorist attacks of 11 September 2001**. *See also* SENATE RESOLUTION 400.

RUTH, SAMUEL (1818–1872). As superintendent of the Richmond, Fredericksburg, and Potomac Railroad, a vital transportation route for Confederate forces, Samuel Ruth conducted sabotage operations for the Union by engaging in delaying tactics, deliberate inefficiency, and slowdowns. Ruth eventually became a member of the Union intelligence network in Richmond, Virginia.

– S –

SAFEHAVEN (PROJECT). An operation initiated in May 1944 to track down and block German assets in neutral and nonbelligerent countries throughout Europe and the Americas. The fear was that the Nazi leaders, sensing defeat, would secretly transfer industrial and fiscal capital to neutral countries, thereby escaping confiscation by the victors. In addition, the victors feared that, if this happened, German economic and industrial power would be largely intact and would provide the power base from which unrepentant Germans might rebuild another Reich and spark another war.

The **Department of State** took the lead in SAFEHAVEN, although the **Office of Strategic Services** (OSS) came to play an important role in gathering intelligence from clandestine sources in neutral and German-occupied Europe. Headquartered in the U.S. Embassy in London, the operation tracked Nazi assets throughout Europe, thereby acquiring the capability to use the intelligence information to restore some of the assets looted by the Nazis. SAFEHAVEN also had a **counterintelligence** component, in that it sought also to prevent postwar German economic penetration in foreign economies, in which OSS also played a significant role.

SAFEHAVEN became a casualty of the postwar dismantling of the U.S. intelligence apparatus. The information gathered during the operation was used in negotiations with neutral governments, such as Switzerland, but those talks became sidetracked by the onset of the **Cold War**. None of the intelligence collected for SAFEHAVEN was useful in identifying assets stolen from the Jews and other victims of the Nazi regime.

SALOMON, HAYM (1740–1785). Salomon was a financier of the American Revolution and one of **George Washington's** spies in New York City during 1776–1777. Salomon occasionally served as spymaster to the French forces in the United States and as banker to ministers of various foreign governments. The U.S. government never repaid Salomon for the substantial amounts of money he spent on the American cause.

SANDINISTA (FSLN/Frente Sandinista de Liberacion Nacional). The Sandinistas were the main Nicaraguan rebel group that opposed the dictatorship of Anastasio Somoza Debayle, whom they overthrew on 17 July 1979. On assuming power, the Sandinistas nationalized the principal industries and began to impose their own brand of Marxism in Nicaragua that infuriated the newly elected administration of President **Ronald Reagan** in the United States. In 1981, President Reagan accused the Sandinistas of supporting Marxist revolutionary movements in Latin America and authorized the **Central Intelligence Agency** (CIA) to finance, arm, and train the **Contra** rebels to fight the Sandinista regime. The civil war raged until 1988 when a truce brought the fighting to an end. The FSLN lost the elections of 25 February 1990 and has remained the leading opposition party to the current centrist Nicaraguan government.

SAVAK. Formed under the guidance of United States and Israeli intelligence officers in 1957, SAVAK developed into an effective secret agency of the Iranian shah, Reza Pahlavi. Attached to the Office of the Prime Minister, its director assumed the title of deputy to the prime minister for national security affairs. Despite its allegiance to the monarch, the shah did not trust SAVAK's directors and changed them on a regular basis. Although officially a civilian agency, SAVAK also had close ties to the military; many of its officers served simultaneously in branches of the armed forces.

Founded to round up members of the outlawed Iranian Communist Party, Tudeh, SAVAK expanded its activities to include gathering intelligence and neutralizing the regime's opponents. It established an elaborate system to monitor all facets of political life, including journalists, literary figures, and academics. It also conducted surveillance of universities, labor unions, and peasant organizations. Abroad, SAVAK monitored Iranian students who publicly opposed the Pahlavi rule.

Over the years, SAVAK became a law unto itself, having legal authority to arrest and detain suspected persons indefinitely. It operated its own prisons in Tehran and, many suspected, throughout the country as well. Many of these activities were carried out without any institutional checks. SAVAK was officially dissolved by Ayatollah Khomeini shortly after he came to power in 1979. The Islamic revolutionaries particularly singled out former SAVAK operatives for reprisals, and virtually all of them were purged between 1979 and 1981.

SCHLESINGER, JAMES R. (1929–). Ninth **director of central intelligence** (DCI) between 5 February 1973 and 2 July 1973. After his reelection in 1972, President **Richard M. Nixon** fired DCI **Richard M. Helms**, who had been DCI throughout his first term. Intent on reforming intelligence, President Nixon appointed James Schlesinger as DCI on 21 December 1972. Educated as an economist, Schlesinger also brought to his new position an appreciation of the high cost of intelligence. Schlesinger was also critical of the **intelligence community** (IC), particularly of the quality of intelligence directed at policymakers.

In his five-month term as DCI in 1973, Schlesinger sought to cut personnel and reduce costs. To coordinate the activities of the departmental intelligence services and to maximize his role as DCI, Schlesinger almost immediately put a number of non-CIA personnel on the **Intelligence Community Staff** (ICS). Believing that the day of the spy was over, Schlesinger also focused his efforts on increasing technical collection and reducing the personnel levels in the **Directorate of Plans** (DP). He ordered **William Colby**, the newly appointed deputy director for plans (DDP), to purge the ranks of covert operatives and paramilitary specialists. Consequently, Schlesinger fired or forced to resign or retire nearly 7 percent of the CIA's total staff, predominantly from the clandestine side of the house—whose name he also changed from Directorate of Plans to **Directorate of Operations** (DO). He also sold off the CIA's **proprietary companies**, **Air America** and **Southern Air Transport** (SAT).

Soon after Schlesinger's appointment, the **Watergate scandal** exposed the CIA to charges of involvement in that affair. Determined not to be blindsided, Schlesinger on 9 May 1973 ordered all CIA employees to report any activities they were aware of that might in any way appear inconsistent with the CIA's charter. Later in May, the office of the inspector general gave Schlesinger a 693-page list of "potential flap activities," which detailed CIA involvement in numerous misdeeds. This document came to be known as the "**Family Jewels**" and was turned over to the Congress by Schlesinger's successor as DCI, William Colby.

SECRET SERVICE. Established on 5 July 1865, the United States Secret Service carries out two vital missions: protection of very important persons and criminal investigations. According to its mission statement, the secret service protects the president and vice president, their families, heads of state, and other designated individuals; investigates threats against those it protects; provides protection service to the White House, vice president's residence, foreign missions, and other buildings within Washington, D.C.; and plans and implements security designs for special events. The secret service also investigates violations of laws relating to counterfeiting of currencies and securities, financial fraud, identity theft, computer fraud, and computer-based attacks on the United States.

The **USA PATRIOT Act**, passed in 2002, increased the role of the secret service in investigating computer fraud and related activities.

It also authorized the director of the secret service to establish nationwide electronic task forces to assist law enforcement, the private sector, and academia in detecting and suppressing computer-based crime; increased the statutory penalties for the manufacture, possession, dealing in, and passing of counterfeit U.S. or foreign obligations; and allowed protection of the nation's financial systems. The **Department of Homeland Security** (DHS) absorbed the secret service on 1 March 2003.

SECRET SERVICE BUREAU. The Secret Service Bureau was the Union's short-lived intelligence organization created by **Allan Pinkerton** in mid-1861. Because of Pinkerton's self-styled intelligence missions behind Confederate lines and his outlandish and dubious reports on Confederate movements, the Secret Service Bureau quickly languished and simply disappeared without making much of a contribution to the Union's intelligence effort.

SECURITY POLICY BOARD. Established in 1994 by **Presidential Decision Directive** (PDD) 29, it sought to develop government-wide integrated security policies across a broad range of security disciplines, from classification to personnel security. The Security Policy Board was composed of prominent Americans outside of government who brought an independent, nongovernmental, public interest perspective to security policy initiatives and the **intelligence community** (IC). It was also a national-level security policy committee, which provided leadership, structure, and coherence to the U.S. government's personnel, physical, technical, and procedural policy, practices, and procedures. The Security Policy Board was abolished on 24 April 2001, pursuant to **National Security Presidential Directive** (NSPD) 1.

SELECT COMMITTEE ON INTELLIGENCE TO INVESTIGATE ALLEGATIONS OF ILLEGAL OR IMPROPER ACTIVITIES OF FEDERAL INTELLIGENCE AGENCIES. Impaneled in February 1975, the committee of the House of Representatives had a mandate to investigate allegations of illegal and improper activities by U.S. intelligence agencies, especially the **Central Intelligence Agency** (CIA). Also known as the Pike Committee, after its chairman representative Otis Pike, it focused on the cost of U.S. intelligence, its effectiveness, and its management. The committee's staff did not develop the same cooperative relationship with CIA officials as had its counterpart in the Senate, the **Church Committee**, and so its investigations were mired in disputes with the CIA over access to documents and declassification of information.

The final report of the committee was highly critical of U.S. intelligence and of the CIA in particular. CIA officials countered that the report was factually erroneous, was based on bias, lacked any semblance of balance, and was highly pejorative. On 29 January 1976, the House of Representatives voted not to release the report, but it was nonetheless leaked to *The Village Voice*, which published it on 16 February 1976. Despite the recriminations and the acrimony surrounding the House investigations, the Pike Committee evolved into the **House Permanent Select Committee on Intelligence** (HPSCI), the **intelligence oversight** committee in the House of Representatives. *See also* SENATE RESOLUTION 400; SENATE SELECT COMMITTEE ON INTELLIGENCE.

SELECT COMMITTEE TO STUDY GOVERNMENTAL OPER-ATIONS WITH RESPECT TO INTELLIGENCE ACTIVITIES. *See* CHURCH COMMITTEE.

SENATE ARMED SERVICES COMMITTEE (SASC). Created by the Legislative Reorganization Act of 1946, the committee merged the Senate Military Affairs Committee and Naval Affairs Committee, both of which had been in existence since 1816. The new committee's jurisdiction was based on the Constitution's grant to Congress to provide for the general defense. The 13-member committee met for the first time on 13 January 1947.

The SASC quickly became an important conduit for national security legislation. It was heavily involved in the passage of the 1947 **National Security Act** and the amendments to it in 1949 that established the **Department of Defense** (DOD). It passed, among others, the Selective Service Act of 1948, the Armed Services Procurement Act of 1948, the Air Force Composition Act of 1948, the Uniform Code of Military Justice Act of 1950, the Universal Military Training Program Act of 1952, and the Armed Forces Reserve Act of 1952.

In its early years, the SASC lacked jurisdiction and professional staff and so largely reacted to, rather than initiated, legislation. The committee passed general authorization bills that provided little guidance for the annual funding decision of the Defense Subcommittee of the Senate Committee on Appropriations, which doled out the money for authorized programs. However, the SASC gradually began accruing important powers, first, by assuming control over presidential nominations and, then, by asserting its oversight responsibilities over defense and intelligence matters. In 1959, for example, the committee started requiring authorization of missiles, aircraft, and naval vessels prior to appropriations, all in the face of opposition by the **Dwight D. Eisenhower** White House and the Department of Defense.

During the 1960s, the committee enhanced the authorization process by broadening its access to information. In 1969, the chairman established a system of regular quarterly Pentagon reports on major weapons programs, cost overruns, and performance tests. In 1973, the committee received for the first time the Pentagon's five-year plan for procurement of major weapons systems. In the meantime, the committee continued to expand the items in the defense budget requiring authorization, such as weapons, manpower, and personnel issues.

In addition, the committee began asserting jurisdiction over **arms control** issues in the late 1960s and early 1970s. In 1969, for example, the committee held hearings on the military implications of the Treaty on the Nonproliferation of Nuclear Weapons. It also held hearings on the **Strategic Arms Limitation Talks** (SALT) that led to the Treaty on the Limitation of Anti-Ballistic Missiles (ABM) and an interim agreement on the Limitation of Strategic Offensive Arms. In 1975, a subcommittee held hearings on Soviet compliance with the SALT I agreements.

In the late 1970s, the committee also played a significant role in the debate over ratification of the Panama Canal Treaty. During July through October of 1979, the committee held hearings on the SALT II agreement and on 20 December 1979 recommended that the treaty not be ratified, claiming that it, as negotiated, "is not in the national security interests of the United States."

During this time, the committee exercised limited oversight responsibilities over intelligence matters that, to some experts, were tantamount to no oversight at all. In May 1976, the committee lost some of its jurisdiction over intelligence when the Senate established the **Senate Select Committee on Intelligence** (SSCI) with responsibility for oversight of the **Central Intelligence Agency** (CIA) and the

intelligence community (IC). The SASC, however, retained jurisdiction over tactical intelligence with military applications.

By the time Arizona senator Barry Goldwater became chairman of the committee in 1985, the committee's work was well on its way to being sidelined by the momentous changes taking place in world politics. The **Ronald Reagan** defense buildup, for example, began to wane, and a long period of real decline in the defense budget began. However, Senator Goldwater was instrumental in putting together a bill to reorganize America's defense establishment. Congress passed the **Goldwater-Nichols Act of 1986** over the opposition of the Pentagon and the secretary of defense. Today, the committee is an important arbiter of national security policy, especially since the **terrorist attacks of 11 September 2001**. *See also* HOUSE ARMED SERVICES COMMITTEE.

SENATE FOREIGN RELATIONS COMMITTEE (SFRC). The Senate Foreign Relations Committee was established in 1816 as one of the original 10 standing committees of the Senate. Throughout its history, the committee has been instrumental in developing and influencing United States foreign policy. The committee has considered, debated, and reported important treaties and legislation, ranging from the purchase of Alaska in 1867 to the establishment of the United Nations in 1945. It also holds jurisdiction over all diplomatic nominations.

Through these powers, the committee has helped shape foreign policy of broad significance, such as in matters of war and peace and international relations. Members of the committee have assisted in the negotiation of treaties and at times have helped to defeat treaties they felt were not in the national interest. The SFRC was instrumental in the rejection of the Treaty of Versailles in 1919 and 1920, and in the passage of the **Truman Doctrine** in 1947 and the Marshall Plan in 1948.

For much of the **Cold War**, the SFRC experienced a bipartisan spirit. However, the state of almost constant crisis spawned by the ideological conflict with the **Soviet Union** resulted in the vast expansion of presidential authority over foreign policy. Since the 1960s, the committee has sought to redress this imbalance of powers.

The SFRC has had only limited jurisdiction over intelligence matters. During the Cold War, the committee exercised intelligence jurisdiction only as it affected American foreign relations. The committee lost that role when the Senate established the **Senate Select Committee on Intelligence** (SSCI) in May 1976. Since the **terrorist attacks of 11 September 2001**, the SFRC has assumed a secondary role to that of the SSCI and the **Senate Armed Services Committee** (SASC) on matters pertaining to counterterrorism and intelligence. *See also* HOUSE INTERNATIONAL RELATIONS COMMITTEE.

SENATE RESOLUTION 400. A resolution of the U.S. Senate passed in May 1976 that established the **Senate Select Committee on Intelligence** (SSCI) to oversee the activities of U.S. intelligence agencies. The resolution empowered the SSCI to conduct studies of intelligence activities and programs of the U.S. government, submit to the Senate appropriate proposals for legislation, and report to the Senate concerning intelligence activities and programs. *See also* CHURCH COMMITTEE; RULE X; SELECT COMMITTEE ON INTELLIGENCE TO INVESTIGATE ALLEGATIONS OF ILLEGAL OR IMPROPER ACTIVITIES OF FEDERAL INTELLIGENCE AGENCIES.

SENATE SELECT COMMITTEE ON INTELLIGENCE (SSCI). The SSCI was established in 1976 by **Senate Resolution 400** to provide congressional **oversight** of the programs and activities of U.S. intelligence agencies. The SSCI evolved from the **Church Committee**, which in the mid-1970s investigated the activities of the U.S. intelligence, particularly the **Central Intelligence Agency** (CIA). The SSCI performs an annual review of the **intelligence budget** submitted by the president and prepares legislation authorizing appropriations for the various civilian and military agencies and departments comprising the **intelligence community** (IC). The committee makes recommendations to the **Senate Armed Services Committee** (SASC) on authorizations for the intelligence-related components of the army, navy, air force, and marines. The committee also conducts periodic investigations, audits, and inspections of intelligence activities and programs.

In February 2002, the SSCI and the **House Permanent Select Committee on Intelligence** (HPSCI) agreed to conduct a joint inquiry into the activities of the U.S. intelligence community in connection with the **terrorist attacks of 11 September 2001**.

SENIOR BOWL (OPERATION). *See* TAGBOARD (OPERATION).

SENIOR EXECUTIVE INTELLIGENCE BRIEF (SEIB). A SEIB is a **current intelligence** publication of the **Central Intelligence Agency** (CIA) delivered to a select group of government officials usually six days a week. Formerly known as the **National Intelligence Daily** (NID), this publication was former **Director of Central Intelligence** (DCI) **William Colby's** idea, who recommended during the mid-1960s that the CIA's daily intelligence report, known as the **National Intelligence Digest**, be issued in newspaper format. In doing so, Colby sought to offer readers a choice between a headline summary and in-depth reports. Judging that the newspaper format was too inflexible, the NID was subsequently produced in magazine format. The SEIB is produced by the CIA's **Directorate of Intelligence** (DI), in coordination with the **Defense Intelligence Agency** (DIA), the State Department's **Bureau of Intelligence and Research** (INR), and the **National Security Agency** (NSA) and is distributed to several hundred officials. The text notes dissenting views either in the text of the article or in a separate paragraph. There is no classification limit, although the SEIB is produced in various versions with different classifications and is tailored to different consumers, with some versions cabled to major U.S. posts overseas and some U.S. military commands.

SENIOR INTERDEPARTMENTAL GROUP (SIG). *See* SPECIAL GROUP (COUNTERINSURGENCY).

SHAMROCK (OPERATION). During **World War II**, military intelligence and three American private cable companies came to an arrangement whereby the companies shared some telegraph traffic involving foreign targets with military intelligence, despite the prohibition of such sharing by section 605 of the Communications Act of 1934. In time, the arrangement also included telegrams sent by suspicious American citizens. The secretary of defense renewed the deal in 1947 under the code name SHAMROCK. The companies—RCA Global, ITT World Communications, and Western Union International—believed that the arrangement had the approval of the president of the United States. The **Army Security Agency** (ASA) and subsequently the **National Security Agency** (NSA) scanned hundreds of thousands of communications under SHAMROCK until Secretary of Defense **James R. Schlesinger** discontinued it in May 1975. *See also* YARDLEY, HERBERT O.

SHOOTDOWN OF KAL 007. On 1 September 1983, **Soviet** air defense forces shot down Korean Air Line flight 007, a Boeing 747, in Soviet airspace. The commercial flight apparently had veered off-course for unexplained reasons, but Soviet authorities claimed that the airplane flew erratically and ordered it shot down. Soviet authorities at this time were already suspicious of U.S. intentions, fueled by anti-Soviet rhetoric in the United States, and were already on alert to detect a surprise American nuclear attack. The incident also sparked numerous conspiracy theories, some of which claim that KAL 007 was actually on an intelligence mission for the United States. Investigations have been unable conclusively to explain the reasons why the commercial flight strayed off its course, but Russian president Boris Yeltsin acknowledged in mid-1990s that the Soviet Union was to blame for shooting down the civilian airliner. *See also* IVY BELLS (OPERATION); SOVIET WAR SCARE.

SIGNALS INTELLIGENCE (SIGINT). Signals intelligence is the interception and decoding of foreign electronic communications. It is comprised of three subsidiary collection disciplines: communications intelligence (COMINT), which is the interception of communications traffic; electronic intelligence (ELINT), which is the interception of electronic emissions; and telemetry intelligence (TELINT), which is the interception of signals from test vehicles or weapons systems. Although many of America's intelligence agencies engage in SIGINT collection, the **National Security Agency** (NSA) is the official manager of the country's SIGINT programs.

Signals intelligence as a collection discipline has a long and storied past. The British pioneered signals intelligence measures in the interwar years, but SIGINT's modern era dates to **World War II**, when the U.S. broke the Japanese military code and learned of plans to invade Midway Island, allowing the United States to defeat Japan's superior fleet. The use of SIGINT probably contributed directly to shortening the war by at least one year. The establishment of the NSA in 1952 gave coherence to the government's scattered signals intelligence programs. Some intelligence agencies, such as the **Central Intelligence Agency** (CIA), conduct their own specialized form of signals collection, but even these activities must be performed within NSA guidelines.

SIGNALS INTELLIGENCE CORPS. The Signals Intelligence Corps was the U.S. Army's **signals intelligence** (SIGINT) operation in the interwar years that assumed the work of the **Black Chamber** after its closure in 1929. The corps later worked closely with other elements of the U.S. government to break Japan's "**Purple**" code and listen in on Japanese communications during **World War II**. After the war, the **Army Security Agency** (ASA) assumed the duties of the Signals Intelligence Corps.

SKYHOOK SYSTEM. Skyhook was a navy aerial retrieval system, perfected in 1958, that employed some of the principles of the **All American system**. It featured a harness, for cargo or person, that was attached to a 500-foot, high-strength, braided nylon line. A portable helium bottle inflated a dirigible-shaped balloon, raising the line to its full height. The pickup aircraft, with two tubular "horns" on its nose, would fly into the line, snag it, and secure it to the aircraft by means of an anchor. As the line streamed under the fuselage, the crew snared it and brought it onboard by using a winch. The **Central Intelligence Agency** (CIA), in cooperation with the navy, incorporated the system into packages dropped from aircraft for agents. *See also* TROPIC (OPERATION).

SMITH, GENERAL WALTER BEDELL (1895–1961). Fourth **director of central intelligence** (DCI) between 7 October 1950 and 9 February 1953, General Smith presided over the growing **intelligence community** (IC) and the **Central Intelligence Agency** (CIA) during the **Korean War**. His appointment in October 1950 marked the **Harry S. Truman** administration's acceptance of the CIA as a permanent feature of the bureaucratic landscape.

General Smith made his reputation during **World War II** as General **Dwight D. Eisenhower's** chief of staff for the European theater. President Truman sent General Smith, considered an efficient administrator, to Moscow as his ambassador after the war. The surprise attack on South Korea in June 1950 raised fears of a third world war. President Truman appointed General Smith to be DCI in order to prevent future surprises and to wage clandestine war on the **Soviet Union** and **People's Republic of China** (PRC).

During General Smith's tenure as DCI, Congress expanded the national security budget, tripling intelligence spending in the process.

General Smith also adopted the recommendations of an early 1949 report to the **National Security Council** (NSC) by a commission chaired by **Allen W. Dulles** to streamline procedures for gathering and disseminating intelligence. He also created a new **Office of National Estimates** (ONE) specifically dedicated to producing national estimates. The newly established Board of Estimates (BOE), moreover, set the procedures for the estimative process that lasted over two decades. DCI Smith stepped up efforts to obtain current economic, psychological, and photographic intelligence (PHOTINT).

By the end of 1950, DCI Smith had reorganized the CIA by forming, on 1 December 1950, the Directorate of Administration, beginning a process of reorganization that divided CIA operations by function into three directorates—Administration, Plans, and Intelligence. The **Office of Policy Coordination** (OPC), formed in 1948, continued to exercise control over **covert action**, but DCI Smith began its gradual assimilation under his control. In early January 1951, DCI Smith made Allen Dulles the first deputy director for plans (DDP), to supervise both the OPC and the CIA's separate **espionage** organization, the Office of Special Operations (OSO). In January 1952, the DCI unified all analytic functions under a deputy director of intelligence (DDI). He also merged the OSO and the OPC—each of which had its own culture, methods, and pay scales—into an effective, single **Directorate of Plans** (DP) in August 1952. DCI Smith left an enduring legacy as a director who shaped U.S. intelligence effectively to fight the **Cold War**.

SONS OF LIBERTY. A radical patriotic association of colonists during the American Revolution, Sons of Liberty organizations came into existence in 1765 in reaction to the Stamp Act. The first chapter was located in Connecticut, but local groups quickly sprang up in all the colonies, with New York and Massachusetts being most active. Through mob action, the Sons of Liberty intimidated British officials, and through **propaganda,** they stimulated the patriots to action. In some instances, local groups engaged in intelligence collection and assumed government functions. *See also* COMMITTEE OF SECRET CORRESPONDENCE.

SOUERS, REAR ADMIRAL SIDNEY (1892–1973). First **director of central intelligence** (DCI) between 23 January and 10 June 1946. President **Harry S. Truman** appointed Souers the first chief of the

Central Intelligence Group (CIG), America's first post–**World War II** central intelligence processing organization. DCI Souers served a mere five months, but in that time, he set some important precedents for U.S. intelligence. As former deputy chief of **naval intelligence** and one of the authors of the directive establishing the CIG, Souers was aware of the need for central coordination of intelligence. He gathered a cadre of experienced intelligence professionals, mostly from the military, around him, and he successfully engineered to acquire the substantial foreign intelligence capability the **Office of Strategic Services** (OSS) had built up during World War II.

At President Truman's request, the CIG collated the vast amounts of army, navy, and **Department of State** cables, dispatches, and reports that arrived daily and produced a comprehensive intelligence summary for the White House. Souers was unable to get much cooperation from the State Department, and the military services refused even to provide the CIG with information on their capabilities and intentions. **Lieutenant General Hoyt Vandenberg** succeeded Souers as DCI in June 1946.

SOURCES AND METHODS. *See* PROTECTING SOURCES AND METHODS.

SOUTHERN AIR TRANSPORT. Southern Air Transport was a **proprietary company** of the **Central Intelligence Agency** (CIA) acquired in August 1960 to support CIA's **covert actions**. Southern Air Transport grew quickly to have semiautonomous corporate divisions for Atlantic and Pacific operations. It also won an air force contract to move cargo and passengers on interisland routes to the Far East. The company absorbed many of the personnel and aircraft of **Air America**, another CIA proprietary, which had supported CIA operations in the 1950s and early 1960s.

In 1972, a **director of central intelligence directive** (DCID) ordered that Air America be retained only until the end of the **Vietnam War**. The same directive ordered that Southern Air Transport be sold off immediately, which was done to private concerns at the end of 1973.

SOVIET UNION (SSSR/Soyuz Sovetskikh Sotsialisticheskikh Respublik). Established officially in 1922, the **Soviet Union** was the first state to be based on Marxist principles. Until 1989, the Communist

Party controlled all levels of government, the party's politburo effectively ruled the country, and its general secretary was the country's most powerful leader. The state owned and managed all industry, and agricultural land was divided into state farms, collective farms, and small, privately held plots.

From 1940 until 1991, the USSR was divided politically into 15 constituent or union republics ostensibly joined in a federal union, but until the final year or so of the Soviet Union's existence, the republics had little real power. The Soviet Union's intelligence services—the **KGB** and the **GRU**—and their clients were the principal intelligence threats during the **Cold War**.

The Soviet Union dissolved in 1991 into its constituent republics, with Russia assuming the obligations of the former Marxist state. The Russian Federation's security services—the **FSB** and **SVRR**—now cooperate extensively with U.S. intelligence on a variety of issues, but they also constitute a significant intelligence threat.

SOVIET WAR SCARE. The Soviet war scare refers to the 1983 alert in the **Soviet Union** of a possible war with the United States. Alarmed over the hard-line rhetoric of the **Ronald Reagan** administration that had come into office in 1981, Soviet intelligence had been placed on alert to monitor indications of a U.S. surprise nuclear attack on the USSR and its allies and to provide early warning of U.S. intentions. The Soviet intelligence collection program, known by the acronym RYAN, came to dominate the work of the **KGB** and **GRU** during this time. Soviet intelligence officers in the West received requirements in November 1981 and January 1982 to collect, on a priority basis, information on: key U.S. and **North Atlantic Treaty Organization** (NATO) political and strategic decisions regarding the **Warsaw Pact**; early warning of U.S./NATO preparations for launching a surprise nuclear attack; and new U.S./NATO weapons systems intended for use in a surprise attack.

Although the origins of RYAN are unclear, it may have been in response to a set of events that, taken together, alarmed the Soviet leadership: a series of new psychological operations against the Soviet Union and its client states; naval exercises near and incursions into Soviet maritime approaches; and ongoing covert operations within Soviet territorial waters, such as **Operation Ivy Bells**.

President Reagan's 23 March 1983 announcement of the **Strategic Defense Initiative** (SDI) probably was the catalyst for the emerging

Soviet war scare. Soviet leaders became very skittish after the announcement, which may have contributed to the erroneous **shootdown of Korean Air Lines 007** on 1 September 1983. Coupled with suspicions over a NATO command exercise in November 1983, codenamed ABLE ARCHER 83, that simulated release of nuclear weapons, the Soviet leadership perceived a genuine threat and whipped the Soviet public in late 1983 into a frenzy of fear. Radio Liberty (RL) interviews with Soviet citizens traveling abroad suggested that the Soviet public was genuinely alarmed. Even though the alert gradually subsided, RYAN continued until the dissolution of the Soviet Union in 1991. *See also* RADIO FREE EUROPE/RADIO LIBERTY.

SPACE SIGINT. *See* NATIONAL RECONNAISSANCE OFFICE.

SPANISH-AMERICAN WAR OF 1898. The Spanish-American War took place between April and August 1898, with the goal of liberating **Cuba** from Spanish occupation. At its end, the U.S. had acquired the territories of Guam, Puerto Rico, and the Philippine Islands. The war also elevated the United States to a world power.

The United States, through its Monroe Doctrine, which stipulated U.S. opposition to any European colonial encroachment into the Americas, had long been concerned over Spanish misrule of Cuba. In 1895, a revolution broke out on the island, possibly encouraged by the U.S. government and private interests, which Spanish forces were not equipped to quell. American newspapers, through their sensational accounts and exaggerated reports of Spanish oppression, did much to stir up popular sentiment for the war. Americans also began to demand that the United States should also become an imperial power by acquiring naval and military bases.

In March 1898, President William McKinley sent demarches to Spain, demanding full independence for Cuba. On 19 April 1898, Congress passed a joint resolution asserting that Cuba was independent. The resolution also authorized the use of the army and navy to oversee the Spanish withdrawal. Based on this resolution, the U.S. on 25 April 1898 formally declared war against Spain.

During the brief conflict, the **Office of Naval Intelligence** (ONI) tapped into the undersea Spanish cables running in and out of Havana, Cuba, enabling the ONI to read Spain's war plans, an operation credited with the American win. In addition, American military units on the island fought beside the rebel forces. As part of the American war effort, U.S. naval vessels landed in Puerto Rico and the Philippines and defeated the Spanish occupation forces. The war ended on 10 December 1898 after the conclusion of a treaty in Paris, which granted Cuba its independence and ceded Guam, Puerto Rico, and the Philippines to the United States. The United States, in turn, paid Spain $20 million for the Philippine Islands.

SPECIAL ACTIVITIES. "Special activities" is the formal phrase denoting **covert actions**. The **1947 National Security Act** authorizes the **Central Intelligence Agency** (CIA) to engage in special activities that the **National Security Council** (NSC) may from time to time direct. Legal experts have interpreted this provision of the law to grant covert operations authority to the CIA.

SPECIAL COMPARTMENTED INTELLIGENCE FACILITY (SCIF). SCIFs are specially constructed and vaulted installations designed to protect classified information and intelligence activities. "SCIFed" facilities encompass not only physical security components, such as guards and combination locks, but also mechanisms intended to prevent electronic emissions out of the facility or remote penetration of the facility from the outside. All intelligence installations containing classified and compartmented intelligence information are "SCIFed." *See also* COMPARTMENTATION.

SPECIAL GROUP (AUGMENTED). The Special Group (Augmented) was a committee of the **National Security Council** (NSC) established in November 1961 to review and approve covert actions associated with **Operation Mongoose**, the program aimed at overthrowing **Cuba's Fidel Castro**. The committee consisted of the **national security advisor**, representatives of the secretary of defense and the secretary of state, the chairman of the **Joint Chiefs of Staff** (JCS), and the attorney general. President **John F. Kennedy** appointed Brigadier General **Edward G. Lansdale** to act as chief of operations. The Special Group (Augmented) was disbanded in October 1962. *See also* 5412 SPECIAL GROUP.

SPECIAL GROUP (COUNTERINSURGENCY). Established on 18 January 1962 by National Security Action Memorandum (NSAM) 124, the Special Group (CI) was a committee of the **National Security Council** (NSC) set up to coordinate counterinsurgency activities separate from other **covert action** mechanisms, previously established by NSC directive 5412/2 on 28 December 1955. The Special Group (CI) was to confine itself to establishing broad policies aimed at preventing and resisting subversive insurgency and other forms of indirect aggression in friendly countries. In early 1966, President **Lyndon B. Johnson** assigned responsibility for the direction and coordination of counterinsurgency activities abroad to the secretary of state, who established a Senior Interdepartmental Group (SIG) to assist in discharging these responsibilities. *See also* 5412 SPECIAL GROUP; SPECIAL GROUP (AUGMENTED).

SPECIAL INTELLIGENCE SERVICE (SIS). Mandated by order of President **Franklin D. Roosevelt** on 24 June 1940, the SIS was established within the **Federal Bureau of Investigation** (FBI) on 1 July 1940 to engage in foreign intelligence collection activities in Latin America. FBI Director **J. Edgar Hoover** found the mandate far removed from the bureau's main mission of fighting crime and internal subversion and tried on repeated occasions, without success, to divest the FBI of foreign intelligence responsibilities. Resigned to having to conduct **espionage** in Latin America, Director Hoover demanded and received assurances that the SIS would be unfettered in its activities abroad. Consequently, SIS agents, who numbered in the hundreds during the course of **World War II**, became experts in tracking down Axis agents, breaking up Axis **signals intelligence** (SIGINT) channels, and identifying laundered Axis funds. SIS agents were also highly successful in tracking down German clandestine radio stations that were used to send wartime intelligence back to Germany. The **Central Intelligence Group** (CIG), established on 22 January 1946, assumed the responsibilities of the SIS, which were then transferred to the **Central Intelligence Agency** (CIA) in 1947.

SPECIAL NATIONAL INTELLIGENCE ESTIMATE (SNIE). SNIEs are **national intelligence estimates** (NIEs) that focus on a specific policy issue or intelligence problem within a short time frame.

SNIEs usually look into the immediate future, defined as up to two months ahead. However, they do go through the same production process as NIEs, including **coordination**. *See also* NATIONAL INTELLIGENCE COUNCIL.

SPECIAL OPERATIONS EXECUTIVE (SOE). The SOE was a secret British unit established in June 1940 to conduct guerrilla warfare against Nazi Germany. SOE agents, including women, were trained in the use of guns, explosives, sabotage, and infiltration. They were sent to any country under Nazi occupation, in part to organize resistance against the occupiers and in part to control operations against German forces. SOE representative in Washington, D.C., **William S. Stephenson**, also known by his code name INTREPID, is generally credited with convincing President **Franklin D. Roosevelt** to establish the position of coordinator of information (COI) in 1941 and later the **Office of Strategic Services** (OSS) in 1942. The SOE was fully incorporated into Britain's Secret Intelligence Service (SIS) at the end of **World War II**.

SPOT (SYSTEM). SPOT is a French commercial imaging satellite whose images are at times employed by **North Atlantic Treaty Organization** (NATO) peacekeeping forces. The first SPOT satellite was launched in 1986 and was followed by later versions in 1988, 1993, and 1998. The latest version, launched on 4 May 2002, has increased resolution and spectral capabilities.

SPOT satellites have the capability to view areas that are under different orbital tracks. According to Jeffrey Richelsen, a noted observer of satellite capabilities, color and black and white images can be recorded simultaneously with the satellite's two imaging sensors and then digitally merged.

SPUTNIK. Sputnik refers to a series of artificial satellites launched by the **Soviet Union** beginning on 4 October 1957. The first four Sputniks were unmanned, but Sputnik 5, launched on 15 May 1960, carried animals that were recovered alive after their return to earth the next day.

The launch of the first Sputnik satellite shocked the United States and contributed to the "missile gap" controversy in the late 1950s. In response, the U.S. government undertook a crash program to catch up with the Soviet Union, first establishing the National Aeronautics and

Space Administration (NASA) and then beginning to develop the first of the **photographic intelligence** (PHOTINT) satellites, **CORONA**, which went into service in 1960.

SR-71 BLACKBIRD. *See* U-2.

STALIN, JOSEF (1879–1953). Born as Josif Vissarionovich Dzhugashvili to illiterate peasants in Georgia, Stalin—whose nickname refers to steel—became enamored of socialism while attending seminary school and honed his Marxist skills as an underground agitator in the Russian Caucasus. Soon after, he joined up with Vladimir Lenin but took no active part in the 1917 October Revolution that ousted the Russian czar and brought into being the **Soviet Union**.

After the revolution, Stalin became general secretary of the new Soviet Communist Party and secretly began consolidating power. Soon after Lenin's death in 1924, Stalin took over the reins of power, began undoing Lenin's market socialist policies by implementing a program of draconian industrialization, and forced agricultural collectivization. Stalin blamed the resulting resistance and food shortages on rich peasants (kulaks) and forced them into prison camps (gulags) in Siberia. In the 1930s, Stalin also consolidated his power by purging his opponents from the Communist Party and either killing or imprisoning them.

In 1939, Stalin agreed to a nonaggression pact with Nazi Germany. However, Nazi Germany's leader, Adolph Hitler, abrogated the pact and invaded the Soviet Union in 1941. Stalin, who was unprepared for the invasion, reorganized the Soviet Red Army and launched a massive resistance effort that forced German occupation forces from Soviet territory and drove them into Germany, while Western forces marched into Germany from the west. Germany surrendered to Allied forces in May 1945.

Following **World War II**, Stalin established a series of communist governments in East European satellite countries, which later formed the backbone of the **Warsaw Pact**. Stalin's actions sparked the **Cold War**—the ideological and military competition between the East and the West—that lasted until 1991. To fight the Cold War effectively, Stalin sought military power, first by strengthening the role of the Red Army internally and externally and then building and maintaining strategic nuclear forces. Stalin died in March 1953, officially from a cerebral hemorrhage, and unofficially from poisoning.

STAR GATE (OPERATION). From 1972 until the mid-1990s, the **Central Intelligence Agency** (CIA) and some other agencies of the U.S. government funded parapsychological research, such as remote viewing, mental telepathy, and extrasensory perception (ESP), at the Stanford Research Institute and Science Applications International Corporation. The highly classified project sought to discover the applications of such methods in clandestine and covert operations. *See also* OPERATION MKULTRA.

STARLITE (SYSTEM). Starlite is a constellation of radar satellites, first proposed in 1997, to provide near-continuous, day and night, all-weather, imaging support to battle commanders in the field. The acronym stands for Surveillance, Targeting, and Reconnaissance Satellite, which was developed by the **Defense Advanced Research Projects Agency** (DARPA).

STEPHENSON, WILLIAM SAMUEL (1896–1989). Prior to America's entry into **World War II**, Sir William Stephenson, a Canadian entrepreneur, headed the New York Office of British Security Coordination and was the representative of **Special Operations Executive** (SOE) in Washington, D.C. Stephenson, code-named INTREPID, was instrumental in pressing President **Franklin D. Roosevelt** to establish the coordinator of information (COI) position to coordinate U.S. intelligence activities and lobbied for **William J. Donovan** to head it.

COI Donovan, having recently toured British defenses at the behest of William S. Stephenson and President Roosevelt, had gained the trust of British prime minister Winston Churchill. When America entered the war, Donovan became head of the **Office of Strategic Services** (OSS), which worked closely with and learned from British and Canadian intelligence officials. Stephenson was highly regarded by the Americans who worked with him. In 1946, General Donovan awarded Sir William Stephenson the Medal for Merit, the highest civilian decoration awarded by the United States (and never before awarded to a foreigner). One of William S. Stephenson's legacies was that former OSS officers formed the core of the **Central Intelligence Agency** (CIA) when established in 1947.

STRATEGIC ARMS LIMITATION TALKS (SALT). These **arms control** negotiations between the United States and the **Soviet Union**

were initiated on 17 November 1969. The first round of talks, alternating between Helsinki and Vienna, produced a set of agreements (SALT I) on 26 May 1972—the Anti-Ballistic Missile (ABM) Treaty and the Interim Agreement on Strategic Offensive Arms, both of which restricted the parties in the type and quantity of weapons each could possess. For example, the Interim Agreement limited the United States to 1054 intercontinental ballistic missiles (ICBMs) and the Soviet Union to 1607 ICBMs. The second round of negotiations resulted in a set of agreements (SALT II) restricting the number of each side's strategic weapons. The U.S. Senate did not ratify SALT II because of the Soviet invasion of **Afghanistan** in 1979, but both sides observed its major limitations until 1986.

Both SALT I and SALT II provided verification regimes that included the use of **national technical means**, consisting of overhead reconnaissance, **imagery intelligence** (IMINT), and **signals intelligence** (SIGINT) activities. The agreements specified that neither side could obstruct monitoring activities. SALT II prohibited the use of **telemetry** encryption if it impeded verification compliance with provisions of the treaty.

STRATEGIC ARMS REDUCTION TREATY (START). The first agreement, START I, signed in 1991 by President **George H. W. Bush** and Soviet president Mikhail Gorbachev, reduced the number of U.S. and Soviet ballistic missiles by about one-third and one-half, respectively. Because of the dissolution of the USSR in 1991, implementation was delayed until 1994 when agreements were reached with former Soviet republics. The second agreement, START II, signed in 1993 by President George H. W. Bush and Russian president Boris Yeltsin, proposed more intense reduction in strategic warheads than START I, but could be implemented only after START I targets were met. The Russian parliament eventually ratified START II, and the U.S. Senate ratified START II in January 1996.

The two sides agreed in late 1990s to negotiate START III, which would address Russian concerns with START II. The goal of START III is further to reduce the strategic arsenals of each party to a level of 2,000 to 2,500 deployed strategic nuclear warheads. This lower level supposedly is to assist Russia in avoiding a massive missile buildup in order to maintain the high START II ceilings. Presidents **William J. Clinton** and Boris Yeltsin also agreed to negotiate the problem of nuclear warheads, not just delivery systems. Doing so would mean that intelligence verification would extend to warheads removed from downloaded carriers, or even the dismantling of those warheads.

STRATEGIC DEFENSE INITIATIVE (SDI). The SDI was a plan for a ground- and space-based laser armed antiballistic missile (ABM) system that would have created a shield for U.S. land-based missiles. President **Ronald Reagan** announced the plan on 23 March 1983, and his administration poured substantial sums of money into the program, administered by the Strategic Defense Initiative Office (SDIO). Although there was considerable research under the project's auspices, congressional and public opposition to it—on the grounds that the concept would have meant scrubbing some key **arms control** agreements at significant financial and reputation costs—essentially derailed the program. President **George H. W. Bush** discontinued plans to deploy the SDI when he came to office in 1989. However, the introduction of the SDI into the volatile mix of the **Cold War** probably was the catalyst for such crises as the 1983 **Soviet war scare** and the dissolution of the **Soviet Union** in 1991. Succeeding administrations have recommended modified versions of the SDI at the theater level, such as the high altitude theater defense program President **George W. Bush** authorized on coming to office in 2001.

STRATEGIC SUPPORT BRANCH. Established in 2002, the **Defense Intelligence Agency** (DIA) created the Strategic Support Branch on the orders of Defense Secretary Donald Rumsfeld to boost the Defense Department's **espionage** capabilities by deploying small teams of case officers, linguists, interrogators, and technical specialists alongside the military's special operations forces. According to insiders, the Strategic Support Branch was established to lessen the Defense Department's dependence on **human intelligence** (HUMINT) supplied by the **Central Intelligence Agency** (CIA). In addition, the idea behind the Branch was to give combat forces more and better information about their enemy on the battlefield and to find new tools that could be used to penetrate and destroy nonstate groups, such as **terrorist** organizations, that pose threats to U.S. global interests. In a memorandum to the Chairman of the **Joint Chiefs of Staff** (JCS) in late 2001, Secretary of Defense Rumsfeld reportedly indicated that the units would focus on emerging target countries, such as Somalia, Yemen, Indonesia, the Philippines, and Georgia. According to press reports, the units have been operating within Iraq, **Afghanistan**, and other places for more than two years.

STUDEMAN, WILLIAM O. (1940–). A lifelong intelligence officer, Admiral Studeman was appointed **deputy director of central intelligence** (DDCI) in 1992 after a distinguished career as an intelligence officer in the navy. Between 1992 and 1995, Studeman served as deputy to **Directors of Central Intelligence** (DCI) **Robert M. Gates**, **R. James Woolsey Jr.**, and **John Mark Deutch** and served twice for extended periods as the acting director of central intelligence.

Between 1988 and 1992, Admiral Studeman was director of the **National Security Agency** (NSA), and, in 1985–1988, director of the **Office of Naval Intelligence** (ONI). In addition, he has held posts ranging from vice chief of naval operations and officer in charge of the Atlantic Fleet Ocean Surveillance Information Center to commanding officer of the Navy Operational Intelligence Center and assistant chief of staff for sixth fleet intelligence.

SUCCESS (OPERATION). Operation Success was a **covert action** by the **Central Intelligence Agency** (CIA) in 1954 to overthrow the democratically elected government of **Jacobo Arbenz Guzman** in Guatemala. Arbenz was elected in 1950 on a platform of land reform, and soon after his election, he expropriated the lands of the United Fruit Company, the largest employer in Guatemala at the time, which magnified calls in Washington for his ouster by painting him as a communist and a Soviet sympathizer. The CIA set up training camps in Nicaragua, planted Soviet weaponry in Guatemala, and broadcast alarming reports of massive defections within the Guatemalan army. Operation Success groomed a "liberator" and fomented subversion within the Guatemalan army by **propaganda**, sabotage, and commando raids. Expecting an invasion, Arbenz requested Soviet help, thus giving the CIA the pretext for intervention. Arbenz resigned on

2 June 1954 and took sanctuary in the Mexican Embassy. Following the coup, the CIA undertook a follow-up covert action, **Operation History**, to gather and exploit the documents of the Guatemalan Communist Party. Arbenz's overthrow ushered in a decades-long period of successive dictatorships and human rights abuses.

SVRR (Sluzhba Vneshney Rasvedki Rossii). The SVRR is the external intelligence service of the Russian Federation and a direct successor of the **Soviet KGB**. The SVRR's sister agency, the **FSB**, also a direct successor of the KGB, focuses primarily on domestic intelligence and security. The SVRR handled many of the American spies in the 1990s, including **Aldrich Ames** and **Robert Hanssen**.

– T –

TACTICAL INTELLIGENCE AND RELATED ACTIVITIES (TIARA). One of the three **intelligence budgets**, TIARA programs are a diverse array of reconnaissance and target acquisition programs that provide direct intelligence support to military operations. TIARA actually includes both tactical intelligence programs and other intelligence activities serving both tactical and national requirements.

TIARA evolved from the budget authorization category called *intelligence-related activities* (IRA) to consolidate **Department of Defense** (DOD) tactical intelligence activities, which, prior to 1982, were outside the **National Foreign Intelligence Program** (NFIP). Beginning with the fiscal year 1982 authorizations, IRA was renamed *tactical intelligence and related activities* to emphasize the tactical nature of many of the programs in this category. *See also* JOINT MILITARY INTELLIGENCE PROGRAM.

TAGBOARD (OPERATION). TAGBOARD was a research and development program initiated in 1963 to create a pilotless aircraft to collect national-level intelligence. The resulting Lockheed D-21 was a "drone" aircraft designed to fly over hostile territory at an altitude of over 90,000 feet, at three time the speed of sound, and with a range of over 3,400 nautical miles. TAGBOARD drones initially were designed to be launched from aircraft based on carriers, but the program encountered operational problems from the beginning. In the late 1960s, some B-52 bomber airplanes were modified to serve as launching platforms for the drones, at which point the entire program was renamed SENIOR BOWL. Despite consistent operational difficulties, SENIOR BOWL drones flew several successful missions for two years beginning in 1969. The program, however, was cancelled in 1971 because of mounting costs and operational setbacks. *See also* UNMANNED AERIAL VEHICLES.

TALLMADGE, BENJAMIN (1754–1835). Benjamin Tallmadge was a Continental Army officer who in 1778 established the **Culper Spy Ring** in New York and ran it until the end of the Revolutionary War. He did so at the behest of General **George Washington**, with whom Tallmadge maintained a steady correspondence. Tallmadge also played a role in the **Benedict Arnold** affair, during which he had custody of Arnold's **case officer**, British Major John Andre.

TASK FORCE 157. In 1966, the navy established a covert **human intelligence** (HUMINT) collection unit, designated the Naval Field Operations Support Group (NFOSG). The navy changed the name to the task force designation because of resentment over its work by navy commands. Some of its operations, moreover, assumed notoriety during the **Vietnam War**. Nonetheless, Task Force 157 was a highly regarded clandestine collection intelligence organization that fell victim to the pressures generated during the **Church Committee** hearings in 1976. Task Force 157 was disbanded in 1977.

TAYLOR, ZACHARY (1784–1850). The 12th president of the United States between 1849 and 1859 and a hero of the Mexican-American War. President Taylor spent most of his life in the army and was one of the few military men of his day not to make good use of intelligence. In fact, Zachary Taylor ignored intelligence almost to the point of dereliction, especially when invading northern Mexico during the Mexican-American War. Yet, General Taylor received a commendation from the U.S. Congress on 18 July 1846, congratulating him "for the fortitude, skill, and enterprise and courage which have distinguished the recent operations on the Rio Grande." His colleague, General Winfield Scott, who landed in Vera Cruz and occupied central

Mexico, displayed better intelligence sense and organized a crude but effective secret service known as the **Mexican Spy Company**.

TEAM A–TEAM B EXERCISE. Authorized in June 1976 during the tenure of **Director of Central Intelligence** (DCI) **George H. W. Bush**, the exercise sought to determine whether **Central Intelligence Agency** (CIA) analysts over- or underestimated **Soviet Union's** military capabilities. The exercise examined three different aspects of Soviet capabilities: air defenses, missile accuracies, and strategic objectives. CIA analysts, Team A, prepared their analyses normally. Team B, comprised of independent experts using the same information available to CIA analysts, drew their conclusions independently. The two teams were required to complete their analyses by early December 1976, to enable **National Intelligence Estimate** (NIE) 11-3/8, on Soviet military capabilities, to reflect the outcome of the exercise.

The two teams worked separately of each other, but on meeting in October, it became clear that the same data set had yielded substantially different conclusions. Team A foresaw a mild increase in Soviet defense spending, whereas Team B estimated a much larger increase in military expenditures. Team B believed Soviet missiles to be much more accurate than did Team A. On the subject of Soviet air defenses, there was general agreement that the Soviets did not possess the ability to neutralize an incoming bomber attack, although Team B felt that the Soviets had greater ability than did Team A.

On the issue of Soviet strategic objectives, Team A steadfastly believed that the Soviets did not seek nuclear superiority, but rather only nuclear parity with the United States. Team B, on the other hand, estimated that the Soviet Union sought nuclear superiority, not parity, and that Moscow not only believed that it could win a nuclear war, it was preparing for such a war. In a **coordination** meeting between the two teams in December, Team A gave in virtually to all of Team B's views.

The exercise demonstrated that the CIA's analytic methodologies needed reevaluation. It showed that relying on a single point of view produced faulty estimates and that good estimation could only be the result of considering and addressing all views. The exercise also pointed to the necessity of not only interpreting Soviet capabilities but also its intentions. Consequently, the CIA revised its methodological practices, incorporating the suggestion that the final estimative product be the result of internal debate and discussion among all points of view. *See also* ESTIMATIVE INTELLIGENCE; INTELLIGENCE ANALYSIS; RED CELL.

TELEMETRY INTELLIGENCE (TELINT). *See* SIGNALS INTELLIGENCE.

TELEVISION MARTI. Television Marti was established on 27 March 1990 to provide Cuban viewers with quality programming available in other countries in the western hemisphere, including news, features on life in the United States and other nations, entertainment, and sports. The station now provides commentary and other information about events in **Cuba** and elsewhere. The **Fidel Castro** regime has successfully jammed the station's transmissions, claiming that the broadcasts, transmitted from a blimp, violate international law forbidding the use of another nation's airspace. *See also* RADIO MARTI.

TENET, GEORGE JOHN (1953–). The 18th **director of central intelligence** (DCI), serving from 11 July 1997 until 11 July 2004. Prior to his service as DCI, George J. Tenet was sworn in as senior director for intelligence programs at the **National Intelligence Council** (NSC), where he coordinated policy issues and guidance on intelligence and security matters. He also was responsible for coordinating all interagency activities concerning **covert action**. Before serving at the NSC, Tenet served on President **William J. Clinton's** national security transition team in 1992 and early 1993, where he coordinated the evaluation of the **intelligence community** (IC). Previously, Tenet served as staff director of the **Senate Select Committee on Intelligence** (SSCI) for over four years, during which he worked on the committee's oversight and legislative activities, including the strengthening of covert action reporting requirements, the creation of a statutory inspector general at the CIA, and the introduction of comprehensive legislation to reorganize U.S. intelligence. In 1985, Tenet was appointed to the staff of the SSCI as a legislative director.

DCI Tenet resigned for personal reasons effective on 11 July 2004, but there was general speculation that he was pushed out by the **George W. Bush** White House for intelligence failures over the Iraqi weapons of mass destruction and the **terrorist attacks on 11 September 2001.**

TERRORISM. The numerous definitions of terrorism generally agree that it involves the threat or use of violence, often against the civilian population, to achieve political or social ends, to intimidate opponents, or to publicize grievances. Terrorism employs myriad activities such as assassinations, random killings, hijackings, and bombings. Once used for political purposes mostly by groups too weak to mount open assaults, it is now increasingly becoming a tactic of choice for the alienated or those with deep grievances. Some governments have also used political terrorism to eliminate the opposition or as an effort to overthrow another regime. In addition, terrorist attacks are also now a common tactic in guerrilla warfare. Because of its indiscriminate nature, terrorism has a vast psychological impact, amplified by extensive media coverage.

International terrorism reaches back to ancient times and has occurred throughout history. The term dates from the Reign of Terror (1793–1794) that followed the 1789 French Revolution, but in the post–**World War II** era, terrorism has generally been associated with such violent groups as the Italian Red Brigades, the Irish Republican Army (IRA), the Palestine Liberation Organization (PLO), Peru's Shining Path, Sri Lanka's Liberation Tigers of Tamil Eelam, and the weathermen and some members of U.S. "militia" organizations. Religiously inspired terrorism also has a long pedigree, dating back to biblical times. Its modern manifestations include such diverse groups as the extremist Muslims associated with Hamas, Osama bin Laden's **al Qai'da**, and other organizations; extremist Sikhs in India; and Japan's Aum Shinrikyo, which released nerve gas in Tokyo's subway system in 1995. The **terrorist attacks of 11 September 2001**, the Madrid, Spain, bombings in March 2004, the downing of the Russian airliners in August 2004, and the 2005 London bombings have set a new level of violence in international terrorism. Experts worry that the potential use of biological, chemical, radiological, or nuclear weapons of mass destruction may elevate the psychological impact of international terrorism even further.

In 1999, the United Nations Security Council unanimously called for better international cooperation in fighting terrorism and asked governments not to aid terrorists. However, international cooperation and the use of the military in the struggle against terrorism has had only mixed results, in part because some key governments have little at stake in eradicating terrorism and in part because the general strategy ignores the fact that some governments are heavily involved in sponsoring terrorism for their own purposes. Furthermore, states tend to define terrorism differently, oftentimes lending support to "freedom fighters" with whom they empathize while condemning the others as terrorists.

TERRORISM THREAT INTEGRATION CENTER (TTIC). The TTIC, established by President **George W. Bush** in early 2003 as part of his "war on terrorism" strategy, marshaled resources from across the intelligence, law enforcement, and homeland security communities in a common fight against **terrorism**. Specifically, the TTIC brought intelligence analysts from across the **intelligence community** (IC) together to assess, analyze and disseminate terrorist threat information. Under the terms of its mandate, TTIC analysts were responsible for assessing, integrating, and expeditiously disseminating available threat information and analysis; maintaining an all-source database on known and suspected terrorists; and identifying collection requirements related to the terrorist threat. The TTIC's establishment was a tacit acknowledgment that there was little cooperation and **coordination** among U.S. intelligence agencies on terrorism issues prior to the **terrorist attacks of 11 September 2001**. The TTIC, along with the **Federal Bureau of Investigation's** (FBI's) counterterrorism division and the **Counterterrorism Center** (CTC) of the **Central Intelligence Agency** (CIA), is slated eventually to be entirely absorbed by the **National Counterterrorism Center** (NCC) announced by President Bush in August 2004.

TERRORIST ATTACKS OF 11 SEPTEMBER 2001. The terrorist attacks of 11 September 2001, commonly referred to as the 9/11 attacks, were a series of coordinated suicide attacks against the World Trade Center towers in New York City and the Pentagon in suburban Washington, D.C. The attacks included the hijacking of three commercial airliners and flying them into the buildings. A fourth hijacked aircraft crashed into a field in rural Pennsylvania. The U.S. government is convinced that **al Qai'da** (also commonly referred to as al Qaeda) was responsible for the attacks, in which an estimated 3,000 people perished.

The attacks sparked the "war on terrorism," part of which was the invasion of **Afghanistan** in the fall of 2002 and the ouster of the ruling Taliban Islamist government. President **George W. Bush** also tried to justify the 2003 war on Iraq with the 9/11 events, but the link has been tenuous at best and totally unconvincing to a majority of U.S. allies, who have refused to cooperate with Washington in Iraq.

The attacks also sparked numerous investigations, particularly of the performance of U.S. intelligence prior to the attacks, most notably the joint inquiry by the congressional **oversight** committees and the independent **National Commission on Terrorist Attacks upon the United States**, also known as the 9/11 Commission. Ensuing reports illustrated numerous causes of the intelligence failure, including inadequate intelligence collection, insufficient policy and intelligence attention to the **terrorism** issue, lack of effective **coordination** and cooperation among the intelligence agencies, faulty intelligence structures, and many more dysfunctions, all of which contributed, after **Pearl Harbor**, to the second most devastating surprise attack on the United States in its history.

THREAT ASSESSMENT. A threat assessment is an evaluation of the harm that might be done by a foreign entity or its agents to the interests of the United States.

303 COMMITTEE. On 2 June 1964, President **Lyndon B. Johnson** authorized changing the name of the **5412 Special Group**—which reviewed and authorized **covert actions**—to the 303 Committee but did not alter its composition, functions, or responsibility. This committee considered 142 covert operations during the Johnson administration. *See also* 40 COMMITTEE.

TOWER COMMISSION. Known formally as the President's Special Review Board, the Tower Commission—so named because of its chairman, Senator **John G. Tower**—was established on 1 December 1986 to investigate the **Iran-Contra Affair**. The commission's report was highly critical of President **Ronald Reagan's** management of the crisis, which allowed **National Security Council** (NSC) staffers to conduct private covert operations. The report absolved the **Central Intelligence Agency** (CIA) from complicity in the affair, asserting that the CIA had refused to undertake the operations without proper presidential authorization.

TOWER, JOHN GOODWIN (1925–1991). Senator John G. Tower, Republican from Texas, chaired the **President's Special Review Board** that in 1987 investigated the **Iran-Contra Affair**. First elected to the Senate in 1961, John Tower spent most of his career in the Senate. In 1989, President **George H. W. Bush** appointed him secretary of defense but the Senate declined to confirm him. Subsequently, Senator Tower served as the chair of the **President's Foreign Intelligence Advisory Board** (PFIAB).

TRICYCLE AFFAIR. German spy **Dusko Popov**, who also doubled for Britain, claimed that Berlin had asked him to procure information about **Pearl Harbor** in mid-1941. In his 1974 book, *Spy, Counterspy*, Popov claimed that when in the United States to spy for the Germans, he relayed the requirements from his German masters, including the their curiosity about Pearl Harbor, to **Federal Bureau of Investigation** (FBI) director **J. Edgar Hoover**, who passed the information on to military intelligence. Neither the FBI nor military intelligence did anything with Popov's information, which during the **Cold War** fueled the theory that President **Franklin D. Roosevelt** knew about the Pearl Harbor attack beforehand but did nothing to stop it in order to have the United States enter the war on the side of the Allies.

TROPIC (OPERATION). In the summer of 1952, the **Central Intelligence Agency** (CIA) tried to establish a resistance network in the Manchuria district of the **People's Republic of China** (PRC). **Civil Air Transport** (CAT), the CIA's **proprietary** airline, dropped two agents and supplies into Kirin province, intending to retrieve the agents by using the **All American system**. However, the operation was betrayed, the retrieval aircraft shot down, and the crew killed. The Chinese captured the two CIA agents who had been dropped, and they were incarcerated until 1971 and 1973, respectively. Such drops and pickups continued into the early 1960s. *See also* COLDFEET (OPERATION); SKYHOOK SYSTEM.

TRUJILLO (MOLINAS), RAFAEL LEONIDAS (1891–1961). Rafael Trujillo was the Dominican Republic strongman from 1930 until his assassination in 1961. Trujillo, a Dominican military officer, rose through the ranks quickly, becoming a general in 1927. He seized political power during a revolt against President Horacio Vasquez in 1930 and wielded absolute control for the next 30 years through his command of the army, by placing his family members in key offices, and by murdering his opponents. Trujillo served officially as president from 1930 to 1938 and from 1942 to 1952.

An astute and ruthless politician, Trujillo brought stability to the island nation at the expense of civil and political liberties. He looted the national treasury, tortured and murdered his political opponents, and brutalized the population. His brutality was well known and documented. In the late 1950s, he began losing the support of the army and was assassinated on 30 May 1961. Some critics of U.S. policies in the Caribbean have argued that the **Central Intelligence Agency** (CIA) was behind the **assassination**, but there is no evidence to support the allegation.

TRUMAN DOCTRINE. Proclaimed by President **Harry S. Truman** before Congress on 12 March 1947, the doctrine said that "it must be the policy of the United States to support free peoples who are resisting attempted subjugation by armed minorities or by outside pressures." At the time, Greece was in the throes of civil war between royalists and communists, and the **Soviet Union** was threatening Turkey with aggression. President Truman argued that if such governments did not receive U.S. assistance, they would fall under the communist yoke, which "would be disastrous not only for them but . . . [also] for neighboring peoples striving to maintain their freedom and independence." He asked Congress to appropriate $400 million for economic and military assistance to Greece and Turkey, which Congress authorized in May 1947.

TRUMAN, HARRY S. (1884–1972). Thirty-third president of the United States between 1945 and 1953, Truman presided over the formative years of America's approaches to the **Cold War**. Trained as a lawyer, Harry S. Truman was elected in 1922 to be one of three judges of the Jackson County (Missouri) Court. In that role, he built a reputation for honesty and efficiency in the management of county affairs. He lost reelection in 1924 but won election as presiding judge in 1926. He won reelection in 1930.

In 1934, Truman won a seat as senator from Missouri and distinguished himself as a tough politician interested in ensuring that defense contractors delivered quality goods at fair prices. In July 1944, the Democratic Party chose Harry S. Truman to be President **Franklin D. Roosevelt's** vice president, and after President Roosevelt's unexpected death on 12 April 1945, he was sworn in as the nation's 33rd president. In 1948, President Truman won reelection despite widespread predictions of his defeat.

President Truman's domestic programs were generally nonmemorable but included desegregating the armed forces; forbidding racial discrimination in federal employment; and encouraging the U.S. Supreme Court to hear cases brought by plaintiffs fighting against segregation.

President Truman's foreign policy had a lasting impact on America's Cold War posture. He oversaw the end of **World War II** in Europe; approved the dropping of two atomic bombs on Japan on 6 and 9 August 1945; accepted the resulting Japanese surrender; presided over the founding of the United Nations; and took the first steps in countering the emerging threat from the **Soviet Union**. Although he dismantled the wartime **Office of Strategic Services** (OSS), Truman established the **National Intelligence Authority** (NIA) in 1946, which led to the drafting of the **National Security Act of 1947** and the creation of the **Central Intelligence Agency** (CIA) on 18 September 1947.

President Truman firmly believed in blocking Soviet expansion. The **Truman Doctrine** was a manifestation of this belief, through which the United States pledged to provide military aid to countries resisting communist insurgencies. In addition, the Marshall Plan sought to revive the war-torn economies of European nations in the hope that communism would not thrive in the midst of prosperity. President Truman was also instrumental in the creation of the **North Atlantic Treaty Organization** (NATO) in 1949, which enunciated the doctrine of collective defense against possible Soviet military incursions into Europe. He also waged an undeclared but United Nations (UN)–approved war against communist forces that, in June 1950, had invaded South Korea.

TRUST (OPERATION). Operation Trust was a covert deception operation initiated in 1923 by Soviet intelligence against Western intelligence services. It created a phony White Russian group called the Monarchist Association of Central Russia, which succeeded in passing itself off to Western governments as an anti-Bolshevik resistance group operating inside the **Soviet Union**. At a time when the Bolshevik regime was starved for hard currency, the intelligence services of Britain, France,

Poland, Finland, and other anticommunist countries channeled funds to the association, unaware the money was going to the Kremlin. Worse, the association lured genuine anti-Soviet resistance fighters to their deaths. Moscow kept the ruse going for six years before being found out. *See also* DENIAL/DECEPTION OPERATION.

TURNER, STANSFIELD (1923–). Twelfth **director of central intelligence** (DCI) between 9 March 1977 and 20 March 1981. A career naval officer with little intelligence training, Turner brought an apolitical and professional management style into the **intelligence community** (IC) in the wake of the congressional investigations into misdeeds by the **Central Intelligence Agency** (CIA) and other intelligence agencies. As part of his managerial reforms, Turner downplayed **human intelligence** (HUMINT) collection in favor of technical means of intelligence collection, arguing that they were more efficient and less controversial. Consequently, he eased many **case officers** out of the CIA. Turner's moves probably destroyed the CIA's ability to clandestinely collect information from human assets in the Middle East and elsewhere, which resulted in the CIA's failure to forecast the Islamic Revolution in **Iran** and the Soviet invasion of **Afghanistan**, both in 1979.

In addition to refocusing intelligence, DCI Turner opened up the world of intelligence to increased public scrutiny. To underscore greater openness, Turner established the Office of Public Affairs in the CIA and initiated the practice of giving press briefings and allowing the media to interview intelligence officers. Stansfield Turner is now an author and Senior Research Scholar at the Center for International and Security Studies at the University of Maryland.

– U –

U-2. The U-2, which stands for Utility-2, is a high altitude photoreconnaissance airplane that in the 1950s was initially designed to elude **Soviet** antiaircraft missiles. When the **Cold War** began in the late 1940s, the U.S. government sought various ways to gather information about Soviet military and economic capabilities. A 1954 presidential commission recommended that the United States build an aircraft that would fly at altitudes beyond the reach of Soviet missiles. Lockheed Aircraft Corporation won the contract to manufacture the U-2 to **Central Intelligence Agency** (CIA) design and use specifications.

The U-2 began flights in 1956, bringing back extraordinarily detailed photographs of targets, especially of Soviet defenses. President **Dwight D. Eisenhower** retained final say on whether or not each flight would occur. When the Soviets shot down a U-2 flight piloted by **Francis Gary Powers** on 1 May 1960, President Eisenhower discontinued the flights, claiming that they were interfering with U.S.–Soviet relations. The A-12 and its successor, the SR-71 Blackbird, replaced the U-2 as the principal photoreconnaissance asset in the mid-1960s.

Beginning in the 1960s, satellite collection of intelligence began to overshadow **photographic intelligence** (PHOTINT) collected by airborne platforms like the U-2 and SR-71. These two aircraft are still in service despite decommissioning in the past. In their current configurations, U-2 aircraft carry **imagery intelligence** (IMINT) equipment as well as sensors that gather **signals intelligence** (SIGINT) that can be transmitted by means of satellite link to intelligence analysts in as little as four minutes. The U.S. government now employs the airplanes in treaty verification, antiterrorism, counternarcotics, and patrolling truce lines in areas where U.S. forces are engaged in peacekeeping duties.

ULTRA. *See* ENIGMA.

UNION OF SOVIET SOCIALIST REPUBLICS (USSR). *See* SOVIET UNION

UNITED STATES INFORMATION AGENCY (USIA). The United States Information Agency, which existed from August 1953 until October 1999, was established to engage in "public diplomacy," which to some people is synonymous with **propaganda**. The agency was known as the United States Information Service (USIS) overseas but could not use that abbreviation in order to avoid confusion with the United States Immigration Service.

The USIA's mission was to understand, inform, and influence foreign publics in promotion of the national interest and to broaden the dialogue between Americans and U.S. institutions and their counterparts abroad. In addition, the USIA's goals were to increase understanding and acceptance of U.S. policies and American society by foreign audiences; broaden dialogue between Americans and U.S. institutions and their counterparts overseas; and increase U.S. government knowledge and understanding of foreign attitudes and their implications for U.S. foreign policy.

The USIA operated under its name until April 1978, when its functions were consolidated with those of the Bureau of Educational and Cultural Affairs of the **Department of State**. Following a brief period during the **Jimmy Carter** administration when it was called the International Communications Agency (USICA), the agency's name was restored to USIA in August 1982. The Foreign Affairs and Restructuring Act abolished the USIA effective 1 October 1999.

UNITED STATES INTELLIGENCE BOARD (USIB). The United States Intelligence Board provided executive oversight of intelligence matters, including the estimative process, during the administration of President **Dwight D. Eisenhower**. In 1956, President Eisenhower established the President's Board of Consultants on Foreign Intelligence Activities. Shortly after it was formed, it issued a critical review of the management of the **intelligence community** (IC) by the **director of central intelligence** (DCI). In 1957, on the board's recommendation, President Eisenhower established the USIB as the single forum for all intelligence chiefs to provide advice to the DCI on intelligence activities. President **John F. Kennedy** changed the USIB's name to the **President's Foreign Intelligence Advisory Board** (PFIAB).

Following up on the recommendations in November 1971, President **Richard M. Nixon** issued a directive calling for improvements in intelligence resource management as well as in intelligence analysis. The directive made the DCI responsible for "planning, reviewing, and evaluating all intelligence programs and activities and in the production of national intelligence." It also reconstituted the PFIAB not only to advise but also to assist the DCI, and set up the intelligence committee of the **National Security Council** (NSC) to coordinate and to review intelligence activities.

UNMANNED AERIAL VEHICLES (UAV). Unmanned aerial vehicles are pilotless craft, operated remotely by ground controllers, that can fly independently and are capable of carrying lethal and nonlethal payloads. Initially, they were designed to replace manned aerial platforms like the **U-2** and **SR-71** aircraft for reconnaissance photography, but technological limitations associated with their development made such substitution unfeasible. UAVs have been employed for reconnaissance and intelligence gathering purposes since the 1950s, but they became commonplace in the 1990s in such operational environments as Kosovo, when their ability to linger over hostile territory enabled them to provide surveillance information that would otherwise be unavailable. They now come in a variety of forms, such as the medium-altitude **Predator** and the high-altitude **Global Hawk**. *See also* TAGBOARD (OPERATION); SENIOR BOWL (OPERATION).

USA PATRIOT ACT. Officially known as the Uniting and Strengthening America by Providing Appropriate Tools Required to Intercept and Obstruct Terrorism (USA PATRIOT) Act, the legislation was adopted by Congress on 25 October 2001 as the legislative response to the **terrorist attacks of 11 September 2001**. Its intent was to provide law enforcement officials with enhanced authorities to investigate and prosecute **terrorism**. The law expanded the definition of terrorist activity to include providing support to groups that the individual "knew or should have known were terrorist organizations." In addition, the act enabled the use of search warrants, rather than wiretap orders, to read opened voice mail messages and electronic Internet mail. Furthermore, the law expanded the list of toxins that are classified as dangerous and requires background checks of scientists who work with them.

In the intelligence area, the USA PATRIOT Act also expanded intelligence authorities to enable better information gathering about terrorists. It modified the **Foreign Intelligence Surveillance Act of 1978** to permit surveillance warrants whose purpose is "significant" foreign intelligence information gathering. The act broadened the authority of intelligence agencies to deal with individuals who have had human rights violations or other transgressions. It also sought to promote intelligence sharing and cooperation among intelligence agencies on criminal matters, which had heretofore been subject to the strict separation of law enforcement from intelligence information.

The USA PATRIOT Act went through Congress with unaccustomed speed, without much public debate, and with few oversight authorities for Congress. Consequently, the provisions of the law have been subject to a great deal of criticism, particularly those that may be interpreted as threatening civil liberties and freedoms. Expanding intelligence authorities, moreover, have been condemned by civil libertarians as harkening back to the days of intelligence excesses. Some of the act's sections contain the sunset date of 31 December 2005, thereby ensuring that the controversial aspects of the law remain in the public limelight for quite some time.

USSR. *See* SOVIET UNION.

– V –

VANDENBERG, LIEUTENANT GENERAL HOYT (1899–1954). Lieutenant General Hoyt Vandenberg was the second **director of central intelligence** (DCI) between on 10 June 1946 and 1 May 1947. A former intelligence chief for wartime general **Dwight D. Eisenhower**, DCI Vandenberg came to head the **Central Intelligence Group** (CIG), fully aware of the need for central coordination and analysis. Consequently, his short tenure as DCI witnessed many changes that later were incorporated into the **National Security Act of 1947** establishing the **Central Intelligence Agency** (CIA). Initially, Vandenberg focused simply on increasing the CIG's budget and expanding its staff. However, he was continually dogged by the pervasive influence of the **Department of State** and the military in intelligence matters. He gradually sought and got some additional authorities for the CIG, and he was able to win, over the objections of the State Department and **J. Edgar Hoover's Federal Bureau of Investigation** (FBI), control over clandestine collection, foreign **counterintelligence**, and the right to conduct independent research and analysis.

In July 1946, DCI Vandenberg established the Office of Special Operations (OSO) and the Office of Reports and Estimates (ORE) and, in the same month, took over intelligence operations in Latin America from the FBI. To manage this growing structure, he reorganized and strengthened the director's office, subjecting it to the kind of military discipline to which he was accustomed in the service. When President **Harry S. Truman** asked the CIG to assess the **Soviet Union's** worrisome behavior, Vandenberg presided over the first

national intelligence estimate (NIE), produced on 23 July 1946, judging that **Josef Stalin** had neither the capabilities nor the desire for a war with the West and would therefore follow an opportunistic foreign policy.

By early September 1946, Vandenberg had acquired the right for the CIG to have its own budget and personnel. He also began a campaign to place the CIG on a firmer legal footing, an aspiration fulfilled early in his successor's term by the passage of the **National Security Act of 1947**. *See also* HILLENKOETTER, REAR ADMIRAL ROSCOE.

VAN LEW, ELIZABETH L. (1818–1900). Arguably the best Union spy during the American **Civil War**, Elizabeth van Lew organized a spy ring in Richmond, Virginia, known as the Richmond Underground, to work against the Confederacy. She is reputed to have had superb tradecraft skills, including the protection of her spies, such that the identities of her agents have never been revealed.

VEGA (SYSTEM). *See* LACROSSE.

VEIL (OPERATION). A deception and disinformation **covert action** against Libya in the early 1980s, carried out jointly by the **Central Intelligence Agency** (CIA) and the **Department of Defense** (DOD), to dissuade Libyan strongman Muammar Qaddafi from engaging in **terrorism**; bring about a change of leadership; and minimize the possibility of Soviet gains in Libya. VEIL called for encouraging internal dissidents to act in order to increase psychological pressure on Qaddafi. To augment the operation, the DOD conducted unilateral and joint military exercises designed to deceive, overburden, and "spook" Libyan defenses. Part of the plan also was the placement of **propaganda** items in the media that would focus attention on infighting among Libyan groups jockeying for position against Qaddafi, the general plight of Libyan society, speculation about successors to Qaddafi, and rumors of foreign planning for renewed actions against Qaddafi.

VENONA (OPERATION). Project VENONA was set up secretly in February 1943 by the U.S. Army Signals Intelligence Corps, predecessor of the **Army Security Agency** (ASA) and **National Security Agency** (NSA). Its mission was to intercept and analyze Soviet diplomatic communications. By doing so, the United States could discern Soviet intentions toward the U.S. and the West. However, VENONA intercepts also played a central role in identifying Julius and Ethel Rosenberg, Klaus Fuchs, and **Alger Hiss**, who, along with others, constituted a Soviet "atom spy" ring that penetrated the Manhattan Project and passed secret information about the atomic bomb to the Soviets.

Julius and Ethel Rosenberg, husband and wife, were convicted of spying for the Soviet Union in 1951 and were executed in 1953. Both steadfastly proclaimed their innocence. Their case sparked domestic and international protests that they had been falsely convicted as part of an upswing in anti-Semitic and anticommunist hysteria that gripped the United States during the **McCarthy Era** in the early 1950s. The case remains controversial, although VENONA evidence suggests their guilt. VENONA came to an end in 1980, and the U.S. government made VENONA intercepts public in 1995. *See also* SIGNALS INTELLIGENCE.

VIETNAM WAR. The Vietnam War was a **Cold War** confrontation between the U.S.-backed South Vietnamese regime and communist North Vietnam and its guerrilla allies, the Viet Cong, that began in 1956 and lasted until 30 April 1975. Vietnam had been divided in 1954 by an agreement that pledged a plebiscite on unification by 1956. South Vietnam, with the support of its ally, the United States, backed out of the deal, sparking an insurgency by the Viet Cong, previously the Viet Minh, who had battled French occupation forces and defeated them in 1954.

Direct U.S. military involvement in the war began in the early 1960s. Throughout 1961, President **John F. Kennedy** came under intense pressure from his military chiefs and political advisors to send American troops to Laos and South Vietnam to stem the flood of communist military successes and prop up the faltering South Vietnamese regime. President Kennedy committed U.S. advisors, training, and equipment to the South Vietnamese armed forces later that year, hoping to stiffen South Vietnamese resolve. By the time of President Kennedy's assassination on 22 November 1963, however, it had become clear that the situation was rapidly deteriorating in favor of communist forces. The U.S.-sanctioned overthrow of South Vietnamese president Ngo Dinh Diem and the installation of successor puppet regimes had cast further doubt on the legitimacy of the South Vietnamese government.

President **Lyndon B. Johnson** used the **Gulf of Tonkin Resolution**, passed by Congress on 7 August 1964, as justification to escalate the war and introduce large numbers of American military personnel into South Vietnam. By April 1969, the United States had 543,000 troops on the ground in Southeast Asia. However, growing domestic and international opposition to the war and the inability of armed force to subdue the communists, especially after the January 1968 Tet offensive by communist forces, had cast doubt on America's ability to win the war.

During much of the Vietnam War, U.S. intelligence was split on the prospects for a successful military outcome. The **Central Intelligence Agency** (CIA) took the pessimistic view, often claiming that the war could not be won militarily. President Johnson, consequently, began to ignore CIA assessments in favor of the military intelligence agencies, such as the **Defense Intelligence Agency** (DIA), which echoed the military chiefs in asserting that the heavy commitment of armed forces and increasing "body count" of enemy casualties would bring about a positive outcome.

Peace negotiations to resolve the war began in 1968 but did not conclude until 1974. The United States suffered the bulk of its casualties in the intervening years. Despite the peace treaty that brought about a cease-fire, North Vietnamese forces swept into South Vietnam and occupied the country on 30 April 1975, effectively bringing the Vietnam War to an end.

VOICE OF AMERICA (VOA). Founded in February 1942, Voice of America has carried United States, regional, and world news to listeners around the globe for more than 60 years. VOA has prided itself on reporting the news accurately and objectively, no matter what the subject. To do it, a vast satellite network and a series of relay stations around the globe carry VOA programming to an estimated 100 million people.

In 1994, VOA entered the world of television when it inaugurated China Forum TV, a Chinese-language TV program beamed by satellite to viewers in the **People's Republic of China** (PRC). In 1996, a new television studio was completed, and VOA now simulcasts portions of some programs on radio and TV in nearly a dozen languages—Albanian, Arabic, Bosnian, English, Indonesian, Mandarin, Persian, Russian, Serbian, Spanish, and Ukrainian. VOA also puts text, audio, and audio/video on its two Internet sites and has an aggressive targeted e-mail program to countries where the Internet site is blocked. *See also* RADIO FREE EUROPE/RADIO LIBERTY; RADIO MARTI.

VORTEX (SYSTEM). Known as the Mercury-Advanced Vortex satellite, it is a classified **signals intelligence** (SIGINT) satellite capable of intercepting transmissions from radios, radars, and other electronic networks. First launched on 10 June 1978 under the code name CHALET, VORTEX has intercepted telemetry and communications from target areas. For example, the U.S. government made use of VORTEX satellites to monitor communications traffic during the nuclear accident in the **Soviet** city of Chernobyl in April 1986.

– W –

WALKER, JOHN ANTHONY, JR. (1937–). John A. Walker was a navy employee who in the late 1960s began spying for the **Soviet Union**. Specifically, he gave the Soviets information about the navy's **cryptologic** programs, code machines, and various "keylists" of specific codes that are used for only a specified period. In the 1970s, he recruited his friend, Jerry Alfred Whitworth, also a navy employee, to help in spying. In the early, 1980s, Walker also convinced his son, Michael Lance Walker, a corpsman stationed on an American aircraft carrier, to hand classified materials over to him to relay to his Soviet handlers. The **Federal Bureau of Investigation** (FBI) arrested the "Walker Ring" in 1985. According to official assessments, the damage done by Walker and his associates has cost the **Department of Defense** (DOD) nearly one billion dollars to replace code machines and make other changes to secure military hardware.

WALK-IN. A "walk-in" is a person who walks into an official facility, such as an embassy, and volunteers information or his services to an intelligence service. During the **Cold War**, **Soviet** walk-ins were the most productive intelligence sources for the West. However, there are several problems associated with employing walk-ins as spies. For one thing, determining the bona fides of a walk-in is difficult and so the volunteered information is suspect. Adversary intelligence services also sometimes have employed walk-ins as double agents to test defenses and capabilities and to spread false information.

WALTERS, VERNON ANTHONY (1917–2002). General Vernon Walters was the **deputy director of central intelligence** (DDCI) during the administrations of **Richard M. Nixon** and **Gerald R. Ford**. Walters joined the U.S. army in 1941, retiring in 1976 as a lieutenant general. In the intervening years, he had a colorful government career.

In the early years of the **Cold War**, Vernon Walters was aide to **Averill Harriman**; accompanied President **Harry S. Truman** to a meeting with an insubordinate General Douglas MacArthur during the **Korean War**; shuttled with President **Dwight D. Eisenhower** to a series of summit meetings; and served as translator to Vice President Richard M. Nixon during his goodwill tour of Latin America in 1958. Later, as a military attaché in Paris, General Walters reportedly borrowed a private airplane from French president Georges Pompidou to smuggle **Henry A. Kissinger** in and out of France for clandestine meetings with North Vietnamese negotiators. President Richard M. Nixon appointed Walters to be deputy to **Director of Central Intelligence** (DCI) **Richard Helms** in 1972.

In 1981, President **Ronald Reagan** appointed General Walters as ambassador at large and, in 1985, named him to be U.S. ambassador to the United Nations. President **George H. W. Bush** appointed General Walters U.S. ambassador to West Germany in 1989. Fluent in several languages, General Walters served as translator to many U.S. presidents and was one of America's more experienced intelligence officers.

WAR POWERS RESOLUTION. Passed by Congress on 7 November 1973, the War Powers Resolution sought to reaffirm congressional authority in decisions regarding war and peace and in the use of American armed forces abroad. Under the terms of the resolution, the president can introduce U.S. forces into hostilities only after a declaration of war, upon specific statutory authorization, or in a national emergency created by an attack on the United States or its forces. However, it requires the president to consult with Congress before introducing military forces. It also requires the president to report to Congress any introduction of forces into hostilities or imminent hostilities, into foreign territory while equipped for combat, or in numbers that substantially enlarge U.S. combat forces already in a foreign country. Once a report is submitted, Congress must authorize the use of forces within 60 or 90 days or the forces must be withdrawn.

Since its passage, many constitutional experts have questioned the act's usefulness, pointing out that Congress has tended to defer to the president when conducting war. More importantly, every president since 1973 has declared the act to be unconstitutional, even though no president since the act's passage has challenged the act in court. Finally, every president since 1973 has asked for, and received, authorization for the use of force consistent with the provisions of the War Powers Resolution.

WARSAW PACT. The **Soviet Union** and its client states in Eastern Europe established the Warsaw Pact alliance on 14 May 1955 in order to counterbalance the **North Atlantic Treaty Organization** (NATO). The Warsaw Pact dissolved on 1 July 1991.

WASHINGTON, GEORGE (1732–1799). The first president of the United States from 1789 to 1797, setting precedents in all areas of the presidency, including the use and management of intelligence activities. Although George Washington's military and political exploits have received more attention than his intelligence activities, he was a deep believer in the value and effective use of intelligence. Washington developed his appreciation of intelligence in the French and Indian War (1754–1763), during which he gathered intelligence and ran spies.

It was during the Revolutionary War that General Washington brought his intelligence skills to bear on winning the patriotic cause. He utilized agents behind enemy lines, recruited both Tory and patriotic sources, interrogated travelers for intelligence information, and launched scores of agents on both intelligence and **counterintelligence** missions. His most successful spy operation in New York City, the **Culper Spy Ring**, employed all these skills.

As an intelligence manager, Washington insisted that the terms of an agent's employment and his instructions be precise and in writing, composing many letters of instruction himself. He instructed his generals to do their utmost to gather intelligence and urged those employed for intelligence purposes to have integrity and be loyal. He was adept at deception operations and tradecraft and was a skilled propagandist. He also practiced sound operational security. He emphasized his desire for receiving written, rather than verbal, reports. He demanded repeatedly that intelligence reports be expedited so that they remain relevant. He also recognized the need for developing many different sources so that their reports could be cross-checked and so that the compromise of one source would not cut off the flow of intelligence from an important area. Washington sought and obtained a "secret service fund" from the Continental Congress. In accounting for the sums in his journals, he did not identify the recipients, thus beginning the tradition of protecting sources and methods. *See also* HONEYMAN, JOHN; SALOMON, HAYM; TALLMADGE, BENJAMIN.

WATERGATE SCANDAL. The Watergate scandal refers to the break-in at the Democratic Party headquarters at the Watergate complex in Washington, D.C., on 17 June 1972 and the ensuing revelations that the White House had authorized the break-in. In addition, the scandal involved several White House officials who tried to cover up their roles. Subsequent investigations implicated Vice President Spiro Agnew, who resigned in October 1973, on charges of tax evasion. Eventually, the scandal reached President **Richard M. Nixon** and his inner circle. Following impeachment hearings broadcast over television to the American public throughout 1974, President Nixon resigned on 9 August 1974. Vice President **Gerald R. Ford** was sworn in as president that same day. President Ford granted President Nixon an unconditional pardon a month later.

Director of Central Intelligence (DCI) **Richard M. Helms** successfully kept the CIA out of the scandal, even though many of the Watergate burglars had worked for the CIA. Helms even went so far as to refuse to cooperate when President Nixon tried to enlist Helms's help in blocking the investigation by the **Federal Bureau of Investigation** (FBI). When DCI Helms refused to cooperate, President Nixon fired him and installed **William Colby** as the new DCI.

WEBSTER, WILLIAM HEDGECOCK (1924–). The 14th **director of central intelligence** (DCI) between 26 May 1987 and 31 August 1991. William Webster became DCI at a critical time for U.S. intelligence. During the early 1980s, DCI **William J. Casey** had infused the **Central Intelligence Agency** (CIA) with resources that had greatly expanded covert operational as well as analytic capabilities. At the same time, the CIA was beset by charges of illegal activity arising out of the **Iran-Contra scandal**. Moreover, Webster's deputy, **Robert M. Gates**, whom the inexperienced DCI required for analytical support and expertise, was himself suspected in the Iran-Contra Affair.

Webster's mandate was to restore the CIA's credibility. A former federal judge, he had successfully played a similar role as director of the **Federal Bureau of Investigation** (FBI). His task was made easier by the **Tower Commission** report, which, while critical of the CIA, made it clear that the Iran-Contra Affair was a **National Security Council** (NSC) initiative and that the CIA as an institution—as opposed to the actions of specific individuals—was not involved.

In his first 100 days, Webster worked hard to make the CIA accountable, insisting that the CIA be subordinate to national policy. In addition to strengthening ties to Congress, DCI Webster tightened up the internal review process, defining rigorous standards by which **covert action** would be judged for competence, practicality, and consistency with American foreign policy and values.

DCI Webster was in office during the cataclysmic changes taking place in world politics, such as the dissolution of the **Soviet Union**, the collapse of communism, and the rise of **terrorism** and international drug traffic as new national security threats. Consequently, he created new **fusion centers**—interdisciplinary task forces—to cope with the new problems. For the rest of his tenure, DCI Webster navigated cautiously in a complex world dominated by long-service professionals and employed a detached and conciliatory management style.

WHITE PROPAGANDA. *See* PROPAGANDA.

WINTER HARVEST (OPERATION). On 17 December 1981, Colonel James Dozier, the highest ranking American army officer in the **North Atlantic Treaty Organization** (NATO) southern European Command, was kidnapped by members of the Red Brigade terrorist faction. Under Operation Winter Harvest, a small team of Delta Force technicians was dispatched to Italy to provide assistance with the search for Dozier. After a massive effort turned up nothing, the U.S. sent a team of **signals intelligence** (SIGINT) specialists to Italy.

The team brought sophisticated equipment and specially outfitted helicopters and was subsequently successful in tracking the Red Brigade terrorists and uncovering the location of Dozier. Colonel Dozier was rescued by Italian security on 28 January 1982.

WISNER, FRANK G. (1909–1965). A former **Office of Strategic Services** (OSS) operative in Eastern Europe, Frank Wisner was the first head of U.S. **covert actions** before and after the establishment of the **Central Intelligence Agency** (CIA) in 1947. Trained as a lawyer, Wisner ran spies in Rumania, Turkey, and Italy during **World War II**. After the war, he became assistant director of policy coordination with the specific mission of combating **Soviet** covert actions, especially those by Soviet front organizations. In 1949, Wisner conceived of and set up **Radio Free Europe** (RFE). He also masterminded the recruitment and establishment of the **Gehlen Organization**, which was comprised of former German military and intelligence officers. Wisner was one of the CIA chiefs responsible for **Operation Success**, the coup in Guatemala in 1954.

Wisner reveled in his ability to mastermind and run covert operations. As head of the CIA's Office of Special Operations (OSO), he initiated **Operation Gold**, the Berlin Tunnel caper, which monitored all military and diplomatic phone calls in East Berlin. He was also responsible for obtaining the 1956 secret speech Premier **Nikita S. Khrushchev** gave in the Kremlin in which he denounced **Josef Stalin**. In addition, Wisner and his operatives subsidized anticommunist West German politician Willy Brandt and supported organized guerrilla bands in Eastern Europe.

Wisner helped direct radio **propaganda** into Soviet-occupied Hungary in 1956, causing the Hungarians to revolt against Soviet occupation forces, driving them briefly out of power. At the time, Hungarian anticommunist leaders had been promised that American forces would come to the aid once they revolted. Wisner had envisioned a widespread anticommunist revolt that would unseat the Soviets in all of the Eastern Bloc countries. When this did not happen, the Russians returned in force and crushed the Hungarian revolt. Wisner consequently had numerous nervous breakdowns. He stayed on with the CIA for a time, even becoming chief of station (COS) in London, but resigned from the CIA in 1962 and shot himself dead in 1965.

WORLD WAR II • 221

WOOLSEY, R. JAMES, JR. (1941–). The 16th **director of central intelligence** (DCI), serving between 5 February 1993 and 10 January 1995, James Woolsey became DCI with no experience in intelligence. However, his previous positions had given him substantial policy experience, which Woolsey used to better the intelligence analyses. Prior to becoming DCI, Woolsey served as ambassador to the Negotiation on Conventional Armed Forces in Europe (CFE), Vienna, 1989–1991; undersecretary of the navy, 1977–1979; general counsel to the Senate Committee on Armed Services (SASC), 1970–1973; and advisor to the U.S. delegation to the **Strategic Arms Limitation Talks** (SALT) I in Helsinki and Vienna, 1969–1970. In 1983, President **Ronald Reagan** appointed James Woolsey a delegate at large to the U.S.-Soviet **Strategic Arms Reduction Treaty** talks (START) and Nuclear and Space Arms Talks (NST) in Geneva, a position he held until 1986.

WORLD WAR I (1914–1918). Known also as the Great War and the War to End All Wars, World War I was sparked by imperial ambitions, nationalistic fervor in the Balkans, and power politics among the Great Powers. The global conflict was the first to mobilize and employ stupendous numbers of soldiers in the field and to have enormous casualty rates. Over nine million men reportedly died on the battlefield, and nearly that many more people died on the home front from food shortages, starvation, genocide, and being caught up in the fighting. In addition, chemical weapons, widespread use of trench warfare, and new and highly lethal conventional weapons, such as the machine gun, made their debut during this conflict. The United States was a latecomer to the conflict, entering the war in early 1917. U.S. intelligence, which was virtually nonexistent at the time, had a small and inconsequential role in supporting American forces in the field. It also had a limited role in supporting American diplomats during the peace conferences following the end of the war on 11 November 1918. *See also* MILITARY INTELLIGENCE DIVISION.

WORLD WAR II (1939–1945). Also known as the Second World War, this was the costliest and most extensive conflict in the history of human warfare. The global war was sparked by Nazi Germany's leader, Adolph Hitler, who sought to undo the humiliating surrender terms of **World War I**, substantially increase Germany's military power, and acquire territories in Europe and elsewhere. The war officially began with Germany's attack on Poland on 1 September 1939 and ended on 9 May 1945 with Germany's surrender.

The United States entered World War II immediately after the surprise Japanese attack on **Pearl Harbor** on 7 December 1941 and fought alongside its European allies in the European and the Pacific theaters until the end of the war. It led the "D-Day" invasion and spearheaded the drive into Germany that, together with the Soviet push from the East, culminated in Germany's capitulation. While the fighting in Europe stopped upon Germany's surrender, the war continued for the United States in the Pacific until Japan's surrender following the dropping of atomic bombs on the Japanese cities of Hiroshima and Nagasaki on 6 and 9 August 1945, respectively.

Because of the war in Europe, President **Franklin D. Roosevelt** had authorized the establishment of the coordinator of information (COI) position in 1941 to coordinate intelligence information for the United States government. Its director, **William J. Donovan**, was appointed to head the newly established **Office of Strategic Services** (OSS) in early 1942. The OSS conducted sabotage and guerrilla warfare operations in all theaters of the global conflict, but there is general disagreement among historians about its contributions to the war effort. At the end of the war, President **Harry S. Truman** disbanded the OSS, but its veterans later formed the core of the **Central Intelligence Agency** (CIA) when it was established in 1947.

– Y –

YARDLEY, HERBERT O. (1889–1958). Herbert Yardley is generally regarded as the father of American **cryptology**. Born in Indiana, Yardley moved to Washington, D.C., in 1912 where he obtained work as a telegrapher and code clerk in the **Department of State**. Working on his own and with no formal training, Yardley was able to break the codes used by the department. When the United States entered **World War I**, Yardley convinced the head of military intelligence to have him assigned to the War Department, where he was put in charge of MI-8, and a newly created cryptological section of military intelligence. Under his supervision, MI-8 succeeded in breaking most of the codes used in German diplomatic and army communications and established new codes for use by the American army. Yardley accompanied the American mission to the Paris Peace Conference in 1919 as chief cryptologist.

With the war over, the American government considered disbanding MI-8 but instead renamed it the Cipher Bureau and placed Yardley in charge of it. The Cipher Bureau was funded jointly by the War Department and the State Department. As a **covert action**, the cipher bureau set up operations in New York City under cover as the Code Compilation Company, which produced commercial codes. Its New York location gave it easy access to message sources, such as Western Union, that later became participants in **Operation Shamrock**.

Yardley, who had named his cryptologic operations the **Black Chamber**, enjoyed great success. In December 1919, it broke the Japanese diplomatic code, which allowed the United States to have access to the negotiating instructions given to Japanese delegations. He was also hired in 1928 by Chiang Kai-shek's government in China and then by the Canadian government to make and break codes. However, Yardley's bureau was closed in 1929 when Secretary of State Henry Stimson concluded, "gentlemen do not read each other's mail." By that time, the Cipher Bureau had read more than 45,000 secret telegrams from more than 20 countries.

Now unemployed, Yardley wrote his memoir, *The American Black Chamber.* It was first serialized in the *Saturday Evening Post* and then published as a book. The U.S. government denied the existence of the Cipher Bureau, and the Japanese government quickly redesigned its communications codes. Later in his life, Yardley would go on to write several novels that involved cryptology.

YURCHENCKO, VITALY SERGEYEVICH (1936–). Vitaly Yurchenko was a Soviet **KGB** officer who defected to the United States in August 1985 and later redefected to the **Soviet Union** in November 1985. Yurchenko gave the **Central Intelligence Agency** (CIA) information that identified Ronald Pelton, an officer of the **National Security Agency** (NSA), as the person who betrayed **Operation Ivy Bells** to the Soviet Union. Yurchenko also gave the CIA valuable information on KGB operatives around the world.

Following his defection, Yurchenko became increasingly disenchanted with the CIA's restrictions on his movement around Washington, D.C. He also worried about the fate of his wife and child in the Soviet Union. On 2 November 1985, he evaded his CIA minders and redefected to the Soviet Embassy in Washington. There he claimed to have been kidnapped and drugged by CIA agents, and four days after he was flown back to Moscow. Subsequently, some CIA officials considered the possibility that Yurchenko was a false defector, but, given the information he provided, this theory appeared farfetched. The CIA has concluded that Yurchenko's was a genuine case of a real defector having changed his mind and deciding to return home to face the consequences.

– Z –

ZAPATA (OPERATION). *See* BAY OF PIGS INVASION.

ZIMMERMAN TELEGRAM. The Zimmerman telegram was an official cable, intercepted in February 1917, from the German foreign minister, Arthur Zimmerman, to the German ambassador in Mexico, Heinrich von Eckardt, disclosing a scheme to seek an alliance with Mexico in a war with the United States. If Mexico acceded to the plan, then it would reconquer the lost territories of Texas, New Mexico, and Arizona upon the defeat of the United States. Because the telegram was conveyed to President Woodrow Wilson by the British, some speculate that the telegram was a forgery, intended to persuade President Wilson to bring the United States into **World War I** on the side of the Allies.

Appendix A
Directors of Central Intelligence

Name	Service Dates
Sidney W. Souers	23 January 1946–10 June 1946
Hoyt S. Vandenberg	10 June 1946–1 May 1947
Roscoe H. Hillenkoetter	1 May 1947–7 October 1950
Walter Bedell Smith	7 October 1950–9 February 1953
Allen W. Dulles	26 February 1953–29 November 1961
John A. McCone	29 November 1961–28 April 1965
William F. Raborn Jr.	28 April 1965–30 June 1966
Richard M. Helms	30 June 1966–2 February 1973
James R. Schlesinger	2 February 1973–2 July 1973
William E. Colby	4 September 1973–30 January 1976
George H. W. Bush	30 January 1976–20 January 1977
Stansfield Turner	8 March 1977–20 January 1981
William J. Casey	28 January 1981–29 January 1987
William H. Webster	26 May 1987–31 August 1991
Robert M. Gates	6 November 1991–20 January 1993
R. James Woolsey	5 February 1993–10 January 1995
John M. Deutch	10 May 1995–15 December 1996
George J. Tenet	11 July 1997–11 July 2004
Porter Goss	22 September 2004–Present*

*DCI Goss, in 2005, relinquished his intelligence community responsibilities and became the first sole director of the Central Intelligence Agency.

Appendix B
Deputy Directors of Central Intelligence

Name	Service Dates
Kingman Douglass	2 March 1946–11 July 1946
Edwin Kennedy Wright	20 January 1947–9 March 1949
William Harding Jackson	7 October 1950–3 August 1951
Allen W. Dulles	23 August 1951–26 February 1953
Charles Pearre Cabell	23 April 1953–31 January 1962
Marshall S. Carter	3 April 1962–28 April 1965
Richard M. Helms	28 April 1965–30 June 1066
Rufus Lackland Taylor	13 October 1966–1 February 1969
Robert Everton Cushman Jr.	7 May 1969–31 December 1971
Vernon Anthony Walters	2 May 1972–2 July 1976
Enno Henry Knoche	7 July 1976–1 August 1977
John F. Blake	1 August 1977–10 February 1978
Frank Charles Carlucci	10 February 1978–5 February 1981
Bobby Ray Inman	12 February 1981–10 June 1982
John Norman McMahon	10 June 1982–29 March 1986
Robert M. Gates	18 April 1986–20 March 1989
Richard James Kerr	20 March 1989–2 March 1992
William Oliver Studeman	9 April 1992–3 July 1995
George J. Tenet	3 July 1995–11 July 1997
John Alexander Gordon	31 October 1997–28 June 2000
John E. McLaughlin	28 June 2000–6 December 2004

Bibliography

INTRODUCTION

Popular perception to the contrary, a vast body of literature on or about U.S. intelligence is available to those who want to delve into its complexities and myriad manifestations. This is so because the United States is one of the few countries on the globe that allows—in fact, at times encourages—the public to discuss and debate American intelligence activities. Admittedly, this perspective is a recent one, dating only to the 1980s, but the generally permissive environment in the United States has found expression in excellent works on all periods in the history of American intelligence.

While "openness" is now a general principle of American intelligence, there are limits to what can be disclosed without jeopardizing the country's security. Most works about American intelligence tend to be general in nature. Because intelligence activities take place within a legally sanctioned culture of secrecy, there are fewer works on specific intelligence operations. This gap is beginning to close as intelligence agencies continue to declassify greater number of documents as part of their historical review programs. However, some national security secrets will never see the light of day, either as declassified materials or as grist in books and journal articles.

The United States still maintains secrecy over a substantial number of intelligence operations, some dating back to World War I. There are good reasons for doing so, although some scholars allege that the American government has a penchant for overclassification. One reason for maintaining secrecy is that the information in question may, if revealed, embarrass governments that cooperated with the United States on specific secret actions. Most governments are very sensitive about their historical recollections, even if they date back a hundred years. However, the main reason the United States classifies information is to "protect sources and methods." Any information that compromises a specific intelligence gathering methodology or a person serving as a source of intelligence information must be protected from disclosure. Not doing so would bring into question the entire raison d'etre of the intelligence enterprise.

My view is that the more information available to the public, the better the public understands and appreciates the role of intelligence in the governmental process. American intelligence is blessed with a rich literature—perhaps more voluminous than any other country's—that is available to the public. The Central Intelligence Agency, the country's premier spying organization, must be thinking along the same lines, since in the last decade or so, it has begun declassifying relevant historical documents and publishing them in volumes that are available to the public. In 1976, the CIA published a volume on *Intelligence in the War of Independence* that is particularly useful for those interested in the early history of American intelligence.

For the modern beginnings of the central intelligence enterprise in the United States, particularly noteworthy are Douglas J. MacEachin's monogram on *The Final Months of the War with Japan: Signals Intelligence, U.S. Invasion Planning, and the A-Bomb Decision* and Michael Warner's *The CIA under Harry Truman*. The CIA has also published volumes on technical methods of collecting intelligence, such as *The CIA and the U-2 Program, 1954–1974* and Kevin C. Ruffner's *CORONA: America's First Satellite Program*.

In 1996, the CIA issued a volume on one of the more esoteric and successful interception programs that began prior to World War II and continued until the late 1950s: *VENONA, Soviet Espionage and the American Response, 1939–1957*. It also published documents and commentary on several of the Cold War's confrontations between the East and the West: Mary S. McAuliffe, CIA Documents on the *Cuban Missile Crisis, 1962*; Harold P. Ford, *CIA and the Vietnam Policymakers: Three Episodes, 1962–1968*; *CIA Activities in Chile*; and *U.S. Intelligence and the Polish Crisis, 1980–1981*.

Finally, since the CIA has come under intense criticism for failing to call the breakup of the Soviet Union, it has issued several volumes on its analyses of Soviet developments, the most important of which are Scott A. Koch's *Selected Estimates on the Soviet Union, 1950–1959*; Donald P. Steury's *Intentions and Capabilities: Estimates on Soviet Strategic Forces, 1950–1983*; and Gerald K. Haines's and Robert E. Leggett's *CIA's Analysis of the Soviet Union, 1947–1991*.

The historical dictionary series initiated by Scarecrow Press in 2005, of which this book is an integral part, would be useful to students of comparative intelligence. The series, an ongoing project spanning several years, will eventually cover the principal intelligence services around the globe. For now, the series's important contributions are Robert W. Pringle's *Historical Dictionary of Russian/Soviet Intelligence* and Nigel West's *Historical Dictionary of British Intelligence* and *Historical Dictionary of International Intelligence*.

The historical development of American intelligence has been a popular theme among scholars outside the intelligence community. Of particular interest in this area are Charles D. Ameringer's *U.S. Foreign Intelligence: The Secret Side of American History*; G. J. A. O'Toole's *Honorable Treachery: A His-*

tory of U.S. Intelligence, Espionage, and Covert Action from the American Revolution to the CIA; and Jeffrey T. Richelsen's *A Century of Spies: Intelligence in the Twentieth Century*. Nathan Miller's *Spying for America: The Hidden History of U.S. Intelligence* is also useful in this regard, although many of the stories are anecdotal and therefore subject to historical inaccuracies.

The more recent history of U.S. intelligence as well as the intelligence process it spawned are the subjects of several excellent works that are essential in any syllabi on U.S. intelligence. Among the most important are Christopher Andrew's *For the President's Eyes Only: Secret Intelligence and the American Presidency from Washington to Bush*; Angelo Codevilla's *Informing Statecraft, Intelligence for a New Century*; Allen Dulles's *The Craft of Intelligence*; Rhodri Jeffrey-Jones's *The CIA and American Democracy*; Loch K. Johnson's *America's Secret Power: The CIA in a Democratic Society*; William M. Leary's *The Central Intelligence Agency: History and Documents*; Mark M. Lowenthal's *Intelligence: From Secrets to Policy*; and Jeffrey T. Richelsen's *The U.S. Intelligence Community*. Of course, Sherman Kent's *Strategic Intelligence for American World Policy* remains the "bible" of intelligence analysis. Since intelligence is a foreign policy tool against strategic surprise, its role is explored in detail in Ephraim Kam's *Surprise Attack* and Ariel Levite's *Intelligence and Strategic Surprise*.

Several general works on American national security put U.S. intelligence in its context. The volumes of Amos A. Jordan, William J. Taylor Jr., and Michael J. Mazarr, *American National Security*, and Donald M. Snow, *National Security*, are particularly relevant in this regard. Other volumes deal with specific intelligence community agencies, among which are James Bamford's *The Puzzle Palace: A Report on NSA, America's Most Secret Agency* and *Body of Secrets: Anatomy of the Ultra-secret National Security Agency* as well as Ronald Kessler's *Inside the CIA: Revealing the Secrets of the World's Most Powerful Spy Agency* and *The Bureau: The Secret History of the FBI*. H. Bradford Westerfield's *Inside CIA's Private World: Declassified Articles from the Agency's Internal Journal, 1955–1992* is a superb resource for insights into how intelligence professionals perceive their own profession. The intelligence agenda in the post–Cold War period is laid out in Loch K. Johnson's *Bombs, Bugs, Drugs, and Thugs*, while Ronald Kessler's *The CIA at War: Inside the Secret Campaign against Terror* and Paul R. Pillar's *Terrorism and U.S. Foreign Policy* specifically speak to the war on terror.

Sources on specific historical periods are too numerous to cover adequately here. Instead, I would prefer listing one or two of significant works in each historical period and leave the reader to explore the other works in the extensive, albeit limited, bibliography that follows. For the role of intelligence during the War of Independence, I would recommend Helen Augur's *The Secret War of Independence* and Stephen F. Knott's *Secret and Sanctioned: Covert Operations and the American Presidency*. Intelligence played a minor, but significant, role in America's continental expansion, explored in Stephen E. Ambrose's *Undaunted Courage: Meriwether Lewis, Thomas Jefferson, and the Opening of the American West* and A. Brooke Caruso's *The Mexican Spy Company: United States Covert Operations in Mexico, 1845–1848*. In my view, the definitive work on the role of intelligence during the Civil War is Alan Axelrod's *The War between the Spies: A History of Espionage during the American Civil War*.

Most scholars trace the founding of modern American intelligence to the period just following the end of the Civil War. Significant works in this are James C. Bradford's *Crucible of Empire: The Spanish-American War and Its Aftermath* and Brian M. Linn's *The U.S. Army and Counterinsurgency in the Philippine War, 1899–1902*. American policymakers began viewing American intelligence, and its specific aspects, as worthy enterprises only after World War I, covered in Herbert O. Yardley's *The American Black Chamber*. Of course, the authoritative work on the failure of American intelligence to predict the Japanese Pearl Harbor attack is Roberta Wohlstetter's *Pearl Harbor: Warning and Decision*. For insights into the Office of Strategic Services and its director, "Wild Bill" Donovan, I would recommend Stewart Alsop and Thomas Braden's *Sub Rosa: The OSS and American Espionage* and Thomas F. Troy's *Wild Bill and Intrepid: Bill Donovan, Bill Stephenson, and the Origin of CIA*.

Since there is a plethora of good sources on intelligence during and after the Cold War, I am restricting myself to recommending books on and the memoirs of some notable personages of American intelligence as starting points for research in this area. Edward G. Lansdale's *In the Midst of Wars: An American's Mission to Southeast Asia* and Thomas Powers's *The Man Who Kept the Secrets: Richard Helms and the CIA* are worthy for the period from the 1950s until the early 1970s. Richard Helms and William Hood's *A Look over My Shoulder: A Life in the Central Intelligence Agency* is an excellent source for the troubles of the 1970s. Duane R. Clarridge's *A Spy for All Seasons: My Life in the CIA* and Joseph E. Persico's *Casey* cover the Iran-Contra Affair and the Nicaragua debacle in reasonable detail, while Robert M. Gates's *From the Shadows: The Ultimate Insider's Story of Five Presidents and How They Won the Cold War* is a good resource for materials on the dissolution of the Soviet Union and the role of intelligence in bringing down America's Cold War foe.

Scholarship in intelligence studies also comes in the form of journal articles. The *International Journal of Intelligence and Counterintelligence*, *Intelligence and National Security*, *American Intelligence Journal*, *Cryptologia*, and *Studies in Intelligence*, the CIA's house journal, all contain superb source materials on intelligence in all its aspects. Moreover, journalists have made an immense contribution to the literature of American intelligence. Space limitations prevent me from listing important journalistic sources, but I have found that the more recent and controversial an intelligence issue, the more likely that the print media is the principal source of information on that issue. The *Christian Science Monitor*, the *Los Angeles Times*, and the *New York Times*, and the *Washington Post* all provide deep coverage of recent intelligence developments. Finally, there are several comprehensive websites that are a must for students of intelligence. Of particular note in this area are the sites of the CIA, www.cia.gov, where *Studies in Intelligence* can also be accessed; the Federation of Atomic Scientists, www.fas.org; and Loyola University's superb collection of intelligence and other government documents on www.loyola.edu/dept/politics/intel.html#docs.

U.S. intelligence went into a tailspin during the 1990s, owing largely to the lack of an identifiable enemy against which it could mobilize its extensive resources. The search for new targets and new ways of doing intelligence work are explored in Wesley K. Clark's *Waging Modern War: Bosnia, Kosovo, and the Future of Combat* and in Frederick H. Hartmann and Robert L. Wendzel's *America's Foreign Policy in a Changing World*. The fast-paced changes taking place in the role of American intelligence are also amply illustrated and made most illuminating in the exhibits of the Spy Museum in Washington, D.C., which opened its doors just about when the United States was attacked for the second time in its modern history.

The terrorist attacks of 11 September 2001 changed everything by making U.S. intelligence the centerpiece both of accusations of failure to anticipate terrorist attacks and of the new national security strategy of counterterrorism at home and abroad. There are no better sources for these perspectives than the reports of the joint congressional inquiry and the report of the independent 9/11 Commission.

CONTENTS

A. GENERAL

1. Bibliographies

Bennett, James R. "The Agencies of Secrecy: A Bibliographic Guide to the U.S. Intelligence Apparatus." *National Reporter* 9, nos. 3–4 (1986): 41–47.

Blackstock, Paul W., and Frank L. Schaf Jr., eds. *Intelligence, Espionage, Counterespionage, and Covert Operations: A Guide to Information Sources.* Detroit, Mich.: Gale Research Company, 1978.

Calder, James D., comp. *Intelligence, Espionage, and Related Topics: An Annotated Bibliography of Serial Journal and Magazine Scholarship, 1844–1998.* Westport, Conn.: Greenwood, 1999.

Cline, Marjorie W., Carla E. Christianson, and Judith M. Fontaine, eds. *Scholar's Guide to Intelligence Literature: Bibliography of the Russell J. Bowen Collection in the Joseph Mark Lauinger Memorial Library, Georgetown University.* Frederick, Md.: University Publications of America, 1983.

Constantinides, George C. *Intelligence and Espionage: An Analytical Bibliography.* Boulder, Colo.: Westview, 1983.

Dearth, Douglas H. *Strategic Intelligence and National Security: A Selected Bibliography.* Carlisle Barracks, Pa.: Army War College, 1992.

Department of State. Office of the Historian. *Foreign Relations, 1945–1950: Emergence of the Intelligence Establishment—List of Documents.* Washington, D.C.: Government Printing Office, 1997.

Devore, Ronald M. *Spies and All That: Intelligence Agencies and Operations; A Bibliography.* Los Angeles: California State University, Center for the Study of Armament and Disarmament, 1977.

Farson, Stuart, and Catherine J. Matthews. *Criminal Intelligence and Security Intelligence: A Selected Bibliography.* Toronto, Ontario, Canada: Center of Criminology, University of Toronto, 1990.

Goehlert, Robert, and Elizabeth R. Hoffmeister, eds. *The CIA: A Bibliography.* Monticello, Ill.: Vance Bibliographies, 1980.

Harris, William R. *Intelligence and National Security: A Bibliography with Selected Annotations*. Rev. ed. Cambridge, Mass.: Harvard University, Center
for International Affairs, 1968.

Lowenthal, Mark M. *The U.S. Intelligence Community: An Annotated Bibliography*. New York: Garland, 1994.

Petersen, Neal H., ed. *American Intelligence, 1775–1990: A Bibliographic
Guide*. Claremont, Calif.: Regina Books, 1992.

Pforzheimer, Walter, ed. *Bibliography of Intelligence Literature: A Critical and
Annotated Bibliography of Open-Source Intelligence Literature*. 8th ed.
Washington, D.C.: Defense Intelligence College, 1985.

Pinck, Dan C., Geoffrey M. T. Jones, and Charles T. Pinck, eds. *Stalking the
History of the Office of Strategic Services: An OSS Bibliography*. Boston:
Donovan Press, 2000.

Smith, Myron J., Jr. *Cloak-and-Dagger Bibliography*. Metuchen, N.J.: Scarecrow Press, 1976.

———. *The Secret Wars: A Guide to Sources in English*. 3 vols. Vol. 1, *Intelligence, Propaganda and Psychological Warfare, Resistance Movements, and
Secret Operations*. Vol. 2, *Intelligence, Propaganda and Psychological Warfare, Covert Operations, 1945–1980*. Vol. 3, *International Terrorism,
1969–1980*. Santa Barbara, Calif.: ABC-Clio, 1980–1981.

Tuterow, Norman. *The Mexican-American War: An Annotated Bibliography*.
Westport, Conn.: Greenwood, 1981.

Wilcox, Laird M., comp. *Bibliography on Espionage and Intelligence Operations*. Kansas City, Mo.: Editorial Research Service, 1988.

———. *Terrorism, Assassination, Espionage and Propaganda: A Master Bibliography*. Olathe, Kans.: Laird Wilcox, 1988.

2. Dictionaries

Becket, Henry S. A. *The Dictionary of Espionage: Spookspeak into English*.
New York: Stein & Day, 1986.

Burton, Bob. *Top Secret: A Clandestine Operator's Glossary of Terms*. Boulder, Colo.: Paladin Press, 1986.

Carl, Leo D. *The CIA Insider's Dictionary of U.S. and Foreign Intelligence,
Counterintelligence and Tradecraft*. Washington, D.C.: NIBC Press, 1996.

———. *The International Dictionary of Intelligence*. McLean, Va.: Maven
Books, 1990.

Central Intelligence Agency. "Glossary of Intelligence Terms and Definitions."
In U.S. Congress. House. Permanent Select Committee on Intelligence. *An-
nual Report*. 95th Cong., 2nd sess. Washington, D.C.: Government Printing
Office, 1978.

Department of Defense. *DOD Dictionary of Military Terms*. www.dtic.mil/doc
trine/jel/doddict/ (accessed 19 July 2005).
———. *Glossary of Intelligence Terms and Definitions*. Washington, D.C.: Defense Intelligence College, 1987.

Dobson, Christopher, and Ronald Payne. *The Dictionary of Espionage*. London: Harrap, 1984.

Mader, Julius. *Who's Who in CIA*. East Berlin, East Germany: Julius Mader, 1968.

Mahoney, M. H. *Women in Espionage: A Biographical Dictionary*. Santa Barbara, Calif.: ABC-CLIO, 1994.

National Security Agency. *Basic Cryptologic Glossary*. Washington, D.C.:
Government Printing Office, 1971.

Parrish, Michael. *Soviet Security and Intelligence Organizations, 1917–1990:
A Biographical Dictionary and Review of Literature in English*. Westport,
Conn.: Greenwood, 1991.

Payne, Ronald, and Christopher Dobson. *Who's Who in Espionage*. New York:
St. Martin's Press, 1984.

Quirk, John P. *FBI Glossary*. Guilford, Conn.: Foreign Intelligence Press, 1988.

Shulman, David. *A Glossary of Cryptography*. New York: 1981.

West, Nigel. *Historical Dictionary of British Intelligence*. Lanham, Md.: Scarecrow Press, 2005.

3. General Works

Ameringer, Charles D. *U.S. Foreign Intelligence: The Secret Side of American
History*. Lexington, Mass.: Lexington Books, 1990.

Andrew, Christopher. *For the President's Eyes Only: Secret Intelligence and
the American Presidency from Washington to Bush*. New York: HarperPerre-
nial, 1995.

Bamford, James. *Body of Secrets, Anatomy of the Ultra-secret National Secu-
rity Agency*. New York: Doubleday, 2001.
———. *The Puzzle Palace: A Report on NSA, America's Most Secret Agency*.
Boston: Houghton Mifflin, 1982.

Codevilla, Angelo. *Informing Statecraft: Intelligence for a New Century*. New
York: Free Press, 1992.

Conboy, Kenneth J., and James Morrison. *The CIA's Secret War in Tibet*.
Lawrence: University Press of Kansas, 2002.

Dulles, Allen. *The Craft of Intelligence*. New York: Harper and Row, 1963.

Handel, Michael I., ed. *Leaders and Intelligence*. London: Frank Cass, 1989.
———. *War, Strategy and Intelligence*. London: Frank Cass, 1989.

Holt, Pat M. *Secret Intelligence and Public Policy*. Washington, D.C.: Congressional Quarterly Press, 1995.

Jeffreys-Jones, Rhodri. *The CIA and American Democracy*. New Haven, Conn.: Yale University Press, 1989.

——. *Cloak and Dollar: A History of American Secret Intelligence*. New Haven, Conn.: Yale University Press, 2002.

Johnson, Loch K. *America's Secret Power: The CIA in a Democratic Society*. New York: Oxford University Press, 1989.

——. *Bombs, Bugs, Drugs, and Thugs: Intelligence and America's Quest for Security*. New York: New York University Press, 2000.

Johnson, Loch K., and James J. Wirtz, eds. *Strategic Intelligence: Windows into a Secret World*. Los Angeles, Calif.: Roxbury Publishing Company, 2004.

Jordan, Amos A., William J. Taylor Jr., and Michael J. Mazarr. *American National Security*. Baltimore, Md.: Johns Hopkins University Press, 1999.

Kam, Ephraim. *Surprise Attack*. Cambridge, Mass.: Harvard University Press, 1988.

Kent, Sherman. *Strategic Intelligence for American World Policy*. Hamden, Conn.: Archon Books, 1965.

Kessler, Ronald. *The Bureau: The Secret History of the FBI*. New York: St. Martin's Press, 2002.

——. *The CIA at War: Inside the Secret Campaign against Terror*. New York: St. Martin's Press, 2003.

——. *Inside the CIA: Revealing the Secrets of the World's Most Powerful Spy Agency*. New York: Pocket Books, 1992.

Lacqueur, Walter. *A World of Secrets: The Uses and Limits of Intelligence*. New York: Basic Books, 1985.

Leary, William M. *The Central Intelligence Agency: History and Documents*. Tuscaloosa: University of Alabama Press, 1984.

Levite, Ariel. *Intelligence and Strategic Surprise*. New York: Columbia University Press, 1987.

Lowenthal, Mark M. *Intelligence: From Secrets to Policy*. Washington, D.C.: Congressional Quarterly Press, 2000.

Miller, Nathan. *Spying for America: The Hidden History of U.S. Intelligence*. New York: Paragon House, 1989.

O'Toole, G. J. A. *Honorable Treachery: A History of U.S. Intelligence, Espionage, and Covert Action from the American Revolution to the CIA*. New York: Atlantic Monthly Press, 1991.

Pillar, Paul R. *Terrorism and U.S. Foreign Policy*. Washington, D.C.: Brookings Institution Press, 2001.

Richelsen, Jeffrey T. *A Century of Spies: Intelligence in the Twentieth Century*. New York: Oxford University Press, 1995.

———. *The U.S. Intelligence Community*. Boulder, Colo.: Westview, 1999.

Shulsky, Abram N., and Gary J. Schmitt. *Silent Warfare: Understanding the World of Intelligence*. Washington, D.C.: Brassey's, 2002.

Snow, Donald M. *National Security: Defense Policy in a Changed International Order*. New York: St. Martin's Press, 1998.

Westerfield, H. Bradford, ed. *Inside CIA's Private World: Declassified Articles from the Agency's Internal Journal, 1955–1992*. New Haven, Conn.: Yale University Press, 1995.

B. THE AMERICAN REVOLUTION

1. General

Augur, Helen. *The Secret War of Independence*. Westport, Conn.: Greenwood, 1976.

Bakeless, John. "Spies in the Revolution." *American History Illustrated* 6 (June 1971): 36–45.

———. *Turncoats, Traitors and Heroes*. New York: Da Capo Press, 1998.

Berger, Carl. *Broadsides and Bayonets: The Propaganda War of the American Revolution*. Philadelphia: University of Pennsylvania Press, 1961.

Bowers, Ray L. "The American Revolution: A Study in Insurgency." *Military Review* 46, no. 7 (1966): 64–72.

Burnett, Edmund C. "Ciphers of the Revolutionary Period." *American Historical Review* 22 (January 1917): 329–34.

Butterfield, Lyman H. "Psychological Warfare in 1776: The Jefferson-Franklin Plan to Cause Hessian Desertions." *American Philosophical Society, Philadelphia, Proceedings* 94 (20 June 1950): 233–41.

Casey, William J. *Where and How the War Was Fought: An Armchair Tour of the American Revolution*. New York: Morrow, 1976.

Central Intelligence Agency. *Intelligence in the War of Independence*. Washington, D.C.: Government Printing Office, 1976.

Cummings, Light. "Spanish Espionage in the South during the American Revolution." *Southern Studies* 19 (1980): 39–49.

Davidson, Philip. *Propaganda and the American Revolution*. Chapel Hill: University of North Carolina Press, 1941.

Knott, Stephen F. *Secret and Sanctioned: Covert Operations and the American Presidency*. New York: Oxford University Press, 1996.

Patrick, Louis S. "The Secret Service of the American Revolution." *Journal of American History* 1 (1907): 497–508.

Pennypacker, Morton. *General Washington's Spies on Long Island and in New York*. Brooklyn, N.Y.: Long Island Historical Society, 1939.

Rose, P. K. "The Founding Fathers of American Intelligence." *Intelligencer* 11, no. 2 (Winter 2000): 9–15.

Thompson, Edmund R., ed. *Secret New England: Spies of the American Revolution*. Portland, Maine: Provincial Press, 2001.

Van Doren, Carl. *Secret History of the American Revolution*. Garden City, N.Y.: Garden City Publishing, 1941.

2. Benjamin Franklin

Bemis, Samuel Flagg. *The Diplomacy of the American Revolution*. Bloomington: Indiana University Press, 1957.

Clark, William Bell. *Ben Franklin's Privateers*. New York: Greenwood, 1956.

Currey, Cecil B. *Road to Revolution: Benjamin Franklin in England, 1765–1775*. New York: Anchor, 1969.

O'Toole, George J. A. "Benjamin Franklin: American Spymaster or British Mole." *International Journal of Intelligence and Counterintelligence* 3, no. 1 (Spring 1989): 45–53.

Poteat, S. Eugene. "Benjamin Franklin: The Spy No One Knew, for Sure." *Intelligencer* 10, no. 3 (December 1999): 21–24.

Srodes, James. *Franklin: The Essential Founding Father*. Washington, D.C.: Regnery, 2002.

3. Benjamin Tallmadge

Hall, Charles S. *Benjamin Tallmadge: Revolutionary Soldier and American Businessman*. New York: Columbia University Press, 1943.

Johnston, Henry P., ed. *Memoir of Colonel Benjamin Tallmadge*. New York: Society of Sons of the Revolution in the State of New York, 1904.

4. Culper Ring

Currie, Catherin. *Anna Smith Strong and the Setauket Spy Ring*. Port Jefferson Station, N.Y.: C. W. Currie, 1992.

Groh, Lynn. *The Culper Spy Ring*. Philadelphia: Westminster Press, 1969.

5. George Washington

Bakeless, John E. "General Washington's Spy System." *Manuscripts* 12, no. 2 (1960): 28–37.

Freeman, Douglas Southall. *George Washin gton: A Biography*. 7 vols. New York: Scribner, 1948–1957.

Kross, Peter. "George Washington: America's First Spymaster." *Military Intelligence*, January–March 1991, 6–8.

Thompson, Edmund R. "George Washington, Master Intelligence Officer." *American Intelligence Journal* 5 (July 1984): 3–8.

Wise, William. *The Spy and General Washington*. New York: Dutton, 1965.

6. Nathan Hale

Hagman, Harlan L. *Nathan Hale and John Andre: Reluctant Heroes of the American Revolution*. Interlaken, N.Y.: Empire State Books, 1992.

Lossing, Benson J. *The Two Spies: Nathan Hale and John Andre*. New York: Appleton, 1904.

7. Other Prominent Personalities

André, John. *Major André's Journal*. New York: New York Times, 1968.

Arnold, Isaac N. *The Life of Benedict Arnold: His Patriotism and His Treason*. Chicago: Jansen McClurg, 1880.

Boylan, Brian R. *Benedict Arnold: The Dark Eagle*. New York: Norton, 1973.

Brandt, Clare. *The Man in the Mirror: A Life of Benedict Arnold*. New York: Random House, 1994.

Decker, Malcolm. *Benedict Arnold: Son of the Havens*. New York: Antiquarian, 1961.

Fischer, David Hackett. *Paul Revere's Ride*. New York: Oxford University Press, 1994.

Flexner, James Thomas. *The Traitor and the Spy: Benedict Arnold and John André*. Syracuse, N.Y.: Syracuse University Press, 1992.

Forbes, Esther. *Paul Revere and the World He Lived In*. Boston: Houghton Mifflin, 1942.

Fryer, Mary Beacock. *Loyalist Spy: The Experiences of Captain John Walden Meyers during the American Revolution*. Brockville, Ontario, Canada: Besancourt, 1974.

James, Coy Hilton. *Silas Deane—Patriot or Traitor?* East Lansing: Michigan State University Press, 1975.

Martin, James Kirby. *Benedict Arnold, Revolutionary Hero: An American Warrior Reconsidered*. New York: New York University Press, 1997.

O'Brien, Michael J. *Hercules Mulligan: Confidential Correspondent of General Washington*. New York: P. J. Kennedy, 1937.

O'Dea, Anna, and Samuel A. Pleasants. "The Case of John Honeyman: Mute Evidence." *New Jersey Historical Society* 84 (July 1966): 174–81.

Pickering, James H. "Enoch Crosby, Secret Agent of the Neutral Ground: His Own Story." *New York History* 47 (January 1966): 61–73.

Randall, Willard Sterne. *Benedict Arnold: Patriot and Traitor*. New York: Barnes & Noble, 2003.

Russell, Charles Edward. *Haym Salomon and the Revolution*. New York: Cosmopolitan Book Corporation, 1930.

Sellers, Charles Coleman. *Patience Wright: American Artist and Spy in George III's London*. Middletown, Conn.: Wesleyan University Press, 1976.

C. AMERICAN EXPANSION AND THE MEXICAN WAR

Abernathy, Thomas Perkins. *The Burr Conspiracy*. New York: Oxford, 1954.

Ambrose, Stephen E. *Undaunted Courage: Meriwether Lewis, Thomas Jefferson, and the Opening of the American West*. New York: Simon & Schuster, 1996.

Bauer, Karl J. *The Mexican War, 1846–1848*. New York: Macmillan, 1974.

Beach, Moses S. "A Secret Mission to Mexico." *Scribner's Monthly* 18 (May 1879): 136–40.

Beirne, Francis F. *Shout Treason: The Trial of Aaron Burr*. New York: Hastings House, 1959.

——. *The War of 1812*. New York: Dutton, 1949.

Berton, Pierre. *The Invasion of Canada*. Vol. 1, *1812–1813*. Boston: Little, Brown, 1980.

Bill, Alfred H. *Rehearsal for Conflict: The Story of Our War with Mexico*. New York: Knopf, 1947.

Brown, Charles H. *Agents of Manifest Destiny*. Chapel Hill: University of North Carolina, 1980.

Caruso, A. Brooke. *The Mexican Spy Company: United States Covert Operations in Mexico, 1845–1848*. London: McFarland, 1991.

Croffut, W. A., ed. *Fifty Years in Camp and Field: Diary of Major-General Ethan Allen Hitchcock, U.S.A.* New York: Putnam's, 1909.

Elliott, Charles W. *Winfield Scott: The Soldier and the Man*. New York: Macmillan, 1937.

Knott, Stephen F. "Covert Action Comes Home: Daniel Webster's Secret Operations against the Citizens of Maine." *International Journal of Intelligence and Counterintelligence* 5, no. 1 (Spring 1991): 77–87.

——. "Thomas Jefferson's Clandestine Foreign Policy." *International Journal of Intelligence and Counterintelligence* 4, no. 3 (Fall 1990): 325–55.

D. THE AMERICAN CIVIL WAR

1. Air Reconnaissance

Crouch, Tom D. *The Eagle Aloft: Two Centuries of the Balloon in America.* Washington, D.C.: Smithsonian Institution Press, 1983.

Davis, Daniel T. "The Air Role in the War between the States." *Air University Review* 27 (July–August 1976): 13–29.

Evans, Charles M. *War of the Aeronauts: The History of Ballooning in the Civil War.* Mechanicsburg, Pa.: Stackpole, 2002.

Infield, Glenn B. *Unarmed and Unafraid: The First Complete History of the Men, Missions, Training, and Techniques of Aerial Reconnaissance.* New York: Macmillan, 1970.

MacCloskey, Monro. *From Gasbags to Spaceships: The Story of the U.S. Air Force.* New York: Richards Rosen, 1968.

2. Campaigns and Battles

Byrne, Robert. "Combat Intelligence: Key to Victory at Gettysburg." *Military Intelligence* 2 (Fall 1976): 5–9.

Canan, Howard V. "Influence of Military Intelligence (Second Manassas)." *Armor* 64 (September–October 1955): 34–41.

Curts, Bob. "U.S. Grant Goes to Shiloh: More Thoughts on Warning and Surprise." *Naval Intelligence Professionals Quarterly* 5, no. 1 (Winter 1989): 5–8.

Elley, B. L. *Grant's Final Campaign: Intelligence and Communications Support.* Fort Leavenworth, Kans.: Army Command and General Staff College, 1992.

Feis, William B. "Neutralizing the Valley: The Role of Military Intelligence in the Defeat of Jubal Early's Army of the Valley, 1864–1865." *Civil War History* 39, no. 3 (September 1993): 199–215.

Luvaas, Jay. "Lee at Gettysburg: A General without Intelligence." *Intelligence and National Security* 5, no. 2 (April 1990): 116–35.

———. "The Role of Intelligence in the Chancellorsville Campaign, April–May 1963." *Intelligence and National Security* 5, no. 2 (April 1990): 99–115.

Sears, Stephen W. *To the Gates of Richmond: The Peninsula Campaign.* New York: Ticknor & Fields, 1992.

3. The Confederacy

Andrews, J. Cutler. *The South Reports the Civil War.* Princeton, N.J.: Princeton University Press, 1970.

Axelrod, Alan. *The War between the Spies: A History of Espionage during the American Civil War*. New York: Atlantic Monthly Press, 1992.

Bakeless, John. "Three Who Chose Death: Part 1. The Sam Davis Tragedy." In *Spies of the Confederacy*. Philadelphia: Lippincott, 1970.

Beymer, William Gilmore. *On Hazardous Service: Scouts and Spies of the North and South*. New York: Harper, 1912.

Campbell, Helen J. *Confederate Courier*. New York: St. Martin's Press, 1964.

Carter, Samuel, III. *The Riddle of Dr. Mudd*. New York: Putnam's, 1974.

Fishel, Edwin C. "The Mythology of Civil War Intelligence." *Civil War History* 10, no. 4 (December 1964): 344–67.

——. "Myths That Never Die." *International Journal of Intelligence and Counterintelligence* 2, no. 1 (Spring 1988): 27–58.

——. *The Secret War for the Union: The Untold Story of Military Intelligence in the Civil War*. Boston: Houghton Mifflin, 1996.

Foster, G. Allen. *The Eyes and Ears of the Civil War*. New York: Criterion, 1963.

Harlow, Alvin F. *Brass-Pounders: Young Telegraphers of the Civil War*. Denver, Colo.: Sage, 1962.

Humphreys, David. *Heroes and Spies of the Civil War*. New York: Neale, 1903.

Jones, John B. *A Rebel Clerk's War Diary*. 2 vols. New York: Old Hickory Bookshop, 1935.

Kane, Harnett T. *Spies for the Blue and Gray*. Garden City, N.Y.: Hanover House, 1954.

Klement, Frank L. *Dark Lanterns: Secret Political Societies, Conspiracies, and Treason Trials in the Civil War*. Baton Rouge: Louisiana State University Press, 1984.

Markle, Donald E. *Spies and Spy Masters of the Civil War*. New York: Hippocrene, 1995.

Pittenger, William. *Capturing a Locomotive: A History of Secret Service in the Late War*. Philadelphia: Lippincott, 1884.

Sears, Stephen W. "Raid on Richmond." *Quarterly Journal of Military History* 11, no. 1 (Autumn 1998): 88–96.

Stern, Philip Van Doren. *Secret Missions of the Civil War: First-Hand Accounts by Men and Women Who Risked Their Lives in Underground Activities for the North and South*. Avenel, N.J.: Wings Books, 1990.

Tidwell, William A. *April '65: Confederate Covert Action in the American Civil War*. Kent, Ohio: Kent State University Press, 1995.

——. *Come Retribution: The Confederate Secret Service and the Assassination of Lincoln*. With James O. Hall and David W. Gaddy. Jackson: University Press of Mississippi, 1988.

4. Covert Actions

Ayer, I. Winslow. *The Great Treason Plot in the North during the War*. Chicago: U.S. Publishing, 1895.

Bovey, Wilfrid. "Confederate Agents in Canada during the American Civil War." *Canadian Historical Review* 2 (March 1921): 46–57.

Brandt, Nat. *The Man Who Tried to Burn New York*. New York: Berkley, 1990.

Fesler, Mayo. "Secret Political Societies in the North during the Civil War." *Indiana Magazine of History* 14 (1918): 183–286.

Headley, John William. *Confederate Operations in Canada and New York*. Alexandria, Va.: Time-Life Books, 1984.

Horan, James D. *Confederate Agent: A Discovery in History*. New York: Crown, 1954.

Lester, Richard I. *Confederate Finance and Purchasing in Great Britain*. Charlottesville: University of Virginia Press, 1975.

Milton, George Fort. *Abraham Lincoln and the Fifth Column*. Washington, D.C.: Infantry Journal, 1943.

Rehnquist, William H. "The Milligan Decision." *Quarterly Journal of Military History* 11, no. 2 (Winter 1999): 44–49.

Smith, Bethania Meradith. "Civil War Subversives." *Journal of the Illinois State Historical Society* 45 (1952): 220–40.

Treadway, Gilbert R. *Democratic Opposition to the Lincoln Administration in Indiana*. Indianapolis: Indiana Historical Bureau, 1973.

Wubben, H. H. "The Maintenance of Internal Security in Iowa, 1861–1865." *Civil War History* 10, no. 4 (December 1964): 401–15.

5. Guerrillas

Brownlee, Richard S. *Gray Ghosts of the Confederacy: Guerrilla Warfare in the West, 1861–1865*. Baton Rouge: Louisiana State University Press, 1958.

Curry, Richard O., and F. Gerald Ham. "The Bushwhackers' War: Insurgency and Counter-insurgency in West Virginia." *Civil War History* 10, no. 4 (December 1964): 416–33.

6. The Union

Andrews, J. Cutler. *The North Reports the Civil War*. Pittsburgh, Pa.: University of Pittsburgh Press, 1955.

Baker, Lafayette C. *Daring Exploits of Scouts and Spies*. Chicago: Thompson & Thomas, 1894.

——. *History of the United States Secret Service*. Philadelphia: King & Baird, 1868.

Bates, David Homer. *Lincoln in the Telegraph Office: Recollections of the U.S. Military Telegraph Corps during the Civil War*. New York: Appleton-Century, 1939.

Brown, J. Willard. *The Signal Corps U.S.A. in the War of the Rebellion*. Boston: U.S. Veteran Signal Corps, 1896.

Burnham, George P. *Memoirs of the United States Secret Service*. Boston: Lee & Shephard, 1872.

Byrne, Robert. "Combat Intelligence: Key to Victory at Gettysburg." *Military Intelligence* 2 (Fall 1976): 5–9.

Cuthbert, Norma B., ed. *Lincoln and the Baltimore Plot, 1861, from Pinkerton Records and Related Papers*. San Marino, Calif.: Huntington Library, 1949.

Feis, William B. "A Union Military Intelligence Failure: Jubal Early's Raid, June 12–June 14, 1964." *Civil War History* 36, no. 3 (September 1990): 209–25.

——. "Neutralizing the Valley: The Role of Military Intelligence in the Defeat of Jubal Early's Army of the Valley, 1864–1865." *Civil War History* 39, no. 3 (September 1993): 199–215.

Finnegan, John P. "The Union's Blind Eyes: HUMINT in the Civil War." *Military Intelligence* 15 (July–September 1989): 38–39.

Horan, James D. *The Pinkertons: The Detective Dynasty That Made History*. New York: Crown, 1967.

Horan, James D., and Howard Swiggett. *The Pinkerton Story*. New York: Putnam's, 1951.

Milton, David Hepburn. *Lincoln's Spymaster: Thomas Haines Dudley and the Liverpool Network*. Mechanicsburg, Pa.: Stackpole, 2003.

Mogelever, Jacob. *Death to Traitors: The Story of General Lafayette C. Baker, Lincoln's Forgotten Secret Service Chief*. Garden City, N.Y.: Doubleday, 1960.

Morn, Frank. *"The Eye That Never Sleeps": A History of the Pinkerton National Detective Agency*. Bloomington: Indiana University Press, 1982.

Newcome, Louis A. *Lincoln's Boy Spy*. New York: Putnam, 1929.

Ormont, Arthur. *Master Detective: Allan Pinkerton*. New York: Julian Messner, 1965.

Owsley, Harriet C. "Henry Shelton Sanford and Federal Surveillance Abroad, 1861–1865." *Mississippi Valley Historical Review* 48, no. 2 (September 1961): 211–28.

Pinkerton, Allan. *The Spy of the Rebellion: Being a True History of the Spy System of the United States Army during the Late Rebellion*. Lincoln: University of Nebraska Press, 1989.

Rose, P. K. "The Civil War: Black American Contributions to Union Intelligence." *Studies in Intelligence* (Winter 1998–1999): 73–80.

Schultz, Duane. *The Dahlgren Affair: Terror and Conspiracy in the Civil War.* New York: Norton, 1998.

Smith, Henry Bascom. *Between the Lines: Secret Service Stories Told Fifty Years After.* New York: Booz Brothers, 1911.

Wubben, H. H. "The Maintenance of Internal Security in Iowa, 1861–1865." *Civil War History* 10, no. 4 (December 1964): 401–15.

7. Women Spies

Boyd, Belle. *Belle Boyd in Camp and Prison, Written by Herself.* Baton Rouge: Louisiana State University Press, 1996.

Burger, Nash. *Confederate Spy: Rose O'Neal Greenhow.* New York: Franklin Watts, 1953.

Burgess, Lauren Cook, ed. *An Uncommon Soldier: The Civil War Letters of Sarah Rosetta Wakeman, Alias Pvt. Lyons Wakeman. 153rd Regiment, New York State Volunteers, 1862–1864.* New York: Oxford University Press, 1995.

Castleman, John B. *Active Service.* Louisville, Ky.: Courier-Journal Company, 1917.

Conrad, Thomas N. *A Rebel Scout.* Washington, D.C.: National Publishing, 1904.

Dannett, Sylvia G. L. *She Rode with Generals: The True and Incredible Story of Sarah Emma Seelye, Alias Franklin Thompson.* New York: Thomas Nelson, 1960.

Davis, Curtis Carroll. "The Civil War's Most Over-Rated Spy." *West Virginia History* 28, no. 1 (October 1965): 1–9.

Edmonds, S. Emma E. *The Female Spy of the Union Army: The Thrilling Adventures, Experiences, and Escapes of a Woman, as Nurse, Spy, and Scout, in Hospitals, Camps, and Battle-Fields.* Boston: De Wolfe, Fiske, 1864.

Galbraith, William, and Loretta Galbriath, eds. *A Lost Heroine of the Confederacy: The Dairies and Letters of Belle Edmondson.* Jackson: University of Mississippi Press, 1990.

Hall, Richard. *Patriots in Disguise: Women Warriors of the Civil War.* New York: Paragon House, 1993.

Hergesheimer, Joseph. *Swords and Roses.* New York: Knopf, 1929.

Holt, Patricia L. "Emma Edmonds." *Military History* 5, no. 1 (1988): 8, 64–66.

Ross, Ishbel. *Rebel Rose: The Life of Rose O'Neal Greenhow, Confederate Spy.* New York: Harper, 1954.

Sarmiento, F. L. *Life of Pauline Cushman, the Celebrated Union Spy and Scout: Comprising Her Early History; Her Entry into the Secret Service of the Army of the Cumberland, and Exciting Adventure with the Rebel Chieftains and Others While within the Enemy's Lines; Together with Her Capture and Sentence to Death by General Bragg and Final Rescue by the Union Army under General Rosecrans.* Philadelphia: John E. Potter, 1865.

Scarborough, Ruth. *Belle Boyd: Siren of the South.* Macon, Ga.: Mercer University Press, 1983.

Sigaud, Louis A. *Belle Boyd, Confederate Spy.* Richmond, Va.: Dietz, 1944.

Stevens, Bryna. *Frank Thompson, Her Life and Times: A Civil War Story.* New York: Macmillan, 1992.

Velazquez, Loreta J. *The Woman in Battle: A Narrative of the Exploits, Adventures, and Travels of Madam Loreta Janeta Velazquez, Otherwise Known as Lieutenant Harry T. Buford, Confederate States Army.* Edited by C. J. Worthington. Hartford, Conn.: Belknap, 1876.

E. THE UNITED STATES, 1865–1918

Bigelow, Michael E. "The Apache Campaigns under General Crook: A Historical Perspective on Low-Intensity Conflict." *Military Intelligence* 16, no. 3 (1990): 38–40.

Bradford, James C., ed. *Crucible of Empire: The Spanish-American War and Its Aftermath.* Annapolis, Md.: Naval Institute Press, 1992.

Burnham, Philip. "Unlikely Recruits: Indians Scouting for America." *Quarterly Journal of Military History* 17, no. 3 (Spring 1999): 78–85.

Harris, Charles H., III, and Louis R. Sadler. *The Border and the Revolution: Clandestine Activities of the Mexican Revolution, 1910–1920.* Silver City, N.M.: High-Lonesome Books, 1988.

Jeffreys-Jones, Rhodri. "The Montreal Spy Ring of 1898 and the Origins of 'Domestic Surveillance' in the United States." *Canadian Review of American Studies* 5 (Fall 1974): 119–34.

Linn, Brian M. "Intelligence and Low-Intensity Conflict in the Philippine War, 1899–1902." *Intelligence and National Security* 6, no. 1 (January 1991): 90–114.

——. *The U.S. Army and Counterinsurgency in the Philippine War, 1899–1902.* Chapel Hill: University of North Carolina Press, 1989.

O'Toole, George J. A. "Our Man in Havana: The Paper Trail of Some Spanish War Spies." *Intelligence Quarterly* 2, no. 2 (1986): 1–3.

——. *The Spanish War: An American Epic.* New York: Norton, 1984.

F. THE INTERWAR YEARS

Aldrich, Richard J. *The Key to the South: Britain, the United States, and Thailand during the Approach of the Pacific War, 1929–1942*. Oxford: Oxford University Press, 1993.

Alvarez, David. *Secret Messages: Codebreaking and American Diplomacy, 1930–1945*. Lawrence: University Press of Kansas, 2000.

Barker, Wayne G., ed. *The History of Codes and Ciphers in the United States during the Period between the World Wars*. 2 vols. Laguna Hills, Calif.: Aegean, 1979.

Borg, Dorothy, and Shumpei Okamoto, eds. *Pearl Harbor as History: Japanese-American Relations, 1931–1941*. New York: Columbia University Press, 1973.

Challener, Richard D., ed. *United States Military Intelligence, 1917–1927*. New York: Garland, 1977.

DeFalco, Ralph Lee, III. "Blind to the Sun: U.S. Intelligence Failures before the War with Japan." *International Journal of Intelligence and Counterintelligence* 16, no. 1 (Spring 2003): 95–107.

Egerton, George. "Diplomacy, Scandal, and Military Intelligence: The Craufurd-Stuart Affair and Anglo-American Relations, 1918–20." *Intelligence and National Security* 2, no. 4 (October 1987): 110–34.

Elphick, Peter. *The Far Eastern File: The Intelligence War in the Far East, 1930–1945*. London: Hodder & Stoughton, 1997.

Hannant, Larry. "Inter-War Security Screening in Britain, the United States and Canada." *Intelligence and National Security* 6, no. 4 (October 1991): 711–35.

Hessen, Robert, ed. *Berlin Alert: The Memoirs and Reports of Truman Smith*. Stanford, Calif.: Hoover Institution Press, 1984.

Komatsu, Keiichiro. *Origins of the Pacific War and the Importance of "Magic."* New York: St. Martin's, 1999.

Leshuk, Leonard. *US Intelligence Perceptions of Soviet Power, 1921–1946*. London: Frank Cass, 2002.

Mahnken, Thomas G. "Gazing at the Sun: The Office of Naval Intelligence and Japanese Naval Innovation, 1918–1941." *Intelligence and National Security* 11, no. 3 (July 1996): 424–41.

———. *Uncovering Ways of War: U.S. Intelligence and Foreign Military Innovation, 1918–1941*. Ithaca, N.Y.: Cornell University Press, 2002.

Maurer, Alfred. "A Delicate Mission: Aerial Reconnaissance of Japanese Islands before World War II." *Military Affairs* 26, no. 2 (Summer 1962): 66–75.

Murphy, John F. "The Alaskan Mystery Flights." *International Journal of Intelligence and Counterintelligence* 9, no. 1 (Spring 1996): 97–111.

Parker, Frederick D. *Pearl Harbor Revisited: United States Communications Intelligence, 1924–1941*. Ft. George Gordon Meade, Md.: Center for Cryptologic History, National Security Agency, 1994.

Rowan, Richard W. *Secret Agents against America*. New York: Doubleday, Doran, 1939.

———. *Spy and Counterspy: The Development of Modern Espionage*. New York: Viking, 1928.

Rowlett, Frank B. *The Story of Magic: Memoirs of an American Cryptologic Pioneer*. Laguna Hills, Calif.: Aegean Park Press, 1998.

Wilhelm, Maria. *The Man Who Watched the Rising Sun: The Story of Admiral Ellis M. Zacharias*. New York: Watts, 1967.

Yardley, Herbert O. *The American Black Chamber*. Mattituck, N.Y.: Amereon, 1999.

———. *The Chinese Black Chamber: An Adventure in Espionage*. New York: Houghton Mifflin, 1983.

———. *Yardleygrams*. Indianapolis, Ind.: Bobbs Merrill, 1932.

Zacharias, Ellis M. *Secret Missions: The Story of an Intelligence Officer*. New York: Paperback Library, 1961.

G. WORLD WAR II

1. The Office of Strategic Services (OSS)

Alcorn, Robert Hayden. *No Bugles for Spies: Tales of the OSS*. New York: David McKay, 1962.

———. *Spies of the OSS*. London: Robert Hale, 1973.

Alsop, Stewart, and Thomas Braden. *Sub Rosa: The OSS and American Espionage*. New York: Harcourt, Brace & World, 1964.

Bentley, Elizabeth. *Out of Bondage: The Story of Elizabeth Bentley*. New York: Ivy Books, 1988.

Booth, Waller B. *Mission Marcel-Proust: The Story of an Unusual OSS Undertaking*. Philadelphia: Dorrance, 1972.

Breaks, Katherine. "Ladies of the OSS: The Apron Strings of Intelligence in World War II." *American Intelligence Journal* 13, no. 3 (Summer 1992): 91–96.

Breuer, William B. *War and American Women: Heroism, Deeds, and Controversy*. Westport, Conn.: Praeger, 1997.

Brown, Anthony Cave, ed. *The Secret War Report of the OSS*. New York: Berkley, 1976.

Brunner, John W. *OSS Weapons*. Williamstown, N.J.: Phillips, 1994.

Casey, William J. *The Secret War against Hitler*. New York: Berkley Books, 1989.

Chalou, George C., ed. *The Secret War: The Office of Strategic Services in World War II*. Washington, D.C.: National Archives, 1992.

Clauseen, Martin P., ed. *The OSS-NKVD Relationship, 1943–1945*. New York: Garland, 1989.

Coon, Carleton S. *North Africa Story: An Anthropologist as OSS Agent, 1941–1943*. Ipswich, Mass.: Gambit,1980.

Corvo, Max. *The OSS in Italy, 1942–1945: A Personal Memoir.* New York: Praeger, 1990.

Dawidoff, Nicholas. *The Catcher Was a Spy: The Mysterious Life of Moe Berg.* New York: Vintage, 1995.

DeCoster, Bryan Donald. "OSS Estimate of German Logistics on the Eastern Front, 1941–1942: An Early Example of Strategic Warning." *Defense Intelligence Journal* 3, no. 1 (Spring 1994): 107–31.

Dessants, Betty Abrahamsen. "Ambivalent Allies: OSS' USSR Division, the State Department, and the Bureaucracy of Intelligence Analysis, 1941–1945." *Intelligence and National Security* 11, no. 4 (October 1996): 722–53.

Dulles, Allen. *Germany's Underground.* New York: Macmillan, 1947.

———. *The Secret Surrender*. New York: Harper & Row, 1966.

Dunlop, Richard. *Behind Japanese Lines, with the OSS in Burma.* New York: Rand McNally, 1979.

Field, Edward L. *Retreat to Victory: A Previously Unknown OSS Operation.* Surfside Beach, S.C.: EDMA Historical Consultants, 1991.

Ford, Corey, and Alastair MacBain. *Cloak and Dagger: The Secret Story of the OSS.* New York: Grosset & Dunlap, 1945.

Gould, Jonathan S. "The OSS and the London 'Free Germans.'" *Studies in Intelligence* 46, no. 1 (2002): 11–29.

Heideking, Jürgen, and Christof Mauch, eds. *American Intelligence and the German Resistance to Hitler: A Documentary History*. Scranton, Pa.: Westview, 1996.

Heimark, Bruce H. *The OSS Norwegian Special Operations Group in World War II.* Westport, Conn.: Praeger/Greenwood, 1994.

Hilsman, Roger. *American Guerrilla: My Life behind Japanese Lines.* New York: Brassey's, 1991.

Hodgson, Lynn-Philip. *Inside-Camp X.* Toronto, Ontario, Canada: Blake Books, 1999.

Hymoff, Edward. *The OSS in World War II.* New York: Richardson & Steirman, 1986.

Jakub, Jay. *Spies and Saboteurs: Anglo-American Collaboration and Rivalry in Human Intelligence Collection and Special Operations, 1940–45.* New York: St. Martin's, 1999.

Jeffreys-Jones, Rhodri. "The Role of British Intelligence in the Mythologies Underpinning the OSS and Early CIA." *Intelligence and National Security* 15, no. 2 (Summer 2000): 5–19.

Jespersen, Knud J. V. *No Small Achievement: Special Operations Executive and the Danish Resistance, 1940–1945.* Odense, Denmark: University Press of Southern Denmark, 2002.

Katz, Barry M. *Foreign Intelligence: Research and Analysis in the Office of Strategic Services 1942–1945.* Cambridge, Mass.: Harvard University Press, 1989.

Kehoe, Robert R. "1944: An Allied Team with the French Resistance." *Studies in Intelligence* (Winter 1998–1999): 15–50.

Ladd, James, and Keith Melton. *Clandestine Warfare: Weapons and Equipment of the SOE and OSS.* London: Blandford, 1988.

Langer, Walter C. *In and Out of the Ivory Tower: The Autobiography of William L. Langer.* New York: Neale Watson Academic Publications, 1978.

———. *The Mind of Adolf Hitler: The Secret Wartime Report.* New York: Basic Books, 1972.

Lankford, Nelson D., ed. *OSS against the Reich: The World War II Diaries of Colonel David K. E. Bruce.* Kent, Ohio: Kent State University Press, 1991.

Lees, Lorraine M. "DeWitt Clinton Poole, the Foreign Nationalities Branch and Political Intelligence." *Intelligence and National Security* 15, no. 4 (Winter 2000): 81–103.

Lovell, Mary S. *Cast No Shadow: The Life of the American Spy Who Changed the Course of World War II.* New York: Pantheon Books, 1992.

Lovell, Stanley P. *Of Spies and Strategems.* Englewood Cliffs, N.J.: Prentice-Hall, 1963.

Lowenthal, Mark M. "Searching for National Intelligence: U.S. Intelligence and Policy before the Second World War." *Intelligence and National Security* 6, no. 4 (October 1991): 736–49.

MacPherson, B. Nelson. *American Intelligence in Britain During the Second World War.* Portland, Ore.: Frank Cass, 2003.

———. "Inspired Improvisation: William Casey and the Penetration of Germany." *Intelligence and National Security* 9, no. 4 (October 1994): 695–722.

———. "*Reductio Ad Absurdum*: The R&A Branch of OSS/London." *International Journal of Intelligence and Counterintelligence* 15, no. 3 (Fall 2002): 390–414.

Marquardt-Bigman, Petra. "Behemoth Revisited: The Research and Analysis Branch of the Office of Strategic Services in the Debate of U.S. Policies towards Germany, 1943–46." *Intelligence and National Security* 12, no. 2 (April 1997): 91–100.

———. "Project Communication: An Oral History of the Office of Strategic Services." *Intelligence and National Security* 12, no. 2 (April 1997): 161–62.

McIntosh, Elizabeth P. *Sisterhood of Spies: The Women of the OSS*. Annapolis, Md.: Naval Institute Press, 1998.

Melton, H. Keith. *OSS Special Weapons and Equipment: Spy Devices of WWII*. Foreword by William Colby New York: Sterling, 1991.

Mendelsohn, John, comp. *Covert Warfare: Intelligence, Counterintelligence and Military Deception during the World War II Era*. New York: Garland, 1988.

Mills, Robert., and John W. Brunner. *OSS Special Operations in China*. Williamstown, N.J.: Phillips, 2002.

Moon, Thomas M. *This Grim and Savage Game: OSS and the Beginning of U.S. Covert Operations in World War II*. Los Angeles: Burning Gate Press, 1991.

Padover, Saul K. *Experiment in Germany: The Story of an American Intelligence Officer*. New York: Duell, 1946.

Paillole, Colonel Paul. *Fighting the Nazis: French Intelligence and Counterintelligence, 1935–1945*. New York: Enigma Books, 2003.

Parnell, Ben. *Carpetbaggers—America's Secret War in Europe: A Story of the World War II Carpetbaggers 801st/492nd Bombardment Group (H) U.S. Army, Eighth Air Force*. Rev. ed. Austin, Tex.: Eakin, 1993.

Peake, Hayden B. "OSS and the Venona Decrypts." *Intelligence and National Security* 12, no. 3 (July 1997): 14–34.

Peers, William R., and Dean Brelis. *Behind the Burma Road: The Story of America's Most Successful Guerrilla Force*. Boston: Little, Brown, 1963.

Persico, Joseph E. *Piercing the Reich: The Penetration of Nazi Germany by American Secret Agents during World War II*. New York: Barnes & Noble, 1997.

Petersen, Neal H., ed. *From Hitler's Doorstep: The Wartime Intelligence Reports of Allen Dulles, 1942–1945*. University Park: Pennsylvania State University Press, 1996.

Rossiter, Margaret. *Women in the Resistance*. New York: Praeger, 1991.

Sacquety, Troy J., ed. "Behind Japanese Lines in Burma." *Studies in Intelligence* 11 (Fall–Winter 2001): 67–79.

Schwab, Gerald. *OSS Agents in Hitler's Heartland: Destination Innsbruck*. Westport, Conn.: Praeger, 1996.

Smith, Bradley F. *The Shadow Warriors: O.S.S. and the Origins of the C.I.A.* New York: Basic Books, 1983.

Stafford, David. *Camp X: Canada's School for Secret Agents, 1941–45*. Toronto, Ontario, Canada: University of Toronto Press, 1986.

Steury, Donald P. "Tracking Nazi 'Gold': The OSS and Project SAFEHAVEN." *Studies in Intelligence* 9 (Summer 2000): 35–50.

Tomkins, Peter. "Intelligence and Operational Support for the Anti-Nazi Resistance: The OSS and Italian Partisans in World War II." *Studies in Intelligence* (Spring 1998): 95–103.

——. *A Spy in Rome*. New York: Avon, 1962.

Troy, Thomas F. "Knifing of the OSS." *International Journal of Intelligence and Counterintelligence* 1, no. 3 (1986): 95–108.

——, ed. *Wartime Washington: The Secret OSS Journal of James Grafton Rogers, 1942–1943*. Frederick, Md.: University Press of America, 1987.

Tyson, James L. "The EOU vs. Hitler's Mini-Missiles." *International Journal of Intelligence and Counterintelligence* 12, no. 1 (Spring 1999): 80–87.

Ward, James R. "The Activities of Detachment 101 of the OSS." *Special Warfare*, October 1993, 14–21.

Whiting, Charles. *The Battle for Twelveland: An Account of Anglo-American Intelligence Operations within Nazi Germany, 1939–1945*. London: Leo Cooper, 1975.

——. *The Spymasters: The True Story of Anglo American Intelligence Operations within Nazi Germany, 1939–1945*. New York: Dutton, 1976.

Windmiller, Marshall. "A Tumultuous Time: OSS and Army Intelligence in India, 1942–1946." *International Journal of Intelligence and Counterintelligence* 8, no. 1 (Spring 1995): 105–24.

Winks, Robin W. *Cloak and Gown: Scholars in the Secret War, 1939–1961*. New Haven, Conn.: Yale University Press, 1996.

Yu, Maochun. "OSS in China—New Information about an Old Role." *International Journal of Intelligence and Counterintelligence* 7, no. 1 (Spring 1994): 75–96.

——. *OSS in China: Prelude to Cold War*. New Haven, Conn.: Yale University Press, 1996.

2. Pearl Harbor

Albright, Harry. *Pearl Harbor: Japan's Fatal Blunder*. New York: Hippocrene, 1988.

Bachrach, Deborah. *Pearl Harbor: Opposing Viewpoints*. San Diego, Calif.: Greenhaven, 1989.

Barker, Arthur J. *Pearl Harbor*. New York: Ballantine, 1978.

Barkin, Edward S., and L. Michael Meyer. "COMINT and Pearl Harbor: FDR's Mistake." *International Journal of Intelligence and Counterintelligence* 2, no. 4 (Winter 1988): 513–31.

Bartlett, Bruce R. *Cover-Up: The Politics of Pearl Harbor, 1941–1946*. New Rochelle, N.Y.: Arlington House, 1978.

Beach, Edward L. *Scapegoats: A Defense of Kimmel and Short at Pearl Harbor*. Annapolis, Md.: U.S. Naval Institute Press, 1995.

Beard, Charles. *President Roosevelt and the Coming of the War, 1941: A Study of Appearances and Reality*. New Haven, Conn.: Yale University Press, 1948.

Brownlow, Donald G. *The Accused: The Ordeal of Rear Admiral Husband Edward Kimmel, U.S.N.* New York: Vantage, 1968.

Burtness, Paul S., and Warren U. Ober. *The Puzzle of Pearl Harbor.* Evanston, Ill.: Row, Peterson, 1962.

Chapman, John W. M. "Pearl Harbor: The Anglo-Australian Dimension'" *Intelligence and National Security* 4, no. 3 (July 1989): 451–60.

Clausen, Henry C., and Bruce Lee. *Pearl Harbor: Final Judgement.* New York: Crown, 1992.

Department of Defense. *The "Magic" Background of Pearl Harbor.* 8 vols. Washington, D.C.: Government Printing Office, 1979.

Farago, Ladislas. *The Broken Seal: The Story of "Operation Magic" and the Pearl Harbor Disaster.* New York: Random House, 1967.

Fish, Hamilton. *Tragic Deception—FDR and America's Involvement in World War II.* Greenwich, Conn.: Devin-Adair, 1983.

Fishel, Edwin C., and Louis W. Tordello. "FDR's Mistake? Not Likely." *International Journal of Intelligence and Counterintelligence* 5, no. 3 (Fall 1991): 360–72.

Goldstein, Donald, and Katherine V. Dillon, eds. *The Pearl Harbor Papers: Inside the Japanese Plans.* Washington, D.C.: Brassey's, 1993.

Howard, Michael E. "Military Intelligence and Surprise Attack: The 'Lessons' of Pearl Harbor." *World Politics* 15 (July 1963): 701–11.

Jacobsen, Philip H. "Who Deceived Whom?" *Naval History* 17, no. 6 (December 2003): 27–31.

Kahn, David. "The Intelligence Failure of Pearl Harbor." *Foreign Affairs* 70, no. 5 (Winter 1991/1992): 136–52.

Kirkpatrick, Lyman B., Jr. *Captains without Eyes: Intelligence Failures in World War II.* New York: Macmillan, 1969.

Morgenstern, George. *Pearl Harbor: The Story of the Secret War.* Chicago: Devin Adair, 1947.

Prange, Gordon W. *At Dawn We Slept: The Untold Story of Pearl Harbor.* New York: McGraw-Hill, 1981.

——. *Pearl Harbor: The Verdict of History.* New York: McGraw-Hill, 1986.

Rusbridger, James, and Eric Nave. *Betrayal at Pearl Harbor: How Churchill Lured Roosevelt into World War II.* Old Tappan, N.J.: Simon & Schuster, 1992.

Stillwell, Paul, ed. *Air Raid: Pearl Harbor.* Annapolis, Md.: Naval Institute Press, 1981.

Stinnett, Robert. *Day of Deceit: The Truth about FDR and Pearl Harbor.* New York: Free Press, 1999.

Theobold, Robert A. *The Final Secret of Pearl Harbor: The Washington Contribution to the Japanese Attack.* New York: Devin-Adair, 1954.

Thompson, Robert Smith. *A Time for War: Franklin D. Roosevelt and the Path to Pearl Harbor*. Englewood Cliffs, N.J.: Prentice Hall, 1991.

Thorpe, Elliott R. *East Wind Rain: The Intimate Account of an Intelligence Officer in the Pacific, 1939–1949*. Boston: Gambit, 1969.

Toland, John. *Day of Infamy: Pearl Harbor and Its Aftermath*. Garden City, N.Y.: Doubleday, 1982.

U.S. Congress. *Investigation of the Pearl Harbor Attack: Report of the Joint Committee, Congress of the United States, Pursuant to Senate Concurrent Resolution 27, 79th Congress*. Laguna Hills, Calif.: Aegean Park Press, 1994.

West, Nigel. *A Thread of Deceit: Espionage Myths of World War II*. New York: Dell, 1987.

Wilford, Timothy. *Pearl Harbor Redefined: USN Radio Intelligence in 1941*. Lanham, Md.: University Press of America, 2001.

———. "Watching the North Pacific: British and Commonwealth Intelligence before Pearl Harbor." *Intelligence and National Security* 17, no. 4 (Winter 2002): 131–64.

Winton, John. *ULTRA in the Pacific: How Breaking Japanese Codes and Cyphers Affected Naval Operations against Japan, 1941–45*. Annapolis, Md.: Naval Institute Press, 1993.

Wohlstetter, Roberta. *Cuba and Pearl Harbor: Hindsight and Foresight*. Santa Monica, Calif.: Rand Corporation, 1965.

———. *Pearl Harbor: Warning and Decision*. Stanford, Calif.: Stanford University Press, 1962.

Worth, Roland H., Jr. *Secret Allies in the Pacific: Covert Intelligence and Code Breaking Cooperation between the United States, Great Britain and Other Nations prior to the Attack on Pearl Harbor*. London: McFarland, 2001.

3. The Tricycle Affair

Bratzel, John F., and Leslie B. Rout Jr. "Pearl Harbor, Microdots, and J. Edgar Hoover." *American Historical Review* 87 (December 1982): 1342–51.

Bruce-Briggs, B. "Another Ride on Tricycle." *Intelligence and National Security* 7, no. 2 (April 1992): 77–100.

Chapman, John W. M. "Tricycle Recycled: Collaboration among the Secret Intelligence Services of the Axis States, 1940–41." *Intelligence and National Security* 7, no. 3 (July 1992): 268–99.

Masterman, J. C. *The Double-Cross System in the War of 1939–1945*. New York: Ballantine, 1982.

Popov, Dusko. *Spy/Counterspy: The Autobiography of Dusko Popov*. Greenwich, Conn.: Fawcett, 1975.

Troy, Thomas F. "The British Assault on J. Edgar Hoover: The Tricycle Case." *International Journal of Intelligence and Counterintelligence* 3, no. 2 (1989): 169–209.

4. William Donovan

Brown, Anthony Cave. *The Last Hero: Wild Bill Donovan*. New York: Times Books, 1982.

Campbell, Kenneth J. "William J. Donovan: Leader and Strategist." *American Intelligence Journal* 11, no. 1 (Winter 1989–1990): 31–36.

Dunlop, Richard. *Donovan, America's Master Spy*. Chicago: Rand McNally, 1982.

Ford, Corey. *Donovan of OSS*. Boston: Little, Brown, 1970.

Smith, Bradley F. "Admiral Godfrey's Mission to America, June/July 1941." *Intelligence and National Security* 1, no. 3 (September 1986): 441–50.

Sullivan, Brian R. "'A Highly Commendable Action': William J. Donovan's Intelligence Mission for Mussolini and Roosevelt, December 1935–February 1936." *Intelligence and National Security* 6, no. 2 (April 1991): 334–66.

Troy, Thomas F. "The Coordinator of Information and British Intelligence: An Essay on Origins." *Studies in Intelligence* 18, no. 1 (Spring 1974).

——. *Donovan and the CIA: A History of the Establishment of the Central Intelligence Agency*. Frederick, Md.: University Publications of America, 1981.

——. *Wild Bill and Intrepid: Bill Donovan, Bill Stephenson, and the Origin of CIA*. New Haven, Conn.: Yale University Press, 1996.

Wilhelm, Maria. *The Fighting Irishman*. New York: Hawthorne, 1964.

H. THE ONSET OF THE COLD WAR, 1945–1950

Aarons, Mark, and John Loftus. *Unholy Trinity: How the Vatican's Nazi Networks Betrayed Western Intelligence to the Soviets*. New York: St. Martin's Press, 1991.

Acheson, Dean. *Present at the Creation: My Years in the State Department*. New York: Norton, 1969.

Anderson, Elizabeth E. "The Security Dilemma and Covert Action: The Truman Years." *International Journal of Intelligence and Counterintelligence* 11, no. 4 (Winter 1998–1999): 403–27.

Bar-Zohar, Michel. *The Hunt for German Scientists*. London: Arthur Barker, 1967.

Best, R. A. *"Cooperation with Like-Minded Peoples": British Influences on American Security Policy, 1945–1949.* Westport, Conn.: Greenwood, 1986.

Bower, Tom. *The Paperclip Conspiracy: The Battle for the Spoils and Secrets of Nazi Germany.* London: Michael Joseph, 1987.

Crabb, Cecil V., Jr., and Kevin V. Mulcahy. "The National Security Council and the Shaping of U.S. Foreign Policy." *International Journal of Intelligence and Counterintelligence* 3, no. 2 (Summer 1989): 153–68.

Critchfield, James H. *Partners at the Creation: The Men behind Postwar Germany's Defense and Intelligence Establishments.* Annapolis, Md.: Naval Institute Press, 2003.

Darling, Arthur B. *The Central Intelligence Agency: An Instrument of Government, to 1950.* University Park: Pennsylvania State University Press, 1990.

Department of State. Office of the Historian. *Foreign Relations of the United States, 1945–1950—Truman Series: Emergence of the Intelligence Establishment.* Edited by C. Thomas Thorne Jr. and David S. Patterson. Washington, D.C.: Government Printing Office, 1996.

Falk, Stanley L. "The National Security Council under Truman, Eisenhower, and Kennedy." *Political Science Quarterly* 79 (September 1964): 403–34.

Friedman, Hal M. "The 'Bear' in the Pacific? US Intelligence Perceptions of Soviet Strategic Power Projection in the Pacific Basin and East Asia, 1945–1947." *Intelligence and National Security* 12, no. 4 (October 1997): 75–101.

Gimbel, John. "German Scientists, United States Denazification Policy, and the 'Paperclip Conspiracy.'" *International History Review* 12, no. 3 (August 1990): 441–65.

———. "Project Paperclip: German Scientists, American Policy, and the Cold War." *Diplomatic History* 14, no. 3 (1990): 343–65.

Grose, Peter. *Operation Rollback: America's Secret War behind the Iron Curtain.* Boston: Houghton Mifflin, 2000.

Heuser, Beatrice. *Western "Containment" Policies in the Cold War: The Yugoslav Case, 1948–53.* London: Routledge, 1989.

Hogan, Michael J. *A Cross of Iron: Harry S. Truman and the Origins of the National Security State, 1945–1954.* New York: Cambridge University Press, 1998.

Hunt, Linda. *Secret Agenda: The United States Government, Nazi Scientists, and Project Paperclip, 1945 to 1990.* New York: St. Martin's, 1991.

Inderfurth, Karl F., and Loch K. Johnson. *Decisions of the Highest Order: Perspectives on the National Security Council.* Pacific Grove, Calif.: Brooks/Cole, 1988.

Lasby, Clarence G. *Project Paperclip: German Scientists and the Cold War.* New York: Atheneum, 1971.

Loftus, John J. *The Belarus Secret.* New York: Knopf, 1982.

MacEachin, Douglas J. *The Final Months of the War with Japan: Signals Intelligence, U.S. Invasion Planning, and the A-Bomb Decision.* Washington, D.C.: Central Intelligence Agency, 1998.

May, Ernest R., ed. *American Cold War Strategy: Interpreting NSC 68.* Boston: Bedford Books, 1993.

Milano, James V., and Patrick Brogan. *Soldiers, Spies, and the Rat Line: America's Undeclared War against the Soviets.* Washington, D.C.: Brassey's, 1996.

Mitrovich, Gregory. *Undermining the Kremlin: America's Strategy to Subvert the Soviet Bloc, 1947–1956.* Ithaca, N.Y.: Cornell University Press, 2000.

Prados, John. *Keepers of the Keys: A History of the National Security Council from Truman to Bush.* New York: Morrow, 1991.

Sander, Alfred Dick. *A Staff for the President: The Executive Office, 1921–1952.* Boulder, Colo.: Greenwood, 1989.

Sibley, Katherine A. S. *Red Spies in America, Stolen Secrets and the Dawn of the Cold War.* Lawrence: University Press of Kansas, 2004.

Simpson, Christopher. *Blowback—America's Recruitment of Nazis and Its Effects on the Cold War.* New York: Weidenfeld & Nicolson, 1988.

Steury, Donald P. "Tracking Nazi 'Gold': The OSS and Project SAFEHAVEN." *Studies in Intelligence* 9 (Summer 2000): 35–50.

Valero, Larry A. "An Impressive Record: The American Joint Intelligence Committee and Estimates of the Soviet Union, 1945–1947." *Studies in Intelligence* 9 (Summer 2000): 65–80.

Warner, Michael. *The CIA under Harry Truman.* Washington, D.C.: Central Intelligence Agency, 1994.

Wilford, Hugh. *The CIA, the British Left, and the Cold War.* Portland, Ore.: Frank Cass, 2003.

Zegart, Amy B. *Flawed by Design: The Evolution of the CIA, JCS, and NSC.* Stanford, Calif.: Stanford University Press, 1999.

Ziegler, Charles A. "Intelligence Assessments of Soviet Atomic Capability, 1945–1949: Myths, Monopolies and Maskirovka." *Intelligence and National Security* 12, no. 4 (October 1997): 1–24.

I. THE GOLDEN AGE OF INTELLIGENCE: THE 1950s

1. General

Alin, Erika. *The United States and the 1958 Lebanon Crisis.* Lanham, Md.: University Press of America, 1994.

Alsop, Joseph W. *"I've Seen the Best of It": Memoirs.* With Adam Platt. New York: Norton, 1992.

Alsop, Stewart. *The Center: People and Power in Political Washington*. New York: Harper & Row, 1968.

Ambrose, Stephen E. *Eisenhower*. Vol. 2, *The President*. New York: Simon and Schuster, 1984.

———. *Ike's Spies: Eisenhower and the Espionage Establishment*. With Richard H. Immerman. Garden City, N.Y.: Doubleday, 1981.

Barrett, David M. "Glimpses of a Hidden History: Sen. Richard Russell, Congress, and Oversight of the CIA." *International Journal of Intelligence and Counterintelligence* 11, no. 3 (Fall 1998): 271–98.

Benson, Robert Louis. *VENONA, Soviet Espionage and the American Response, 1939–1957*. With Michael Warner. Washington, D.C.: Central Intelligence Agency, 1996.

Beschloss, Michael R. *May-Day: Eisenhower, Khrushchev and the U-2 Incident*. New York: Harper & Row, 1986.

Bohlen, Charles E. *Witness to History, 1929–1969*. New York: Norton, 1973.

Brands, H. W., Jr. *Cold Warriors: Eisenhower's Generation and American Foreign Policy*. New York: Columbia University Press, 1988.

Cook, Blanche W. *The Declassified Eisenhower: A Divided Legacy*. Garden City, N.Y.: Doubleday, 1981.

Currey, Cecil B. *Edward Lansdale: The Unquiet American*. Washington, D.C.: Brassey's, 1998.

Divine, David A. *The Sputnik Challenge: Eisenhower's Response to the Soviet Satellite*. New York: Oxford University Press, 1993.

Divine, Robert A. *Eisenhower and the Cold War*. New York: Oxford University Press, 1981.

Dockrill, Saki. *Eisenhower's New-Look National Security Policy, 1953–61*. London: Macmillan, 1996.

Eisenhower, Dwight D. *The White House Years: Mandate for Change, 1953–1956*. Garden City, N.Y.: Doubleday, 1963.

———. *The White House Years: Waging Peace, 1956–1961*. Garden City, N.Y.: Doubleday, 1965.

Fry, Michael Graham. "The Uses of Intelligence: The United Nations Confronts the United States in the Lebanon Crisis, 1958." *Intelligence and National Security* 10, no. 1 (January 1995): 59–91.

Garthoff, Raymond L. "Intelligence Aspects of Early Cold War Summitry (1959–60)." *Intelligence and National Security* 14, no. 3 (Autumn 1999): 1–22.

Holober, Frank. *Raiders of the China Coast: CIA Covert Operations during the Korean War*. Annapolis, Md.: Naval Institute Press, 1999.

Hopkins, Robert S., III. "An Expanded Understanding of Eisenhower, American Policy and Overflights." *Intelligence and National Security* 11, no. 2 (April 1996): 332–44.

Koch, Scott A. *Selected Estimates on the Soviet Union, 1950–1959*. Washington, D.C.: Central Intelligence Agency, 1993.

Laird, Thomas. *Into Tibet: The CIA's First Atomic Spy and His Secret Expedition to Lhasa*. New York: Grove, 2002.

Lansdale, Edward Geary. *In the Midst of Wars: An American's Mission to Southeast Asia*. New York: Harper & Row, 1972.

Leary, William M. *Perilous Missions: Civil Air Transport and CIA Covert Operations in Asia*. Birmingham: University of Alabama Press, 1984.

Marchio, Jim. "Resistance Potential and Rollback: US Intelligence and the Eisenhower Administration's Policies toward Eastern Europe, 1953–56." *Intelligence and National Security* 10, no. 2 (April 1995): 219–41.

Montague, Ludwell Lee. *General Walter Bedell Smith as Director of Central Intelligence, October 1950–February 1953*. University Park: Pennsylvania State University Press, 1992.

Murphy, David E., Sergei A. Kondrashev, and George Bailey. *Battleground Berlin: CIA vs. KGB in the Cold War*. New Haven, Conn.: Yale University Press, 1997.

Pedlow, Gregory W., and Donald E. Welzenbach. *The CIA and the U-2 Program, 1954–1974*. Washington, D.C.: Central Intelligence Agency, 1998.

Reese, Mary Ellen. *General Reinhard Gehlen: The CIA Connection*. Fairfax, Va.: George Mason University Press, 1990.

Roman, Peter J. *Eisenhower and the Missile Gap*. Ithaca, N.Y.: Cornell University Press, 1995.

Scott-Smith, Giles. *The Politics of Apolitical Culture: The Congress for Cultural Freedom, the CIA, and Post-war American Hegemony*. London: Routledge, 2002.

Steury, Donald P. *Intentions and Capabilities: Estimates on Soviet Strategic Forces, 1950–1983*. Washington, D.C.: Central Intelligence Agency, 1996.

Taubman, Philip. *Secret Empire: Eisenhower, the CIA, and the Hidden History of America's Space Espionage*. New York: Simon and Shuster, 2003.

Yoder, Edwin M., Jr. *Joe Alsop's Cold War: A Study of Journalistic Influence and Intrigue*. Chapel Hill: University of North Carolina Press, 1995.

2. Guatemala

Aybar de Soto, Jose M. *Dependency and Intervention: The Case of Guatemala in 1954*. Boulder, Colo.: Westview, 1978.

Barrett, David M. "Congress, the CIA, and Guatemala, 1954." *Studies in Intelligence* 10 (Winter–Spring 2001): 23–31.

Bowen, Gordon L. "U.S. Foreign Policy toward Radical Change: Covert Operations in Guatemala, 1950–1954." *Latin America Perspectives* 10 (Winter 1983): 88–102.

Cullather, Nick. *Secret History: The CIA's Classified Account of Its Operations in Guatemala, 1952–1954.* Stanford, Calif.: Stanford University Press, 2000.

Department of State. Office of the Historian. *Foreign Relations of the United States, Eisenhower Administration, 1952–1954, Guatemala.* Edited by Susan Holly. Washington, D.C.: Government Printing Office, 2003.

Gleijeses, Piero. *Shattered Hope: The Guatemalan Revolution and the United States, 1944–1954.* Princeton, N.J.: Princeton University Press.

Immerman, Richard H. *The CIA in Guatemala: The Foreign Policy of Intervention.* Austin: University of Texas Press, 1982.

Marks, Frederick W., III. "The CIA and Castillo Armas in Guatemala, 1954: New Clues to an Old Puzzle." *Diplomatic History* 14, no. 1 (1990): 67–86.

Schlesinger, Stephen, and Stephen Kinzer. *Bitter Fruit: The Untold Story of the American Coup in Guatemala.* Garden City, N.Y.: Anchor, 1983.

3. Iran

Abrahamian, Ervand. "The 1953 Coup in Iran." *State & Society* 66, no. 2 (Summer 2001): 182–215.

Bamberg, J. H. *The History of the British Petroleum Company.* Vol. 2, *The Anglo-Iranian Years, 1928–54.* Cambridge: Cambridge University Press, 1994.

Gasiorowski, Mark J. "The 1953 Coup D'Etat in Iran." *International Journal of Middle East Studies* 19, no. 3 (1987): 261–86.

Heiss, Mary Ann. *Empire and Nationhood: The United States, Great Britain, and Iranian Oil, 1950–1954.* New York: Columbia University Press, 1997.

Kinzer, Stephen. *All the Shah's Men: The Hidden Story of the CIA's Coup in Iran.* New York: Wiley, 2003

Kisatsky, Deborah. "Voice of America and Iran, 1949–1953: US Liberal Developmentalism, Propaganda and the Cold War." *Intelligence and National Security* 14, no. 3 (Autumn 1999): 160–85.

Roosevelt, Kermit. *Countercoup: The Struggle for the Control of Iran.* New York: McGraw-Hill, 1981.

Ruehsen, Moyara De Moraes. "Operation 'Ajax' Revisited: Iran, 1953." *Middle Eastern Studies* 29, no. 3 (July 1993): 467–86.

Wilber, Donald N. *Adventures in the Middle East: Excursions and Incursions.* Princeton, N.J.: Darwin, 1986.

4. Korea

Aid, Matthew M. "US Humint and Comint in the Korean War [Part I]: From the Approach of War to the Chinese Intervention." *Intelligence and National Security* 14, no. 4 (Winter 1999): 17–63.

——. "American Comint in the Korean War (Part II): From the Chinese Intervention to the Armistice." *Intelligence and National Security* 15, no. 1 (Spring 2000): 14–49.

Appleman, Roy E. *Disaster in Korea.* College Station: Texas A&M University Press, 1989.

Bigelow, Michael E. "Disaster along the Ch'ongch'on: Intelligence Breakdown in Korea." *Military Intelligence* 18, no. 3 (July–September 1992): 11–16.

Breuer, William B. *Shadow Warriors: The Covert War in Korea.* New York: Wiley, 1996.

Cagle, Malcolm W. "Errors of the Korean War." *U.S. Naval Institute Proceedings* (March 1958): 31–35.

Cohen, Eliot A. "'Only Half the Battle': American Intelligence and the Chinese Intervention in Korea, 1950." *Intelligence and National Security* 5, no. 1 (January 1990): 129–49.

De Weerd, Harvey A. "Strategic Surprise in the Korean War." *Orbis* 6 (Fall 1962): 435–52.

Dwyer, John B. "Secret Naval Raids in Korea." *Military History* 19, no. 5 (December 2002): 66–72.

Evanhoe, Ed. *Darkmoon: Eighth Army Special Operations in the Korean War.* Annapolis, Md.: Naval Institute Press, 1995.

Foot, Rosemary. "The Sino-American Conflict in Korea: The U.S. Assessment of China's Ability to Intervene in the War." *Asian Affairs* 14 (June 1983): 160–66.

——. *The Wrong War: American Policy and the Dimensions of the Korean Conflict, 1950–1953.* Ithaca, N.Y.: Cornell University Press, 1985.

Goulden, Joseph C. *Korea: The Untold Story of the War.* New York: Time Books, 1982.

Haas, Michael E. *In the Devil's Shadow: U.N. Special Operations during the Korean War.* Annapolis, Md.: Naval Institute Press, 2000.

Hallion, Richard P. *The Naval Air War in Korea.* Baltimore, Md.: Nautical & Aviation, 1986.

Hatch, David A. *The Korean War: The SIGINT Background.* With Robert Louis Benson. Washington, D.C.: Government Printing Office, 2000.

Holober, Frank. *Raiders of the China Coast: CIA Covert Operations during the Korean War.* Annapolis, Md.: Naval Institute Press, 1999.

Mobley, Richard A. "North Korea's Surprise Attack: Weak U.S. Analysis?" *International Journal of Intelligence and Counterintelligence* 13, no. 4 (Winter 2000): 490–514.

Nicholas, Jack D. "The Element of Surprise in Modern Warfare." *Air University Quarterly* 8 (Summer 1956): 3–20.

Pease, Stephen E. *PSYWAR: Psychological Warfare in Korea, 1950–1953.* Harrisburg, Pa.: Stackpole Books, 1992.

Rose, P. K. "Two Strategic Intelligence Mistakes in Korea, 1950." *Studies in Intelligence* 11 (Fall–Winter 2001): 57–65.

Stack, Kevin P. "The Role of Intelligence at Inchon." *Naval Intelligence Professionals Quarterly* 14, no. 1 (January 1998): 7–10.

Unsinger, Peter C. "Three Intelligence Blunders in Korea." *International Journal of Intelligence and Counterintelligence* 3, no. 4 (Winter 1989): 549–61.

5. The Suez Crisis of 1956

Cogan, Charles G. "From the Politics of Lying to the Farce at Suez: What the U.S. Knew." *Intelligence and National Security* 13, no. 2 (Summer 1998): 100–122.

Cohen, Raymond. "Israeli Military Intelligence before the 1956 Sinai Campaign." *Intelligence and National Security* 3, no. 1 (January 1988): 100–140.

Drachman, Edward R., and Alan Shank. *Presidents and Foreign Policy: Countdown to Ten Controversial Decisions.* Ithaca: State University of New York Press, 1997.

Hahn, Peter L. *The United States, Great Britain and Egypt, 1945–1956.* Chapel Hill: University of North Carolina Press, 1991.

Lucas, W. Scott. *Divided We Stand: Britain, the US and the Suez Crisis.* London: Hodder & Stoughton, 1991.

——. *Britain and Suez: The Lion's Last Roar.* Manchester, United Kingdom: Manchester University Press, 1996.

Lucas, W. Scott, and Alistair Morey. "The Hidden 'Alliance': The CIA and MI6 before and after Suez." *Intelligence and National Security* 15, no. 2 (Summer 2000): 95–120.

Rawnsley, Gary D. "Overt and Covert: The Voice of Britain and Black Radio Broadcasting in the Suez Crisis, 1956." *Intelligence and National Security* 11, no. 3 (July 1996): 497–522.

J. THE ONSET OF DECLINE: THE 1960s

1. General

Cabell, Charles A., Jr., ed. *A Man of Intelligence: Memoirs of War, Peace, and the CIA.* Boulder, Colo.: Impavide, 1997.

Department of State. Office of the Historian. *Foreign Relations of the United States, 1964–1968.* Vol. 12, *Western Europe.* Edited by James E. Miller. Washington, D.C.: Government Printing Office, 2001.

Dorn, A. Walter, and David J. H. Bell. "Intelligence and Peace-Keeping: The UN Operation in the Congo, 1960–64." *International Peace-Keeping* 2, no. 1 (Spring 1995): 11–33.

Freedman, Lawrence. *Kennedy's Wars: Berlin, Cuba, Laos, and Vietnam*. New York: Oxford University Press, 2000.

Helms, Richard. *A Look over My Shoulder: A Life in the Central Intelligence Agency*. With William Hood. New York: Random House, 2003.

Holm, Richard. "A Close Call in Africa." *Studies in Intelligence*, Winter 1999–2000, 17–28.

Kohli, M. S., and Kenneth Conboy. *Spies in the Himalayas: Secret Missions and Perilous Climbs*. Lawrence: University of Kansas Press, 2003.

Leary, William M. "Robert Fulton's Skyhook and Operation Coldfeet." *Studies in Intelligence* 38, no. 5 (1995): 99–109.

Leary, William M., and Leonard A. LeSchack. *Project Coldfeet: Secret Mission to a Soviet Ice Station*. Annapolis, Md.: Naval Institute Press, 1996.

Lewis, Jonathan E. *Spy Capitalism: Itek and the CIA*. New Haven, Conn.: Yale University Press, 2002.

Meyer, Cord. *Facing Reality: From World Federalism to the CIA*. New York: Harper & Row, 1980.

Powers, Thomas. *The Man Who Kept the Secrets: Richard Helms and the CIA*. New York: Knopf, 1979.

Prados, John. *Lost Crusader: The Secret Wars of CIA Director William Colby*. New York: Oxford University Press, 2003.

Ruffner, Kevin C., ed. *CORONA: America's First Satellite Program*. Washington, D.C.: Central Intelligence Agency, 1995.

Ryan, Henry Butterfield. *The Fall of Che Guevara: A Story of Soldiers, Spies, and Diplomats*. New York: Oxford University Press, 1998.

Tovar, B. Hugh. "The Indonesian Crisis of 1965–1966: A Retrospective." *International Journal of Intelligence and Counterintelligence* 7, no. 3 (Fall 1994): 313–38.

2. The Bay of Pigs, 1961

Aguilar, Luis, ed. *Operation Zapata: The "Ultra-sensitive" Report and Testimony of the Board of Inquiry on the Bay of Pigs*. Frederick, Md.: University Publications of America, 1981.

Bissell, Richard M., Jr. "Response to Lucien S. Vandenbroucke, The 'Confessions' of Allen Dulles: New Evidence on the Bay of Pigs." *Diplomatic History* 8, no. 4 (1984): 377–80.

Blight, James G., and Peter Kornbluh, eds. *The Politics of Illusion: The Bay of Pigs Invasion Reexamined*. Boulder, Colo.: Lynne Rienner, 1998.

Chapman, Robert D. "You Gotta Know When to Hold." *International Journal of Intelligence and Counterintelligence* 11, no. 2 (Summer 1998): 221–39.

Department of State. Office of the Historian. *Foreign Relations of the United States, 1961–1963*. Vol. 10, *Cuba, January 1961–September 1962*. Washington, D.C.: Government Printing Office, 1997.

Feeney, Hal. "The Bay of Pigs Remembered." *Naval Intelligence Professionals Quarterly* 4, no. 3 (Fall 1988): 1–4.

———. "The Night of the White Horse." *Naval Intelligence Professionals Quarterly* 11, no. 1 (Winter 1995): 1–4.

Gleijeses, Piero. "Ships in the Night: The CIA, the White House, and the Bay of Pigs." *Journal of Latin American Studies* 27, no. 1 (February 1995): 1–42.

Hershberg, James G. "Their Man in Havana: Anglo-American Intelligence Exchanges and the Cuban Crises, 1961–62." *Intelligence and National Security* 15, no. 2 (Summer 2000): 121–76.

Higgins, Trumbull. *Perfect Failure: Kennedy, Eisenhower, and the CIA at the Bay of Pigs*. New York: Norton, 1987.

Johnson, Haynes. *The Bay of Pigs: The Leaders' Story of Brigade 2506*. New York: Norton, 1964.

Kornbluh, Peter, ed. *Bay of Pigs Declassified: The Secret CIA Report on the Invasion of Cuba*. New York: New Press, 1998.

Lynch, Grayston L. *Decision for Disaster: Betrayal at the Bay of Pigs*. Washington, D.C.: Brassey's, 1998.

Meyer, Karl E., and Tad Szulc. *The Cuban Invasion: The Chronicle of a Disaster*. New York: Praeger, 1962.

Thomas, Ronald C., Jr. "Influences on Decisionmaking at the Bay of Pigs." *International Journal of Intelligence and Counterintelligence* 3, no. 4 (Winter 1989): 537–48.

Warner, Michael. "The CIA's Internal Probe of the Bay of Pigs Affair." *Studies in Intelligence* (Winter 1998–1999): 93–101.

3. The Cuban Missile Crisis, 1962

Abel, Elie. *The Missile Crisis*. Philadelphia: Lippencott, 1966.

Allison, Graham T. *Essence of Decision: Explaining the Cuban Missile Crisis*. Boston: Little, Brown, 1971.

Allyn, Bruce J., James G. Blight, and David A. Welch. *Back to the Brink: Proceedings of the Moscow Conference on the Cuban Missile Crisis, January 27–28, 1989*. Lanham, Md.: University Press of America, 1992.

———, eds. "Essence of Revision: Moscow, Havana, and the Cuban Missile Crisis." *International Security* 14, no. 3 (Winter 1989/1990): 136–72.

Alvarez, David. "Research Note: American Signals Intelligence and the Cuban Missile Crisis." *Intelligence and National Security* 15, no. 1 (Spring 2000): 169–76.

Amuchastegui, Domingo. "Cuban Intelligence and the October Crisis." *Intelligence and National Security* 13, no. 3 (Autumn 1998): 88–119.

Beschloss, Michael R. *The Crisis Years: Kennedy and Khrushchev, 1960–1963*. New York: HarperCollins, 1991.

Blight, James G. *The Shattered Crystal Ball: Fear and Learning in the Cuban Missile Crisis*. Lanham, Md.: Rowman and Littlefield, 1992.

Blight, James G., and David A. Welch, eds. *Intelligence and the Cuban Missile Crisis*. London: Frank Cass, 1998.

———, eds. "Intelligence and the Cuban Missile Crisis." Special issue, *Intelligence and National Security* 13, no. 3 (Autumn 1998).

———. *On the Brink: Americans and Soviets Reexamine the Cuban Missile Crisis*. New York: Hill & Wang, 1989.

———. "Risking 'The Destruction of Nations': Lessons of the Cuban Missile Crisis for New and Aspiring Nuclear States." *Security Studies* 4, no. 4 (Summer 1994): 811–50.

Blight, James G., Bruce J. Allyn, and David A. Welch. *Cuba on the Brink: Castro, the Missile Crisis, and the Soviet Collapse*. New York: Pantheon, 1993.

Blight, James G., David Lewis, and David A. Welch, eds. *Cuba Between the Superpowers: The Antigua Conference on the Cuban Missile Crisis*. Providence, R.I.: Thomas J. Watson Jr., Institute for International Studies, Brown University, 1991.

Blight, James G., Joseph S. Nye Jr., and David A. Welch. "The Cuban Missile Crisis Revisited." *Foreign Affairs* 60, no. 4 (Fall 1987): 170–88.

Brugioni, Dino A. *Eyeball to Eyeball: The Inside Story of the Cuban Missile Crisis*. New York: Random House, 1991.

———. "The Invasion of Cuba." *Quarterly Journal of Military History* 4, no. 2 (Winter 1992): 92–101.

Brune, Lester. *The Missile Crisis of October 1962: A Review of Issues and References*. Claremont, Calif.: Regina Books, 1985.

Caldwell, Dan, ed. "Cuban Missile Affair and the American Style of Crisis Management." *Parameters* 19 (April 1989): 170–88.

———. "Department of Defense Operations during the Cuban Missile Crisis: A Report by Adam Yarmolinsky, Special Assistant to the Secretary of Defense, 13 February 1963." *Naval War College Review* 32 (July–August 1979): 83–99.

Christol, C. Q., and C. R. Davis. "Maritime Quarantine: The Naval Interdiction of Offensive Weapons and Associated Material to Cuba, 1962." *American Journal of International Law* 57 (July 1963): 525–45.

Cline, Ray S. "The Cuban Missile Crisis." *Foreign Affairs* 68, no. 4 (Fall 1989): 190–96.

Crane, Robert D. "The Cuban Crisis: A Strategic Analysis of American and Soviet Policy." *Orbis* 6 (Winter 1963): 528–63.

Daniel, James, and John G. Hubbell. *Strike in the West: The Complete Story of the Cuban Crisis*. New York: Holt, Rinehart & Winston, 1963.

Detzer, David. *The Brink: The Cuban Missile Crisis, 1962*. New York: Crowell, 1979.

Divine, Robert A., ed. *The Cuban Missile Crisis*. New York: Quadrangle, 1988.

Feeney, Hal. "Eyeball to Eyeball: My View." *Naval Intelligence Professionals Quarterly* 8, no. 4 (Fall 1992): 16–18.

Fischer, Beth A. "Perception, Intelligence Errors, and the Cuban Missile Crisis." *Intelligence and National Security* 13, no. 3 (Autumn 1998): 150–72.

Garthoff, Raymond L. "American Reaction to Soviet Aircraft in Cuba, 1962 and 1978." *Political Science Quarterly* 95, no. 3 (1980): 427–39.

———. "Cuban Missile Crisis: The Soviet Story." *Foreign Policy* 72 (Fall 1988): 61–80.

———. *Reflections on the Cuban Missile Crisis*. Washington, D.C.: Brookings, 1987.

———. "US Intelligence in the Cuban Missile Crisis." *Intelligence and National Security* 13, no. 3 (Autumn 1998): 18–63.

Goodell, Thaxter L. "Cratology Pays Off." *Studies in Intelligence* 8, no. 4 (Fall 1964): 1–10.

Hansen, James H. "Soviet Deception in the Cuban Missile Crisis." *Studies in Intelligence* 46, no. 1 (2002): 49–58.

Hershberg, James G. "Before the Missiles of October: Did Kennedy Plan a Military Strike against Cuba?" *Diplomatic History* 14, no. 2 (Spring 1990): 163–98.

———. "Their Man in Havana: Anglo-American Intelligence Exchanges and the Cuban Crises, 1961–62." *Intelligence and National Security* 15, no. 2 (Summer 2000): 121–76.

Hilsman, Roger. *The Cuban Missile Crisis: The Struggle over Policy*. Westport, Conn.: Praeger, 1996.

———. *To Move a Nation: The Politics of Foreign Policy in the Administration of John F. Kennedy*. Garden City, N.Y.: Doubleday, 1967.

Kennedy, Robert F. *Thirteen Days: A Memoir of the Cuban Missile Crisis*. New York: Norton, 1969.

Kent, Sherman. "A Crucial Estimate Relived." *Studies in Intelligence* 8, no. 2 (Spring 1964): 1–18.

Knorr, Klaus. "Failures in National Intelligence Estimates: The Case of the Cuban Missiles." *World Politics* 16, no. 3 (April 1964): 455–67.

May, Ernest R., and Philip D. Zelikow, eds. *The Kennedy Tapes: Inside the White House during the Cuban Missile Crisis*. Cambridge, Mass.: Harvard University Press, 1997.

McAuliffe, Mary S., ed. *CIA Documents on the Cuban Missile Crisis, 1962*. Washington, D.C.: Central Intelligence Agency, 1992.

Merom, Gil. "The 1962 Cuban Intelligence Estimate: A Methodological Perspective." *Intelligence and National Security* 14, no. 3 (Autumn 1999): 48–80.

Nash, Philip. *The Other Missiles of October: Eisenhower, Kennedy, and the Jupiters, 1957–1963*. Chapel Hill: University of North Carolina Press, 1997.

National Security Agency. *NSA and the Cuban Missile Crisis*. Ft. Meade, Md.: NSA Center for Cryptologic History, 1998.

Rumpelmayer, J. J. "The Missiles in Cuba." *Studies in Intelligence* 8, no. 4 (Fall 1964): 87–92.

Scott, Len. "Espionage and the Cold War: Oleg Penkovsky and the Cuban Missile Crisis." *Intelligence and National Security* 14, no. 3 (Autumn 1999): 23–47.

Scott, L. V. *Macmillan, Kennedy, and the Cuban Missile Crisis: Political, Military and Intelligence Aspects*. London: Macmillan, 1999.

Scott, L. V., and Steve Smith. "Lessons of October: Historians, Political Scientists, Policy-makers and the Cuban Missile Crisis." *International Affairs* 70 (October 1994): 659–84.

Thompson, Robert Smith. *The Missiles of October: The Declassified Story of John F. Kennedy and the Cuban Missile Crisis*. Old Tappan, N.J.: Simon & Schuster, 1992.

Usowski, Peter S. "John McCone and the Cuban Missile Crisis: A Persistent Approach to the Intelligence-Policy Relationship." *International Journal of Intelligence and Counterintelligence* 2, no. 4 (Winter 1988): 547–76.

Welch, David A. "Intelligence Assessment in the Cuban Missile Crisis." *Queen's Quarterly* 100, no. 2 (Summer 1993): 421–37.

Welch, David A., and James G. Blight. "The Eleventh Hour of the Cuban Missile Crisis: An Introduction to the ExComm Transcripts." *International Security* 12, no. 3 (Winter 1987–1988): 5–29.

Wirtz, James J. "Organizing for Crisis Intelligence: Lessons from the Cuban Missile Crisis." *Intelligence and National Security* 13, no. 3 (Autumn 1998): 120–49.

Wohlstetter, Roberta. "Cuba and Pearl Harbor: Hindsight and Foresight," *Foreign Affairs* 43 (July 1965): 691–707.

4. The Liberty Incident

Borne, John E. *The USS Liberty: Dissenting History vs. Official History*. New York: Reconsideration Press, 1995.

Cristol, A. Jay. *The Liberty Incident: The Israeli Attack on the U.S. Navy Spy Ship*. Washington, D.C.: Brassey's, 2002.

Department of State. Office of the Historian. *Foreign Relations of the United States, 1964–1968*. Vol. 19, *Arab-Israeli Crisis and War, 1967*. Edited by Harriet Dashiell Schwar. Washington, D.C.: Government Printing Office, 2004.

Ennes, James M., Jr. *Assault on the "Liberty": The True Story of the Israeli Attack on an American Intelligence Ship*. New York: Random House, 1979.

Fishel, Reverdy S. "The Attack on the Liberty: An 'Accident'?" *International Journal of Intelligence and Counterintelligence* 8, no. 3 (Fall 1995): 345–52.

Hounam, Peter. *Operation Cyanide: Why the Bombing of the USS Liberty Nearly Caused World War III.* London: Vision, 2003.

Jacobsen, Walter L. "A Juridical Examination of the Israeli Attack on the U.S.S. Liberty," *Naval Law Review*, Winter 1986, 1–52.

Pearson, Anthony. *Conspiracy of Silence: The Attack on the USS Liberty.* New York: Quartet Books, 1978.

Rodman, David. "Against Fishel: Another Look at the *Liberty* Incident." *International Journal of Intelligence and Counterintelligence* 9, no. 1 (Spring 1996): 73–80.

Taylor, Jim. *Pearl Harbor II: The True Story of the Sneak Attack by Israel upon the USS Liberty.* Washington, D.C.: Mideast, 1980.

Walsh, David C. "Friendless Fire?" *U.S. Naval Institute Proceedings*, June 2003, 58–64.

5. The Phoenix Program

Andrade, Dale. *Ashes to Ashes: The Phoenix Program and the Vietnam War.* Lexington, Mass.: Lexington Books, 1990.

Blaufarb, Douglas S. *The Counterinsurgency Era: U.S. Doctrine and Performance, 1950 to the Present.* New York: Free Press, 1977.

Brown, F. C. "The Phoenix Program." *Military Journal* 2 (Spring 1979): 19–21, 49.

Colby, William E. *Honorable Men: My Life in the CIA.* With Peter Forbath. New York: Simon & Schuster, 1978.

Hunt, Richard A. *Pacification: The American Struggle for Vietnam's Hearts and Minds.* Boulder, Colo.: Westview, 1995.

Moyar, Mark. *Phoenix and the Birds of Prey: The CIA's Secret Campaign to Destroy the Viet Cong.* Annapolis, Md.: Naval Institute Press, 1997.

Valentine, Douglas. *The Phoenix Program: A Shattering Account of the Most Ambitious and Closely-Guarded Operation of the Vietnam War.* New York: Morrow, 1990.

6. Psychic Experiments

Mandelbaum, W. Adam. *The Psychic Battlefield.* New York: St. Martin's, 2000.

McRae, Ronald M. *Mind Wars: The True Story of Government Research into the Military Potential of Psychic Weapons.* New York: St. Martin's, 1984.

Schnabel, Jim. *Remote Viewers: The Secret History of America's Psychic Spies.* New York: Dell, 1997.

7. The Pueblo Incident

Armbrister, Trevor. *A Matter of Accountability: The True Story of the Pueblo Affair*. New York: Coward-McCann, 1970.

——. "The Pueblo Crisis and Public Opinion." *Naval War College Review* 24 (March 1971): 84–110.

Brandt, Edward. *The Last Voyage of the USS Pueblo*. New York: Norton, 1969.

Bucher, Lloyd M. *Bucher: My Story*. With Mark Rascovich. Garden City, N.Y.: Doubleday, 1970.

——. "The Pueblo Incident: Commander Bucher Replies." *Naval History* 3, no. 1 (Winter 1989): 44–50.

Buhite, Russell D. *Lives at Risk: Hostages and Victims in American Foreign Policy*. Wilmington, Del.: Scholarly Resources, 1995.

Department of State. Office of the Historian. *Foreign Relations of the United States, 1964–1968*. Vol. 29, *Korea*. Edited by Karen L. Gatz. Washington, D.C.: Government Printing Office, 1999.

Gallery, Daniel V. *The Pueblo Incident*. Garden City, N.Y.: Doubleday, 1970.

Lentner, Howard H. "The Pueblo Affair: Anatomy of a Crisis." *Military Review* 49 (July 1969): 55–66.

Lerner, Mitchell B. *The Pueblo Incident: A Spy Ship and the Failure of American Foreign Policy*. Lawrence: University Press of Kansas, 2002.

Liston, Robert A. *The Pueblo Surrender: A Covert Action by the National Security Agency*. New York: M. Evans, 1988.

Murphy, Edward R., Jr., with Curt Gentry. *Second in Command: The Uncensored Account of the Capture of the Spy Ship Pueblo*. New York: Holt, Rinehart & Winston, 1971.

U.S. Congress. House. Committee on Armed Services. Special Subcommittee on the USS Pueblo. *Inquiry into the USS Pueblo and EC-121 Plane Incidents*. 91st Cong., 1st sess., March–April 1969. Washington, D.C.: Government Printing Office, 1969.

8. The Vietnam War

Baker, Bob. "The Easter Offensive of 1972: A Failure to Use Intelligence." *Military Intelligence* 24, no. 1 (January–March 1998): 40–42, 60.

——. "Warning Intelligence: The Battle of the Bulge and the NVN Easter Offensive." *American Intelligence Journal* 17, nos. 3–4 (1997): 71–79.

Bennett, Donald G. "Spot Report: Intelligence, Vietnam." *Military Review* 46, no. 8 (1966): 72–77.

Bjelajac, Stavko N. "A Design for Psychological Operations in Vietnam." *Orbis* 10 (Spring 1966): 126–37.

Browne, Malcolm. "A Reporter Looks Back: The CIA and the Fall of Vietnam." *Washington Journalism Review*, January–February 1978, 18–19.

Burchett, Wilfred G. *The Furtive War: The United States in Vietnam and Laos.* New York: International, 1963.

Cable, Larry E. *Conflict of Myths: The Development of American Counterinsurgency Doctrine and the Vietnam War.* New York: New York University Press, 1986.

———. *Unholy Grail: The U.S. and the Wars in Vietnam.* New York: Routledge, 1991.

Cassidy, Robert M. "Back to the Street without Joy: Counterinsurgency Lessons from Vietnam and Other Small Wars." *Parameters* 36, no. 2 (Summer 2004): 73–83.

Chandler, Robert W. *War of Ideas: The U.S. Propaganda Campaign in Vietnam.* Boulder, Colo.: Westview, 1981.

Colby, William E. *Lost Victory: A Firsthand Account of America's Sixteen-Year Involvement in Vietnam.* With James Mccarger. Chicago: Contemporary Books, 1989.

Davidson, Phillip B. *Secrets of the Vietnam War.* Novato, Calif.: Presidio, 1990.

———. *Vietnam at War: The History 1946–1975.* Novato, Calif.: Presidio, 1988.

DeForest, Orrin, and David Chanoff. *Slow Burn: The Rise and Bitter Fall of American Intelligence in Vietnam.* New York: Simon and Schuster, 1990.

De Silva, Peer. *Sub Rosa: The CIA and the Uses of Intelligence.* New York: New York Times Books, 1978.

Donahue, James C. *Mobile Guerrilla Force: With the Special Forces in War Zone D.* Annapolis, Md.: Naval Institute Press, 1996.

Englemann, Larry. *Tears before Rain: An Oral History of the Last Days of the Fall of South Vietnam.* New York: Oxford University Press, 1990.

Ford, Harold P. *CIA and the Vietnam Policymakers: Three Episodes, 1962–1968.* Washington, D.C.: Central Intelligence Agency, 1998.

Gilbert, James L. *The Most Secret War: Army Signals Intelligence in Vietnam.* Washington, D.C.: U.S. Army Intelligence and Security Command, Military History Office, 2003.

Jensen-Stevenson, Monika. *Spite House: The Last Secret of the War in Vietnam.* New York: Norton, 1997.

Kelly, Francis J. *The Green Berets in Vietnam, 1961–71.* McLean, Va.: Brassey's, 1991.

Lansdale, Edward G. "Vietnam: Do We Understand Revolution?" *Foreign Affairs* 43, no. 1 (1964): 75–86.

Larson, Doyle. "Direct Intelligence Combat Support in Vietnam: Project Teaball." *American Intelligence Journal* 15, no. 1 (Spring/Summer 1994): 56–58.

Lee, Alex. *Force Recon Command: A Special Marine Unit in Vietnam, 1969–1970.* Annapolis, Md.: Naval Institute Press, 1995.

McNamara, Robert S., with Brian VanDeMark. *In Retrospect: The Tragedy and Lessons of Vietnam.* New York: Times Books/Random House, 1995.

Moyar, Mark. "Hanoi's Strategic Surprise." *Intelligence and National Security* 18, no. 1 (Spring 2003): 155–70.

Plaster, John L. *Secret Commandos: Behind Enemy Lines with the Elite Warriors of SOG.* New York: Simon & Schuster, 2004.

———. *SOG: The Secret Wars of America's Commandos in Vietnam.* New York: Simon & Schuster, 1997.

Prados, John. *The Hidden History of the Vietnam War.* Chicago: Ivan R. Dee, 1995.

Scott, Peter Dale. *Lost Crusade: America's Secret Cambodian Mercenaries.* Annapolis, Md.: Naval Institute Press, 1998.

———. *The War Conspiracy: The Secret Road to the Second Indochina War.* Indianapolis, Ind.: Bobbs-Merrill, 1972.

Shultz, Richard H., Jr. *The Secret War against Hanoi: Kennedy and Johnson's Use of Spies, Saboteurs, and Covert Warriors in North Vietnam.* New York: HarperCollins, 1999.

Smith, Eric McAllister. *Not by the Book: A Combat Intelligence Officer in Vietnam.* New York: Ivy Books, 1993.

Smith, Warner. *Covert Warrior: Fighting the CIA's Secret War in Southeast Asia and China, 1965–1967.* Novato, Calif.: Presidio, 1996.

Snepp, Frank. *Decent Interval: An Insider's Account of Saigon's Indecent End.* New York: Random House, 1977.

Stanton, Shelby L. *Green Berets at War: U.S. Army Special Forces in Southeast Asia, 1956–1975.* Novato, Calif.: Presidio, 1985.

———. *Rangers at War: Combat Recon in Vietnam.* New York: Crown/Orion Books, 1992.

Stein, Jeff. *A Murder in Wartime: The Untold Spy Story That Changed the Course of the Vietnam War.* New York: St. Martin's, 1992.

Sullivan, John F. *Of Spies and Lies: A CIA Lie Detector Remembers Vietnam.* Lawrence: University Press of Kansas, 2002.

Tourison, Sedgwick. *Secret Army, Secret War: Washington's Tragic Spy Operation in North Vietnam.* Annapolis, Md.: Naval Institute Press, 1995.

———. *Talking with Victor Charlie: An Interrogator's Story.* New York: Ivy Books, 1991.

Tovar, B. Hugh. "Vietnam Revisited: The United States and Diem's Death." *International Journal of Intelligence and Counterintelligence* 5, no. 3 (Fall 1991): 291–312.

Young, Darryl. *The Element of Surprise: Navy SEALS in Vietnam.* New York: Ivy Books, 1990.

K. TOWARD CONGRESSIONAL INVESTIGATIONS: THE 1970s

1. General

Adler, Emanuel. "Executive Command and Control in Foreign Policy: The CIA's Covert Activities." *Orbis* 23 (Fall 1979): 671–96.

Agee, Philip. "The American Security Services: Where Do We Go from Here?" *Journal of Contemporary Asia* 7 (Spring 1977): 251–59.

Andrianopoulos, Gerry Argyris. *Kissinger and Brezinski: The NSC and the Struggle for Control of U.S. National Security Policy.* New York: St. Martin's, 1991.

Association of the Bar of the City of New York. Committee on Civil Rights. *The Central Intelligence Agency: Oversight and Accountability.* New York: Association of the Bar of the City of New York, 1975.

Baker, Carol M., and Matthew H. Fox. *Classified Files: The Yellowing Pages.* New York: Twentieth Century, 1972.

Baldwin, Hanson W. "The Future of Intelligence." *Strategic Review* 4 (Summer 1976): 6–24.

Blackstock, Paul W. *The CIA and the Intelligence Community: Their Roles, Organization, and Functions.* St. Charles, Mo.: Forum Press, 1974.

———. "The Intelligence Community under the Nixon Administration." *Armed Forces and Society* 1 (February 1975): 231–50.

Blum, Richard H., ed. *Surveillance and Espionage in a Free Society: A Report by the Planning Group on Intelligence and Security to the Policy Council of the Democratic National Committee.* New York: Praeger, 1972.

Brzezinski, Zbigniew. *Power and Principle: Memoirs of the National Security Advisor, 1977–1981.* New York: Farrar, Straus, and Giroux, 1983.

Bush, George H. *Looking Forward.* New York: Doubleday, 1987.

Carter, Jimmy. *Keeping Faith: Memoirs of a President.* New York: Bantam Books, 1982.

Cline, Ray S. "Policy without Intelligence." *Foreign Policy* 17 (Winter 1974–75): 121–35.

Colby, William E. "Can We Do without Secret Intelligence Operations?" *Skeptic* 7 (May–June 1975): 36–39.

———. "Intelligence Secrecy and Security in a Free Society." *International Security* 1 (Fall 1976): 3–14.

Cookridge, E. H. *Spy Trade.* London: Hodder, 1971.

Cooper, Chester L. "The CIA and Decision-Making." *Foreign Affairs* 50 (January 1972): 223–36.

Copeland, Miles. *Beyond Cloak or Dagger: Inside the CIA.* New York: Pinnacle, 1975.

——. "The Functioning of Strategic Intelligence." *Defense and Foreign Affairs Digest*, nos. 2–4 (1977): 29–32, 36–38, 32–35.

Corn, David. *Blond Ghost: Ted Shackley and the CIA's Crusades.* New York: Simon & Schuster, 1994.

Graham, Daniel O. "The Intelligence Mythology of Washington." *Strategic Review* 4 (Summer 1976): 59–66.

——. *U.S. Intelligence at the Crossroads.* Washington, D.C.: United States Strategic Institute, 1976.

Hoffman. Fred. "The Role of Intelligence in President Jimmy Carter's Troop Withdrawal Decisions." *American Intelligence Journal* 21, nos. 1–2 (Spring 2002): 57–60.

Hughes, Thomas L. *The Fate of Facts in a World of Men: Foreign Policy and Intelligence-Making.* New York: Foreign Policy, 1976.

Lindgren, David T. *Trust but Verify: Imagery Analysis in the Cold War.* Annapolis, Md.: Naval Institute Press, 2000.

Szanton, Peter, and Graham Allison. "Intelligence: Seizing the Opportunity." *Foreign Policy* 22 (Spring 1976): 183–215.

Szulc, Tad. *Compulsive Spy: The Strange Career of E. Howard Hunt.* New York: Viking, 1974.

Troy, Thomas F. "Writing History in CIA: A Memoir of Frustration." *International Journal of Intelligence and Counterintelligence* 7, no. 4 (Winter 1994): 397–411.

2. Chile and Salvador Allende

Barry, James A. "Covert Action Can Be Just." *Orbis* 37, no. 3 (Summer 1993): 375–90.

Central Intelligence Agency. *CIA Activities in Chile.* Washington, D.C.: Central Intelligence Agency, 2000.

Davis, Nathaniel. *The Last Two Years of Salvador Allende.* Ithaca, N.Y.: Cornell University Press, 1985.

——. "U.S. Covert Actions in Chile 1971–73." *Foreign Service Journal*, part I (November 1978): 10–14, 38–39; part II (December 1978): 11–13, 42.

Goldberg, Peter A. "The Politics of the Allende Overthrow in Chile." *Political Science Quarterly* 90, no. 1 (Spring 1975): 93–116.

Sigmund, Paul E. *The Overthrow of Allende and the Politics of Chile, 1964–1976.* Pittsburgh, Pa.: Pittsburgh University Press, 1977.

U.S. Congress. House. Subcommittee on Evaluation. Permanent Select Committee on Intelligence. *Iran: Evaluation of U.S. Intelligence Performance prior to November 1978.* 96th Cong., 1st sess., 1979. Washington, D.C.: Government Printing Office, 1979.

U.S. Congress. Select Committee to Study Governmental Operations with Respect to Intelligence Activities. "Covert Action in Chile: 1963–1973." *Staff Report*. Washington, D.C.: Government Printing Office, 1975.

3. Glomar Explorer (Project Jennifer)

Bartlett, Donald L., and James B. Steele. *Empire: The Life, Legend, and Madness of Howard Hughes*. New York: Norton, 1979.
Booth, Marilyn. "The Jennifer Triangle: Hughes, Glomar, and the CIA." *Harvard Political Review* 4 (Spring 1976): 17–25.
Burleson, Clyde W. *The Jennifer Project*. Englewood Cliffs, N.J.: Prentice-Hall, 1977.
Burns, Thomas S. *The Secret War for the Ocean Depths: Soviet-American Rivalry for the Mastery of the Seas*. New York: Rawson Associates, 1978.
Eustis, Frederic A., III. "The Glomar Explorer Incident: Implications for the Law of Salvage." *Virginia Journal of International Law* 16 (Fall 1975): 177–85.
Varner, Roy, and Wayne Collier. *A Matter of Risk: The Incredible Inside Story of the CIA's Hughes Glomar Explorer Mission to Raise a Russian Submarine*. New York: Random House, 1978.
Williams, David L. *Salvage! Rescued from the Deep*. Shepperton, United Kingdom: Ian Allen, 1991.

4. The Mayaguez Incident

Guilmartin, John F., Jr. *A Very Short War: The Mayaguez and the Battle of Koh Tang*. College Station: Texas A&M University Press, 1995.
Messegee, J. A., et al. "Mayday for Mayaguez." *U.S. Naval Institute Proceedings*, November 1976, 93–111.
Rowan, Roy. *The Four Days of the Mayaguez*. New York: Norton, 1975.
Wetterhahn, Ralph. *The Mayaguez Incident and the End of the Vietnam War*. New York: Carroll & Graf, 2001.

L. THE EXPANSION: THE 1980s

1. General

Armstrong, Anne. "Bridging the Gap: Intelligence and Policy." *Washington Quarterly* 12, no. 1 (1989): 23–34.
Barker, Rodney. *Dancing with the Devil: Sex, Espionage, and the U.S. Marines—the Clayton Lonetree Story*. New York: Simon & Schuster, 1996.

Bernstein, Carl, and Marco Politi. *His Holiness: Pope John Paul II and the Hidden History of Our Time*. New York: Doubleday, 1996.

Betts, Richard K. "Intelligence for Policymaking." *Washington Quarterly,* Summer 1980, 118–29.

———. "Policymakers and Intelligence Analysts: Love, Hate or Indifference?" *Intelligence and National Security* 3, no. 1 (January 1988): 184–89.

Cherne, Leo. "Need to Know." *Journal of Defense and Diplomacy* 4 (May 1986): 38–41.

Chomeau, John B. "Covert Action's Proper Role in U.S. Policy." *International Journal of Intelligence and Counterintelligence* 2, no. 3 (Fall 1988): 407–13.

Clarke, Duncan F., and Edward L. Neveleff. "Secrecy, Foreign Intelligence, and Civil Liberties: Has the Pendulum Swung Too Far?" *Political Science Quarterly* 99, no. 3 (1984): 493–513.

Farson, Stuart. "Schools of Thought: National Perceptions of Intelligence." *Conflict Quarterly* 9 (Spring 1989): 52–104.

Gardiner, L. Keith. "Squaring the Circle: Dealing with Intelligence-Policy Breakdowns." *Intelligence and National Security* 6, no. 1 (January 1991): 141–53.

Gates, Robert M. "The CIA and American Foreign Policy." *Foreign Affairs* 66, no. 2 (Winter 1987/88): 215–30.

———. "Future Intelligence Challenges." *Periscope* 13, no. 4 (Fall 1988): 14–19.

———. "An Opportunity Unfulfilled: The Use and Perceptions of Intelligence at the White House." *Washington Quarterly*, Winter 1989, 35–44.

———. "Unauthorized Disclosures: Risks, Costs, and Responsibilities." *American Intelligence Journal* 9, no. 1 (1988): 6–8.

Handel, Michael I. "The Politics of Intelligence." *Intelligence and National Security* 2, no. 4 (October 1987): 5–46.

Hennesy, Peter. *The Secret State: Whitehall and the Cold War*. London: Allen Lane, 2002.

Hilsman, Roger. "On Intelligence." *Armed Forces and Society* 8 (Fall 1981): 129–43.

Howard, Edward Lee. *Safe House: The Compelling Memoirs of the Only CIA Spy to Seek Asylum in Russia*. Bethesda, Md.: National Press Books, 1995.

Hulnick, Arthur S. "Determining U.S. Intelligence Policy." *International Journal of Intelligence and Counterintelligence* 3, no. 2 (1989): 211–24.

———. "The Intelligence Producer-Policy Consumer Linkage: A Theoretical Approach." *Intelligence and National Security* 1, no. 2 (May 1986): 212–33.

Jeffreys-Jones, Rhodri. "American Intelligence: A Spur to Historical Genius?" *Intelligence and National Security* 3, no. 2 (1988): 332–37.

Johnson, Loch K. "Covert Action and Accountability: Decision-Making for America's Secret Foreign Policy." *International Studies Quarterly* 33 (March 1989): 81–109.

———. "Strategic Intelligence: An American Perspective." *International Journal of Intelligence and Counterintelligence* 3, no. 3 (July 1989): 299–332.

Kerr, Richard J., and Peter Dixon Davis. "Ronald Reagan and the President's Daily Brief." *Studies in Intelligence*, Winter 1998–1999, 51–56.

Kessler, Ronald. *Escape from the CIA: How the CIA Won and Lost the Most Important KGB Spy Ever to Defect to the U.S.* New York: Pocket Books, 1991.

———. *Moscow Station: How the KGB Penetrated the American Embassy.* New York: Scribner's, 1989.

Laqueur, Walter. "The Question of Judgment: Intelligence and Medicine." *Journal of Contemporary History* 18 (October 1983): 533–43.

MacEachin, Douglas J. *U.S. Intelligence and the Polish Crisis, 1980–1981.* University Park: Pennsylvania State University Press, 2003.

Matthias, Willard C. *America's Strategic Blunders: Intelligence Analysis and National Security Policy, 1936–1991.* University Park: Pennsylvania State University Press, 2001.

McCarthy, Shaun P. *The Function of Intelligence in Crisis Management: Towards an Understanding of the Intelligence Producer-Consumer Dichotomy.* Brookfield, Vt.: Ashgate, 1998.

Mitchell, Fredric. "Lots of Smoke—Little Fire." *International Journal of Intelligence and Counterintelligence* 1, no. 4 (1986): 111–18.

Nelson, Dick, and Julie Koenen-Grant. "A Case of Bureaucracy 'in Action': The U.S. Embassy in Moscow." *International Journal of Intelligence and Counterintelligence* 6, no. 3 (Fall 1993): 303–17.

Nelson, Harold. "Intelligence and the Next War: A Retrospective View." *Intelligence and National Security* 2, no. 1 (1987): 97–117.

Persico, Joseph E. *Casey: From the OSS to the CIA.* New York: Viking, 1990.

Powell, S. Steven. *Covert Cadre: Inside the Institute for Policy Studies.* Ottawa, Ill.: GreenHill, 1987.

Ransom, Harry Howe. "Being Intelligent about Secret Intelligence Agencies." *American Political Science Review* 74 (Spring 1980): 141–48.

———. "Congress Never Intended the CIA to Spy at Home." *First Principles* 7 (February 1982): 13–16.

Shultz, George P. *Turmoil and Triumph: My Years as Secretary of State.* New York: Scribner's, 1993.

Simmons, Robert Ruhl. "Intelligence Policy and Performance in Reagan's First Term: A Good Record or Bad?" *International Journal of Intelligence and Counterintelligence* 4, no. 1 (Spring 1990): 1–22.

Soyster, Harry E. "The Changing Nature of the American Spy." *American Intelligence Journal* 10, no. 2 (1989): 29–32.

Stafford, David. *The Silent Game: The Real World of Imaginary Spies.* Toronto, Ontario, Canada: Lester & Orpen Dennys, 1988.

Stanik, Joseph T. *El Dorado Canyon: Reagan's Undeclared War with Qadaffi.* Annapolis, Md.: Naval Institute Press, 2002.

Turner, Stansfield, and George Thibault. "Intelligence: The Right Rules." *Foreign Policy* 48 (Fall 1982): 122–38.

U.S. Congress. House. Permanent Select Committee on Intelligence. *Intelligence Support to Arms Control.* Report together with Dissenting Views. House Rept. No. 100–450. 100th Cong., 1st sess., 1987. Committee print.

Vanderbrook, Michael. "UNCTAD V: Intelligence Support at a Major International Economic Conference." *Studies in Intelligence* 24, no. 1 (Spring 1980): 47–56.

Wise, David. *The Spy Who Got Away: The Inside Story of Edward Lee Howard, the CIA Agent Who Betrayed His Country's Secrets and Escaped to Moscow.* New York: Random House, 1988.

Woodward, Bob. *Veil: The Secret Wars of the CIA, 1981–1987.* New York: Simon & Schuster, 1987.

2. The Iran-Contra Affair

Armstrong, Scott. *The Chronology: The Documented Day-to-Day Account of the Secret Military Assistance to Iran and the Contras.* New York: Warner, 1987.

Bradlee, Ben, Jr. *Guts and Glory: The Rise and Fall of Oliver North.* New York: Donald I. Fine, 1988.

Bruemmer, Russell J., and Marshall H. Silverberg. "The Impact of the Iran-Contra Matter on Congressional Oversight of the CIA." *Houston Journal of International Law* 11, no. 1 (1988): 219–43.

Cinquegrana, Americo R. "Dancing in the Dark: Accepting the Invitation to Struggle in the Context of 'Covert Action,' the Iran-Contra Affair and the Intelligence Oversight Process." *Houston Journal of International Law* 11, no. 1 (Fall 1988): 177–209.

Clarridge, Duane R. *A Spy for All Seasons: My Life in the CIA.* With Digby Diehl. New York: Scribner's, 1997.

Cohen, William S., and George J. Mitchell. *Men of Zeal: A Candid Inside Story of the Iran-Contra Hearings.* New York: Viking Penguin, 1988.

Currie, James T. "Iran-Contra and Congressional Oversight of the CIA." *International Journal of Intelligence and Counterintelligence* 11, no. 2 (Summer 1998): 185–210.

Draper, Theodore. *A Very Thin Line: The Iran-Contra Affair.* New York: Hill and Wang, 1991.

Feldman, Daniel L. "Constitutional Dimensions of the Iran-Contra Affair." *International Journal of Intelligence and Counterintelligence* 2, no. 3 (Fall 1988): 381–97.

Kornbluh, Peter, and Malcolm Byrne, eds. *The Iran-Contra Scandal: The Declassified History; A National Security Archive Documents Reader*. New York: New Press, 1993.

Marshall, Jonathan, Peter Dale Scott, and Jane Hunter. *The Iran-Contra Connection: Secret Teams and Covert Operations in the Reagan Era*. Boston: South End Press, 1987.

McCullough, James. "Personal Reflections on Bill Casey's Last Month at CIA: Coping with Iran-Contra." *Studies in Intelligence* 39, no. 5 (1996): 75–91.

North, Oliver L. *Taking the Stand: The Testimony of Lt. Col. Oliver L. North*. New York: Pocket Books, 1987.

Sayle, Edward F. "The Déja Vu of American Secret Diplomacy." *International Journal of Intelligence and Counterintelligence* 2, no. 3 (Fall 1988): 399–406.

Segev, Samuel. *Iranian Triangle: The Untold Story of Israel's Role in the Iran-Contra Affair*. Translated by Haim Watzman. New York: Free Press, 1988.

Tower, John, Edmund Muskie, and Brent Scowcroft. *The Tower Commission Report*. New York: Times Books, 1987.

U.S. Congress. *Joint Hearings before the Select Committee on Secret Military Assistance to Iran and the Nicaraguan Opposition, U.S. Senate, and the Select Committee to Investigate Covert Arms Transactions with Iran, U.S. House*. 100th Cong., 1st sess. Washington, D.C.: Government Printing Office, 1987.

——. *Report of the Congressional Committees Investigating the Iran-Contra Affair, with Supplemental, Minority, and Additional Views*. 100th Cong., 1st sess. Washington, D.C.: Government Printing Office, 1987.

——. Senate. Select Committee on Intelligence. *Preliminary Inquiry into the Sale of Arms to Iran and Possible Diversion of Funds to the Nicaraguan Resistance*. 100th Cong., 1st sess. Washington, D.C.: Government Printing Office, 1987.

U.S. President. *Implementation of the Recommendations of the President's Special Review Board: Message*. Washington, D.C.: Government Printing Office, 1987.

——. *Report of the President's Special Review Board, February 26, 1987*. Washington, D.C.: Government Printing Office, 1987.

Walsh, Lawrence E. *Firewall: The Iran-Contra Conspiracy and Cover-Up*. New York: Norton, 1997.

——. *Iran-Contra: The Final Report*. New York: Time Books/Random House, 1994.

Wroe, Ann. *Lives, Lies, and the Iran-Contra Affair*. London: Tauris, 1991.

3. The Iran Hostage Crisis

Bani-Sadr, Abol Hassan. *My Turn to Speak: Iran, the Revolution and Secret Deals with the U.S.* Washington, D.C.: Brassey's, 1991.

Beckwith, Charles A., and Donald Knox. *Delta Force: The U.S. Counter-Terrorist Unit and the Iran Hostage Rescue Mission*. New York: Harcourt, Brace & Jovanovich, 1983.

Christopher, Warren. *American Hostages in Iran: Conduct of a Crisis*. New Haven, Conn.: Yale University Press, 1985.

Daugherty, William J. "A First Tour like No Other." *Studies in Intelligence* (Spring 1998): 1–45.

———. "Behind the Intelligence Failure in Iran." *International Journal of Intelligence and Counterintelligence* 14, no. 4 (Winter 2001–2002): 449–84.

———. *In the Shadow of the Ayatollah: A CIA Hostage in Iran*. Annapolis, Md.: Naval Institute Press, 2001.

Department of Defense. *Rescue Mission Report* [Holloway report]. Washington, D.C.: Government Printing Office, 1980.

Donovan, Michael. "National Intelligence and the Iranian Revolution." *Intelligence and National Security* 12, no. 1 (January 1997): 143–63.

Houghton, Patrick David. *U.S. Foreign Policy and the Iran Hostage Crisis*. New York: Cambridge University Press, 2001.

Huyser, Robert E. *Mission to Tehran*. New York: Harper & Row, 1986.

Karabell, Zachary. "'Inside the US Espionage Den': The US Embassy and the Fall of the Shah." *Intelligence and National Security* 8, no. 1 (January 1993): 44–59.

Kyle, James H., and John Robert Eidson. *The Guts to Try: The Untold Story of the Iran Hostage Rescue Mission by the On-Scene Desert Commander*. New York: Crown, 1990.

Ledeen, Michael, and William Lewis. *Debacle: The American Failure in Iran*. New York: Knopf, 1981.

Lenahan, Rod. *Crippled Eagle: A Historical Perspective of U.S. Special Operations, 1976–1996*. Charleston, S.C.: Narwhal Press, 1998.

Mendez, Antonio J. "A Classic Case of Deception." *Studies in Intelligence* (Winter 1999–2000): 1–16.

Pelletier, Jean, and Claude Adams. *The Canadian Caper*. New York: Morrow, 1981.

Rhee, Will. "Comparing U.S. Operations Kingpin (1970) and Eagle Claw (1980)." *International Journal of Intelligence and Counterintelligence* 6, no. 4 (Winter 1993): 489–506.

Rivers, Gayle, and James Hudson. *The Tehran Contract*. New York: Doubleday, 1981.

Rubin, Barry. *Paved with Good Intentions: The American Experience in Iran*. New York: Oxford University Press, 1980.

Salinger, Pierre. *America Held Hostage: The Secret Negotiations*. Garden City, N.Y.: Doubleday, 1981.

Sick, Gary. *All Fall Down: America's Tragic Encounter with Iran*. New York: Random House, 1985.

Stemple, John D. *Inside the Iranian Revolution.* Bloomington: Indiana University Press, 1981.

Sullivan, William H. *Mission to Iran.* New York: Norton, 1981.

Taheri, Amir. *Nest of Spies.* London: Hutchinson, 1988.

4. Nicaragua and Contras

Bouchey, L. Francis, ed. *The Real Secret War: Sandinista Political Warfare and Its Effects on Congress.* Washington, D.C.: Council for Inter-American Security and Inter-American Security Educational Institute, 1987.

Cockburn, Leslie. *Out of Control: The Story of the Reagan Administration's Secret War in Nicaragua, the Illegal Arms Pipeline, and the Contra Drug Connection.* New York: Atlantic Monthly Press, 1987.

Cruz, Arturo, Jr. *Memoirs of a Counterrevolutionary: Life with the Contras, the Sandinistas, and the CIA.* Garden City, N.Y.: Doubleday, 1989.

Dickey, Christopher. *With the Contras: A Reporter in the Wilds of Nicaragua.* New York: Simon & Schuster, 1987.

Dillon, Sam. *Commandos: The CIA and Nicaragua's Contra Rebels.* New York: Henry Holt, 1991.

Garvin, Glenn. *Everybody Had His Own Gringo: The CIA and the Contras.* Washington, D.C.: Brassey's, 1992.

Gutman, Roy. *Banana Diplomacy: The Making of American Policy in Nicaragua, 1981–1987.* New York: Simon & Schuster, 1989.

Kagan, Robert. *A Twilight Struggle: American Power and Nicaragua, 1977–1990.* New York: Free Press, 1996.

Kinzer, Stephen. *Blood of Brothers: Life and War in Nicaragua.* New York: Putnam, 1991.

Moore, John Norton. *The Secret War in Central America: The Sandinista Assault on World Order.* Frederick, Md.: University Press of America, 1987.

Turner, Robert F. "The CIA's Nicaragua 'Murder Manual': A Sandinista 'Dirty Trick'?" *International Journal of Intelligence and Counterintelligence* 9, no. 1 (Spring 1996): 33–41.

5. The October Surprise

Ben-Menashe, Ari. *Profits of War: Inside the Secret U.S.-Israeli Arms Network.* Lanham, Md.: Sheridan Square Press, 1992.

Honegger, Barbara. *October Surprise.* New York: Tudor, 1989.

Parry, Robert. *Trick or Treason: The October Surprise Mystery.* New York: Sheridan Square Press, 1993.

Sick, Gary. *October Surprise: America's Hostages in Iran and the Election of Ronald Reagan*. New York: Random House, 1991.

6. The Shootdown of KAL 007

Clubb, Oliver. *KAL 007: The Hidden Story*. Sag Harbor, N.Y.: Permanent Press, 1985.

Dallin, Alexander. *Black Box: KAL 007 and the Superpowers*. Berkeley: University of California Press, 1985.

Gollin, James. "Stirring Up the Past: KAL Flight 007." *International Journal of Intelligence and Counterintelligence* 7, no. 4 (Winter 1994): 445–63.

Gollin, James, and Robert W. Allardyce. *Desired Track: The Tragic Flight of KAL Flight 007*. 2 vols. Findlay, Ohio: American Vision, 1994.

Haslam, Jonathan. "The KAL Shootdown (1983) and the State of Soviet Air Defence." *Intelligence and National Security* 3, no. 4 (October 1988): 128–33.

Hersh, Seymour M. *The Target Is Destroyed: What Really Happened to Flight 007 and What America Knew about It*. New York: Random House, 1986.

Johnson, R. W. *Shootdown: Flight 007 and the American Connection*. New York: Viking, 1986.

Maertens, Thomas R. "'Shootdown' Shotdown." *International Journal of Intelligence and Counterintelligence* 1, no. 2 (1986): 137–45.

Miller, David W. "007's Analysis of KAL's Flight 007." *International Journal of Intelligence and Counterintelligence* 1, no. 1 (Spring 1986): 109–19.

Twining, David T. "The KAL Incident." *Military Intelligence* 10, no. 3 (1984): 7–9.

M. THE POST–COLD WAR ERA AND THE RISE OF NEW THREATS: THE 1990s

Bacevich, Andrew J., and Eliot A. Cohen, eds. *War over Kosovo*. New York: Columbia University Press, 2001.

Bearden, Milt, and James Risen. *The Main Enemy: The Inside Story of the CIA's Final Showdown with the KGB*. New York: Random House, 2003.

Beschloss, Michael R., and Strobe Talbott. *At the Highest Levels: The Inside Story of the End of the Cold War*. Boston: Little, Brown, 1993.

Biddle, Stephen. "The New Way of War? Debating the Kosovo Model." *Foreign Affairs* 81, no. 3 (May–June 2002): 138–44.

Bush, George, and Brent Scowcroft. *A World Transformed*. New York: Knopf, 1998.

Central Intelligence Agency. *CIA Support to the US Military during the Persian Gulf War*. Washington, D.C.: Government Printing Office, 1997.

Clark, Wesley K. *Waging Modern War: Bosnia, Kosovo, and the Future of Combat*. New York: Public Affairs, 2001.

Constantine, G. Ted. *Intelligence Support to Humanitarian-Disaster Relief Operations: An Intelligence Monograph*. Washington, D.C.: Central Intelligence Agency, December 1995.

Dees, Jennifer L. "Joint STARS in Kosovo: Can the Army and the Air Force Blend Their Operational Differences?" *Military Intelligence* 25, no. 4 (October–December 1999): 16–18.

DeMars, William E. "Hazardous Partnership: NGOs and United States Intelligence in Small Wars." *International Journal of Intelligence and Counterintelligence* 14, no. 2 (Summer 2001): 193–222.

Derian, James Der. "Anti-diplomacy, Intelligence Theory and Surveillance Practice." *Intelligence and National Security* 8, no. 3 (July 1993): 29–51.

Donath, Jaap. "A European Community Intelligence Organization." *Defense Intelligence Journal* 2, no. 1 (Spring 1993): 15–33.

Dorn, A. Walter. "The Cloak and the Blue Beret: Limitations on Intelligence in UN Peacekeeping." *International Journal of Intelligence and Counterintelligence* 12, no. 4 (Winter 1999): 414–47.

Eriksson, Pär. "Intelligence in Peacekeeping Operations." *International Journal of Intelligence and Counterintelligence* 10, no. 1 (Spring 1997): 1–18.

Ermarth, Fritz W. "Seeing Russia Plain: The Russian Crisis and American Intelligence." *National Interest* (Spring 1999): 5–14.

Gates, Robert M. *From the Shadows: The Ultimate Insider's Story of Five Presidents and How They Won the Cold War*. New York: Simon & Schuster, 1996.

Gries, David. "New Links between Intelligence and Policy." *Studies in Intelligence* 34, no. 2 (Summer 1990): 1–6.

Haines, Gerald K. *CIA's Analysis of the Soviet Union, 1947–1991*. With Robert E. Leggett. Washington, D.C.: Central Intelligence Agency, 2001.

Hall, Keith. "Challenges Faced by U.S. Intelligence." *American Intelligence Journal* 11, no. 3 (1990): 1–3.

Hartmann, Frederick H., and Robert L. Wendzel. *America's Foreign Policy in a Changing World*. New York: HarperCollins, 1993.

Herman, Michael. "Diplomacy and Intelligence." *Diplomacy & Statecraft* 9, no. 2 (July 1998): 1–22.

Johnson, Loch K. "Smart Intelligence." *Foreign Policy* 89 (Winter 1992): 53–69.

Johnson, Loch K., and Kevin J. Scheid. "Spending for Spies: Intelligence Budgeting in the Aftermath of the Cold War." *Public Budgeting & Finance* 15 (Winter 1998): 543–69.

Johnston, Paul. "No Cloak and Dagger Required: Intelligence Support to UN Peacekeeping." *Intelligence and National Security* 12, no. 4 (October 1997): 102–12.

Jones, Christopher M. "The CIA under Clinton: Continuity and Change." *International Journal of Intelligence and Counterintelligence* 14, no. 4 (Winter 2001–2002): 503–28.

Kay, David. *Denial and Deception: Iraq and Beyond.* Working Group on Intelligence Reform Series. Washington, D.C.: Consortium for the Study of Intelligence, 1994.

Knott, Stephen F. "The Great Republican Transformation on Oversight." *International Journal of Intelligence and Counterintelligence* 13, no. 1 (Spring 2000): 49–63.

Kreib, Mark W. "Intelligence Support to Peacekeeping Operations." *Naval Intelligence Professionals Quarterly* 18, no. 1 (January 2002): 14.

Lambeth, Benjamin S. *NATO's Air War for Kosovo.* Santa Monica, Calif.: Rand Corporation, 2001.

Lowenthal, Mark M. "Tribal Tongues: Intelligence Consumers, Intelligence Producers." *Washington Quarterly* 15 (Winter 1992): 157–68.

Mason, Simon. *Secret Signals: The Euronumbers Mystery.* Lake Geneva, Wisc.: Tiare, 1992.

McCarthy, Gregory C. "GOP Oversight of Intelligence in the Clinton Era." *International Journal of Intelligence and Counterintelligence* 15, no. 1 (Spring 2002): 26–51.

Meyer, Herbert E. "Reinventing the CIA." *Global Affairs* 7, no. 2 (Spring 1992): 1–13.

Miller, Abraham H., and Nicholas Damask. "Thinking about Intelligence after the Fall of Communism." *International Journal of Intelligence and Counterintelligence* 6, no. 3 (Fall 1993): 257–69.

Moynihan, Daniel P. *Secrecy: The American Experience.* New Haven, Conn.: Yale University Press, 1998.

Owens, William A. "Intelligence in the 21st Century." *Defense Intelligence Journal* 7, no. 1 (Spring 1998): 25–45.

Pipes, Richard. "What to Do about the CIA." *Commentary* 99, no. 3 (March 1995): 36–43.

Powers, Thomas. "The Truth about the CIA." *New York Review of Books* 40, no. 9 (13 May 1993): 49–55.

Putney, Diane T. "Reflections on Intelligence and History." *American Intelligence Journal* 13, no. 3 (Summer 1992): 85–87.

Ramsbotham, David. "Analysis and Assessment for Peacekeeping Operations." *Intelligence and National Security* 10, no. 4 (October 1995): 162–74.

Riemann, Robert H. "The Challenge of Glasnost for Western Intelligence." *Parameters* 20, no. 4 (1990): 85–94.

Riley, Patrick R. "CIA and Its Discontents." *International Journal of Intelligence and Counterintelligence* 11, no. 3 (Fall 1998): 255–69.

Runde, Carl P., and G. Voss, eds. *Intelligence and the New World Order: Former Cold War Adversaries Look towards the Twenty-first Century.* London: International Freedom Foundation, 1992.

Russell, Richard L. "CIA: A Cold War Relic?" *International Journal of Intelligence and Counterintelligence* 8, no. 1 (Spring 1995): 11–20.

———. "CIA's Strategic Intelligence in Iraq." *Political Science Quarterly* 117, no. 2 (Summer 2002): 191–207.

Schweizer, Peter. *Victory: The Reagan Administration's Secret Strategy That Hastened the Collapse of the Soviet Union.* New York: Atlantic Monthly, 1994.

Smith, Hugh. "Intelligence and UN Peacekeeping." *Survival* 36 (Autumn 1994): 174–92.

Snider, L. Britt. *Sharing Secrets with Lawmakers: Congress as a User of Intelligence.* Washington, D.C.: Central Intelligence Agency, Center for the Study of Intelligence, 1997.

Snyder, Alvin A. *Warriors of Disinformation: American Propaganda, Soviet Lies, and the Winning of the Cold War—an Insider's Account.* New York: Arcade, 1995.

Stempel, John D. "Error, Folly, and Policy Intelligence." *International Journal of Intelligence and Counterintelligence* 12, no. 3 (Fall 1999): 267–81.

Swenson, Russell G., ed. *Intelligence for Multilateral Decision and Action.* Washington, D.C.: Joint Military Intelligence College, 1997.

Toffler, Alvin, and Heidi Toffler. "Powershift: The World's Most Dangerous Brain Drains." *International Journal of Intelligence and Counterintelligence* 5, no. 3 (Fall 1991): 329–31.

Travers, Russ. "The Coming Intelligence Failure." *Studies in Intelligence* 1 (1997): 35–43.

Turner, Michael A. "Issues in Evaluating U.S. Intelligence." *International Journal of Intelligence and Counterintelligence* 5, no. 3 (Fall 1991): 275–85.

———. "Understanding CIA's Role in Intelligence." *International Journal of Intelligence and Counterintelligence* 4, no. 3 (Fall 1990): 295–305.

Wark, Wesley K., ed. "The Future of Espionage." Special issue, *Queen's Quarterly* 100, no. 2 (Summer 1993).

Waxman, Matthew C. "Emerging Intelligence Challenges." *International Journal of Intelligence and Counterintelligence* 10, no. 3 (Fall 1997): 317–31.

Weinrod, W. B. "U.S. Intelligence Priorities in the Post-Cold War Era." *World Affairs* 159 (Summer 1996): 3–11.

Westerfield, H. Bradford. "American Exceptionalism and American Intelligence." *Freedom Review* 28 (Summer 1997): 27–36.

Wiebes, Cees. *Intelligence and the War in Bosnia, 1992–1995*. New Brunswick, N.J.: Transaction Books, 2003.

N. TERRORISM AND INTELLIGENCE FAILURES: THE 2000s

1. General

Anonymous. *Imperial Hubris: Why the West Is Losing the War on Terror*. Dulles, Va.: Brassey's, 2004.

Betts, Richard K., and Thomas G. Mahnken, eds. *Paradoxes of Strategic Intelligence: Essays in Honor of Michael I. Handel*. London: Frank Cass, 2003.

Bruneau, Thomas C. "Controlling Intelligence in New Democracies." *International Journal of Intelligence and Counterintelligence* 14, no. 3 (Fall 2001): 323–41.

Callamari, Peter, and Derek Reveron. "China's Use of Perception Management." *International Journal of Intelligence and Counterintelligence* 16, no. 1 (Spring 2003): 1–15.

Callum, Robert. "The Case for Cultural Diversity in the Intelligence Community." *International Journal of Intelligence and Counterintelligence* 14, no. 1 (Spring 2001): 25–48.

Carroll, Thomas Patrick. "The Case against Intelligence Openness." *International Journal of Intelligence and Counterintelligence* 14, no. 4 (Winter 2001–2002): 559–74.

Central Intelligence Agency. *The Strategic Investment Plan for Intelligence Community Analysis*. Washington, D.C.: Government Printing Office, 2001.

DeMars, William E. "Hazardous Partnership: NGOs and United States Intelligence in Small Wars." *International Journal of Intelligence and Counterintelligence* 14, no. 2 (Summer 2001): 193–222.

Deutch, John, and Jeffrey H. Smith. "Smarter Intelligence." *Foreign Policy,* January–February 2002, 64–69.

Ennis, Michael E. "The Future of Intelligence." *Naval Intelligence Professionals Quarterly* 16, no. 4 (October 2000): 1–2.

Gertz, Bill. *Breakdown: How America's Intelligence Failures Led to September 11*. Washington, D.C.: Regnery, 2002.

Haass, Richard N. "Supporting US Foreign Policy in the Post-9/11 World." *Studies in Intelligence* 46, no. 3 (2002): 1–13.

Hitz, Frederick P. "The Future of American Espionage." *International Journal of Intelligence and Counterintelligence* 13, no. 1 (Spring 2000): 1–20.

Holm, Richard L. *The American Agent: My Life in the CIA*. London: St. Ermin's Press, 2003.

Johnson, Loch K. "Spies." *Foreign Policy*, no. 120 (September–October 2000): 18–26.

Johnson, Loch K., and James J. Wirtz, eds. *Strategic Intelligence: Windows into a Secret World*. Los Angeles: Roxbury, 2004.

Kessler, Ronald. *The CIA at War: Inside the Secret Campaign against Terror*. New York: St. Martin's, 2003.

Lahneman, William J. "Outsourcing the IC's Stovepipes?" *International Journal of Intelligence and Counterintelligence* 16, no. 4 (Winter 2003–2004): 573–93.

MacDonald, Margaret S., and Anthony G. Oettinger. "Information Overload: Managing Intelligence Technologies." *Harvard International Review* 24, no. 3 (Fall 2002): 44–48.

Powers, Thomas. *Intelligence Wars: American Secret History from Hitler to Al-Qaeda*. New York: New York Review of Books, 2004.

Pringle, Robert W. *Historical Dictionary of Russian/Soviet Intelligence*. Lanham, Md.: Scarecrow Press, 2006.

Quinn, James L., Jr. "Staffing the Intelligence Community: The Pros and Cons of an Intelligence Reserve." *International Journal of Intelligence and Counterintelligence* 13, no. 2 (Summer 2000): 160–70.

Rathmell, Andrew. "Towards Postmodern Intelligence." *Intelligence and National Security* 17, no. 3 (Autumn 2002): 87–104.

Rothkopf, David. *Running the World: The Inside Story of the National Security Council and the Architects of American Power*. New York: Public Affairs, 2005.

Ryan, Maria. "The Myth and Reality of US Intelligence and Policy-Making after 9/11." *Intelligence and National Security* 17, no. 4 (Winter 2002): 55–76.

Shpiro, Shlomo. "The Media Strategies of Intelligence Services." *International Journal of Intelligence and Counterintelligence* 14, no. 4 (Winter 2001–2002): 485–502.

Treverton, Gregory F. "Intelligence and the 'Market State.'" *Studies in Intelligence* 10 (Winter–Spring 2001): 69–76.

Turner, Michael A. *Why Secret Intelligence Fails*. Dulles, Va.: Potomac Books, 2005.

Villadsen, Ole R. "Prospects for a European Common Intelligence Policy." *Studies in Intelligence* 9 (Summer 2000): 81–94.

Vital, David. "Images of Other Peoples in the Making of Intelligence and Foreign Policy." *International Journal of Intelligence and Counterintelligence* 16, no. 1 (Spring 2003): 16–33.

Weller, Geoffrey R. "The Internal Modernization of Western Intelligence Agencies." *International Journal of Intelligence and Counterintelligence* 14, no. 3 (Fall 2001): 299–322.

West, Nigel. *Historical Dictionary of British Intelligence*. Lanham, Md.: Scarecrow Press, 2005.

———. *Historical Dictionary of International Intelligence*. Lanham, Md.: Scarecrow Press, 2006.

Wettering, Frederick L. "(C)overt Action: The Disappearing 'C.'" *International Journal of Intelligence and Counterintelligence* 16, no. 4 (Winter 2003–2004): 561–72.

———. "The Internet and the Spy Business." *International Journal of Intelligence and Counterintelligence* 14, no. 3 (Fall 2001): 342–65.

2. The Iraq War

Bamford, James. *A Pretext for War: 9/11, Iraq, and the Abuse of America's Intelligence Agencies*. New York: Doubleday, 2004.

Cordesman, Anthony H. *The Iraq War: Strategy, Tactics, and Military Lessons*. Westport, Conn.: Praeger, 2003.

Mann, James. *Rise of the Vulcans: The History of Bush's War Cabinet*. New York: Viking, 2004.

Souza, Corrine. *Baghdad's Spy: A Personal Memoir of Espionage and Intrigue from Iraq to London*. Edinburgh, Scotland: Mainstream, 2003.

U. S. Congress. Senate. *Report on the U.S. Intelligence Community's Prewar Intelligence Assessments on Iraq*. Washington, D.C.: Senate Select Committee on Intelligence, 2004.

West, Bing, and Ray L. Smith. *The March Up: Taking Baghdad with the 1st Marine Division*. New York: Bantam, 2003.

Zinsmeister, Karl. *Boots on the Ground: A Month with the 82nd Airborne in the Battle for Iraq*. New York: St. Martin's, 2003.

3. The Terrorist Attacks of 11 September 2001

Anonymous. *Through Our Enemies' Eyes: Osama bin Laden, Radical Islam, and the Future of America*. Dulles, Va.: Brassey's, 2002.

Brooks, Thomas A. "Did Intelligence Fail Us?" *U.S. Naval Institute Proceedings*, October 2001, 54–55.

Clarke, Richard C. *Against All Enemies: Inside America's War on Terror*. New York: Free Press, 2004.

Graham, Bob. *Intelligence Matters: The CIA, the FBI, Saudi Arabia, and the Failure of America's War on Terror*. With Jeff Nussbaum. New York: Random House, 2004.

The 9/11 Commission Report: Final Report of the National Commission on Terrorist Attacks upon the United States. New York: Norton, 2004.

Shelby, Richard C. "September 11 and the Imperative of Reform in the U.S. Intelligence Community: Additional Views of Senator Richard C. Shelby, Vice Chairman, Senate Select Committee on Intelligence." Select Committee on Intelligence, Washington, D.C., 10 December 2002.

Stern, Jessica. *Terror in the Name of God: Why Religious Militants Kill.* New York: Harper Collins, 2003.

Strasser, Steven, ed. *The 9/11 Investigations.* New York: Public Affairs, 2004.

About the Author

Michael A. Turner is a political scientist teaching intelligence and national security matters in San Diego, California. He is a 15-year veteran of the Central Intelligence Agency, where he worked in various analytical and staff positions. He also served rotational assignments on Capitol Hill and for the Department of State and the Department of Defense. Dr. Turner was twice the recipient of CIA's prestigious Exceptional Performance Award. He is the author of *Why Secret Intelligence Fails* and numerous journal articles on intelligence matters, and he serves on the editorial board of the *International Journal of Intelligence and Counterintelligence*.